On the Run in Occupied Poland

Rochester Studies in East and Central Europe

(ISSN 1528–4808)

Senior Editor: Timothy Snyder, University of Toronto

Additional Titles of Interest

A Doctor's Memoir of the Romanian Holocaust: Survival in Lager Vapniarka and the Ghettos of Transnistria
Arthur Kessler, edited by Leo Spitzer, translated by Margaret Robinson

Bulgaria, the Jews, and the Holocaust: On the Origins of a Heroic Narrative
Nadege Ragaru, translated by Victoria Baena and David A. Rich

Individualism and the Rise of Democracy in Poland
Tomek Grabowski

Rethinking Modern Polish Identities: Transnational Encounters
Edited by Agnieszka Pasieka and Pawel Rodak

Seeking Accountability for Nazi and War Crimes in East and Central Europe: A People's Justice?
Edited by Eric Le Bourhis, Irina Tcherneva and Vanessa Voisin

Great Power Competition and the Path to Democracy: The Case of Georgia, 1991–2020
Zarina Burkadze

Toward Xenopolis: Visions from the Borderland
Krzysztof Czyżewski

The Universe behind Barbed Wire: Memoirs of a Ukrainian Soviet Dissident
Myroslav Marynovych, translated by Z. Hayuk, edited by K. Younger, foreword by T. Snyder

Borders on the Move: Territorial Change and Ethnic Cleansing in the Hungarian-Slovak Borderlands, 1938–1948
Leslie Waters

Beyond the Pale: The Holocaust in the North Caucasus
Crispin Brooks, Kiril Feferman

Polish Literature and National Identity: A Postcolonial Perspective
Dariusz Skórczewski, Agnieszka Polakowska

A complete list of titles in the Rochester Studies in East and Central Europe Series may be found on our website, www.urpress.com

On the Run in Occupied Poland

Tales of a Refugee Childhood

Grażyna Gross

Edited by Irene Kacandes
With Joyce Gross and Aleksandra Szczepan

UNIVERSITY OF ROCHESTER PRESS

Copyright © 2026 Grażyna Gross

All rights reserved. Except as permitted under current legislation, no part of this work may be photocopied, stored in a retrieval system, published, performed in public, adapted, broadcast, transmitted, recorded, or reproduced in any form or by any means, without the prior permission of the copyright owner.

First published 2026

University of Rochester Press
www.urpress.com
and Boydell & Brewer Limited
www.boydellandbrewer.com

ISBN: 978-1-64825-147-4 (Hardback)
ISBN: 978-1-64825-150-4 (Paperback)

ISSN: 1528-4808

Our Authorized Representative for product safety in the EU is Easy Access System Europe –Mustamäe tee 50, 10621 Tallinn, Estonia, *gpsr.requests@easproject.com*

Library of Congress Cataloging-in-Publication Data
CIP data is available from the Library of Congress

A catalogue record for this title is available from the British Library

This book is dedicated to the memory of
Grażyna Gross, née Połtowicz (1931–2022),
and to that of all individuals whose childhoods
were indelibly marked by war

Contents

	A Prefatory Note from the Editor	ix
	Map	xiii

On the Run in Occupied Poland: Tales of a Refugee Childhood
Grażyna Gross

1	Maria and Mirek	1
2	Henius	7
3	Maybe Not a Story	15
4	Letter to an Unknown Man	19
5	The Shoemaker's Son	22
6	The Doctor's Daughter	29
7	The Fortune Teller	34
8	The Root Canal	38
9	The Day Papa Left	42
10	Tereska	46
11	The Picture Album, Part One	52
12	Half-Boarders	58
13	Józefina's Mistress	61
14	The Psychic	65
15	The Gloves	69
16	The Ring	73
17	A Boy	81
18	Uncle Kot	82
19	A Dinner	89
20	A Christmas Story	92
21	Letter to Józefina	100
22	The Sled	107

23	The Watch	111
24	Typhus	115
25	Justyna	120
26	Mrs. Kraus	126
27	The Picture Album, Part Two	132
28	Peace	135
29	A Night in Regensburg	137
30	Evhen	143
31	School	156
32	EH	161
33	The Girl from Furth	167
34	Father Zeisel	172
35	Mama	178

Afterwords

Mothers and Daughters—and Grandmothers *Joyce Gross*	201
What is Historic? What is Heroic? *Aleksandra Szczepan*	219
My Friend the Writer *Irene Kacandes*	233

Appendices

Timeline	251
Notes to the Tales	259
Family Photos	275
Extract from the Polish Notebooks	305
Card from Henryk Połtowicz at Gross-Rosen to his Daughter	309
Acknowledgments	311
Notes on Contributors	312
Index	313

A Prefatory Note from the Editor

As I write these words and almost certainly as you read them, too, more individuals have been forcibly displaced from their homes than at any other time since records of refugeedom began to be kept: in mid-2025 that's more than 122 million people since the start of the year, according to the United Nations. Persecution, human rights violations, degradation of the environment, and of course armed conflicts, small and large, have turned mostly homebodies into refugees and displaced persons.

This book is about a Polish child forced to be on the run during the previous great wave of human movement, that was caused by the paroxysms of violence across Europe and the world in the mid-twentieth century. Grażyna Połtowicz (pronounced Gra-ZHI-na Po-TO-vich) was the second child born to Henryk Połtowicz and Waleria Orzyszyńska. Arriving on the first of January in the year 1931 in the town of Sarny—then Poland, now Ukraine—Grażyna was born into a life of displacements in a part of the world that is alas once again today experiencing war, millions of people on the run, and changing borders: Eastern Europe. Grażyna's father's family had been dispossessed of their estate in what is now Moldova, long before her own birth, through what we conveniently call the Russian Revolution, though actually a series of violent conflicts that began before the mass violence referred to then as the Great War—what we now refer to as World War One—had concluded.

Grażyna's own first moves around what used to be eastern Poland and is now Belarus and Lithuania—from Wilno (now Vilnius) to Wołożyn (now Valozhyn) to Oszmiana (now Ashmyany) and then back to Wilno—were peacefully caused by her father's law career. Her first years were lived in relative material comfort, though not untouched by the kind of tragedy in the form of unexpected deaths that can visit any family—in Grażyna's case, of her older brother Henius̀. The "next war" that the child heard adults around her predicting soon caught up with her family, though. And, so, it was fear of execution or deportation to Siberia that put them into flight from Wilno through Kaunus to Warsaw and soon after to Kraków, where Grażyna and her mother spent most of the war before fleeing farther west to Prague, southern Germany, and eventually the midwestern United States.

A PREFATORY NOTE FROM THE EDITOR

I offer readers of this book the above thumbnail sketch to give you a small amount of orientation. I hope you will eventually be grateful that I don't offer more detail now, because the next part of this book will plunge you into the Eastern Europe of almost a century ago through the perspective of a child refugee who did not know much history and could not know what would happen next.

What follows was written by Grażyna Gross, née Połtowicz, over many years of her later adulthood. She referred to them as "stories," and readers might note some similarities to folk tales or even fairy tales in their short titles, limited cast of characters, and narrative thrust. Their content is from memory, though, not invented, which is why we decided against using the word "stories" in the title of this book. In many of the segments, the author stays true to what she could remember by limiting the narrator to what a child could know. Other segments are written as letters to people Grażyna couldn't seem to forget, to achieve some kind of closure where there had been none during the war. Like the great Franz Kafka, Grażyna never intended to publish these writings—or at least that's what she told me when she started showing them to me. I had met Grażyna by starting a conversation with her in a restaurant in Ithaca, New York, where she lived and to which I had come to give a lecture at Cornell University. Quite a few years into our friendship, I managed to convince her that her writing deserved to have more readers than just me. It is on the basis of her permission to me then to help her edit what she'd written, and of her family now, that we are publishing Grażyna's writing posthumously and as memoir or, more exactly, as "paramemoir," which I define below.

First, let me explain something about this "we." Shortly after I learned from her husband Leonard, or Len, as he is known, that Grażyna had passed away at the age of 91 in March 2022, the elder of their two children, Joyce Gross, got in touch with me to let me know that she and her father were okay with me trying to publish her writing. Len had been helping his wife for many years with all things related to the computer, including making sure all her files were backed up and not lost. I had our correspondence and most of the short segments on my computer with some things only in hard copy. Joyce applied her skills in the months and years following her mother's death to organizing and digitizing the numerous types of documents, photographs, correspondence, and drafts of anecdotes, some of which Grażyna had shown me, many of which she had not. Joyce was not just organizing but also reading. She knew only a little of her mother's wartime experiences and had not been given any of the stories to read while her mother was alive. I was delighted when Joyce expressed interest in helping me create a memoir of some kind out of what her mother had left behind. One of Joyce's discoveries concerned notebooks that had been written during the war and were in Polish; that is when I fully realized how beneficial it would be to add to the endeavor someone who could read Polish well and knew from firsthand experience the world of Grażyna's childhood. As if by luck or destiny, based on your worldview, I had recently met a young Polish scholar who like myself researched the Holocaust and related issues. Aleksandra Szczepan had even studied in Kraków where Grażyna had spent the longest part of the war and she knew the city well. Grażyna's life story essentially brought the three of us together via videoconferencing and even occasionally in person. We have wrestled with the best way to share Grażyna's unusual perspective and unique personality with a larger number of people. Our work has been deeply rewarding, and one benefit of this book that has already been realized is the creation of new friendships.

Our final editorial decisions include keeping Grażyna's own writing central and embedding it in other types of personal material, like family photographs. Further, we use our own knowledge, perspectives, and interpretations of the traces of her life to help readers understand how Grażyna's experiences on the run provide some access to everyday life in Occupied Poland for non-Jews for which there are not many sources, at least not in English. Grażyna's writing is also invaluable to my mind for its insights into the experience of refugeedom that transcend a single historical time, place, and identity position. For these reasons, this book has become what I have termed in my earlier work on life writing a *paramemoir*, meaning that it goes beyond the account of a single individual both in content and in the number of voices that are included. Concretely, this book offers readers a series of tales that Grażyna Gross produced about her own life, a map, a timeline we created to help fill in gaps in what the author chose to share about that life, additional notes to some of the references the author makes, a visual record, and three essays offering the perspectives of a daughter, a Polish scholar, and a friend.

Because Grażyna drafted several of the anecdotes multiple times experimenting with style, perspective, and narrative arc, and because she did not write them in the order you will read them here, readers will please indulge her in some overlap in content in more than one segment. Sometimes this repetition offers another angle on an event or at the least indicates how large it loomed for her. While I changed some dates and references to her age that I was positive were incorrect, there also remains some fuzziness of chronology that I did not want to edit out because it reflects so well the way her memory—as it appears to be characteristic of all humans—was controlled by affect more than by facts. Grażyna put tremendous effort into getting the facts right, too, when she was able to track them down.

The order in which Grażyna actually composed the segments remains unknown, despite some effort on my part to reconstruct it. As for the order in which they appear in this paramemoir, well, that mainly follows Grażyna's life from early childhood to shortly before her death in 2022. Whereas the author did originally change a few historical or personal facts, withhold some names, and avoid certain kinds of details to protect some of the dead and their offspring, as the cliché goes, I have added dates, place names, and some personal names where I felt sure of them from other information I or Grażyna's family was in possession of. As editor of the segments and of this volume overall, I accept responsibility for any mistakes that might somehow someday come to light.

Grażyna's creation of numerous drafts for the same narrative kernel resulted in much variation in the names of people and places she did choose to include. I mostly regularized these to the Polish and the personal, so, for instance, "Kraków" for an occasional "Cracow," and "Runia" for the more formal "Renata," the first name of her best friend. After consulting with my co-contributors, we decided to use the Polish names for towns that now have names in the languages of the countries they are currently located in: hence Wołożyn (now Valozhyn in Belarus); Oszmiana (now Ashmyany in Belarus); Wilno (now Vilnius in Lithuania); whereas other place names appear in the English forms by which they are currently known.

One other name and naming deserves mention here. Grażyna had a complicated and mostly negative view of her mother's lover. During the war, observers often asked her if he was her "uncle," and she would vehemently reply that he was her mother's tenant. I have retained some of those mentions, but eliminated several others because there were simply so many repetitions of these kinds of interchanges with snooping outsiders. I have also mostly used that individual's actual name, "Mykola," since Grażyna used it in a few of the stories, and it will help readers recognize this person at the various times he appears.

There are many other things I want to share about Grażyna's writing, in dialog with reflections by Joyce Gross and Aleksandra Szczepan. We all agreed to let Grażyna speak for herself, however, before you hear more from us.

Irene Kacandes
28 August 2025
La Tour-de-Peilz, Switzerland

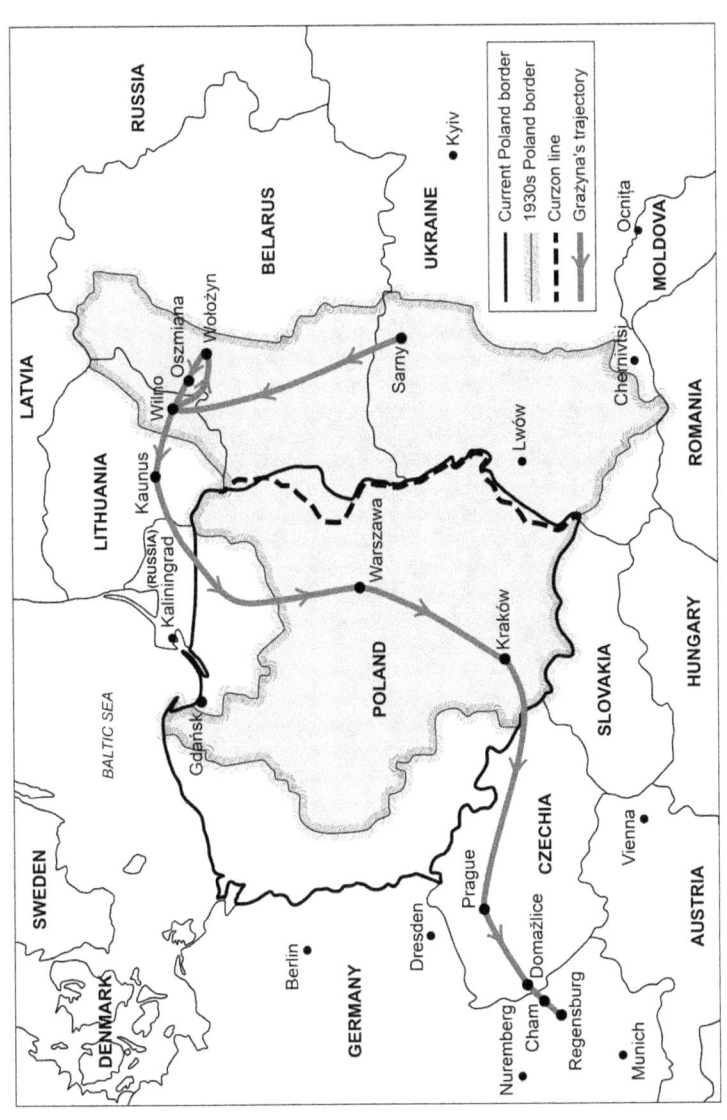

Figure 1. Current map of Poland and neighboring countries, with an overlay of the 1930s Polish border and area indicated by light gray shading. Grażyna Gross's trajectory is shown starting in Sarny and ending in Germany. The Curzon line was a demarcation line proposed in 1919 by Lord Curzon (the British Foreign Secretary) as an armistice line in the Soviet-Polish war of 1919–1920; it became the demarcation line between German-occupied Poland and Soviet-occupied Poland during the Second World War. After the war, most of the area east of the line became part of Soviet Belarus and Ukraine. The western border of Poland shifted westward. Map created by Joyce Gross. 1930s Polish border from: Magocsi, P. R. 2018. *Historical Atlas of Central Europe.* Third Revised and Expanded Edition (Seattle: University of Washington Press). Map 52.

On the Run in Occupied Poland

Tales of a Refugee Childhood

Grażyna Gross

I

Maria and Mirek

At first there was Wilno, where we lived on a narrow street of squat houses, none more than two stories high. Mrs. Brozkowa was our neighbor, and I used to call on her occasionally. She must have been a very kind woman. The cathedral, all white on the outside, was on the main square, a short walk from where we lived. Its beauty made me cry.

When I was three years old, we left Wilno for Wołożyn, a small town on the border. There, Maria was supposed to watch me and Henius, while Papa and Mama were settling into our new apartment on the top floor of the courthouse. She loved children and had five of her own, all but one already old enough to live in faraway places I knew nothing about. Maria's house was at the end of our street at the edge of an endless field where, I thought, the world began.

Maria came with stories and fairytales. She even brought some books to read to us, one of them in French, which she would translate as she read aloud. It was supposed to help us learn French but did not. She may have saved me from electrocution when she convinced my brother Henius not to insist that I stick a pair of scissors into an electrical outlet. We had been told not to do anything like that because… Henius only wanted to see if the grown-ups were telling us the truth. And, besides, it would have been something interesting to watch.

Henius, four years older than I, was allowed to play with the doctor's son who lived near the hospital. The two boys had a lot of fun and refused to let me join them because I was still a baby and a girl besides. Once they managed to climb to the window of the morgue so that they could have a look at a man whose head had been split open with an axe. It must have been quite an exciting sight because it made Henius feel so sick that he threw up on the kitchen floor as soon as he got back home. "Did you touch anything there?" Mama asked him, sniffing the sleeve of his coat, because the dead smell. No, he had not. Listening to Maria's stories was no substitute for action. I was jealous.

Maria must have known every fairytale, even those that were not yet in books, like the one about the magic flower that grows in deep woods and blooms only on the night of Saint John. It is more powerful than Aladdin's lamp because the number of wishes it could grant is infinite. I wanted to find it, of course, but no one would let me wander around in a forest in the middle of the night because of wolves. That Little Red Riding Hood was almost eaten up by one, I already knew. That was scary even just to think about. If I were a boy, would I have been as scared? Probably not and that made me wish to become one, and for this to happen, having the magic flower would help. But how could I find it without being able to go into the woods? The problem had no solution.

When Maria began to run out of fairytales, she would talk about wars—so many of them that I could not keep them straight. Were they wars of long ago or were they fought when she was already alive? She spoke about Napoleon as if she had seen him riding through the fields on his way to save our country. He was not able to do it, and on his retreat—which was not pretty—he had to pass through our town. That his plans did not work out was a great disappointment to people who lived here. Meadows were soaked with blood and the waters of a nearby creek turned red after a battle. Blood Creek it was called. Maria would have taken me to it, had it been closer to home. It was no longer red, she informed me, but would be soon, because a new war was already in the making. And there was this weed growing everywhere that had something to do with blood. Either it would slow down bleeding when put on a wound or it needed blood-soaked soil to thrive. I couldn't keep it straight.

From Maria I learned about Jews to whom I was not paying any attention earlier. Unlike the Gypsies, who came to town for a few days to set up a camp, dance, sing, and cook on bonfires, the Jews, even the ones with tall hats, were a part of the scenery. According to Maria, they put their Christian servant girls into barrels studded with nails, made them bleed—to death or not—and then used the blood for something, but it was not clear to me for what. Could it possibly be true or was it another fairytale? Fairytales were about what one wanted to be true but was not. So, it could not be a fairytale because who would want anyone to bleed to death? Then it had to be either true or false. If true, Jews would be sitting in jail or sent to the gallows. I already knew that killing was against the law, except during a war. Knowing that it had to be a lie was not enough to make me feel safe when Mama began to send me to the Jewish grocery store to pick up some staples she had run out of.

To get there I had to cross a swampy meadow owned by a gaggle of geese. They knew a coward when they saw one and would chase me hissing and nipping my bare legs. Would they have been brave enough to attack a boy if one had tried to wander through their meadow? I never saw a boy being attacked by those geese, but, then again, I never saw a boy crossing that meadow on his way to the grocery store—as if boys always had something more important to do! It was not fair. Yet, I never refused to go there despite the pain, because it was a very interesting place. And that Jews, who could be draining blood from Christian girls, owned it, made it even more alluring. I was curious and wanted to find out what they were like and how they lived.

Only once did I get a peek into one of their rooms when a door between their living quarters and the store had been left open. A peasant servant girl was down on her knees scrubbing the floor. Did she know what could happen to her? Wasn't she afraid? Neat and shiny and unlike Maria's rooms that only had beds in them, the Jewish room even had a china cabinet among its furniture. I was impressed. And there were barrels in the store: one with herring, one with sauerkraut, and one with pickles. I did not see one studded with nails.

I never tired of Maria's tales, even after she had run out of new ones. Still, when summer, the best season of the year, arrived, I turned to the great outdoors for excitement. It was clear to me that I would not have a chance to do what boys somehow managed to do. Ogling a split skull or parachuting into the sand pit with the help of two umbrellas was not anything I was brave enough to undertake, especially not on my own. That they had done it made them into heroes, even though Heniuś ended up vomiting and the parachutist broke his leg on landing. Papa told us to not even dare think about flying. You had to be stupid to try, and the boy who had tried was old enough to know better. What was wrong with him?

Thinking up something heroic to do was not easy. As the saying goes, heroic deeds don't grow on trees, except during a war. The field at the end of our street, the one that started at Maria's house and merged with the sky far away, offered some possibilities. Its immensity and emptiness awed me. I could stand at the edge of it, closest to our house, and stare at it for a long time while all kinds of ideas were brewing in my head. One day, after supper and without saying good-bye to anyone, I walked out onto the street and headed for the great field. I started to run and kept running until the town behind me disappeared. Once I could no longer see the town, I thought to myself, I would no longer have to run. Walking south, even at a slow pace, I would eventually end up in Turkey where people had desserts before the main meal. I knew very well where Turkey was, because Heniuś had an atlas in which all countries appeared in different colors, just like the hard candy in the jar at the Jewish store. If I got to Istanbul, I would be able to continue to the land of 1001 Nights. What an accomplishment that would be! It was not my fault that I did not get there. Before I could get far enough into the field to disappear from view, someone came running after me and dragged me home, shattering my dreams of heroically going into the world.

Even after I got a little older, Heniuś and his friend did not ask me to join them in their games or adventures. They probably thought that I was too weak or too dumb to keep up with them and a sissy besides, fit only for playing with dolls and other girls. That I did not even own a doll and knew no girls—absolutely none!—did not make any difference to them. They were proud of being boys. I found it terribly unfair.

In the summer of our second year in town, a boy about my age—I was four and a half years old by then—began to hang out in our garden looking for company. His name was Mirek. The wooden house he lived in was separated from the courthouse where we were living by a stable and the jail, both very nice buildings of yellow stucco. My parents did not visit his, and his parents did not visit mine. It may have had something to do with the way Mirek's mother called him when she wanted him to come home from wherever he happened to be. She would lean out of a second story window and scream so loud that the whole street could hear her, perhaps even the whole town. To scream like that was a sign of bad manners, and just one more thing I was not supposed to do. People who came to see Papa had to be well-behaved. Mirek was never invited in. If I wanted to spend some time in his company, it had to be outdoors. I overheard Mama warn Andzia, our servant girl, "That child does not look healthy," and that meant that Mirek and I would have to play outside. I had to agree with Mama's assessment but said nothing. With his puffy white face untouched by sun, eyes caked with sleep, and a nose full of snot, he did not look quite right to me. Still, I was not repulsed by him at all. Besides, he was the best I could get for exploring the countryside.

There was so much to learn. We wandered around the sand pit, studied weeds and bugs, stuck sticks into anthills, and tortured flies when we could catch them. We looked for berries and ate too much sorrel. Mirek had few ideas of his own, even of the kind that could get us into trouble. I led, he followed, but I would have preferred to have it the other way around.

Though I did not expect to learn anything from him, I did. He taught me how to put my bare feet into steaming cow pies and enjoy it. I could not have learned that from anyone else. From him I also received my first lesson on worms. That he didn't seem to plan any of these lessons seemed to me to make them even better.

All stables come with manure piles, so the stable across the driveway from the courthouse had one too. When we were passing it one day while returning home from an expedition, Mirek got a sudden urge to use it. With walls on three sides, it was a very private place. I knew that some men used it for peeing, but I never saw anyone pooping there. Mirek would be the first. He climbed halfway up the pile, pulled down his pants and squatted; instead of walking away when he was done, he just stood there looking at whatever he was leaving behind, as if it was some kind of rarity. I became curious and joined him to see if there was something unusual about what he had made. What I saw wasn't like anything I had seen before: a pile of wriggling worms as long as earthworms but white. It was not a pretty sight. "So, you have worms," I announced. Mirek nodded in agreement. He could not deny it, they had to be his. I already knew that people could have worms inside and that poor children are more likely to have them than those better off. I had heard some mothers talk about worms and how to get rid of them but had not seen any yet. Mirek's were the first. "Did your mother give you a lot of garlic to eat?" I asked. No, she had not, and so they must have come out on their own because he had so many. Poor Mirek, so dumb and sickly because of worms. I did not tell anyone that he had them. It was our secret.

Did I feel sorry for him? If I did, it was not the way I felt sorry for beggars, dirty and old, deformed and hungry. They were not going to get any better, but I thought that Mirek could. Some day he could look like other boys I saw strutting around, healthy and smart.

After living in this great little town for three years, we were going to move. Not that Heniuś and I wanted to, but of course no one had asked for our opinion. Opinions were not something children were supposed to have. Had it been up to us, we would have stayed. To make the move less painful, Papa told us that we were moving to a better place: a bigger town, closer to the city. And it had a river we would be able to see from our house. He convinced us that we would end up in paradise. Papa was trustworthy.

It happened in the early afternoon of a glorious day when the sky was cloudless and the sun so bright that it made the western wall of the courthouse glow. Mirek and I were hanging out between Mama's famous beds of pansies when I began telling him about all those terrible wars Maria had told me about. He seemed to listen, but I did not think he understood how bad they were. His face often looked kind of dumb and sleepy. Not much of a talker, he was of little help when I tried to figure out if he understood what I was saying.

A few days earlier, I had come upon a brilliant idea and was about to make him an offer, even though I hadn't worked out the details yet. With so little time left, I had to act quickly, and act I did while standing in Mama's pansies. "Would you like to become a girl?" I asked. It was not unusual for Mirek to look puzzled, and he sure looked puzzled at my question. He thought very hard for a few minutes and said "no."

"If you agree to become a girl, I'll be able to turn into a boy," I explained. "As a girl you won't have to fight in a war and you will not get killed," I promised. Perhaps he still did not understand how bad wars were, so I began to dig up all the gore Maria had regaled me with. The blood-soaked fields strewn with bodies, the rivers whose waters turned red, prisoners beaten and tortured, and finally the upcoming war people were already talking about. Didn't he know what would happen? I had not yet solved all the problems such a switch would create—I still needed to acquire Aladdin's lamp or Saint

John's magic flower. Would I have to live with Mirek's mother? Would he have to move in with my parents? Would they notice that I was no longer who I used to be? As for that thing Mirek had to keep hidden in his pants, yes, I would have to have it, because if I did not, people would keep telling me that girls can't do the things I wanted to do. Besides, with it, I would be able to piss standing up and standing up was superior to squatting.

I could see how hard he was thinking about what I was saying. He may have been close to tears and kept repeating "no." To decide which of the two evils was worse—becoming a girl or getting killed in a war—was not easy. That a boy of Mirek's quality—dumb, sickly, and infested with worms—did not want to become me was not flattering, but I did not care. It was not flattery I was after. That he would rather be dead than become a girl worried me and did not bode well for my future.

His refusal of my offer didn't change our relationship. We were still playmates when we parted and would have kept exploring the countryside had my family only stayed in that town.

2

Heniuś

The new town, Oszmiana, was like Papa promised: bigger than the old one, closer to the city, and it had a river. He did not tell me that some of its houses were falling apart or that most of them were built of wood. A few buildings were stucco, all lining the market square, but none was a palace.

In late summer, when we arrived, I found beauty in everything I saw.

We were going to live in the courthouse, a building not much different from those along the main street. Low and long, its wooden siding blackened by weather, it came with a garden full of weeds. From one of its windows, I could look down into the valley on a meadow of forget-me-nots and, when the sun was right, see the shimmer of the river's elusive waters hiding in the willows. I loved the view.

The new town had trees, giant trees, that Papa had also not mentioned. Some were in the park across the driveway from the courthouse: their immense crowns black except for some spots of pink when the sun was rising behind them in the morning. The park was an enchanted place with wide paths of fine gravel and wooden benches with words carved into them, words we were not allowed to repeat. The field on the west side of the courthouse was not endless, framed as it was by a hedgerow of scrubby trees that formed a curtain for the upcoming storms until they were ready to come out and rage right above us. The black sky, the deafening thunder, and the enormous lightening scared me. Andzia, the servant who had moved with us, told me that a holy picture in the window would keep us from getting struck. Perhaps it did, but it did not keep me from being afraid.

The long driveway led to the main street, the main street led to the market square which had its share of giant trees with benches underneath. A few times I saw Papa sitting on one, a newspaper in his hands. Somewhere in Africa, a war was being fought. I knew all about it because people talked, and I listened. Another war was already on the way and that one was going to be bad for us. The news made Papa look worried and sad.

Soon I had a friend, a boy my age, to play with! Heniuś did not have anyone because older boys were in the city attending school and came home only on holidays. So, except when they were in town, Heniuś had to hang out with me and my friend and treat us as if we were boys of the same age. We were having fun, and I learned to do what boys do, though not as well.

My dresses kept getting caught on branches and posts when I climbed trees and fences.

I met many very nice people, and now being old enough, I was allowed to visit some of them on my own. They treated me as if I were already grown-up and often offered tea. Their houses impressed me, even when they had almost no furniture. My favorite was the one that had only chairs along the walls of an immense room and came with a park of giant trees, with some already toppled over from old age. This is how paradise must look, I thought.

The fields surrounding the town were as beautiful as the town: the deep blue of flax, the pink of buckwheat, the purples of lupine and clover, and finally the gold of grains before the harvest. Autumn was foggy and smelled of fire. After the potato harvest, the fields were brown until the snows came and made them look pretty again.

When not raging, winter could be beautiful, too. Rolling in fresh, fluffy snow was a special delight and so was scratching out peepholes in the rime on the window to have a peek at the weather. That spring with its brave little flowers would arrive one day was not just a silly hope but a certainty.

I should have sensed the danger but did not.

I heard about the warnings while hanging out in the kitchen where some very interesting activities were taking place. I tried not to miss watching the degutting of chickens, an enlightening ritual that taught me what a chicken's innards were made up of.

Often Andzia had the company of peasant women who came to help with some chores or simply to chat. They talked, I listened, and this was how I learned that the house we were living in was cursed because a child had died in it. And then there was the owl living in the old barn across the driveway. It hooted all night I learned, though I never heard it. The bird was letting people know that someone was going to die nearby: perhaps the nice old man across the valley, perhaps someone we did not know. The Gypsy woman with a baby used to come often to read cards to Mama, get some money and a meal for that. Everyone in the kitchen, including Mama, believed in Gypsies: they were the best at divining the future. She, too, said that trouble was on its way but did not say what the trouble would be. I always left the kitchen when she came because I was afraid of the future.

Henius and I were no longer supposed to believe in omens, ghosts, signs, and seers. As for miracles, those approved by the church were true, and those that were not were lies. It had something to do with the saints, but I did not understand the connection. Had I asked Papa to explain it, he would have said "nonsense" and that would have been the end of it. He was probably right, but since one can never be absolutely sure of anything, there was always the possibility that omens happened and therefore it was safer to believe in them, even if just a little bit.

I did believe! Yet I kept missing the signs.

All was well 'til that memorable summer when Heniuś tried to convince me of the existence of ghosts. We were left alone a lot because an election was going to take place, and everyone was busy working on it. I had no idea what elections were about, but they sure came with long shadows and made our rooms fill with strange lighting. Heniuś warned me that a ghost was waiting for me in every room I was about to enter. Since what is repeated often enough becomes true, I was getting scared.

Towards the end of the year, I got sick with what the other little girl had died of. I must have stayed in bed for a whole month. The doctor kept coming to give me shots, and Heniuś got one too to make sure that he did not catch what I had. When I was in the magic land of high fever, I had wonderful dreams and saw things I had not seen before. I sort of enjoyed being there, but as soon as I felt better, I just wanted to get out of bed and start moving again. At Christmas, I was up peeping through the keyhole to catch sight of Santa Claus who could be arriving in the living room where we had a Christmas tree. No luck with seeing him, but someone did leave a teddy bear under the tree to make me feel better after the long illness.

After Christmas Mama and Papa left for a vacation, leaving us with a woman who was supposed to be a governess. Heniuś and I could see that she was just a dumb young woman who would not have known what to do if we got into trouble. We were on our best behavior for her sake and ours. We thought that we had to look out for her, as if she were a child, and never asked her to read to us because we were not sure that she knew how.

That winter was unusual and because it was so unusual it would have to be followed by some extraordinary events. Andzia, who could neither read nor write but knew a lot about omens, told us that. She had no idea what they would be and was sure that anything extraordinary had to be bad. To us winter meant snow and more snow, sometimes coming down so thick that one could get lost after a few steps and then start walking in circles and drop dead from the cold and exhaustion. On sunny days, the air was icy and the snow so bright that one had to walk with eyes half-closed and feel snot in one's nose freeze solid.

In February it got warm, and the snow began to melt. No one could remember ever having a thaw in the middle of winter. It was one of those "once in a lifetime" events. The field behind our house turned into a lake with ice at its bottom. It did not take Heniuś long to come up with a brilliant idea: standing on our sled, a long wooden pole in his hands, he would slide around the field as if walking on water. I was not allowed to join him because I had been sick and still not well enough to play outdoors in strange weather. With my nose glued to the window, I kept watching Heniuś amuse himself. He was having so much fun while I was rotting in our bedroom. It was not fair.

The world came in various shades of gray: light gray for the fields covered with snow, dark gray for the lake that had been a field before the thaw and almost black for the hedgerow at the lake's far end. Henius was interested in ships and wanted to become a seaman. Seeing him dashing around the field, the waters not deep enough to reach the top of the sled, I imagined that he was trying to save people from drowning. My brother the hero. In some book I must have seen a drawing with a lone figure like his on a rescue mission battling a raging sea. I liked to look at rivers and lakes, but I was deathly afraid of water.

There were signs that Henius was getting sick, though the woman taking care of us did not pay any attention to them, and Henius kept spending the days on his boat while I watched him from the window. When I woke up one morning, I heard voices as if there were people in every room of the house talking loudly, perhaps even shouting. I went from room to room trying to find out what had happened, just by listening and not asking questions no one would have been in the mood to answer.

Papa and Mama arrived while I was asleep, the woman who had been taking care of us was gone for good, Henius was very sick, and some nice people came to tell Papa and Mama that everything would turn out all right. Some of them kept watch at Henius's bedside when he no longer knew what was happening around him.

The weather turned again. The water on the lake froze and made it into a skating ring. Henius knew how to skate, I did not. Had he been well, he would have been out skating. After the hard freeze, snows came, sometimes with a howling wind. Once again, everything beyond the porch remained hidden behind the curtain of white fluff. No one was paying any attention to me, and I was afraid to disturb anyone with questions. Everyone looked worried and I did not really want to know what it meant. Unable to go outside because of the weather, I wandered around the house clutching my new teddy bear. Henius had been moved to the big bed in Papa's room. Every time I passed through it I would have a look at him, but only from a distance, because I did not want him to see how worried I was. I did not think he really saw me, even with his eyes wide open. People kept coming to see him, their coats covered with snow, and I began to hang out near the entrance door to get a peek at the weather which was not letting up. I got into the habit of staying in the hallway where the furs of the guests were hanging, petting them as if they were live animals, soft, smooth, and snuggly.

The priest came when it was still light outside. Of the three priests in the parish, it was the one Henius and I disliked. I would run into him while passing through the dining room where he sat at the big table playing solitaire that was not coming out. That was a bad sign, he told me. I was not sure what he meant by that. Was it his way of telling me that Heniuś was going to die? Even though he was a priest, he, like the Gypsy woman, needed cards to divine the future. God was not speaking to him directly. I never did see the owl whose hooting was a warning to us. Was it black like the priest's cassock or was it some other color? If black, it could have been a raven, and ravens like owls were also carriers of bad news.

It was a black car that took Heniuś to the hospital in the city. It pulled up as close to the front of our house as possible. It was still snowing. I saw Heniuś being carried out and put onto the back seat. He did not even have a chance to feel the snow; he was being kept out of it on purpose. I had been told that he was going to the best hospital, the children's clinic at the university, and that he would get well there. I was convinced he would. Papa and Mama went with him just to make sure that he got there safely.

As for me, I was left behind, feeling unwanted.

I stopped keeping track of hours and days. Someone was taking care of me—it was not just Andzia—so that I would not get into any trouble, like go wandering in the snow when it was coming down too hard. To stay indoors was the order and stay I did, once again walking from room to room with the teddy bear in my arms. Perhaps Heniuś was right, and a ghost really was waiting for me behind every door. It's not good to have ghosts in the house, and I was hoping that they would move out as soon as Heniuś returned.

Papa came back, without Mama and Heniuś. To have Papa home made me feel a little better. Mama sent letters from the hospital, Papa answered them. Everything was going well, he told me. Soon I would be able to see Heniuś. Indeed, one day the black car arrived to take Papa and me to the city. It was snowing, it had been for days.

An endless hallway, a room with walls so high that it does not look quite right. Several beds in it but all of them empty except the one Heniuś is lying in. He is alone, all alone, no children to play some games with. The ceiling is like a sky, so far above him and me, and it may even be painted blue. We look at each other. I am afraid to say anything, and he may no longer be able to speak. Perhaps a hospital is like a church, one is not supposed to talk there. A minute or two passes. I am out in the hallway again. Its wall of windows faces a snow-covered courtyard several stories below. It seems that people around me are trying to decide what to do with me. No one needs me, no one wants me, home is too far away, and it is snowing. Finally, a woman I have not seen before takes me by the hand. "I'll take her," she says. She and I get into another black car, not the same one that brought me to the city. When I wake up on a couch in somebody's study the next morning, I have no idea where I am or how I had gotten there. Somewhere along the way I must have fallen asleep.

I was not able to keep track of time. How long did I stay in that house on a hill that had many rooms and many closed doors? It came with a father, a mother, two sons, and servants I did not get to know. I wandered between the study, the boys' room, and a vast dining room, looking out of the windows at the snow in the garden. I did not open any closed doors. The father, a tall man with bushy eyebrows, did not smile. I was afraid of him. The mother tried to be kind and would occasionally ask me how I was doing. Fine, fine, always fine. I did not cry or complain and did my best to stay out of her way and not be a nuisance. I would just wait for the boys to come home from school. I adored them, especially Janek, the older one who was fifteen. They kept me so well entertained that I even stopped thinking about Henius. It was wrong, of course, and I should have known better.

From the time Henius got so sick, it snowed every day, sometimes just an ordinary snow, sometimes a howling blizzard like the one that came down on the city while the boys were still taking care of me. When it was over, the sun came out and it got very cold. Paths were dug out on the hill so that people, like me and the boys, could get into town where I would have been able to buy myself a book, a real book with a hard cover and not one of those things that cost only a few pennies and could be finished in minutes. I should have known that it was a sign that something bad was about to happen or already had. Mama would be paying for the book I was told, and Mama was very careful with money. She did not spend it on stuff that children didn't really need. So, why did she agree to pay for a book? I should have thought about it and seen the sign. I did not. The two boys must have been on my mind, not Mama. They distracted me from thinking about all the terrible events that could have been happening.

We walked down the slope carefully, through a tunnel in the snow, its walls way above my head. When we reached the bottom, we ended up next to an announcement column and right then and there I learned from the black letters on white paper with black edges that Henius had died. We turned around, with me in tears.

Once inside the house, I just let myself go and kept crying until I could no longer cry and had only hiccups left. All that time Janek kept holding me in his arms, feeling my pain.

Papa and Mama arrived. Yes, Henius was dead. A posted death announcement could not be wrong.

What else is there to this story?

That I wasn't supposed to find out? That everyone was supposed to be telling me that he would stay in the hospital 'til he had fully recovered? Were they going to just keep telling me that forever?

I was allowed to go to his funeral: first the church whose glassy decorations were like pellets of ice, the procession to the cemetery along the river, the horse-drawn hearse because Heniuś liked horses and horse carts were superior to cars, a hill with pine trees and a view of the city, and finally a hole in the ground in which he was supposed to stay forever. It snowed on that day with big, wet snowflakes, the kind that mixed well with tears. I kept crying. Papa looked terribly sad. Mama's face was hidden by a black veil.

We returned home after the funeral. Our house no longer felt like a home though I tried to pretend that it did. That the blue room Heniuś and I had shared became all mine did not feel right. I did not want to sleep in it alone. Of course, I had to—together with my nightmares. One night, Heniuś came to the scorched threshold where the adults had tried to ward off the evil eye when we had moved into this house. He was warning me of the upcoming war and ordering me not to give away his toy soldiers. I didn't want to hear this. Enraged, I screamed at him and tried to crush him with the door. Terrified, I woke up.

The inevitable thaw arrived. It got too warm too fast with too much snow on the ground. The river overflowed, the field of forget-me-nots we had to pass through to get to it was under water. Heniuś would have enjoyed seeing the changed landscape: new, different, and scary. I could watch it from the windows but had to stay inside, because a child could drown in deep snow filled with water. A little girl had drowned in a ditch in front of her home.

A priest came to explain to me why Heniuś had died. God, he told me, loves good children and takes them to heaven before they grow old. Heniuś was there now, an adoring angel floating around God, and heaven was the best place to end up in. I already knew something about it from pictures of naked babies flying around an old man seated on a throne. They could not have been having fun and that the man looked angry and mean did not reassure me. So, that I was still alive meant that God did not love me. Should I have been thanking Him for not loving me? I wanted to believe that Heniuś was in a good place, but what the priest was telling me did not make any sense.

The summer that followed the floods had cloudless skies and a sun so bright that it made the countryside glitter as if it were on fire. The blues, pinks, purples, and golds of the fields glowed. I was not the only one noticing it, people were talking about it. The boy I used to play with was away for the summer, so grown-ups became my company. I became special because of Heniuś. They invited me to their homes, served tea and cookies, and showed me their treasures. Someone taught me how to ride a bicycle or at least tried to. I wondered if Heniuś could see me, but I didn't think his hole in the ground came with a view. If, on the other hand, he had become an angel, like the priest promised, he could have been watching. I felt sure that even if he had wanted to join me—and he probably did—God would not have let him.

And then, as if Papa and Mama had not yet suffered enough, I got sick, very sick, while playing ball all by myself in front of the old barn on a sunny day in August. The black car that had taken Heniuś to the hospital took us to the city. In the examining room at the children's hospital, during a moment of consciousness, I heard the doctor say, "If she lives through the night, she will live." I understood what he had said and found it very interesting. His words did not frighten me. I was beyond caring what could happen to me. That God did not love me enough to make an angel out of me was a little disappointing, but unkind as He was, adoring Him was not something I would want to do forever and ever anyway.

Just as I was getting out of the hospital, the war broke out.

I was right. The Almighty, the All-Knowing, was not kind.

3

Maybe Not a Story

This is a story about nothing. Very little will happen in it.

First comes the house, long and low. It has a giant thatched roof and whitewashed stucco walls. It does not look strange because at one time in that part of the world many houses were built like that. They may have burned down during the war, or they caved in on their own since then. It comes with a circular gravel driveway, not for cars but for carriages, and a bouquet of jasmine bushes at the center of the circle. I remember their scent. Behind the house there is magic: an ancient park with enormous trees. No, it is not a forest. There is no undergrowth in it, just short, sparse grass one can easily walk on in summer. I think the park is like a church—sacred and much more beautiful, though. When allowed to stroll through it, I sometimes stop under one of these giant trees, look up and try to find heaven above its crown.

After Henius died, I used to go to that house and sit in the vast parlor where the only pieces of furniture were the chairs lined up against the long walls. An old lady would come in, sit down across from me, and talk as if I were a grown-up. How are you? What have you been doing lately? And then she would tell me about some events that happened when she was still young, many, many years ago. They were as good as fairytales. Sometimes she would even offer me tea in a fine China cup. The tea and the way we talked to each other made me feel important. It is very sad that Henius had to die before people began to treat me like that. I did not know who this woman was. Somebody's grandmother? A relative of the owner of the house? Details like that were not important to me, but her soothing voice was. She did not speak about wars, hers was a peaceful world. I was eight then. It was the summer of 1939.

A man, old by my standards, also lived in that house with his son and daughter-in-law. He was the owner. I don't know who else lived in it, as I never ventured into its depths and always stayed in the empty parlor seated in one of the chairs along the walls. Before I got the chance to learn the secrets of this mysterious place, we left that town and could not go back to it because of the war.

Before Henius got sick, we both were fascinated by the owner's son. He worked at the courthouse and would sometimes stop by after work. Every time he did, Henius and I learned something. "Our father snores," we bragged to him laughing. "Do you think your father wants me to know that he snores?" he asked, making me think: right, perhaps he does not. He showed us the park—his park—and told us about its trees. Some of them, like the ones lying on the ground dead, came with a history of nests built in their branches or of the hurt they had suffered during storms. The man had a name, of course, but strangely enough I do not remember it. I know it started with a "c," so I'll call him C. I have a picture of him and me taken at a picnic at the country house of an old couple I hardly ever saw but whose name I do still remember. Why? We are sitting on the grass next to a brook, he and I. A big, strong man with blond hair, a square jaw, and blue eyes. What would I think of him now? The second picture is of the group sitting on the grass under a tree: our hosts, Mama, C. and his wife, and, finally, me with a big dog in my arms. That was in the summer of 1939, too. Time was about to run out.

C.'s wife, who is as nice and caring as C., is going to have a baby. I know about it because people are saying that she is. I do not see any connection between her big belly and the baby. As far as I can tell, she is just getting fatter and fatter. One day soon a stork will bring it, I am told. That must be one of those lies grown-ups are so good at. In all my life I have seen plenty of storks but none carrying a baby. When I ask Mama to explain, she answers me with a smile. A smile means that she has nothing to say. Mama is not good at explaining. Papa and C. are, but, for some reason, I do not dare to ask them. I don't think men like to talk about babies.

To help me forget about Henius, C. takes me on a trip to the lake country, the likes of which I have not yet seen. We all squeeze into a kayak—C., I, and his wife with her big belly—and glide through a maze of reeds and water lilies. Off and on I can spot the tops of willow trees somewhere far away. Land! It makes me feel safer to know that it is still there. Deep waters frighten me and the lake we are on must be deep. In my many nightmares, rivers, seas, and lakes swallow me before I have a chance to wake up. Of course, C. will not let anything bad happen here, he knows how to row. It is a beautiful landscape, but not as beautiful as C.'s magic park with its rabbit holes, bird nests, and ancient trees. I like the reeds and how they stand up in the water straight, strong, and green. I like the lilies whose round brownish green leaves rest on water, and I like the pink and white of their flowers. What I do not like is the color of the water. It is dark gray, almost black in places, except for the patches where it seems to be on fire. There must be other people on the lake. I hear their voices mingling with the screeches of birds. And just because we are sitting so close to each other, I can see how C. and his wife look at each other when C. takes a short break from rowing.

He was born or delivered by a stork that same summer of 1939. His mother brought him over in a baby carriage so that we could see how beautiful he was. Even I, who had never before seen a baby from so close up, thought that he was beautiful. But what did I know then? Papa's friends who were his age had old children and no babies. The only young married people we knew were C. and his wife. Gypsies, on the other hand, had large families and a lot of babies to carry around. Almost every Gypsy woman held a bundle of rags in her arms, a bundle whose face I could not see, since I was afraid to get close enough. So, actually I had no baby to compare this one to.

I remember very clearly the three of us, Mama, C.'s wife and I, standing in the driveway, between the house and the old barn, admiring the baby in his carriage. "What a beautiful baby! He looks so smart, as if he were older than he is! And he can already smile!" Mama is really impressed and promises him a great future. He has long dark hair and blue eyes, but I don't know about the smile. His lips move as if he were trying to speak. The day is sunny. I feel that Heniuś is standing next to me, admiring the baby, because he, too, thought that C. was a great man. Of course, he can't be here with us. And yet, I still sometimes ask myself if he could be looking on from above…

Soon after meeting the baby, I got sick and had to be taken to a hospital in the city. Papa was transferred for work, and we had to move, and finally the war broke out as promised. The baby in his carriage was the last highlight of our life in the unforgettable little town where I had spent two years learning a lot, though not much of it was of any importance to grown-ups. The war placed that town in a different country and a border now separated us from it. I already knew that borders were hard to cross—if they were not, most people we knew would have already fled from Wilno—but the border to get away from there was particularly hard to get over. I imagined that the crossing had to be done on a moonless night by crawling on all fours. Yet, some people, brave enough to do it, were bringing news of what was happening in what once upon a time was my home. Scores were getting settled: arrests, death sentences, deportations, betrayals, firing squads, and finally famine. No mail from there could reach us, and it would not have been safe to write, neither for C. and his wife nor for us. The messengers of bad news spoke to Mama in whispers perhaps because I was not supposed to hear what they were saying or perhaps because, with walls having ears, one had to be careful. No one was allowed to criticize the state. At first, whispers made me want to listen, but, after a few doses of very bad news that made me feel like disappearing, I made a mistake, a terrible, terrible mistake. When I heard about the hunger and children dying from it, I was stupid enough to ask "And C.'s baby, that beautiful boy? How is he doing?" I was sure that C. and his wife would be taking great care of him. The question had to be safe.

It was not.

"He has died," came the answer.

After that, I stopped listening to whispers. I stopped asking questions. I even forgot the name of the family. I no longer wanted to know.

Maybe that's what this story is about.

4

Letter to an Unknown Man

If this message could get to you somehow, it would probably, as people say here, make your day. If there are days where you are. You did not leave a forwarding address, so I cannot mail it to you. Besides, I no longer remember your name. It is possible that I never really knew it or I may have heard it, but it never sunk in. You did stick with me, though, and that's all that matters at the moment. I wish I could still believe in the superstitions and tall tales I was exposed to in my childhood, but I gave that up a long time ago. So, as far as I am concerned, there is no way of reaching you. Still, in case I am wrong, and the superstitions are right, I will go ahead and try to explain why you have been on my mind for so many years. It certainly was not love at first sight or something equally silly.

I saw you only once, so you may be wondering what all this fuss is about. We were going up the stairs, my mother and I, and you were coming down. We were then living two flights above you, so we must have met near the ground floor. The stairwell was well lit because it had large windows, and the day was distressingly bright. That September the sky was always cloudless as if God, from his throne in heaven, was smiling at the earth below in expectation of great entertainment. The sun was on you when we met, we had our backs to it. Young as I was then, and small, I could look at people carefully without being noticed. I was too insignificant to attract attention and that I rarely had anything to say must have helped. Very likely you did not even see me, not with my mother smiling at you. She had a charming smile and knew how to use it. I did not think that it was working on you, you were in a big hurry. A gray suit, a white shirt, and a tie the color of red wine. Right? See how well I remember? In a moment you will understand why. Your face? I found it rather ordinary, though all its parts fitted together nicely and added up to a kind of handsomeness I had not yet learned to appreciate. A soft face, flat and round. Your eyes were blue, your blond hair was straight, stringy, and plastered down with sweat. I noticed a touch of inconsistency in your appearance and had to study you harder. A well-dressed man in a rumpled suit and in a great hurry, sweating on a cool day.

My mother turned on her charm even harder. She knew how to make her eyes sparkle when circumstances called for it. "We have just moved to the top floor... My husband is a judge," she told you. She may have said "was" instead of "is" because by then the war was already doing away with the legal profession. You must have told her your name, the usual introduction, but probably I was not paying attention because of my habit of taking in the world only with my eyes until someone made a pronouncement that aroused my curiosity. Then I would listen and try to figure out what it really meant. After a brief handshake, you smiled the kind of smile that lets people know that one is in a hurry.

Were you running away or trying to? Everyone we knew then wanted to get away and so did we, but there was no place that would take us in. You had a reason to be afraid and did not want to show us your fear.

After our meeting on the stairs, my mother told my father at dinner that she had met the lawyer from downstairs. By then we were already eating our meals in the kitchen, quick meals of soup and bread, sometimes without even sitting down properly at the table. Our kitchen was just like yours: a dead-end place without an exit, its only window facing the cobbled courtyard, a long, long way down. Every time I looked out through it, I saw myself lying splattered on the stones below. Your apartment was so much closer to the ground that you would have been able to escape through the kitchen window when the wrong kind of people were pounding on your door.

My father told us that he knew you from the courthouse and that you were a White Russian exile from the other side of the border. Your family name was well-known—I already knew the significance of that—and if you had not escaped in time, you would have been killed or sent to Siberia. Here you became a very successful state prosecutor in charge of political cases. It was clear to me that everything my father was saying was not adding up to anything good. Though I was only eight years old and not very bright, I did know a lot about politics. Yes, indeed, you were in for a bad time. Very likely they would get you before they got us. We would feel sorry for you—we were sure to—but, at the same time, we would have to be glad that it was your turn and not ours.

You lived alone, whatever the reason, and your apartment was larger than ours. That one person had so much space to live in was a crime and that was likely another strike against you. You may have had relatives in faraway cities, like Paris or Geneva, where many people from your country had sought refuge some twenty years earlier. My father had told me that wars and revolutions had a way of breaking families apart and scattering them around the globe. So, someone somewhere may still be taking out the precious family album, if it survived the flight, and is showing it to your grandnephew or niece. "This is your great-uncle, a man to be proud of. He did not get out in time…" Your photograph has turned yellow and brittle, its edges are beginning to split, but you are being remembered and will be for many years. Maybe I am not the only person who still remembers you.

One day in October, after the weather had turned cold and the skies had grown gray, my mother and I were going up the stairs while the janitor was coming down. We happened to meet at exactly the same spot where we had met you the month before. Yes, it was a strange coincidence. "He has been arrested," the janitor said. I knew right away that he meant you. My mother's eyes grew wide, her lips twitched, as if she was trying to say, I do want to know, but don't tell me. Yet the janitor did tell her. "He has been shot already," he added. At that moment I saw you again clearly as you stood there in the sun for a few minutes looking down at us: a gray suit, a white shirt, a tie the color of red wine, and the smile of a man who was in a rush and thinking about getting away.

Your apartment was ransacked after your arrest and then turned over to a group of soldiers who did not know what indoor plumbing was for. When they moved out—I never found out why—the toilet was overturned, the sink was sitting on the floor, and there were dead fish in the bathtub. They had used some of the wood from the parquet floors to make a fire in the kitchen stove. There was no furniture in any of the rooms, no pictures on the walls, the colors of which were startling to me. Our walls usually were some shade of beige, one of your rooms was cinnamon red. How did I learn all this, you may be wondering. Once again, my mother and I were going up the stairs when we ran into the janitor on his way down. He insisted on showing my mother what was left of your home after the barbarians had gone over it. At first she hesitated, perhaps because it was not nice to snoop, but then she agreed, perhaps because she wanted to see how you had lived or perhaps because it was no longer right to say no to a janitor. That's how we happened to get a look. "It was such a beautiful place… such a beautiful place…," he kept repeating, as he mourned for its vanished beauty while we were walking through the empty rooms that did not even smell right. I never got a clear look at him and so now, to me, he is just a faceless man in a dark coat, moved almost to tears by the sight of the destruction. He was a good man who, later on, may have saved our lives.

I remember you and the strange cinnamon red color of one of your rooms, and I wish you well wherever you are.

5

The Shoemaker's Son

When the war I had been hearing about for some five years finally arrived, people were expecting bullets, bombs, and poison gas, but that's not what happened. Tanks came. Only one was attacked with a Molotov cocktail, and Papa did not approve. Strips of white paper on windowpanes turned out to be useless decorations. The airtight rooms and the one gas mask allotted to us were not needed. Mama was wise not to spend any time climbing windowsills and gluing the paper that was supposed to prevent the glass from shattering. Had it been necessary, we would have gone to the neighbors who had spent more time and effort preparing themselves for death.

For me the beginning of war was taking place at the railroad station: trains, soldiers, weeping women, and songs. To see so much love in one place at the same time was new to me.

It was Papa who made sure that I would not miss what he called "History." One day, at sunrise, he made me get out of bed and lie down on the cold floor of the balcony. "Just wait, and History will arrive," he told me, before going back into the living room, as if he himself didn't need or want to see its arrival. How did he know? There I was, all alone, shivering from the cold or my fear. But he was right. History did come. Two tanks with red flags rolled down our street. The sky glowed from the rising sun and so did the walls of the building.

The enemy having arrived, everyone stayed home until the looting was over. People began to trickle out of their apartments, slowly and cautiously. I was able to watch them by looking out of a window. Bread, they must have been after. Though I had heard a lot about previous wars—of which there were many—I still had a lot to learn. This time from experience.

I did not see anyone being shot in the street, but when the janitor told Mama that the lawyer who lived on the first floor had been arrested and shot, it was immediately clear to me why: he was a White and we were now living under the Reds. It was as simple as that.

When the apartment below us grew silent, I knew right away that its owners had disappeared leaving everything behind. Did they flee or were they arrested? Mama may have known, but I did not feel like asking her. I preferred to think that they had fled to Sweden, because it was such a nice country and so close to us. War was about fleeing to a safe place, if you could find one that would let you in. Papa thought that we too should try to leave, but Mama wanted to stay a little bit longer and we did, until it was too late. Safe places were so expensive that very few people could afford them. It seemed to me that we did not have that kind of money, not when Mama had been saying for years "we can't buy this or that because it costs too much."

War was also about hunger, not just about shooting and killing. But hunger was not happening, at least not yet. Instead, stuff was disappearing from the shelves of the grocery store where Mama would send me sometimes when she did not feel like going out. The store, which was in the basement of the house next door, used to have some chocolate bars on display to tempt me and make my mouth water. One day there were none and there would not be any in the near future because chocolate did not grow in our part of the world. It was not fair that it did not. Though chocolate was "beyond our means," it had made me feel good just to be able to stare at it. Since Papa was no longer working, because, as the laws changed, judges were no longer needed, we could only buy what Mama called "the essentials," and chocolate had not been one of them. Now, I couldn't even look at it.

I realized that my view of what was happening was not the same as that of the grown-ups. To them, who was disappearing was more important than an empty shelf in the grocery store. It wasn't that I didn't care. I definitely did. But hearing that "so and so" had been arrested did not make me cry as long as I didn't know who "so and so" was. We had moved to Wilno only a few weeks earlier, and almost everyone here was a stranger to me. On the other hand, when I heard that someone from the little town we had come from had been dragged out of bed in the middle of the night and taken to no one knew where, it hurt me so much that soon I stopped listening. The news from there was always bad—tragic as Papa would say—and gave me nightmares.

After what felt to me like a few weeks, there was a change under the Reds. It seemed, at least on the surface, as if life was getting back to what had been normal before. Soldiers, always in groups of three or four, were rarely seen during the day and that helped me imagine that they were gone. Well, apparently, they were not. Instead of strolling through the streets in daylight, they were up in the early morning hours putting people on cattle trains that were waiting at the station. "The age of deportations has returned," Papa would say. Because of the curfew, no one was supposed to know what was happening, but it did not actually work that way. By morning, news would bubble up from the underground about who, when, and where. The destination of the trains was unknown, except that they were always heading east. Papa was sure that our turn would come, sooner or later, and he did not even try to convince me that the place we would be taken to was going to be a place where someone in his right mind would want to end up. Hunger and disease and either very, very severe cold or unbearable heat meant we would probably die before getting there. Yet, he would always add, it was a land of endless forests and fields and of great rivers, famous and beautiful, whose names sounded strange. That didn't seem so bad to me.

It was then and there, that for the first time in my life I was sent to school. At eight years old, I was put into fourth grade even though I knew next to nothing. The children in that school were from very good homes, while I, a stranger, did not even have a real home. They came to class well-prepared and looked down on me, the dumb girl from some crumbling village. We had nothing to say to each other. I sat at my desk not listening to the teachers because, after all, they were not talking to me, but to a class I was not really a part of. Instead, I kept thinking about everything I had lost that year. And I had lost a lot.

Even before school recessed for the summer—early that year to give children a chance to learn a new language—I joined a gang of street children from my neighborhood. I was aware that once I became one of them, no child from a good family would be allowed to play with me. Since I was already an outcast in school, that didn't seem to me like a big step. With the street children, I began to roam—never straying very far from home, looking for treasures though never finding any, and getting excited over some unusual sight, however insignificant, be it a dead bird, a mouse or a strange-looking beetle. The clothes we wore were dirty and tattered, our feet bare, our knees covered with scrapes. It was a life of freedom. These children lived in the cellars of apartment buildings where walls were moldy, the air cold, damp, and filled with germs. "The breeding ground for tuberculosis," Mama used to warn me. Men also beat their wives and drank themselves to death in those depths.

I, in contrast, lived on the third floor in an airy apartment overlooking the park. Life was not fair. The children who lived in our kind of apartment were well-behaved because someone was always watching them, and that made them boring. The street children were also well-behaved even with no one looking after them, because if they tried to do anything outrageous or destructive and got caught at it, their fathers would give them the kind of beating a child could not forget. So, they were boring, too. To come up with something to do, very naughty and foolproof, was not easy. You had to think long and hard, and these children did not seem to be good at it. I knew all that from experience.

I loved to build sandcastles in the sandlot at the bottom of the hill right across the street from our house. Perhaps they did, too, since they would come and watch me build mine and then try to build their own. I thought that mine were better than theirs, more complicated and bigger. I was able to keep working on them for a long time, whereas they would get bored quickly and give up. And once that happened, they would stand around my masterpiece staring at it until one of the kids gave it a kick. Mostly, I did not really care. Sandcastles were meant to crumble. But I didn't always see it that way. When a boy from a good family kicked one I was still working on, I hit him just to make sure that he would not do it again. His governess saw it and told Papa that my behavior was unacceptable, and that the boy would no longer be allowed to play with me. Indeed, I was a very bad child and could even end up in prison someday.

I liked the feel of the sand: how it slid between my fingers when dry, how it stuck to my hands when wet. One day I was digging in search of sand that would be just right for building a castle, moist but not runny. I ended up with a hole big enough to bury a child in. I was sitting inside it throwing the perfect sand over its edge when one of the children came up with the brilliant idea that it would be fun to see me buried in a hole I had dug for myself. I did not object and was soon covered up to my shoulders with sand, some still damp, some dry. The kids and I were amused until I began to wonder if the hole I found myself in was about to turn into one of those sandpits no one ever gets out of. I did not dwell on that thought for long. A stream of warm liquid hit my neck and shoulders. The children behind me were laughing. The shoemaker's son, a dumb, scrawny kid, was trying to add spark to an entertaining event and was pissing on me. When I got out of the pit, he was still standing near its edge waiting for the second act. The stupid kid, what did he expect? Did he think that I would thank him for the gift of his piss because he was so scrawny and younger than I? Well, I punched him in the chest and that sent him running for home. I should have known what would happen next but somehow didn't.

This was my first spring in the city. I had yet to figure out if it was different from the springs I knew from the countryside. Sometimes, while walking along a street, I would pick up an unfamiliar scent that I was unable to identify. I finally decided that in a city even stones smell in spring. Their scent was not as good as that of the soil warming up in the sun. And no big skies here unless one went to the top of the mountain. Often the sky was only a strip as wide as the street below it and that made it impossible to see an oncoming storm until it was too late to get out of its way. A night rain would leave the sandlot smooth and glistening. It did not seem right to mar it with footsteps, but I had to if I wanted to build castles and trace magic figures in the sand.

It was dumb of me not to head right home after the unfortunate incident. Probably no one would have been in because Papa and Mama were very busy with what they called "liquidating." Liquidating meant that they were somewhere in town trying to sell things we would never use again.

I only caught sight of the little pisser's mother when she was already crossing the street, running towards me, waving her arms and screaming. I knew who she was because Mama would talk to her sometimes when they ran into each other in the street. Mama, whom someone had called a great diplomat, would tell the woman that she had beautiful children. The pisser's mother was big and wide but not fat. If she gave me a beating, it would have hurt. Mama had seen her at the May Day celebration shouting "down with the bourgeoisie," her arms raised, her hands rolled into fists.

The situation did not look good to me. I had no place to hide and trying to run away would have been rude and an admission of guilt when I was not the one who started it all. So, I just stood there, next to my grave, holding my ground—not because I was brave, but because I did not know what else to do. She came to a halt in front of me, close enough for a beating. But instead of putting her hands on me, she began to call me names I knew from park benches and was not supposed to repeat. Her face was white, her eyes pale, her bright red hair covered her head with curls that reminded me of worms. I did not like her looks. When she ran out of bad words, she got into politics. I was a bourgeois leech. It was time to put an end to people like me, so that they would no longer drink the blood of the proletariat. She promised to see to it that justice was done and report me to the authorities. Her son had weak lungs—Mama was right—and a blow to the chest could kill him. We are in charge now, and you, little bitch, should know it. I did know that, actually, because Papa and his friends talked about it most of the time. A way of life was being turned upside down, and we all knew it.

Her threats left me terrified. I wished she had given me a beating instead. I did not tell Papa about them. Already worried that any night we could be arrested and deported, he did not have to know that now it was even more likely to happen. Mama was too preoccupied with the liquidation and probably would not have listened to me. The burden was on me. I had no one to share it with.

I was spending most of the time outdoors, avoiding the little pisser, but was so worried about Papa that I had to keep checking on him several times a day either by running home—he was hardly ever there—or by wandering through some nearby streets where, by some miracle, I would catch sight of him, should he have been passing by. And I did a few times: a stooping figure with a bundle under his arm filled with stuff he was trying to sell. The more we sold, the better off we would be. He was not very good at it, and Mama was convinced that buyers were taking advantage of him.

One night they did come for us. By then, there were only two tenants in the building: my family and a neighbor with what was called "connections." The pounding on the entrance door three floors below was so loud that it woke even me up. Why wasn't the janitor, whose duty it was to unlock it, letting them in? Was he sleeping so soundly or was he pretending not to hear them? They must have been kicking the door with their heavy boots and hitting it with the butts of their rifles, it was so loud. "They will be angry when they break in and find us," Papa whispered. "Let's wait," Mama whispered back, though there was no chance that anyone would hear us three floors below. And wait we did—for what felt like forever—till they gave up and walked away from our door. I heard their steps grow dimmer as they went west, towards the river, to look for someone they could get instead of us. Did the shoemaker's wife report on us? Was it her way of getting even with me? At least we were not put before a firing squad. After that night Papa went into hiding and that meant sleeping wherever he could and coming home during the day to prepare for our flight. As for me, I only came home for the night. Our furniture was gone—not sold, but rather put into storage—and we were sleeping on the floor.

One morning, I was out at dawn wearing only a bathing suit because dresses had to be saved for more normal times. The sky was pink, the sand wet with dew, the air cold, the streets empty. I wanted to see what the city looked like when people were still sleeping or just beginning to wake up. Well, it looked like a dream in which half of the sky is light, half of it dark, and you can sense that in spite of all that light, darkness is going to win and change a happy dream into a nightmare. Suddenly, the damn piss boy appeared at my side, for real. He must have just crawled out of his cellar in search of an adventure and wearing his usual outfit: oversize short pants held up by suspenders, no shirt, and no shoes. I could not tell him not to follow me because we were not on speaking terms, so I just pretended that he was not there. Had he already forgotten what had happened?

The borders of the two long sides of the rectangular sandlot were formed by our street and the mountain across from it. On one of the two short sides was a newly constructed apartment building which, according to what Papa had told me, a bomb would not have been able to blow to pieces because it was made of steel-reinforced concrete. Its strength intrigued me, and I almost wished that it would get hit so that I could see for myself if what he was telling me was true. The border of the remaining side was a street whose houses were climbing up the hill almost all the way to the convent where nuns ran an expensive boarding school for girls from good families. A sand-colored masonry wall surrounded its vast secret gardens which I wanted to see badly because they were off limits. There was little chance that I ever would: the wall was too high to climb, and I was not the kind of girl the school would take as a pupil.

The street was very pretty—I sledded down it in winter—and it had a good view of the mountain. That morning it lured me with its colors and lights. I couldn't figure out where the pink on the windows was coming from, and, like in the nightmares I had been having, the brown of the walls was darker than it would have been in sunlight. The pisser followed me when

I turned the corner and headed for the convent. Suddenly there it was, right in the middle of the sidewalk in front of one of the fancy houses that lined the street, a big pile of books damp from dew and a treasure trove of questions I could not answer. Who? Why? When? I already knew that some books could get one into trouble, like those Papa burned in the kitchen stove the night we learned that we had lost the war. They did not burn easily. I could see pictures of eagles and flags on some of the books on the sidewalk. To touch any of them didn't seem right. The shoemaker's son, standing next to me, must have also been wondering what it was all about. Probably he did not know how to read, so books did not have much meaning to him. Neither he nor I said anything. After a little while, he let me know what his thoughts were: he took his little thing out of his pants, the thing I was not supposed to see, and let out a stream of piss onto the pile. That was when I decided to run down the hill as fast as I could, so that I would get home before he was able to stop pissing.

Before Papa, Mama, and I fled the city, I learned that Mama was giving a lot of my stuff to the shoemaker's wife. Even the sled, my most prized possession, ended up with the little pisser. As we were saying good-bye to our apartment, I had, from the window of our living room, my last look at the sandlot down below. Specks of dust were floating in the ray of sun cutting through the room.

6

The Doctor's Daughter

It happened on the day Papa was planning to say good-bye to Wilno, saying good-bye as if the city were some kind of a friend we were about to lose forever. To make sure that I would always remember this place, he insisted that I come along for his farewell. In honor of the occasion that promised to be solemn, I was cleaned up, dressed up, and even given shoes to wear so that I could look like a nice little girl from a good home. It felt strange after weeks of running around barefoot and wearing only my old bathing suit.

We took a final look at our house. Its windows were staring down at us with a warning that we had to keep out, that we no longer belonged. From there we went to the main street—a short, pleasant walk—and were lingering in front of the department store whose window displays disappeared with the arrival of the war. When we still lived in the countryside, Mama used to take Henius and me there so that we could see and admire the toys that she was not going to buy because they were too expensive. She must have known in advance that we would need money to survive the upcoming war and that the few toys we had would have to be given away.

Across the street from the store was the courthouse that had turned into a forbidding kind of place. Papa was no longer going there. It was better to say good-bye to it from a distance and that's what we did before continuing our walk towards the main square. It was right there and then, as I was holding on to Papa's hand, not for guidance but to be close to him, that I felt someone behind me grab my elbow. I turned and there was this little girl asking, "Do you remember me?" A moment earlier the street had been empty. She must have just slipped out from one of the houses. Skinny and smaller than I, her brown hair in two thin braids, a cotton dress identical to mine with tiny white flowers on a background of blue.

Of course, I remembered her!

She was the doctor's daughter. Her father's house was on the main street of the town where we lived when Henius got sick. It wasn't called "Main" then. Its names depended on which country owned it, and when and if you were going east or west. Old people called it by one name, the young by another. It was confusing to a child who did not yet know history.

I had noticed the house because it was big and complicated and not just a simple box like ours. It had gables, two floors, and possibly a third where the gables were. Looking at it from outside one could not be sure. It also had a big front porch and green shutters. Like most houses in town it had wooden siding that had aged to a dark gray. Overgrown bushes filled the space in front of the house, but a picket fence kept them from invading the sidewalk. There may have been flowers in the backyard that could not be seen from the street. I liked to think that there really had been, filling the secret garden of the house of green gables. Two tales combined into one.

It was the doctor's house: that is where he lived and had his office which I saw once when Mama took me there, because the doctor was willing to give her a certificate of vaccination without sticking a needle into me. The office was a fascinating place with its glass cabinets, tools lined up on their shelves, and here and there a jar with what looked like pickled body parts. The doctor himself was a jolly kind of a fellow, his width rather than his height made him look big. I don't think Mama trusted him, though, because, when Henius or I actually got sick, the Jewish doctor came to see us.

The doctor had a daughter whom I did not know until Papa, Mama, Henius, and I were invited to a New Year's party at his house. Parties are not events children get invited to, so it was a big surprise that Henius and I would be going along.

Once upon a time many years ago, when we were still living in Wołożyn, we did go to a party by sled, through deep woods and falling snow, but as soon as we arrived there, we were put to bed in a room that smelled of pine. I fell asleep to the sound of voices and laughter, of grown-ups having a wonderful time. By morning, when I woke up, all the magic had already disappeared. We were driven home again in a sled, because there was no other way to get through the forest.

To the doctor's party we could have walked, but a sled picked us up because the evening was so cold that I had to keep my nose under the furs. It was not snowing, and the sky was covered with stars. Once there, Henius and I were taken into a room where children were having fun because no grown-ups were there telling them to behave. A real freedom it was, everything was allowed. Henius, who was not shy, joined some boys who were playing tag around furniture, often crashing into it, while I climbed to the top of a cabinet and sat on it right under the ceiling. From there I had a good view of what was happening below. Where did all these children come from, I wondered. I did not know any of them. One was the doctor's daughter. She lived in the city with her mother, at least so I heard, and visited her father only now and then. I had seen her before near his house, a girl about my age with bones finer than mine and no sign of her father's bulk. Since I did not know any girls, I wanted to meet her badly but had no idea how. I would only glance at her in passing. Maybe she glanced at me too.

And then there we were, together in one room, where, from my perch high up, I could keep my eye on her. She was wearing a blue velvet dress, the kind I would have liked to have but was not going to get because it would have been too expensive. Her hair was braided into two pigtails so as not to be in the way when some game got rough. Though smaller and younger than most of the guests, she was in charge. Every time she said "no," the other kids listened. Like in a picture in a children's book, she was the lion tamer and a very good one at that. I was impressed. What a girl! I knew there was no chance that I would ever be like her, but we could at least become friends if she were living in my town.

Not much got broken in the room while children were partying, but I did hear the din of breaking glass coming from the depth of the house where grown-ups were celebrating the arrival of the New Year. I must have been half asleep when the party ended yet awake enough to notice the smell of vodka on my way out through the haze of cigarette smoke. Some guests were probably drunk. All in all, it was a party to remember.

Why didn't she and her mother live with the doctor? I was curious enough to ask, though I already knew from experience that the answers would not get me any closer to the truth. First came the smiles, and then the word "divorced," the meaning of which I did not know. When I asked what it meant, I got more smiles and finally the inevitable "someday you will understand." By overhearing what I was not supposed to hear, I learned that the doctor was friendly with a woman who had two daughters and a small country estate nearby. That the word "friendly" had a hidden meaning, I did not yet know.

When Henius got sick, about one month after the party, our Jewish doctor happened to be out of town and Mama had to call the girl's father, the man with the big gabled house on main street. What more is there to write about what happened next? Henius died, and Papa and Mama blamed the doctor. He was an idiot and worse. Mama's hunch not to trust him had been correct. And what did God have in mind when He sent the good doctor out of town on some errand so that Henius would not be treated right? God's ways are mysterious, I was told.

I began to avoid passing the doctor's house. I would do it on the run or cross the street. What would I say to the girl if I ran into her? What did she know, if anything? I still wanted to become friends with her, but I knew somehow that that would be awkward. What would Papa say if I began to play with her? Did her father know that we were blaming him for what had happened?

Then followed that beautiful summer of cloudless deep blue skies and a burning sun when Papa was transferred to the city, because someone thought that we would not want to stay in the town where we had lived with Henius, and when the long-promised war finally broke out and changed our way of life. The weather that fall, too, was perfect.

In difficult times there should be no winter, but it did come that year, with its long nights, short dark days, and snow that did not stay white for long. A gray snow with black edges. We had to save on electric lights and coal. The fear of being arrested and sent into exile was constant. It was going to happen one night, and all we could do was wait.

Papa thought that we should flee. Mama finally agreed, though, according to what I overheard, it was like jumping from "the frying pan into the fire." We had been preparing for it for months until everything we were going to take along fit into three suitcases. The rest was sold, given away, or put into storage to be picked up after our return. There was no way to prepare for an arrest: everything we owned would have been left behind.

The last two days we spent in the city, before finally getting on the train, we stayed with Papa's friends from the court. They were real friends, not just acquaintances, and had a wonderful apartment with a secret passage from the entry to the backdoor. I loved the design. While soldiers enter through the front door, you slip out through the back. After climbing a few fences, you could keep running into the wilderness. I wished we had an apartment like that.

And now, on what was to be our very last walk through the city, the doctor's daughter, the girl I had wanted so badly to be my friend, suddenly appears at my side and asks me if I remember her. I do, though she has changed. Quickly, as if she were out of breath, she tells me that she lives just around the corner from us and knows that we will be leaving the next day. Something is wrong. How does she know that when it is supposed to be a secret? What does it mean?

And then she just kept walking with us as if she belonged.

It seemed to be all right with Papa—he was always kind to children—and she even took his hand when we were crossing the street. It looked as if we were about to have fun together, the three of us, and she would finally be the friend I had wished for when we were still living in Oszmiana.

Our threesome now established for the farewell walk, our first stop was the café, once very fancy, where Papa bought us cake. I had been to that place before the war—going there was one of the highlights of our trips from the country to the city—but I hadn't been there lately because we could not afford it. The glass tops of its tables were no longer as shiny as they were before the war, the cake not as good. Yet it was still a great treat. Papa sure knew what was important.

The linden trees lining the main street were getting ready to bloom and the scent of their blossoms was filling the air. We would stop every now and then to inhale the fragrance and give Papa time to rest. We sat on some chairs in front of the cathedral and had a long look at the castle on the hill and the white crosses that glowed in the sun. We played hopscotch while

Papa was taking his time saying good-bye to the scenery. The small park near where the little river was swallowed up by the big one was my favorite because it was unkempt. A wilderness. The waters of the little river gurgled over stones and plants that grew at its bottom and, after a bend, flowed into a mystery. Papa left us there and went to say another good-bye to Henius, since the cemetery was not far away. We climbed trees and played tag, hide and seek, and hopscotch, all those boring childhood games that turn into great entertainment when played with someone. That they made us laugh together added to the fun. It did not even occur to me to think about what was going to happen the following day.

On the way back, soon after leaving the park, the doctor's daughter began to whine—which was something a girl of her age who had once been a princess at a party should not have been doing! It was so undignified. Finally, she whispered that she had to pee badly and would not be able to hold it any longer. By then we were in the center of the square in front of the cathedral with no bush anywhere in sight for privacy. Why hadn't she peed in the park, I wondered. Her need could not have become so urgent in a few minutes. We were approaching rows of chairs in front of the parliament building, all unoccupied. Papa will want to rest, I told her. I'll see to it that he does. You go to some chair, they all have slatted seats, sit down with your dress out of the way and pee. Actually, her dress, just like mine, was already so short that sitting on it would have been impossible. All of us kids had been outgrowing our clothes and getting replacements was difficult.

My friend did exactly what I told her and came back relieved. She thanked me for coming up with such a brilliant idea. For a moment I felt bad. That brilliant idea should have been hers. She was so clever at the party where I was the dumb one watching from the top of a wardrobe. We walked back, with her holding on to my hand. She seemed to need to. But I wasn't used to being so close to other children. We were making plans to meet the next day, though I knew it was unlikely to happen. It was all about hoping, pretending, dreaming, and even believing in miracles. When we got near the old department store, she suddenly disappeared from my side. Did she enter one of the houses? Did she not want me to know where she lived?

That evening, I gave some thought to gain and loss. I had a friend for only one day and that was terribly unfair. Why did she change so much since the party? Cling to me? Expect me to solve her simple problems? Could it have something to do with her father, the doctor, being a spy who turned people in? I learned later that those were not just rumors. Her father was one of the crooks our little old town had to thank for the reign of terror after the outbreak of the war.

The next day, we fled as planned.

7

The Fortune Teller

The train trip was very long. When it was finally over, I thought that it had lasted two weeks, but it could not have. The confusion must have come from not having a watch and a calendar. The rocking of the train and the sound of its wheels were making me doze off during the day when I should have been awake. Plus, the din and lights of railroad stations in the middle of the night were waking me up when I should have been asleep. In my mind, days and nights merged and I could not keep track of time.

As far as I could tell, the passenger part of the train was empty except for the compartment we were in. The freight part carried pigs, lots of them, and they stunk. Soldiers kept coming to check our papers. The sky and the greenery were pale, sandy patches dappled the fields and there was no hill anywhere in sight. A pale flatland. And if it were not for an occasional river, the scenery would have been boring. Every time the train went over a bridge I asked for the name of the river, and the grown-ups found my questions annoying because they couldn't answer them. I was supposed to sit still and keep quiet so that they would be less anxious about the trip. We had four borders to cross. From what I had heard borders were dangerous, even the legal ones.

I must have been half asleep when we finally arrived. The station? I could not have seen it. Perhaps there was no station. Perhaps it had been bombed out. I simply don't remember it. Papa promised me a beautiful city, but I did not find Warszawa so: no castle on a hill and its great lazy river had no sparkle. I wanted to be back home and was afraid to admit it. I didn't want to disappoint him, since Papa had gone through so much trouble to get us here. I had to pretend.

Had it not been for Maria's daughter Irena, who took us in, we would have had no place to stay. Irena's apartment was filled with splendor like in a fairytale. I never learned how many rooms it had and who lived in it. Maria with her husband, who never smiled, and their youngest daughter Nina— they had fled before we did—and then Irena with her husband, two small children, and a father-in-law. The boy, not much younger than I, had temper tantrums until his face turned purple. The year-old baby screamed most of the time. The noise the two of them made used to put the grown-ups in a bad mood. Sometimes I was asked to distract the baby from crying and when it did not work, I got scolded for not doing it right. The children were still suffering from bombs and air raids of the year before, I heard someone say. Was the rest of Maria's family living there, too? I already knew that one of their two sons had been killed in the early fighting at the western front. No one spoke of the other one as dead, but I never learned where he was. Could he or their third daughter be living in rooms I had not seen?

I quickly learned how to be almost invisible, even if it meant sometimes hiding behind the dark blue velvet curtains that draped the many glass doors that opened onto the terrace. Most of the time I stayed in our room reading and rereading the book I was allowed to take along when we fled—*The Eye of the Prophet* was its title. Papa would take me to the park across the street where there were swings shaped like boats. If I swung for too long, I would get sick to my stomach. Around the corner was the ministry of defense in ruins, with weeds growing between the cracks in the rubble. The Church of the Holy Cross had a part of its roof missing, so even Jesus could not keep the bombs out. Papa showed me all the embassies and palaces lining the street we were living on, except that it was not called a street but a boulevard. There were no boulevards back home. Sometimes we joined Maria's family for meals. Sometimes, sitting on a bench in the park, we ate whatever could be bought from street vendors. I liked that: it was like having a picnic, and we did not have to hear the children cry. Mama, when she was not out on business, would lie on the bed resting, planning our next move and looking miserable. We could not stay with Maria's family for long—it would have been impolite. Besides, there was talk that the entire building would be taken over by the authorities and the family would lose their apartment. The grown-ups were worried, the children cried, and, with their apartment gone, we would become homeless and end up sleeping at the railroad station.

That we were living on a powder keg I kept hearing again and again. The future did not look good. Yet, people were trying very hard to have some fun and put on parties. The pineapple party was one of them. I did not really know what a pineapple was, except that it was some rare fruit one could live without. It came in tin cans with blue labels that pictured Robinson Crusoe's island. That island looked like a paradise I would have liked to get to. Just like chocolate, pineapples did not grow in our part of the world. That there would soon not be any to buy made them extra special. Our hosts had a couple of cans and decided to celebrate their existence with a dessert party. It had to take place in the afternoon because of the curfew and turned into a solemn affair at the big dining room table with a white tablecloth and crystal plates, like a Christmas eve dinner when people break wafers and wish each other the best. But it was only July—or it could have been August. Just like on the train, I could not seem to keep track of time. The pineapple itself did not have much flavor. I would have preferred gooseberries.

The only friend I had then was a servant girl, four or five years older than I. I had seen her briefly at the New Year's party in the big house in the forest which could only be reached by sleigh. She was the owners' daughter who, when the war broke out, was able to flee with her mother and sister. Her father was somewhere else, dead or alive. I hung out with her mostly in the bathroom while she was cleaning it. The girl had to work hard. I liked to think that her father would come one day and take her back to their beautiful house in the woods, a prince charming saving his Cinderella.

The old man, Irena's father-in-law, was small and spritely. Misfortunes seemed to amuse him. He laughed at the news, no matter how bad, as if they were not real but some kind of a joke. He carried a fancy cane with a sharp end though he did not need one to help him walk. I thought that for him the cane was like a fancy hat to a woman: it made him look more important if not any prettier, and he could poke people with it to make them get out of his way. He did not act like anyone Papa used to be friendly with. I liked to watch him because he was so different from anyone I knew, though, in the street I did see men who reminded me of him and, probably because of a picture I had seen or a story I had read, made me think of devils in disguise. Irena's father-in-law could have been one too, tiny horns hiding under his hat, hooves instead of feet in his fancy shoes. But he looked too distinguished to be just a plain devil, and so I had to find a better word to describe him. I came up with "Lucifer." As I understood it, Lucifers were the nobility in the land of devils. This man could have been a count or even a prince there.

After spending so much time going from office to office, Mama finally managed to get a permit to move to Kraków where life was supposed to be better. Better than what, I wondered. Once there, would we get a place of our own to live in or just windows to look at while walking the streets? To celebrate the permit, which was so hard to get, or our upcoming departure—by then Maria's family may have been glad to see us off—a dinner was being planned for a Sunday afternoon to which people I did not know were going to be invited. Friends of Maria's family, I was told. On that day the air was yellowish, the sky milky blue with patches of gray here and there. The sun was hiding behind a haze and somewhere far away a thunderstorm was brewing. It seemed that the guests were having a good time, but since I was sitting between Mama and Papa at a long table, I could not hear much of what was being said so far away from me and everyone talking at the same time trying to outdo each other. I heard them laugh and thought that they must have been joking about the great leaders who were in charge of the war. Irena's father-in-law was sitting at the far end of the table and people were listening to him as if what he was saying was of great importance, and perhaps it was. To make the dinner even more entertaining, he offered to read the palms of those present, guests and family. It was going to be fun, he must have promised, and those sitting near him must have agreed. And so, he started out on his memorable journey around the table looking at hands, sometimes saying something aloud, sometimes whispering. Some guests responded with laughter, some with a puzzled look. I could not hear anything until he got to Nina, whom he told to stop worrying about ending up an old maid because she would get married soon. I knew that that was exactly what Nina wanted to hear. But because she was not as beautiful as her sisters, her husband would not be handsome or come from an illustrious rich family. Nevertheless, Nina looked pleased. It must be the nice young man who often hung around the apartment, I thought. I had already noticed that he and Nina liked each other. Even before Lucifer got to Mama, I was making plans to leave the room unnoticed. If he had something bad to say, I did not want to hear it. If he tried to tell me my fortune, I did not want to know it. He took only a brief look at Mama's hand and, even before I had the time to get out of my seat, said, "And you, my lady, will end up on the other side of the ocean." I should have gotten up and run right then, but I was too absorbed in what I'd just heard. What did it mean? What ocean? Mama seemed pleased. I could see a little smile budding around her lips. A moment later it became clear that Lucifer was not interested in "nobody's" fortune and was going to skip me. I was definitely a "nobody." So, he turned to Papa, looked quickly at his hand and said, "And you, my honorable judge, will not survive the war." People sitting near us must have heard it. I saw Maria's cranky husband across the table from us open his mouth as if he was about to say something. I don't know if he did. As I was walking out of the room following Papa, I heard voices behind me. Did someone say, "Oh my God, how could he have told him that"? Once we were home, if the room we were staying in *was* a home, I lay down on the bed and cried, while Papa kept pacing back and forth. "What a dreadful man, what a dreadful, dreadful man..." I heard him repeat.

A couple of days later we took the train to our next garden of Eden, without seeing Lucifer again.

8

The Root Canal

We are in the city where life is supposed to be better. We have been looking for days but have not found anything better yet. We are homeless and trying to find a place to live. Maria and her family are not here to help us. I miss Cinderella, but I am glad to be rid of Lucifer who was so unkind to Papa. Kraków itself is very nice and filled with history. I like it despite having to walk its streets, looking at the windows that reflect the lights of the day and not knowing where we are going to spend the night. Will it be the railroad station again? Papa was counting on two of his relatives with apartments, but only one of them has offered to put us up for a few nights. Both of them have German tenants and don't want to annoy them. People think that a German tenant will save them from being thrown into the street. This may be the reason why we can't find a room to rent.

One of Papa's relatives is a very nice man. His wife is a real lady, perfumed and very well-dressed. They live in the new part of the city where streets are lined with poplar trees that grow fast and don't live for long. Papa and I take walks with the nice man in the park, and he teaches me about the many different trees that grow there, trees I have not seen before. He can tell funny stories and has pictures of the estate Papa's family lost during the Revolution. The other relative with an apartment is a White Russian woman with a Nansen passport which makes her special. Nansen passports are good to have, because even the Germans respect them. Her husband, a colonel or a general, was killed by the Reds during the civil war and that is why she ended up in this town and is now living in a fancy apartment with her daughter, a son-in-law, and a German tenant. She must have come with a lot of money, Mama says, and that's probably right. The woman has a mouthful of gold teeth I can see when she laughs, and she laughs often. I think she is Papa's first cousin, but her mother was Russian and so she does not speak Polish very well. We have a dinner at her place, good food served on fancy plates. That is all she can do for us. After dinner we sit in their living room for a conversation I can listen to, but her daughter—is she my second cousin?—distracts me. She has climbed onto her husband the doctor's lap and puts her arm around his neck, kissing him every now and then. I don't know what to make of it. That is what park benches are for, not a chair in a living room when guests are present. Should I keep looking at them when they kiss or find something else less interesting to look at? Maybe it's a White Russian custom.

Mama is not pleased with Papa's relatives. They don't do enough for us, she complains, and it may be Papa's fault because he does not know how to insist. Papa's other cousin—the nice one who loves trees—lets us sleep in his apartment when his German tenant is away on business. But most of the time we sleep in strange rooms which Mama rents here and there for a few nights. We lug our suitcases from place to place, always worried that someone may steal them, and we end up with nothing. Without a kitchen to cook in, we are not eating properly, but that is the least of our problems. We are not starving.

Success! Papa's cousin finds us a room in an apartment that belongs to a refugee couple who have no children. They fled or were displaced from the western part of the country at the beginning of the war, when one could still rent an apartment in this city, probably from someone who had fled in the other direction. So now we live in an ancient two-story building on an old narrow street not far from the main square. A very convenient location, I heard someone say, but I have no idea what it is convenient for. Is it the paper store at the nearby corner which still sells boxes of coloring pencils, the expensive kind, which I would like to have but will not be given? Our room has a small balcony and grayish pink walls, black in the corners from soot. Mama can use the kitchen, at least that is what she has been told. The landlord, a big man with a booming voice, wears riding britches because he used to administer a landed estate that, after the outbreak of the war, stopped belonging to its rightful owners. I can imagine him carrying a whip. A large picture of a hunting party hangs in the hallway. His wife is tiny and speaks in a whisper. I don't trust either of them.

There is something about our room that frightens me. In my dreams—I have many, all of them bad—I try to get out of it while being chased by something shapeless and black. The opening in the window is too small to squeeze through and I wake up crying. I know I should stop acting like a spoiled child, but I have no say over what happens in my dreams. Mama keeps complaining about Papa, that he has no business sense, that he will never learn how to work the black market or how to cheat and lie. He is a drone now, a useless drone. Life was supposed to be better here. It is not. At least we are no longer a burden to Maria's family and do not have to put up with Lucifer.

It should not have happened. I am ashamed that it did. One night I wake up with a terrible toothache. We are all in one bed, Papa, Mama, and me between them. Not for cuddling, of course, because we do not cuddle anymore, but because we are trying to keep warm. It has turned cold, and we have no coal for the stove. Though our bed is nowhere near the wall that, according to Mama, has ears, I have to cry into the pillow because if I wake up the landlord, there will be hell.

A dentist has an office on the ground floor, to the right as one enters the hallway from the street, and that is where Papa takes me in the morning to have the tooth pulled. The dentist is a small blond woman in a white coat. She takes a look inside my mouth and tells Papa that the tooth is permanent and should not be pulled. She will do root canal work on it, which is going to take time and will hurt, but at the end I will still have my tooth. Then she tells Papa that many ignorant parents think that that molar is a baby tooth and let it decay because it will come out on its own when the permanent tooth appears. They hope to save money that way and it's a real shame.

Poor Papa, I feel sorry for him. I wish I could say something so that he won't feel guilty—a death, an illness, the war, the flight, now this aching tooth of mine—but children are not supposed to speak unless asked to and I don't say anything.

If one has to be crazy to like going to the dentist, then I must have lost my mind. No one will see to it that I keep my appointments, so I have to keep track of them on my own and make sure that I have the dates and times straight. I do all of that as if I were a grown-up. The office is in her apartment, and, sometimes, when the door at the end of the hallway is left open, I can catch a glimpse of another life. I like to snoop, and I like to see the dentist. She explains to me what she is going to do and when. Yes, there will have to be some drilling, she warns me, and it is going to hurt. Once that is done, some poison will be put into the hole which will then be covered with a temporary filling. I'll have to be careful and not eat anything hard on that side so that the filling does not come out. If it does, I could swallow the poison by accident and that would not be good for me. All that may have to be repeated for a second time if the nerve is not quite dead after the first attempt to kill it. This is a fascinating story, and I wish I knew a child I could share it with. Having poison in my tooth makes me special.

I tell the dentist about Henius and where we come from. I try not to cry. She tells me that her husband may be in a POW camp. If he is not, I wonder but do not ask, then where is he? She also tells me that her daughter is one year old. I have already seen her by the time she tells me this. Being carried piggyback through the hallway by the dentist's German tenant with her arms around the man's neck, the little girl is laughing. The other German tenants I have seen are puny, wear dark suits and sometimes a black coat, but the dentist's tenant is tall and wears a uniform. The child must like him because she holds on to him as if he were her daddy. So far, I have only seen the man's back as he carries the child through the hallway into the mysterious depths of the apartment. Will I see his face one day?

My visits to the dentist will have to come to an end. One day, she takes the nerve out with an itsybitsy screwdriver which she lets me see first. Then she fills the tooth and tells me to come back in a week for a checkup. When I do, she gives me a going-away present, a souvenir: my nerve between two pieces of gauze in a tiny container that once upon a time must have held some pills. I almost cry when we part. I'll miss my visits.

After Papa leaves town—his reason for leaving belongs to another story—our lives go from bad to worse. The landlady does not like what has happened and turns against Mama and me, though I have not done anything wrong. Sometimes, when I run into her while passing through the hall on the way to our room, she calls me names I know only from park benches. Perhaps they are meant for Mama and not for me, but I cannot tell. What is the difference between "a slut" and "a daughter of a slut"? She does not let us use the bathroom when we have to and so we poop on newspapers and pee into a bucket which Mama has to empty once a day. To do that she has to pass through the dining room on the way to the toilet. Of course, the landlady does not like it and I don't blame her. But after Mama threatens to dump the bucket out right next to the dining room table, the woman stops the complaining and the name calling. A bucket of poop does make a good weapon, I realize. We are waiting for a Jewish apartment to be vacated, so that we can move in and take a bath.

One day, I enter the building just after the dentist's German tenant does. He rings the bell. She opens the door. At this point I should have run upstairs but, instead, I hesitate for a moment and see what I do not wish to see. They fall into each other's arms, the door still wide open. She cannot see me because he is in the way, with his broad back to me. When I realize that they are both crying, I begin to climb the stairs as quietly as I can. What could I have done to avoid seeing them? First, I would have had to know what I would be seeing and that is something I did not know. I liked her so much and now I don't know if I still should. It is very confusing. Is she a whore, or isn't she? After everything she has done for me, I want to think that she is not. Why were they crying? Did he get orders to leave? I only saw the man's shoulders and back, so I still don't know what he looks like.

I find out that we will be moving soon to an apartment with a bathroom and no landlady to torture us. I won't be seeing the dentist's German again. If I ran into him in the street, I would not know it. He and what I saw will remain a mystery. This thought makes me sad.

9

The Day Papa Left

When I woke up that morning, Mama and Papa were already gone somewhere, probably to that little store that they had recently opened so that we would be able to survive. I am used to being home alone and have already learned how to entertain myself. When the room is very cold, I stay in bed for a while until it is time to get up for breakfast. Mama always sees to it that I have some bread and some lard to smear on it. I can't make myself tea because Papa has told me not to fool around with the hotplate and so I drink cold water to wash down the bread. Now even water is not easy to come by. To get a pail of it, Mama has to pass through the landlord's dining room on her way to the kitchen sink and his wife objects. She does not want to have to look at Mama. The apartment is hers and hers alone.

I hate this room, though I should be glad that we have a roof over our heads and no longer must spend the nights at the railroad station. The grayish pink of the walls, almost black in the corners from soot, is ugly and I prefer not to look at them. That is why I now spend more time in bed with my eyes closed, trying to slip back into the house we have left behind. In this apartment, the windows face the narrow street and there is no tree anywhere in sight. It is through these windows that I try to escape when a man is chasing me around the room. And though I am flying and staying next to the ceiling, he is so tall that he would catch me if I did not wake up in time.

I don't go to school but will one day, when we get settled. And since I don't yet know any children in this town, I have to play by myself. When the weather is not too bad, I take a long walk, stopping here and there to have a better look at something interesting. First comes the drugstore with a jar of leeches in its window. I watch the disgusting animals as they swim around wagging their tails. At the corner there is the paper store with neat boxes of coloring pencils on display. There is no chance that I will ever have enough money to buy one. To get to the Market Square I have to cross the Planty at the prettiest spot. A pond, a fountain, and a little bridge. Papa used to take me there in the fall, and we would sit on a bench, talking and looking at the waterlilies. A bookstore on the Market Square has books in its window that are for children my age. I study the pictures on their covers and memorize their titles. Next come the German restaurants and the steamy warmth of their insides when someone opens a door to enter or to leave. Even just walking by on the sidewalk I can get a whiff of hot food: cabbage and potatoes or potatoes and cabbage, probably some meat with it. Whatever it is, I like it but don't even slow down to enjoy the smell. A few more steps and I reach the corner of the square where sometimes, when the moment is right, I stop and listen to the bugler play his sad warning from the top of the church tower. Even the Germans want to hear him. A left turn will take me to the street with the toy store. Just a couple of months earlier Mrs. Brozkowa, who had also fled from Wilno to Kraków, took me there on a Sunday morning, so that I could admire the fantastic stuff the store had to offer: teddy bears, board games, porcelain dolls whose blue eyes can open and close, and dollhouses with tiny furniture. None of it would ever be mine, but I could pretend and told Mrs. B. about the one Mark Mama had given me.

"On the black market," I was telling her, "one Mark is worth so much, much more than the official rate. But since it's illegal for us to own Marks, I could get arrested for having one. And besides, the one Mark wouldn't cover the cost of even the tiniest toy." I was so involved with my explanations that I didn't even notice the man who was standing behind us on the otherwise empty street until I heard him say, "It's amazing how fast children grow up during a war."

The bonus is the photographer's shop next door where pictures of beautiful children in beautiful clothes are on display: girls in frilly dresses, boys in suits, white shirts, and ties as if they were no longer boys but men. A true fairytale land on the other side of the glass. To return to our pink room with black corners, I don't go back to the square. I follow a path through the Planty.

This is exactly what I did on that morning and was back in our room by the early afternoon to eat my lunch which was the same as breakfast. I had done nothing bad. I had been a good girl. Because the room was cold, I lay down on the bed without taking off my coat and covered myself with blankets. For a while I was able to read one of the books I was allowed to take along when we fled. By then I must have read *The Eye of the Prophet* at least a hundred times and I knew it almost by heart. Soon it got dark, and I had to stop reading. Hanging a blanket over the window for the blackout wasn't something I could do on my own, and so I just lay there in the dark, thinking about the home we had left behind. Papa and Mama had to be back before the curfew.

Thinking about our old home in the dark is what I was doing when Papa suddenly rushed into the room. Papa does not run because of his bad heart, but this time he was almost running, and so I knew right away that something terrible must have happened. He put a blanket over the window, turned on the lights, and began to pull out suitcases from under the bed. He even got the one from the closet where it was kept under lock and key because it contained our valuables which we had to have for what Mama called "the black hour." A gold watch, some old gold coins, and probably things I do not even know about. Did it mean that the black hour had arrived?

Muttering something under his breath, he emptied them onto the floor—it would have made Mama angry to see it—and he began to pick stuff out of the pile, throwing it into one of the empty suitcases. All that time he hardly looked at me. Since he was so upset, I could not bother him with questions. While watching this frenzy, it finally dawned on me that he was about to leave, and that I had to say something. "I am coming with you!" "No, you are not." I burst into tears, not just ordinary tears that come with scraped knees, but a real deluge with sobbing and wailing. I was so terrified. The landlady must have been listening, her ear to the wall, but I no longer cared. And then Papa had to explain why he was leaving. He had caught Mama at it behind the partition in our little store. I don't know what he meant by "it." And that she did it with a man he had no respect for was particularly insulting. Papa could not take me with him because in his care I would starve, whereas Mama, being so resourceful, would see to it that I had something to eat. Yet, for me, dying from hunger was better than staying with Mama. My crying and screaming did not change Papa's mind. He threw back into the suitcases the stuff that was not his and just walked out after giving me a kiss. "Be good" were his last words to me.

I ran to the window, pushed aside the blackout blanket a little bit, and peered out to catch a glimpse of Papa. He had crossed the street, and I was able to see him until he disappeared around the corner. The railroad station was not far; he would get there before the curfew. Snow was coming down in big wet flakes and melting on the sidewalk. After turning off the light I went back to bed crying, because I already missed Papa and was very much afraid of what was going to happen next. Had I been smarter I would already have guessed that he had to leave. He had been getting sadder and sadder, Mama more and more unpleasant. She kept reminding him how the war had changed the order of everything and that what was bad once is almost good now. Without his judge's robe, Papa did not know what to do and was just a useless drone. He would keep his dignity while we starved. Mama may not have been saying these exact words, but that is what she meant. It hurt me to see what she was doing to Papa who did not even fight back.

Did "it" mean kissing or was it something else I did not know about? I could guess who the man was whom Papa had caught doing it with Mama. We had met him at the boarding house where we sometimes went for a hot meal. His eyes would light up when he saw Mama who was always all smiles for him. We stopped going there when it turned out that one of the guests had lice in his clothing. That should have put an end to the games Mama and the man were playing, but it did not. When they were no longer able to see each other at the dinner table, they met in our little store that had almost nothing to sell. The man is really crude. Even I could see that. He does not know how to blow his nose, swallows his snot, and does not hesitate to spit on the pavement. He has a wife and a daughter my age.

What will happen next? Will Papa come back to get me once he is settled in Warszawa? He did not say that he would. As for Mama, I am afraid of her and for her. She loves me—yes, she does in her own way—and I know it's true that she will see to it that I do not starve. She will take care of my body but not my mind. I can't talk to her the way I talk to Papa, and I never know what she is really thinking. It scares me to see her lying in bed brooding because, when she gets up, she is either in a very bad mood or has hatched some crazy plan that may lead to a disaster. What if she becomes a thief, an informer, or a traitor? Or does something she can get shot for? Though I cannot tell her what to do or not to do—she would not listen to me even if I did—she may not do anything that will endanger her life, because she has to take care of me. And so, just by being with her, I may be able to keep her out of trouble and that is a very big load I have. I don't want anything bad to happen to her. I love her, in a way. If she does something shameful but not dangerous—like what she did in the back of the store that Papa saw—will people punish me for it with some nasty talk? Am I supposed to be Mama's keeper as much as she is mine?

These thoughts kept going through my mind while I lay in bed in the dark, hiccupping from too many tears. My situation was bad and so was the future—a conclusion I could not escape. When Mama got home, I was asleep. She turned on the light, the one bulb in the center of the ceiling that made the pink walls gray. After a quick glance around the room, she asked, "Where is Papa?" I told her that he had left for Warszawa. She answered with an "oh" or an "ah" which meant that she had nothing to worry about for the moment. And then I saw panic on her face: her eyes wide open, her mouth ready to cry out. She ran to the closet where our treasures are kept, pulled out the suitcase and began to rummage in it with her hands. I watched her from the bed and saw her face relax every time she felt what she was looking for: Papa's gold Longines watch, the old gold coins, and some other treasures I have never actually seen. At the end of her search, she took a big sigh of relief and that meant that Papa did not take any valuables with him, not even his own watch. Only then was she able to say, "Don't worry, everything will be all right." I did not believe her. Nothing will be all right. But I did not cry because I either had run out of tears or did not want Mama to see me cry. There was no supper for me that evening. I could not eat.

That is what happened the day Papa left.

10

Tereska

Mama calmed down, in a way, after Papa left. She began looking for a school for me. Perhaps she had to because of the law: children must go to school for six years and after six years should be ready for work. First, she had to find a tutor who would prepare me for the best school in town, so that I would have a chance to spend some time in the company of girls from very good homes. To Mama it means that I would have what she calls "connections," that are very important for the future. She has plans to put me in the sixth grade in the fall though I have missed grades one, two, and three, almost failed the fourth, and still need to have some fifth-grade lessons. Now I have only three months to learn what I should have been learning in ten. It is so hopeless that I don't even try.

My teacher is Mrs. L., my classmates are two boys, sometimes three, even four. We do not meet in a schoolhouse, but in different apartments whose owners I never see. For the next lesson, Mrs. L. tells us, go to such and such an address at such and such a time, ring the bell, give a password to the person opening the door... That is how it works. Sometimes no one is there to let me in, sometimes the person who opens the door tells me that I have come to the wrong address. Often when all the pupils are at the right place at the right time—not all of us could have been wrong—Mrs. L. fails to arrive. Yes, it is very confusing. We wrestle and fight while waiting. I want them to know that I can be as tough as they are, even if sometimes I get hurt. When the hour is up, we go back to where we came from. The boys are not my friends. They do not tell me where they live. And, as for me, I do not want them to see the one room we live in now, the room that often smells of shit and the piss bucket. They are local boys, while I am from far away. The space I have travelled through keeps us apart.

Mrs. L. teaches us history, a very important subject when one's country is occupied, at least so I am told. One king after another, almost all with the same name, except that one is only elbow-high—a midget? Another has a crooked mouth, while the others must have been normal, because they only have numbers after their names. I am supposed to memorize the dates of their rule and who they fought with and where, but this is hard, since only one of these kings stands out because he killed a bishop, and bishops don't get killed very often. That Mrs. L. is spending so much time on history and almost none on arithmetic, which I am so poor at, means that I may not get into the sixth grade. Perhaps I should be grateful that she is not torturing me with fractions and worse.

When it is not too cold, I wander through the Old Town stopping here and there to look at windows of book and toy stores that display stuff I will never be able to buy. I like days when the snow is coming down in big, wet flakes. It muffles the sounds of the street and makes the city look like a picture on a postcard. Sometimes, when I cannot see more than a few feet ahead, I imagine that I am back home running from the house to the old barn, across the drive, to feed our rabbit. When the snow was coming down so thick, I was not allowed to go any farther than that. Just the other day I must have been thinking that I was on my way to the barn and was running on the sidewalk, my face covered with snow, when I bumped into someone. When I opened my eyes, I saw the clasp of a belt and did not have enough time to get scared before I felt someone's hands on my shoulders. Will I be given a good shake for being so stupid? When I look up, I see a face. The soldier is laughing.

Mrs. L. has a daughter. I have not seen her yet because we do not meet in Mrs. L.'s apartment for class. Teaching history is against the law, and she does not want anyone to find out that she is doing it. Too many children coming to her home would attract attention and someone could denounce her.

Mama keeps telling me that someday soon we may be able to move out of our spooky room and get away from the landlady who thinks that torturing us is patriotic. And perhaps it is. Mama is no longer Polish, but Ukrainian, and has a Ukrainian friend, Mykola the hick. None of it is my fault. I am still Polish, but that does not keep the landlady from calling me names.

I have been trying to find the smell of spring in this city. Sometimes, when crossing the park near the railroad station, I catch for a moment a whiff of the soil waking up after the winter. It's gone as soon as I step onto the pavement. The city does not smell as good as the countryside. Now that it is getting warmer and on some days the city glows under a cloudless sky, I put on my fancy coat and hat bought in Kaunas—the one I am not supposed to wear because we may have to sell it soon—and go to the park, sit on a bench, and wait for Papa to arrive. Miracles do happen sometimes, and I want to be ready. I keep hoping that he will walk through the park when he comes to get me and will recognize the coat.

Mykola visits Mama frequently; sometimes he even eats a meal with us. No china on the table, no fancy food: at best a piece of sausage and a pickle on a piece of newspaper. That is not how we used to eat before the war, but so what? I don't really care. Mykola is very nice to me—I cannot complain—yet nothing he does for me feels right, and when he swallows the snot from his nose, I can see why Papa had no respect for him.

In a couple of days, I am supposed to meet Mrs. L.'s daughter Tereska. With a mother who can teach history and even arithmetic, she must be special. I don't know how it came about that I now have the girl's address and should go to her home for a couple of hours. Either Mama or Mrs. L. must be feeling sorry for me because I spend so much time alone walking the streets.

Yes, Tereska is special. She lives on the good side of town in what must be a huge apartment. It comes with a real servant and a dog. Tereska is thirteen years old, three years older than I and much bigger. She stands tall and straight, her head up as if she were some kind of a leader watching a parade. Her eyes are blue, her hair brown, her skin olive. I can imagine what she thinks of me and realize that she is trying to be nice. Lying on the carpet in her vast dining room we play board games, of which she has many. I don't think she enjoys them as much as I do, and she won't play any of them more than once. "So boring..." she says. I am not sure if she means me or the games. Our meeting does not feel like a success, yet I am invited for another visit and another. Perhaps it is my stupidity that interests her or perhaps she also does not have any friends.

One day, when the weather is gray and damp, she decides to take me for a walk. Not that I wanted to—I'd rather lie on her beautiful carpet and play board games—but who am I to object? We go to the main street which has a few stores and a tram line which could take us to the center of the city I know by heart or to a field I have not been to yet where people go to lie on the grass in summer. I can't go there on my own and, besides, it is not yet summer. We stroll along the street and look at the display windows. There is the pharmacy with a jar of leeches which I like to watch, Tereska does not. Instead, she looks at advertisements I don't even notice. "Do you know what that is?" she asks me, pointing to a small sign with only two words on it and no picture: Ola Gum. No, I don't know, and Tereska laughs at the stupid me.

She tells me that before the war she had a German governess who taught her German and gave her a pair of magic white knee socks which she now wears only on special occasions because, with the governess gone, they are irreplaceable. She puts them on for me and parades around the dining room as if she were a Hitler Youth. I don't know what to make of it. Wearing these socks, she can go into German stores and buy stuff she would not be able to get anywhere else. Even if I had a magic wand, I would not be able to pull off anything like that.

Tereska has a father. I ran into him once in the hallway. He must be very important because he did not even notice that I was there too and just looked up instead of down at me. Had I said "Good day," he would not have heard me. Perhaps the old coat I was wearing then made me invisible. Tereska has not yet told me if her huge apartment has any tenants. Is it possible for four people to have all that space to themselves? Perhaps it is, if one has what Mama calls connections.

Now that the weather is getting warmer, we go to the park, the one near her house, and even sit on a bench for a little while. The tiny purple flowers are already blooming under the naked bushes. They remind me of home. Tereska can't see them because she is studying a piece of trash lying near the bench, she even pokes it with a stick. That is Ola Gum, she tells me. I have no idea what to make of it. How did it get from the pharmacy to the park? Tereska laughs. Shall I tell her that what I see reminds me of what a snake leaves behind after it has molted? I say nothing. Perhaps someday soon she will tell me on her own what Ola Gum is.

She asks me if I know who General von Brauchitsch is. I do not. The name sounds strange. Of the two generals I have heard about, one is already dead, the other fled the country when the war broke out, and no one has anything good to say about him, the coward. Von Brauchitsch is Tereska's hero, even though his name does not sound Polish. Is he a relative of hers?

Mama is going out of town, on business. She thinks that in some nearby village she can find a source of food that will cost less than it does in the city. Since I have never stayed alone overnight, Mama has to find a place where she can leave me and asks Mrs. L. if she would take me in for one night. That is why I happen to end up in Tereska's bedroom. And what a room it is! With so much white lace in it and white walls, it makes me think of freshly fallen fluffy snow when the sun gives it pink misty edges. There must be some pink there because Tereska is a girl. We talk for a while, with me settled on some blankets on the floor, Tereska on her lacy bed. She asks me if I know what a Messerschmitt is, and, of course, I don't. She comes up with these ridiculous questions so that she can laugh at me. I do not ask her what it is just to show her that I am not impressed by her fancy words and names. What is a Messerschmitt? She asks me to get into her bed and lie on top of her, and though I have never done anything like that before, I do it. Once I am on top of her, she asks me to hump her. I do as directed. It is not much fun for me and even not for her because after a few humps she tells me to get off. "You don't have the right gadget to poke me with," she explains. "Only boys do." I know how boys are made down there, but can't imagine how their limp thing would be any good for poking. In the countryside where she spends her summers, she tells me, there is a boy who lies on her tummy and humps her. He has the right gadget, of course, because he is a boy. They both enjoy it immensely, and that is why she is trying it out on me. I have no idea why she would want a boy to lie on top of her, humping and poking. I would rather fight than let one do it to me.

Sunday. I know it is Sunday though there is no calendar to look at. Instead of going to church we go for a little walk past the drugstore with its Ola

Gum and make it almost all the way to the Planty. Just like me, Tereska does not go to mass, and she may not even believe in God, the nasty old man with messy long hair and crazy eyes, pointing a finger at his next victim. But we do not talk about religion. Instead, she asks me again if I know what a Messerschmitt is. I still don't of course. How could I? And then, to make me feel even smaller than I already feel, she asks me if I know what an airplane is. That is Tereska's way of calling me stupid. Of course, I know: they fly very fast, drop bombs and sometimes crash. She does not seem impressed. What about a Heinkel or a Focke-Wulf? I have no idea what she is talking about. Where is she getting these strange names from? I'll have to enlighten you, she promises. The word "enlighten" I know only from having heard some woman ask, "Has this child been enlightened yet?" The tiny smile on the woman's lips and a twinkle in her eyes let me know that the word must have some hidden meaning the grownups don't want to share with children.

When we get home from our walk—the home with the vast dining room and many soft carpets we can lie on—Tereska agrees to play a few games of "little fleas" with me, a game I can't play alone. It bores her, and after a short while she goes into her room and brings out a box of her treasures. Every child and even grownups must have some treasures. Mine are the two books I was allowed to take with me when we fled. Mama's are some gold rubles which, wrapped in a piece of cloth, she hides in strange places. If they get stolen, we may have nothing to eat someday. Since Tereska did not have to flee, at least not yet, her treasure chest is as big as a small suitcase. What a rich girl she is! What does she keep in it? I can barely wait to see what kind of wonders are hiding inside. When she lifts the lid, I can only see paper, lots of it, but I am sure that there must be something more interesting at the bottom of the chest. If there is, she does not show it to me. It's the sheets of paper I am supposed to be looking at. They are deep blue in color, like the rare forget-me-nots that grow under trees in fancy gardens. The sheets are divided into small rectangles, a picture of an airplane—some gray, some black, some even green—embossed on each. "Aren't they beautiful?" Tereska asks me. She wants me to say that they are. Saying "no" would be admitting to being hopelessly stupid, saying "yes" would be lying. So, instead, I tell her that the blue is beautiful, and since she is already talking about the planes, she does not even notice that I did not answer her question. Here is a Messerschmitt, she puts her finger on the picture of one of the planes. And here is a Heinkel, a Henschel, a Focke... Too many names all at once, I am confused. Do you know what Stuka is or Flak? I don't, but she does not wait for me to ask. She already knows how ignorant I am. Some planes are bombers, some fighters, some divers. I am being enlightened. It's clear that bombers bomb, but the other two? And that is how I learn that the divers specialize in machine gunning refugees, the fighters "engage" enemy planes in midair fights. I can't even imagine what that is like. While explaining all that, she is beaming, the way she beamed when telling me about the boy who humped her in a thicket of bushes in the summer of 1940.

In the afternoon, Mama comes to pick me up. It's her way of letting me know that she is back from her trip and that it is safe for me to return to our room. She hands Mrs. L. a package of something that I guess can only be butter, because it is too small to be anything else. Nowadays butter is very expensive and hard to get. That is the price Mama pays for my night at Tereska's.

It turns out that Mama did not go anywhere. She stayed home undisturbed doing books for her business, the tiny store which has almost nothing to sell but keeps her out of forced labor. "It's very important, it had to be done," she tells me. When we get into our bed that night, I find a strange handkerchief right in the middle of it, instead of under the pillow where handkerchiefs are kept. I am puzzled, but I don't ask how it got there.

On my next visit to Tereska, I learn how she gets those pictures of airplanes. I have not seen them in any of the stores I snoop in, stores like the big one at the corner that sells paper and pencils or the one on the main square that still sells children's books. Tereska, being so clever and well-educated, puts on her white knee socks and goes to a German store—I have no idea where it is—and asks for the pictures in German. That she is not afraid to pretend to be a Hitler Youth is a proof of how talented she is. I will never be able to catch up to her.

We no longer meet for lessons very often. It's spring and Mama and I will be moving to another part of town, far away from Tereska. Will I see her again after we move? Now I am sure that I won't because Mama and Mrs. L. had a little fight about me and the school I was about to enter. "You told me that after almost a year of lessons from you, she will not have to take any admission exams. Now I learn that she does," Mama tells Mrs. L. No, I did not tell you... Yes, you did... Their faces turn red and there are sparks in their eyes. I just listen and watch. If I do take the exam, I'll fail and not be able to get into the sixth grade of the best school in town. If I don't take it, but get in through what Mama calls "the backdoor," I'll be at the bottom of the class and all the nice girls from good homes will laugh at me the way Tereska does. But she, at least, is teaching me something: Messerschmitt, Heinkel, Henschel, Focke-Wulf... Will nice girls want to teach me anything? If so, what will it be? Since Mama and Mrs. L. do not part on good terms, it is now certain that I won't be seeing Tereska. I will miss her and her planes that fly in the sky of a beautiful blue.

11

The Picture Album, Part One

June of 1941 and the beginning of another war were so confusing that I did not know if I should cry or rejoice. Choosing between two evils was hard. When I told someone that we may be able to return home, I was accused of collaboration. Me, collaboration? I was only ten years old then. We had just moved into an apartment that became Mama's thanks to her connections to Mykola whom she would not have met in normal times. The apartment was vacant because its owners had been moved to the nearby ghetto. This would not have happened without the war. I was learning about life by watching it unfold at the address we had moved to: 37 Starowiślna Street. Our building and its backyard became the centers of my universe. I would have explored the neighborhood, the way I had done at our old address, but I had been told not to turn right on leaving our building because, by turning right, I could end up seeing something that would be bad for me to look at.

Two rooms of our new apartment had to be rented out, because people were entitled to only so much square footage of space. With refugees and colonists descending upon the city from the east, west, and north, being squeezed became a way of life unless one had connections. Having tenants was a pain because Mama could not find anyone she could get along with. There was war, inside and outside. Mama fought with all her tenants except her friend Mykola. When their voices grew too loud for my ears, I would run into the street. Mykola was getting more and more puffed up with self-importance because he was rising to new heights in a country messed up by the war. He had fought the Bolsheviks during the Revolution and was now going to help the Germans fight the Russians. To show his dedication to the cause, he even hung a Nazi flag out of his window—a treacherous act to which another of Mama's tenants objected by telling Mykola that someday he, too, like his flag, will be hanging from that window. That daring threat brought the Gestapo to our apartment, and I had a chance to watch one of their men question Mama in the kitchen while holding her against the wall. It was an interesting sight. As for the tenant who made the threat, she moved out. No one decent stayed with us for long.

Strange creatures kept visiting Mykola, men in charge of those who were willing to join the Germans in their war. One of them was a tall, slim fellow who must have been Mykola's right hand because he came often and stayed for hours. The two were best friends, at least so I thought. One night I was woken up by the cries of a child: "Papa don't go... Please come down with me... I will take you home... Please, please..." It was a voice of desperation, hoarse and loud. The boy's drunken father was standing in front of our door, screaming. He wanted to have a word with Mykola and perhaps he did before being knocked down the stairs by a blow to his face. I heard the thuds of his fall and nothing more because I put a pillow over my head and eventually fell asleep. In the morning, Mykola strutted around the kitchen like some kind of hero, proud of having saved us from a drunk. And perhaps he did, but something about it did not feel right.

Screams were not rare in our courtyard. Once someone whom I hardly knew kept screaming for help during the night. Did adults know what was happening and were afraid to come out? And then there was the janitor who used to beat up his wife. She did all the hard work around the building, her face black and blue from bruises, while he kept track of the tenants and their rationing cards. His bloodshot eyes sparked with anger, his speech was slurred—he was always drunk. The couple had four daughters and there had been a time when this family of six lived in one tiny room whose walls were black from soot. I could not imagine how they all had fitted into it; the children must have slept on the floor. All kinds of rumors circulated about the three oldest girls, rumors I did not understand. When they came to visit their parents, they were always very well dressed. "How is that possible?" Mrs. Bosak, who lived with a carpenter, would ask the crippled tailor's wife, and both would roll their eyes. Once, the janitor was arrested for beating up his wife, badly or worse than usual. When the poor woman could not move, someone must have called the police. As soon as she had recovered enough to be able to talk, she begged the authorities to release him, and they did.

Not all the families living in the building were bad. Some were very good, some in between. The dentist and his wife gave themselves airs and occasionally would go somewhere, all dressed up and stiff as boards, not seeing any passersby but expecting to be looked at. Snobs, they were, but otherwise very proper and they did not scream. I could only guess what they thought of Mama who also liked to pretend to be a great lady and knew how to dress. Once I beat up their son for hitting a dog. The boy was two years younger than I and a very well-behaved kid with no imagination. That is probably what I did not like about him and sooner or later, I would probably have found another reason for beating him up. But I did care about the dog. Really.

The family next door to us was great: an ancient couple, a middle-aged son, and a servant so old and used-up that she would not have been able to work much longer. They all tried to guide me onto the right path and did it nicely, without talking down to me. By the time the servant disappeared one day, she may not have had any more stories to tell me. I never found out what happened to her. The old couple was the next to leave; supposedly they moved to a country estate of some relatives. After they left, their son became my guardian angel. I heard him ask my mother not to expose me to unnecessary dangers, like taking me to a German restaurant for a meal. Had she been caught at it we would have ended up in prison or worse. And he was able to say it so gently that she did not get angry and even thanked him for his advice. They were both acting very cultured and proper. Yet, she did not take his warnings seriously and not only did we keep going out for lunch, but she also let the new servant Józefina take me to an officer's café for a piece of pastry. Józefina should have known better—neither of us spoke any German—but for her, being able to ogle the handsome officers was worth taking the risk. Some of them even played the piano.

I mostly stayed out of Mykola's way because to me any interaction with him looked like a betrayal of Papa. Sometimes, when he and Mama went for a walk in the park on Sunday, I had to come along so that we could pretend we were a family. Well, we were not, and I did not want us to be mistaken for one. He was not even my "uncle," as some of the tenants asked with a strange smile in their eyes that made me respond emphatically "Papa will be coming back soon." Still, I did not yet wish Mykola ill, like him getting run over by a streetcar on his way somewhere. He was too good a man for that, and I was being fair. After all, his wife and daughter needed him.

One day that summer, Mykola told me that I had to come with him so that he can show me a piece of history. Papa had said exactly the same when, almost two years earlier, he woke me up at dawn and made me lie on the floor of the balcony to witness two squat tanks coming around the corner, with their red flags aflutter. I did not like that Mykola was talking about history and sounding almost like Papa. Had I told him about the tanks I saw in Wilno and he had decided that his too was a very important event, worthy of being called history? No! I could not have dragged Papa into my story—it would have been a sacrilege. So, Mykola was not trying to outdo Papa. There could be no tanks around the corner this time: they had already come and left, at least for now. I had no idea what to expect.

When we came out onto the street, we turned right instead of left, taking the path always forbidden to me. I was not afraid because, if need arose, I would just stand still, watch, and pretend not to be there. When running away was not an option, pretending of this kind was my specialty. We were heading towards the black market square, which was often raided by the police. Since even Mama tried to stay away from it, it became one of Józefina's duties to go there to buy food for us. Józefina could run, Mama could not. That day we skirted the square—perhaps it was too dangerous even for Mykola who was carrying a shopping bag with some food. He did not want to be accused of buying it illegally and having it confiscated. The area around the square was, of course, unfamiliar to me, and because it was such a tangle of narrow, twisted streets and alleys with low, long houses, at most two stories high, the paint on their walls once white but now gray and peeling, I quickly lost my bearings. If I did have to run, would I be able to find my way home?

We ended up in a warehouse, though at that time, inexperienced as I was, I could not have told myself that the vast room I found myself in was one. Except for being differently furnished, it resembled the rooms of the department store I had sometimes been taken to before the war. It was brightly lit by the sun and by electric lights hanging over a multitude of tables, so many of them, packed so close together, and so colorful that they were like a giant carpet extending almost to the walls. Boxes covered the tables with exotic yarns and threads poking out of them. Skeins and balls, spools and bundles, some glossy, some dull. Used as I was only to the basic colors, I was overwhelmed by the multitude of shades. Do they have names or are reds always just red? I had entered a fairytale land, in which yarns lived and ruled.

Mykola dropped off the shopping bag near the entrance door and led me to the center of the room where a woman was sitting at a table, skeins of thread sliding through her hands. He stayed silent while she wrote something in a notebook and, once she finished, the two exchanged a warm greeting. As always, I tried to make sense of what I saw: the woman must be the owner of this place which will be turned over to the Germans when the inventory is completed and then she and her husband will be sent to a camp. I already knew what happens there. Mykola has been talking about it. "What a pity... Such a cultured couple... I wish I could find a way out for them..." But there was no way out—unless there was no end to the counting, because, as if by magic, the skeins kept multiplying.

Mykola signed the notebook, approving of the numbers which, I realized, no longer had any meaning. Whatever the count, the warehouse was going to be closed in a few days, its contents shipped off to Germany, its owners to a camp. The neighborhood would be "cleaned out" so that the displaced from somewhere else could move in.

Mykola introduced us. Mrs. Goldweber was her name, and I became the little girl who lives in the same apartment as he. He just wants to show me history and give me something to remember. We are not related, and he does not claim to her to be my "uncle." The woman is old or perhaps she is not: I was no judge of people's age. To me anyone with some strands of white hair looked like a grandmother. She was neatly dressed, and her hair was not in disarray. I tried to place her in my past for comparison but could not come up with anyone resembling her. Mama and the dentist's wife whom I often saw passing through the courtyard all dressed up, showing off their clothes to the wife of the tailor and the mistress of the carpenter, did not look as elegant as this old lady sitting all by herself in a warehouse filled with yarn. I curtsied properly, and we began to talk while Mykola kept signing the notebook and stacking up boxes to be ready for shipment.

I had so much to learn, and the lady was kind enough to teach me. First came the names of the colors, since to me violet was violet, be it dark or light. The language I had learned so far either did not have names for the different shades or no one was able to teach them to me because they were in French. But the lady knew. And she was able to say them, no matter how strange they sounded to me. Then she talked about the types, a much easier lesson for me to absorb: spools of thread for sewing dresses, skeins for embroidery and crocheting, balls of wool for knitting, all of them beautiful enough to take my breath away. We laughed at my efforts to repeat the French names. However hard I tried, I couldn't get out the "r's" and the "l's." Mrs. Goldweber's dark eyes sparkled, either from tears or eye drops, and when she smiled some of her gold teeth were showing. My mind was on the strands of cotton, silk, and wool, and so, after the brief lesson on the subject, I strolled between the tables with their magical colors, letting my fingers explore the different textures. No one said "don't touch." It no longer mattered if my fingers and the threads were dirty or clean.

Mykola's manners were beyond reproach. Not even once did he swallow his snot, at least not that I was aware of, but I may have been too immersed in colors to pay attention to sounds. He promised to be back the next day. The inventory was almost finished and, even if it were not, the truck would come for it because of the deadline. He hugged the woman, I curtsied again. I was good at curtsying but not at hand kissing. After the bright light of the warehouse, the street looked dark. Whatever portion of the sky was showing between the buildings was white with a yellowish tinge. Did the French have a name for that color? I couldn't run back in to find out even though the old woman with the sparkling eyes and a smile of gold might still be there counting and not even go home for the night. Perhaps she no longer has a home? If she does, how is she going to get there? Is someone going to come and take her there? What could she have been thinking about while putting her final touches to the inventory—the end of the beautiful colors. Was she thinking about the trip to the camp, the camp, and finally death of a special kind? Was she terrified of what was going to happen and yet also able to laugh at my attempts at French?

I could not answer these questions on my own and did not think that bringing them up with Mykola was right. After all, he was not my father. When we got back home, some children were playing ball in the few square feet of the yard the janitor let them use. It was always fun, and though I could neither throw nor catch well and no one ever wanted me on their team, I joined the game and stopped thinking about death and history.

A few days later—or was it a whole week?—Mykola came home carrying under his arm an album so enormous that it piqued my curiosity. Only very rich families would need something so huge for their photographs. When we fled, ours fit into an envelope that hardly took up any space at the bottom of a valise. That is how poor we were. How had Mykola acquired something so huge and bulging, I wanted to know. But I was not going to ask him because he was not my Papa, and I talked to him only when necessary. Besides, Mykola was sniffling, and even wiped a few tears from his eyes while passing through the hallway. I could see all that from the kitchen. Before entering his room, he warned me that I should not touch the album with my dirty fingers. I was not planning to. Later in the day, after Mama had come home, I learned the story: the warehouse had been closed and its contents carted away. Mykola's job as a Treuhänder was finished, and the album was a gift from Mrs. Goldweber to express her gratitude for having been treated so kindly and with respect. She had kept it until the very end because she loved it, and it was so worthless that even thieves did not want it. Its contents of picture postcards from some famous museum in Dresden meant nothing to me. Dresden was a city I had never heard of. It was only a year or so later that I began to take an interest in art, especially winter landscapes with sleighs, horses, and wolves.

Mykola took very good care of Mrs. Goldweber's gift. He kept it locked up in a drawer of his desk along with some very important papers. My interest in it waned—out of sight, out of mind. When I thought of Mrs. Goldweber, and that did not happen often, I imagined her still sitting in that warehouse whose tables burst with colors of fantastic names.

12

Half-Boarders

The summer of 1941 was made up of sun and all the strange neighbors in our apartment building. The fall of 1941, in contrast, was deep gray, and the neighbors stopped parading through the courtyard. Being indoors felt better than being outside. Without knowing how bad it would be, people must have been getting ready for the frigid winter of 1942.

Runia and I met in the fall of 1941 when I entered the sixth grade at the Ursuline school that Tereska's mother, Mrs. L., had been preparing me for in her mysterious way. Up until then I had been in school for one year only, and my performance there was far from brilliant. In fact, it was so bad that I should not have passed into fifth grade in Wilno. But by then the war was in full swing, we were preparing to flee west, and my C's and D's had lost their importance.

Mama took me to school the first day to show me where to enter it and through a stroke of good luck, we ran into another mother at the entrance. She had met my Uncle Kot in Wilno, where, after miraculously escaping from a POW camp, he courted her oldest daughter. Her family was as good as my savior Janek's, perhaps even better, and so, because of my connection to Uncle Kot—and without any effort on my part—her daughter Rozmaryna would be allowed to befriend me, if she wished to. Unfortunately, the girl was three years older than I, very wise, and a snob besides.

Runia's family was famous too. Her aunt was the rightful owner of a palace, conveniently located next to the Ursuline school. Since the costs of its upkeep were too high, it was used as a courthouse even before the war. Runia's mother was a countess and because all the great families knew each other and were more or less related, she knew Rozmaryna's mother and that is how she must have learned that Papa's family had owned land before the Revolution and that Uncle Kot, one of its distinguished offspring, had been allowed to court Rozmaryna's sister in Wilno. This is how my friendship with Runia received her mother's approval. By the time it became clear that my family was no longer respectable because of Mama, it was too late to break us apart. I needed Runia to make me laugh.

We were in the same class as our friendship began to blossom, but sitting far apart—I in the first row because I needed glasses, Runia in the last because she had a pair. Many of the girls were from academic families and always knew their lessons; those who were not, were puny and had nondescript faces. There was also the beautiful Rozmaryna, looking down on everyone with her green eyes. She was in a class by herself, but sometimes joined Runia and me because of our family backgrounds.

For the first couple of months, Runia and I had the distinction of being half-boarders, which meant eating lunch at school and going home in the late afternoon. This arrangement let us have a cursory look at what the full boarders were entitled to. Did they all sleep in one room, we wondered? Did each girl have her own cubicle, like the one Runia and I were assigned to? Ours had only a table and a couple of chairs, but theirs must have had a bed. We couldn't be sure, because ours was located at the very end of a long hallway so that we would not have to pass by those belonging to the rich girls. We were supposed to do our homework there before going home for the night. Instead, we killed flies, chewed on chalk, tried to drink ink, and with our pens drilled holes in the blotter. And, of course, we talked about our past and present lives and the gilded existence of the full boarders who even had bathtubs at their disposal.

Runia's family might have been famous, but she, too, was a refugee. Her father was in a POW camp, her mother worked in a hospital lab, and her brother was sequestered with a group of boys from other famous families on an almost inaccessible estate deep in the forested mountains of Central Poland. There, the boys were being groomed for running the country after the war. Besides being taught everything they had to learn for high school, they were fed very well. One of the boys was a son of the president-in-exile, Raczyński.

As for me, I once had a brother, but he died. Papa had to move to Warszawa, but was going to come back, and Mama tried to run a little store but had recently switched to the black market. And Mykola? Well, Runia did not have to know about him, at least not right away. I was not yet enlightened enough to appreciate her distinguished family and had enough conceit to imagine that, if I dug deep enough into Papa's background, I could come up with some famous people.

A younger girl, whose last name was Helcel, was also a half-boarder. The three of us ate our lunch in the kitchen, while the full boarders ate in a dining room. Runia found this segregation unfair and demeaning and began to express her disapproval by misbehaving at the table. I was impressed by her courage. "Look! Look at this soup! It must have been made from dirty dish towels," she would say loud and clear so that everyone could hear her, including the nuns in charge of the meals. "And what do you think is being served in the dining room?" she would ask me in full voice. Of course I had no idea. She would answer her own question: "It's meat and cake!" Did she really know, I wondered. Sometimes she even let tiny bread pellets fly through the kitchen. Runia's antics fascinated me and shocked the sweet Helcel girl. And because the Helcel girl was so sweet and unassuming, Runia, who must have known more than I about the girl's background, would pick on her. "Your family is made up of penny pinchers," I once heard Runia say. The girl defended herself, "No, it is not, or they would not have founded an old people's home for the poor."

   I had no idea what it was all about. Soon after, I learned that indeed there was a Helcel home for the old and the poor, and that that girl lived in it with her grandmother. I was even invited there for a visit because I was nicer than Runia and did not try to defame the Helcels. The invitation was supposed to lead to a friendship, but it did not. The girl was not as exciting as Runia; being so good made her boring. And there was also a sadness about her and her grandmother. Where were her parents, I wondered—but did not ask. Because, in those days, a question like that could have brought a flood of tears. I don't know what caused the breakup of our group of three. The nuns may have decided that it was too much trouble to take care of half-boarders, especially when one of them was Runia. After a couple of months, Runia and I were on our own. No more hanging out in our cubicle. After school we would go either to Runia's home or to mine where no one was looking after us. Freedom it was. The Helcel girl must have switched schools because I never saw her again.

13

Józefina's Mistress

The servants I have met so far like to talk about the families they used to work for. The richer the family, the more there is to tell. Józefina, too, likes to brag about the family she used to work for. They owned a textile factory and a villa to live in. You should have seen all the beautiful things they had, Józefina tells me. Shiny furniture, Persian carpets, fine china, crystal wine glasses, and embroidered tablecloths. She does not mention a garden, but since every villa has to have one, hers must too and it must be full of beautiful flowers. To me a garden is more important than the other stuff.

And he… and he…, Józefina tries to tell me, he was a real gentleman.

The "he" is the head of the household, but I am not sure what she means by "a real gentleman." Is it a man who does not pick his nose in public or spit onto the pavement? I think she has some other gentlemanly quality in mind but does not tell me what it is. I don't ask because I sometimes like to find my own answers, even though they may be wrong.

To become a servant for a rich family one has to have connections; the rich are picky about whom they hire. Józefina's oldest sister, the one who could read and write, was the connection. Smart as she was, she was able to convince the mistress that Józefina was honest, did not drink or chase after men, and would always return with correct change when sent to the store to buy something. Józefina is not dumb, that's for sure. That she had never learned how to read or write was not her fault. There were too many children in her family—eight of them—and only the oldest had shoes. There must have been a law that a child could not go to school barefoot, and so Józefina had to stay home and help with the two-hectare farm her parents owned, a farm not big enough to feed all of them. To end up working in a house that was almost like a church because it had so many pretty, shiny things to look at, was like winning the lottery jackpot. Józefina was very proud of having been able to pull it off.

The war broke out—why did God let it happen?—and the good life came to an end. The town where Józefina lived was annexed to Germany, and the "real gentleman" she had worked for was arrested and his factory taken over. Since the new owner did not know how to run it, the old owner had to stay around and help. Stay he did, in jail, from where he was taken to the factory every day by car. He was treated well because he was such a gentleman,

Józefina assures me. That makes me imagine that after work he wears a fancy robe and sits in an armchair in his cell, a glass of wine in his hand. Józefina does not tell me what will happen to him once he is no longer needed or if the new owner will ever learn how to run the factory. I do not ask.

And then the inevitable happened: the villa was taken over and the gentleman's wife and daughter had to leave immediately, with only one suitcase per person. They had to pack up in a hurry and did not have time to give much thought to what they should be taking along. Józefina was coming with them, and she too was entitled to one suitcase, but hers was filled with her mistress's stuff because the clothing Józefina owned was not worth anything. It was not much better than rags. That is why, when she came to work for Mama, she had only one dress, a pair of shoes that did not fit, and a beret. Nothing for winter and that was frightening. Though she had promised, the mistress did not pay Józefina for the space in the suitcase she had filled with her expensive clothing. That life is not fair is no surprise to Józefina and she did not complain. That is the story of how Józefina ended up in the same town as we did: I as a refugee, she as a displaced person.

Now that Mama has gotten her a second dress, one made of two old ones, black below the waist, flowers on a black background on the top, Józefina is ready to visit her mistress and show off what she calls "the latest Parisian fashion," a phrase her mistress must have used. She wants the woman to see that she is doing all right, that she has found work with a respectable family, and that she takes care of a nice little girl, namely me, and therefore I have to come along. None of it is quite true. Without a winter coat, Józefina will not be all right, with Papa gone we are not even a family, and I have never heard anyone call me a nice little girl. Yet, Józefina is doing her best to turn me into one and the visit into a big event. She scrubs me clean, and since I no longer have any decent dresses, she makes me wear the coat Mama bought for me while we were passing through Kaunas. I know that it makes me look like a child from a good home. With white ankle socks and a hat that came with the coat, I am no longer myself. But I don't mind, since I know it is not going to last. Józefina puts on her best dress or the better of the two. If she is wearing something under it, I cannot tell; she has not yet shown me if she has any underwear in her bundle of treasures. The shoes are a big problem. They do not fit, and she is not used to wearing what she calls her chains, but going barefoot is unthinkable. A hat, a pair of white gloves—I have no idea what they are for—a purse and a dab of eau de Cologne, both borrowed from Mama, and Józefina is ready to go. Once there she may even ask for some kind of a payment for the space in her suitcase so that she can buy herself a winter coat.

Her mistress lives in the attic of an apartment house, and we have many steps to climb. It is Sunday, late morning, the weather nice but too warm for a coat, and going up the stairs in it makes me sweat and wish that I would not have to play the part of a sweet little girl. Józefina's mistress opens the door for us. She is barely dressed, a pink silk nightgown, a burgundy robe over it not even tied or buttoned. Too much of her is showing. We follow her through the vestibule to an open door at its other end and enter a wood-paneled room with a ceiling that slopes on two sides. There is a small window in the far wall of the room with a view of the sky, a bed along a wall where the ceiling is low, a wardrobe and a dresser where the ceiling is high, a table in the center of the room with chairs around it. I like the wood paneling because it reminds me of houses back home, though this one no longer smells of pine and rather of camphor. A man is sitting at the table. His uncombed hair, damp, red, and sparse, clings to his scalp. His face is round and white, his blue eyes are swimming in tears or sweat. His shirt is unbuttoned. Standing as I am right across the table from him, I can't see if his pants are open too or even if he is wearing pants. He gags, coughs, and gasps for air. It is an interesting performance.

Józefina's mistress rushes over to him with a cup of something and holds it to his lips. She is speaking German to him. It is the first time that I see a German from so close up. In real life, I do my best to avoid them. In a streetcar where they have their section and we have ours, I sit as far away from them as possible. But here we are, all in one room, and because the man is in such a sorry state and is not looking at me, I can watch him as if he were just a bug someone has stepped on. What I see fascinates me. Józefina's mistress offers him another cup of some brew, and he drinks it carefully in small sips to avoid gagging on it should he start coughing again. Is it one of the cups Józefina told me about, the best of the best, that was slipped into one of the suitcases between the fancy dresses?

We have come at the wrong time. Yet, Józefina manages to follow her mistress as she hurries between the hotplate in the corner of the room and the sick man at the table. They do talk, but I am not listening; my attention is on the man who finally looks at me. I think that he is surprised that someone has been watching him. He smiles. I think that we both feel embarrassed: he, because he looks so pitiful, I, because I have been caught staring. Has he noticed how well-dressed I am? Probably not.

It is time for Józefina and me to leave. The visit has not been a success. I don't think that Józefina's mistress was impressed by our clothes, and she may not even have noticed what we are wearing. On our way out, we pass the door that was closed before but is now open. I catch sight of a woman standing in the middle of a room. Dressed in one of those transparent nightgowns, she is facing the high window and the sun, and she may as well be naked. The mistress's daughter? We just hurry by. It seems that Józefina does not want to stop and talk. Two doors only? Do they have a bathroom, or do they have to take their baths in a basin of cold water that has to be brought from somewhere? Do they use a bucket for a toilet? Very interesting. I always want to know how other refugees are getting by.

We would run down the stairs, but Józefina cannot really run because of her killer shoes. It feels good to be outside again in the open on such a nice day. I don't know what to make of what I have just seen. Questions keep buzzing through my mind, questions I am not going to ask. That sickly German, who is he? What was bothering him? Does it mean that Józefina's mistress is not a real lady though she is married to a real gentleman, if he is still alive? Why wasn't she dressed properly? And her daughter almost naked in her flimsy nightgown in the middle of the day? Józefina is not talking. She too must be thinking hard trying to make sense of what we have just seen. After a little while, as we pass a strip of grass along the pavement, she spits onto it. Józefina spits with so much power and such good aim that she can make the spittle land far away and exactly where she wants it. It's amazing. I have asked her to show me how she does it, but no matter how hard I try to follow her instructions, the spittle always lands on my legs or feet. It means that either I have no talent for spitting or one has to start learning it while very young. "Oh, that bitch, that bitch," she mutters. By then I have already guessed what she thinks of her mistress because spitting is often as good as saying a bad word. She has nothing more to add and, as we keep walking in silence, I finally come up with a brilliant idea. "You know that she could be working for the Underground using her German to get information about arrests and raids and whatever else can be useful? Perhaps she receives him in her negligé so that he can take a look at her body in exchange for food." Well, my brilliant idea seems to fall on deaf ears. There can't be any excuses for what her mistress is doing. "And her husband was a real gentleman ..." Józefina keeps repeating. "And she did not even give me a chance to ask for a payback... That damn bitch..."

Somewhere along the way, Józefina takes off her killer shoes and walks home barefoot. Someday soon she will visit her mistress again, but I won't have to come with her. I have already done my part.

14

The Psychic

Still considered a child, I'm not supposed to know anything. But I have already learned a lot from experience and not just from hearing some grown-up say that such and such is true. I know that people used to talk about wars, those of the past and the one that was about to come, but now that we are actually in the midst of a war, they talk about prophesies, some of them hundreds of years old, to find out what is going to happen and how the world will be divided up when the fighting ends someday. Since the war did not end in one month—despite people saying that it would—prophesies are now considered to be most reliable at predicting the future, even with their vague language. I listen to grown-ups argue about the meaning of the prophets' words and learn that they mean different things to different people. That is what makes predictions so confusing, and listening to the arguments themselves does not make me any wiser. I have learned that some people would like to know what fate has in store for them, especially while this war lasts. Finding someone who knows the future must be difficult, though, because it seems that true psychics, if they exist at all, are few and always very busy in bad times. That Józefina ran into one—without even trying!—made her into some kind of a hero. And now, everyone wants to hear what happened. Józefina has always been special to me. Now she is special to others, too.

It all began in the little store Mama had managed to open after we had to flee from our home because of the war and Papa no longer had a job. The store was supposed to help us survive, but things were not looking very promising. Located at the end of a quiet street, next to a church that looks like an ordinary building, it can sell only paper products. The customers are neighbors who suddenly need an envelope or a few sheets of paper they forgot to buy at the big store across the street from the park. Someone has to stand behind the counter during the hours shops must be open, but I don't think it can be Mama who is always occupied with her business on the black market. For the store, she hires young women who need a certificate of employment so that they will not be sent to forced labor. Something else must be going on at the store, but I do not want to know what. And because we now live so far away from it, I rarely see it.

Sometimes Mama has to ask Józefina to play the saleslady. I have no idea how good she can be at it without being able to read and write. But Józefina can talk cleverly, make the correct change, and even stand up for herself, and that is all she may need to be a success behind the counter of an almost empty shop. She was doing exactly that—standing behind the counter—when a man rushed in and asked if she could hide him. Even before he had time to tell her what he was so afraid of, Józefina locked the door and hung the "closed" sign in the window. Without a rear exit, the store is a trap. A set of shelves, right behind the counter, divides it in two, but behind the shelves there is nothing but bare walls. I can imagine what they would look like if someone got caught there. That is where the man and Józefina hid and that is where he told her his story. He is a psychic and can often foresee important events. He was just walking along the street with a briefcase full of compromising documents when suddenly he was able to see what was about to happen. The police were right around the corner heading towards him, so he had either to run or to hide. If he ran, they would shoot him. If he hid, they might not look for him in a tiny store with big windows when there is a church next door with nooks and crannies to slip into.

Józefina does not know how long she and the psychic stayed behind the partition. It could have been an hour. Yes, they did hear steps and voices but without looking out, they could not know whose they were. They waited for the sound of silence and when it finally came, the man calmed down. He was sure by then that he would be safe, that the danger had passed. He slipped out of the store and disappeared. Józefina was so shaken by the incident that she decided to close up for the rest of the day and go straight home to tell Mama what had happened.

Everyone in our apartment was fascinated by her story, and, as the word spread, even some neighbors came over to hear it. I am glad that Józefina, the poor servant girl and my friend, has become a hero and is no longer looked down on, at least not for a little while. She is not used to being the center of attention and something about it seemed to disturb her. That the man was trying to avoid arrest and a likely death was of little interest to the listeners—probably because arrests and executions are now everyday events. What interested them was that the man claimed to be a genuine psychic who could foresee the danger and thus save himself. It would be nice if everyone were able to do that.

I asked Józefina if the man predicted her future while they were stuck behind the partition. He did not because the conditions were not right. Frightened as he was, he would not have been able to concentrate on Józefina. I think she was telling me the truth. Would she have wanted to know what was going to happen a week or a month later when, with all the hard work she has to do, she does not seem to have much time for dreams? As for me, I am afraid to learn about my fate because I can't imagine that there will be anything good in it.

Józefina and I were sick recently and, in a way, it was nice. We had the big room all to ourselves: I stayed in the bed, she on the table instead of on the coal bin in the kitchen. Which was better to lie on, the soft bed with its bed bugs or the hard table without them? We could not agree. At first, it did not matter because we were too sick to care, but later, when we were just coughing, gagging, and spitting, we could joke and laugh about our sleeping arrangements. It took us almost a month to get better—we just had to wait it out because a doctor would have been of no help and would have charged Mama a lot anyway. We had plenty of time to talk, Józefina and I, and we even made up an illustrated story which I wrote down and drew the pictures for. It is about two old maids after whose death a pack of dogs stages a magnificent funeral. The next-door neighbor, the educated one who disappeared recently, read it, even showed it to a friend, and told us that it is a masterpiece. That made us laugh.

After being so sick, Józefina had to take it easy and that is how she ended up in the store not doing much of anything. Mama has two old winter coats which she has bought for resale and is letting Józefina, who does not have one, wear them until a buyer comes along. Two coats! To have a choice makes Józefina feel rich, and she likes that feeling. Someday, I'll have good clothes of my own, she keeps telling me. Clothes are very important to her. Mama was able to sell one of these coats recently and now Józefina no longer has a choice. We worry that someone may want to buy the second one before spring and then Józefina would have only a tattered sweater to keep her warm.

It's winter and we are living through hard times. Coal is expensive and in short supply and so is food. To keep warm in the evening we all gather in one room, the only one that is heated from time to time. We try to socialize. I hardly ever say anything, but I do listen. Mykola, Mama's prize tenant, the one who will not move out, who neighbors say is my uncle, wants to find the psychic and be told that a great future is awaiting him. He has been asking around town and learned that there is indeed someone who fits Józefina's description and often knows what is going to happen. Now I hear that the psychic will come to our apartment for a session with the tenant. He did not want to, but after a lot of prodding finally agreed. I am really curious and want to see him. Does he look like an ordinary human being? I am already waiting in the hallway when the bell rings, and I have a good look at the man as he enters. He is tall, has big, light blue eyes and is wearing a dark coat. In a crowd he would stand out because of his height. That there's something unusual about his eyes would not be noticed. I have not seen a psychic before, not a real one, anyway, and so cannot tell if he has a psychic's eyes. He does look in my direction—not at me but at something above and beyond. Perhaps that is where my future is, the future I do not want to hear about. From the way he walks in, so sure of himself, he must already know that he is not walking into a trap. After a friendly handshake, the two men disappear into the depths of the apartment where the "uncle" lives when not away on business. I wait in our room right next to the door that opens into the hallway so that I will have a second look at the psychic before he leaves. Mama and Józefina hover around, mostly in the kitchen, because they too want to see the psychic again. It's a very long wait—it feels like one hour at least—so, the psychic must have a lot to say. And that must mean that the "uncle's" future is not going to end any time soon. When he finally comes out and passes through the hall, I can only see his back.

When, at last, Mykola enters our big room where Mama and I have been waiting, his face is red, and he is not yet ready to talk. It seems that he is trying to make sense out of what he has just heard and for some reason it is not easy. He paces around the room stopping every now and then and when he does, he shakes his head as if disagreeing with his thoughts. "What did he tell you?" Mama asks. As for me, I am just waiting to hear the big story but do not ask because I have no right to, since to me, he is a stranger. Still, I would like to hear what the psychic had to say. And so does Józefina, because she comes in after a while, when the "uncle" had already enough time to say something, if not yet everything. And finally, he does say, almost on the verge of crying, "He told me that I will never find personal happiness." I am puzzled and so is Józefina. I don't know about Mama. She may be disappointed. What does "personal happiness" mean, I wonder. Does it mean that Mykola will make other people happy? I don't think that he ever will. Perhaps later, when Mama is in his room at night, she will hear what else the psychic had to say, but neither Józefina nor I will ever find out what it was.

15

The Gloves

I know I don't have the whole story, because Mama likes secrets, but I'll try to do my best to write about what I saw and even what I did not see. Perhaps it will help me understand what happened.

On that morning Mama was not going to get out of bed: she was playing sick. She does it when she has a difficult day ahead of her or wants to avoid seeing someone who may be coming with demands and complaints of some kind. Often, I have to lie and tell people that she is not home, even though she is in bed under the covers. I don't mind lying to someone who looks like a crook, but when the person is nice, I feel guilty. Later that day, Mama, still in her bed, ordered Józefina to take me to a bakery which still, on occasion, sold cakes that must have been expensive. I should have guessed right away that Mama had something very special on her mind, because she does not believe in spoiling children, neither with cakes nor useless toys. The day was bitter cold even though the sky was dark gray. On days as cold as that one, I had to stay home, so that my toes would not freeze off in my too small boots. Yet Mama kept insisting that Józefina and I get out in a hurry, as if worried that the cake would be sold out by the time we got to the bakery. Even Józefina was not letting me dawdle.

We were going down the stairs—it is a long haul from the fourth floor to the bottom—when we ran into a man on his way up. That man was Papa. And though I had not seen him for a year I recognized him right away and burst into tears. He must have been starving: his face was just skin and bones. The gray winter coat, made by a tailor before the war, was hanging on him like a sack on a scarecrow. As we hugged and hugged, I saw that it was threadbare around the wrists and buttonholes and that the gloves he had on his hands were in shreds. I cried and cried and through my tears caught sight of Józefina's worried face. She was supposed to get me out of the way in time but failed. Mama is going to be angry. Yet she did not try to drag me away and was just standing there watching my performance that could not go on forever. She knew how important it was for me to greet Papa. Finally, Papa said that he had to see Mama, and Józefina reminded me that Mama wanted me out of the way. I would be able to meet him later, she promised.

We went to the bakery where even Józefina got her piece of cake— Mama's payment to her for not letting me know that Papa was coming.

The bakery had some tables we could sit at. It was a good place for keeping warm. I could not stop crying, because Papa's hands had been ice cold, his gloves as good as nothing. To calm me down, Józefina began to tell me a story that sounded like a fairytale. Somewhere in town there was a place where you could buy new winter clothing at a fraction of what it would cost on the black market. If this were true, why didn't she go there and get some clothing for herself to replace her rags and the borrowed winter coat? I know that grown-ups are liars but did not expect Józefina to lie to me. Therefore, I knew that I would no longer be able to trust her. Since we could not stay in the bakery forever, we went to a church. Churches were surely not built to keep people warm, and so then we went out to walk the streets. The cold dried my eyes and froze the snot in my nose. Józefina kept talking and assured me that that store was for real and even had a name: it was **RGO**. She was not sure where it was, but she was going to find out. The problem with it, she told me, was that it was very hard to get a permit to buy anything there. Many offices to go to, many forms to fill out. When I learned that the path to it is full of bumps, I began to believe her. If it were not for the bumps, people would be lining up for miles to get into the store.

When Józefina decided that Mama had had enough time for her fight with Papa, we went home. By then he had already left. I began to cry again; it was my day of crying. To keep me quiet, Mama assured me that I would see him again before he returned to Warszawa. And I did. We met at his cousin's, who, after the Germans had taken over his fancy apartment, was living in a stable, in a room with a floor of cobble stones. Even with fire in the stove, it does not get warm enough to take off one's coat. A very cold winter it is. Soldiers are freezing to death on the eastern front—not that I feel sorry for them.

To pass the time, Papa and I took walks on the Planty to see the places I know from the previous fall. And because I was spending so much time with Papa, I could not keep track of what Józefina was doing about the gloves and did not even know how to ask her. She did take me to an office once where the papers had to be stamped: men sitting behind desks, annoyed with us for coming. They did not care if Papa's fingers froze off and that made me cry. My wailing attracted their attention. My sobs and hiccups did not sound like music. The men looked at me as if I were a monumental nuisance. Perhaps I was, and that is why they stamped the papers quickly, without asking any questions. Later Józefina thanked me for helping her out with my crying—often she had had to wait for a long time before an official would look up from his desk.

I don't know who filled out the forms needed to buy the gloves. If I ask Józefina, I would be reminding her that she can't read or write and that would hurt us both. Was it the nice neighbor from next door who had once warned Mama that she should not expose me to unnecessary dangers? Or was it Papa himself for whom the gloves were supposed to be a surprise? It could not have been Mama, because, as far as I could tell, she just wanted him to be gone. But why do I care? Does it really matter who filled them out?

How many days did Papa stay in Kraków? I just know that it was long enough to spend some time with me, talk to Mama when I was not home, and to Józefina at the entrance to our building and perhaps also somewhere else. I heard him ask her to watch out for me. Once he told me how glad he was that I had her. Józefina got to know him well enough to be able to tell me that he was a real gentleman. How did she know? Did they talk to each other while I was not there? I could not be everywhere at the same time and what I didn't see or hear was secret. Had I asked, no one would have told me anything, not even Józefina. Mama was spending most of the time in bed, and so I wanted to know what was wrong with her. If she stayed up for too long, she would bleed to death, Józefina told me. Did she really mean that? I must have looked puzzled because she said that someday I will understand and that meant that Mama's illness was another of her many secrets that Józefina did not know how to explain to me.

Had I been smarter, I would have asked right at the beginning who was going to pay for the gloves. Perhaps I even thought that they would be free because Papa was so poor and starving. Perhaps I did not think of it because I did not really expect that Józefina would be able to get the necessary papers. When she did, paying for the gloves became a problem. Neither Józefina nor I had any money, and we could not ask Papa because he did not look as if he had any. Besides, the gloves were supposed to be a gift from me to him. Józefina did think of asking the nice neighbor from next door, but that would have been too embarrassing. And so, finally, without telling me, she decided to ask Mama and, had I not walked into the room at the right time, I would not now know about it. I am sure Józefina would have kept it secret because she knew that I would have objected to Mama paying for the gloves, and perhaps Papa would not even accept them if he found out who had paid for them. It was a matter of pride and us no longer being a family.

Mama was in her bed sitting up facing Józefina. I could not see Józefina's face but could hear her voice. She was not talking to Mama like a servant. "I know that you don't want to do it for him, but you should do it for her. She has been crying for days." Was it an order? I saw fear in Mama's face. What was she afraid of? It took Mama a little while to decide what to do, but she did agree, grudgingly.

Later in the day, as more grayness was descending over the city, we set out to get the gloves. First, we had to find the street and that is never easy. Then we had to find the house with the clothing store. I imagined it to be on the ground floor and have large windows with goods on display. But it was not like that. We had to climb several flights of stairs and pass many closed doors before arriving at the right one. That door was closed too, but after Józefina rang the bell, an old man let us into vast room with shelves along the walls and no customers or windows that I could see. It did not look as if there was much stuff on the shelves. Józefina gave him the documents and he began to study them. His head was as round as a volleyball, and, without any hair on it, it shone even under the dim light of a single bulb. He wore glasses. As he was taking his time to look over the papers to make sure that they were not counterfeit, I panicked and began to cry. What if? What if something goes wrong—a missing signature or an incorrect entry? Then all of Józefina's efforts would have been in vain. He got up from his desk and asked Józefina "Why is this child crying?" She went over to him and said something I could not hear. She almost whispered into his ear and whatever it was made him look at me as if I were about to be run over by a tram. Someday I am going to ask her what magic words she had come up with.

We got the gloves—they are black and so go well with Papa's gray coat. Józefina paid, and I was so moved that I could not stop crying. We delivered them to Papa the next day just before he took the train back to Warszawa. A gift from me because he is my Papa, a gift from Józefina because she thinks that he is a great gentleman.

One day I find the right moment to ask her what she means by that. "A real gentleman," Józefina responds immediately, "does not leave any disgusting hair in the tub for the servant to clean up!"

I wasn't sure if there was a hidden meaning I was missing, but I was very happy to know that my father was a true gentleman.

16

The Ring

When you come back from the country with rosy cheeks, a layer of fat over your ribs, and stories of robbers and seductions, you will ask me what I did while you were away, and I will say "nothing." Yes, "nothing," because, as you know, Runia, I only watch what is happening around me, and that is almost as good as doing nothing. Without you here to help me, I did not even get into trouble: I behaved and was bored. If it were not for the ring, I wouldn't have anything to write about. Should I be letting you in on this story? I don't think it's a good idea, but you, as if able to read my mind, will sense that, in the time you were away, something must have happened and will try to make me talk. Friends should not keep secrets from each other, you will say, and we may even get into a little fight. To avoid all that I am writing you this letter, which may turn out to be long. Once it is written, I will decide which parts of it I should erase to keep Mama looking good.

That morning, she woke up feeling unwell and would not get out of bed until later in the day. I had to boil potatoes for breakfast because we were out of bread. Mama either forgot to buy it or had no money to buy it with or there was no bread available in our part of town. I did not ask. Only the two of us were in the apartment. As you know, the people Mama rents rooms to never stay for long because they either do not fit or are on the run. Even Mama's prize tenant, whom I would like to see move out, was away on business buying up stolen goods in the East to bring them here for resale. The silence these people left behind felt eerie. I wished one of them would come back, preferably with a bucket of coal to start a fire. The apartment, unheated for a few days, felt cold.

I had no books to read. I almost asked our classmate Hanka to lend me some, but did not because I knew that she would have refused. She thinks that they would not be safe in my care in the mess of my home. She is right of course. To entertain myself that morning I kept drawing flowers, but none of them were coming out right. In the meantime, Mama stayed in bed brooding and that was a bad sign. She either really was sick or was hatching some outlandish plan: the longer the brooding, the riskier the plan.

By lunchtime Mama was still in bed. I had good reason to be worried.

We ate cold potatoes left over from breakfast. Mama had me serve her in bed. That must have lifted her spirits and helped her to decide. As soon as she had finished eating, she got up and began to dress. I will be going out and you must come with me, she told me. That she would need me meant that she either had to try to make a good impression on someone or get through a tight spot when some street was closed off for arrests. I am used to helping her out and don't mind it too much as long as my being there keeps her out of trouble. I have either to play dumb—I am very good at that—or pretend to be sick, which is much harder for me.

To figure out what was in store for me, I watched Mama dress for the occasion. After trying on this and that, she settled on a wool coat instead of fur, a hat not fancy enough to attract attention, and shoes with high heels which are a torture to wear, but make her look tall and elegant. Somehow, she already knew that the town was going to be quiet that afternoon and that we would not have to run. As you may have noticed, clothes are very important to her. "Kleider machen Leute" is a saying she really believes in.

After touching up her face with powder and her cheeks with rouge, she deepened the pink of her lips and blackened her eyebrows. All this has to be put on in the right amount: too thick a layer would make her look common, too thin would not do the trick. Once finished with the makeup, she studied her face in the mirror as if trying to decide if the face she saw in it was the right one for the occasion. She could not have known yet what kind of a face she needed, so she had to try out different ones for practice: the saintly, the compassionate, the tough, and the mean. To show anger, an evil spark flashed in her eyes before she narrowed them to a pair of slits. She parted from the mirror with one of her most charming smiles. Every time I see Mama try out her faces, I promise myself never to grow up.

The less I know, the safer we are going to be, so Mama does not tell me where we are going or why. I've learned not to ask. Sometimes I think that she is confused because the instructions that have been given to her are vague: the home of a stranger without a name, an address in an unfamiliar part of town, no map for how to get there, and a code for ringing the bell. Unless one gets it right on the first try, no one will open the door. You may not know all this because your mother has a real job—I wish mine did—but that is how the black market works. It is made up of secrets, unfinished sentences, talk that does not make sense, and leads that may take one nowhere.

On our way out, we ran into the janitor's wife. She was cleaning up vomit some soldier had left in the hallway on his way to the front. Was he too embarrassed to throw up in the street? A fresh bruise under her eye explained why the night before their tiny room was exploding with screams and the racket from whatever was being thrown around by her besotted husband. So evil is the look in his bloodshot eyes, so scary his tottering gait, that I run the other way every time I see him coming.

We took the trolley to Błonia, but got off before the end of the line, even before the bridge, in a part of town I do not know and probably neither do you—you and I have not explored it yet because it is so far away from home. It's a maze of nice buildings, big and solid, that the war must have bypassed: walls without cracks or pockmarks, glass in their windows instead of boards, and no vomit in the hallways. Exactly the kind of neighborhood where happy families live. You know the kind: father, mother, sister, brother, a devoted servant, and sometimes even a purebred dog. They have shelves full of books, eat their meals at a big table, talk cleverly about important events, and know what the different forks and spoons are used for. Their children are well-mannered, always do their homework, and don't cause any trouble, like the nice girls in our class we make fun of behind their backs because we can't be like them, even if we decided to try.

On that day the weather was quite ordinary: the sooty sky hung over the city like a damp, gray blanket as if trying to keep it warm. My back felt cold if not my nose because what was trickling out of it was not changing to ice. Mama was walking as fast as her high heels would allow. They went clop, clop on the pavement and sounded very loud on the empty street. The invisible sun was setting somewhere far away. The windows were reflecting a beautiful, purple light.

In that part of town, the streets have no landmarks and all look the same to a stranger. I could barely keep track of the turns we were making. Mama did not know the way and, more than once, we had to retrace our steps and start out in the opposite direction. If I had to run back to the trolley, I would have gotten lost in that maze. When we finally stumbled upon the street Mama was looking for, I could see how relieved she was. "Aha, that is it. I knew that I would be able to find it." By then we must have been close to the river and its black waters. By the feel, it had to be somewhere behind those houses. If you asked me to find this place, I am not sure I would be able to, though.

The entry door was not locked. The hallway led to the stairs and to an elevator with an "out of order" sign that could have been either true or false. I figured what it probably meant was that electricity could not be used for going up and down. Since I knew that you would ask me what it smelled like in there, I sniffed hard, but not as hard as you would have. I came up with nothing more than the scent of dust and cold stone, clean but dull. No vomit and no food. It seemed that in that building no one was cooking anything.

We climbed the stairs, two flights at least, and arrived at a door Mama was sure was the right one. She stood in front of it for a little while, probably rehearsing the code for ringing the bell, because unless she got it right on the first try, there will be no second chance, and we would have to wander around for a while before trying again. Mama was lucky: I heard the sound of footsteps, as if someone ancient, wearing slippers, was shuffling towards the door at a slow pace. Indeed, it was an old woman who let us in after Mama had explained to her briefly what she had come for. A ring it was, a mysterious ring I knew nothing about.

I find it interesting to go into homes of strangers and have a peek at their lives. As you and I have noticed, God has not been very kind lately and so most of the homes Mama takes me to don't have much to look at. They are spaces for refugees to live in: a part of a stable or a single room filled with bundles their owners don't dare unpack because another train may come and take them somewhere else. I, too, have been waiting for such a train.

And now here we were in the apartment of a family that had not been displaced by the war. It did not feel right to be there, we did not belong. I may as well let you know that the foyer had four doors and did not smell of food. With only one door open I could not see the secrets the apartment was hiding and that disappointed me. There was no long hallway to look into, no door left open at its end, no bed left unmade, and no clothes draped over a chair. I listened for sounds of voices and footsteps but heard nothing. Was the apartment so small that it did not have to be shared with tenants? Was a bribe being paid to keep them out? Or, perhaps, it was occupied by ghosts who, in reality, were living somewhere else? Yes, I did wonder about ghosts.

The room we were taken into had two windows at its far end. They may have faced the river, but I could not see if my hunch was right, because we were staying near the door where there was a couch, two armchairs, and a low table with some books on it. After sizing each other up for a moment, the way strangers do, the women took the chairs while I sat down on the edge of the couch. I always sit on the edge when I feel out of place. Everything in the room was nice, very nice, from the shiny floor to the furniture, a grand piano, and a carpet that should have been rolled up and hidden somewhere because it looked Persian. It is not smart to have something so valuable exposed to view.

The woman—I was able to have a good, long look at her because she was not paying any attention to me—no longer had any spark left in her watery eyes. You've noticed it, too, I think, how the spark disappears when people get old. But her face, round and flat, was not all wrinkled and dried up, her back not bent. She sat as straight as we are supposed to sit in school, her hair in a bun, her eyelids red. She wore a thick wool sweater and kept her hands in the sleeves for warmth. I could not tell how cold the room was because we had just come in from outside and had not been asked to take off our coats. The woman knew that our visit was going to be short. "I am very sorry that my daughter is not home yet. She should be back any moment." And so, I learned that there was a daughter whom Mama was supposed to see. When people talk, I listen, and remember only the important parts of what is being said. When Mama responded with small talk—"The trolleys are not running on time"—I knew that meant she wasn't worried about being outsmarted.

After a few moments, the woman had to tell us the story that was making her cry. Her son-in-law had been arrested. Where, how, and exactly when, she did not say. Someone from the underground let her daughter know what prison he had been taken to. The message was not clear because it must have gone through several people before it reached her daughter. First it may have been the headquarters for interrogation and then the Montelupich prison. There was nothing in writing, for a good reason, and no news since. Her daughter has been looking for him through the back channels, but no one seems to know where he is. He could have been shipped off to a camp already, or, God forbid, shot. Perhaps he could still be found and even released with the help of a bribe. There was always hope. Tears were flowing down the woman's cheeks. She was not really sobbing. Her tears were leaking out on their own.

An everyday story that was, as you and I know. Last summer we amused ourselves by watching people next to the prison wall wait for shreds of paper to come floating down from its tiny windows. They were supposed to carry the names of the newly arrested who were trying to let their families know where they were and that they will not be coming home for dinner. Someone, perhaps a guard, must have been in charge of this postal service—it certainly was not God. When the police arrived, we ran just like everybody else.

A photo album was lying on the table so close to me that, to touch its cover, I only would have had to stretch out my hand. You know how much I like to look at photographs, new and old. I often ask you to show me yours. Yet, in that strange room where I had to be very good, I did not give in to the temptation at least not until the woman got up to turn on a lamp whose light was so dim that she did not have to make the long trip to the windows to cover them up for the blackout. When her back was turned towards me, I let my fingers glide over the album's cover. The suede was smooth and soft. She should not have seen me touch it, but did, as if she somehow had sensed the motion of my hand or had eyes in the back of her head. "You can look at it," she said when she turned back towards me. I was so embarrassed by having been caught in the act, that I did not know what to say or do next and played dumb instead. But as soon as the woman started telling Mama the second half of the story and got involved in it, I opened up the album without taking it off the table. It was too precious to be put in my lap.

Her daughter's husband was everything one would want in a son-in-law: decent, cultured and gifted. He came from a distinguished family and, until the outbreak of the war, had a great job as an engineer. And best of all, he really loved his wife. They were a perfect couple. For all I know, he may have been all that, but, then again, people do exaggerate. One isn't supposed to speak badly of the dead or kick someone who is already down. Even the janitor's wife claimed that her man was an angel when she was trying to get him out of jail where he was locked up for drunkenness. Even when she still had a black eye from one of his blows, she missed him, she would insist.

Bad thoughts began to trickle into my stupid brain: why hasn't this man been arrested earlier? He was guilty because of who he was, and men like him were coming to a bad end. Has he been on the run for years? Does his wife think that Mama could save him somehow? "He was such a good husband. They were so happy together, so much in love..." his mother-in-law kept repeating with so much feeling that I almost became convinced that it was true. Tears continued to run down the woman's cheeks. Her voice was cracking. Then she was really crying. The expression on Mama's face was saintly and compassionate, like the one she had tried out in front of the mirror. I thought that it was real, that she was not pretending—but I could have been wrong.

"Why did it have to happen to them?" the woman kept asking. "Why did God tear them apart?" If she expected Him to answer her, she would have had to wait for a long time because He has not been talking lately, not for thousands of years. Didn't we learn in our religion class that God was jealous and vain? I may not have that quite right because I no longer listen to what the nuns tell us. I stopped listening when I realized that what they say does not make sense and is full of contradictions. Jealous of whom or what was not explained. Perhaps no one knows yet for sure. Isn't it quite odd that He is more petty than we're allowed to be? Perhaps God, being jealous and vain, can't stand seeing people be happy and, to please Himself, has to put them through hard times and make them live through the kind of mess we are in now.

The woman was pouring out her heart to Mama as if she had no one else to talk to. After all, she could not tell her daughter how hopeless she felt. Since she was not saying anything new, I began to leaf through the album. I wanted to see what her son-in-law looked like. Was he as handsome as men in the movies? I can't imagine great love between two homely people. The album was filled with pictures taken during trips abroad. Even I, who does not get much of a chance to look at books, could tell that the couple had travelled a lot: there was Paris with the Eiffel tower, Rome with the Coliseum, and Greece with the Parthenon, skiing in the mountains—of course, I could not tell which mountains they were. Your parents, too, travelled between the wars. Papa did not, because after the Revolution he no longer had money to spare. No picture of the son-in-law as far as I could tell, at least not one with a sign underneath, "This is the man I love." My search for him ended when I heard a door open and close and footsteps pass through the foyer. My heart skipped a beat because something was about to happen, and my fingers let go of the page they were holding open.

The daughter entered the room and filled it with her presence.

Have you ever noticed how some people seem to fill a room, however large and crowded? They can enter discreetly, without any fanfare, but soon everyone is looking at them with awe as if they were some kind of royalty. I have seen my mother pull it off a few times, even with her heavy steps. I have also seen her try and fail. Success depends on the audience and circumstances. The daughter's steps were soft and quiet. The way she moved was not meant to attract attention, yet it did. I kept watching her fill the room.

As I continued to stare at her, I realized that though she had her mother's face, flat and round, and her mother's pale blue eyes, hers were not red from too much crying and had a light in them that, I suppose, comes from looking into the future instead of into the past. She did resemble her mother but, being young, she looked fresh and pretty, her eyes full of life. Brown hair was peeking out from around the edges of her white angora beret which was exactly the kind I want to have but will never get, warm and soft. Her coat was bluish gray, its sides flapping in time with her graceful movements as if they were dancing together. That she did not take it off made it clear that we would be on our way before long.

From the greetings she and Mama exchanged, I could tell that they had not seen each other before. Someone had connected them and all I could do was hope that it was someone decent. I had no idea who it could have been since Mama's business dealings are always wrapped in secrecy. It is impossible for me to keep track of everything she does. I try to be her conscience by telling her what someone has said to me about her, but it does not do much good. She responds not with words but with a look which means that she is terribly hurt by what other people think. They make her suffer. And then I try to reassure myself that, if her business dealings were indeed horrible, she would have been shot by now.

The story of the young woman's husband came out in a few words. As she recited it, she did not cry or whine nor did she mention love. Facts only, fuzzy facts because she did not know enough. From the way her lips twitched and the muscles of her face tensed up from time to time, I could tell that hiding grief and holding back tears was not easy. She was trying hard not to expose herself to a stranger. The expression on Mama's face was exactly what it was supposed to be: saintly and compassionate.

"... if this could be of help..." I heard the woman say as she was taking a ring off her finger. I was too far away to see it, but what else could it have been? She wanted Mama either to sell it so that she would have money for food and coal or use it as a bribe to find out what had happened to her husband or even pay for his release. This is what rings are for, as you know.

Mama is keeping one for "the black hour," the day a loaf of bread is worth a diamond ring. Your mother must have one, too, though you've never mentioned it to me.

Since at our end of the room the sickly lamp was not giving off much light, the women went over to the window where Mama could have a better look at what the woman had to offer. What was said there I do not know. I tried to listen but was too far away to hear enough to make sense out of what I did hear. Besides, they may have lowered their voices because they did not want anyone to know what kind of a rotten deal they were making. Nowadays people rarely talk in normal voices: they prefer to whisper unless they happen to be drunk.

The old woman was still sitting in her chair in some kind of a stupor. Her eyes must have run out of water because her cheeks were no longer wet. I think that she did not want her daughter to see her cry and turned off the faucets as soon as she heard the front door open. As for me, I continued my search for her wonderful son-in-law and, counting on luck—I still do sometimes though I ought to know better—I slid just one of my fingers between the pages of the album and opened it up again. My time was running out and I had to hurry. And there it was, not a picture of him but of her. She faces the camera, her face is dreamy, thoughtful, and beautiful. It is touched by destiny, some people would say. Her hair, dark and slightly wavy, comes down her chest in two thick braids and probably reaches all the way to her waist. Under the picture, on the black page of the album, someone had written in white ink, "At 15, when I did not know her yet..." Can you imagine that? She was only a few years older than you or I and someone already loved her in a way. It made me feel like crying.

When the time came for us to leave, I was still staring at the photo and rereading the words. What he looked like, I did not find out: his face must have been buried among the many faces of relatives, friends, and colleagues. Or, perhaps, the album was meant to be just about her and not about him.

In the trolley, on the way home, I could not get the girl out of my mind. To be loved like that she must have been perfect—could sing, play the piano, dance, swim, and write and even knew what to say and when. Being able to do all that made her look the way she did in that photo.

As for the ring, I was not even sure Mama had it. Perhaps she had been asked only to evaluate it. Had I asked her, she would not have told me the truth. A few days later, still thinking about the girl, I almost did ask, but by then it would have been too late. Mama would have said, "What ring?" as if she no longer remembered. When I find out somehow, I'll let you know.

17

A Boy

It happened in the late winter of 1942–1943, maybe March 1943, when Józefina was still working for my mother, but already conspiring to leave. She and I were walking along the stone wall of the garden where the soil was beginning to smell of spring when suddenly the white houses capped with black became the background for an event that I cannot forget, though I no longer remember the name of that short, narrow street or how I would get to it if I tried. The event could not have lasted more than a minute. First, I heard the steps behind me: a boy was running right in the middle of the street, and he was fast, very fast. It could not have been easy to run so fast on cobblestones. He was being chased by a truck, a small truck with an open top, a truck he would not have been able to outrun. We stopped to watch, tears in our eyes as if we already knew what was going to happen. Turn right into one of the houses where the truck won't be able to follow you. From one of the courtyards into an alley and then another and another and you may end up in a safe place. But there is no time to tell you where to go and you won't be able to hear us if we try. That damn truck is making a racket, and it is not even an army truck. When it stops, you have no choice but to run into the open arms of one of its men. You try to wrestle out of his grip, but a blow to your head with a rifle butt brings you onto the ground. Silence. The men—they are not even in uniform—pick you up and throw you into the back of the truck where your body lands with the thud of a log falling onto a wooden floor hollow underneath.

To me it still sounds like a thunderclap.

A moment later the truck disappears around the corner where that street, short and narrow, runs into the avenue of trees.

We continued on our way home, crying and cursing. We did not try to figure out what we had just seen. Instead of turning left at the end of the street, we went through the park and came out in front of the movie theater, pictures of beautiful people plastered next to its door. Right there and then, Józefina spit onto the ground. She knew how to spit and was able to make the yucky stuff land on the wall under one of the pictures.

That is how Józefina expressed her opinion of what we had just witnessed.

18

Uncle Kot

I have finally made it to Warszawa and am staying with Papa. It took weeks of negotiations and delays before Mama let me go. First the Ghetto Uprising had to end, then the Russians dropped a bomb on a streetcar—they had done it in broad daylight—and that incident made Warszawa look like a very dangerous place. Almost every night there were air raid warnings which would keep me awake at night, and I would not be getting enough sleep. Also, Papa could be arrested and then what would happen to me? Every few weeks he had to move to a new address to keep one step ahead of the Gestapo. For the three weeks I was going to spend with him he had rented a room that was supposed to be safe, at least for as long as I was there.

Mama took me to Warszawa by train, since I was not old enough to travel on my own. On the way there we met a woman with a little boy whose face was deep red from screaming. She was sitting right across from us trying to calm down the child, but it was not working. He was not giving up. Mama, too, tried to distract him, without success. Everyone in our crowded compartment must have been relieved when he finally gave up on his own, probably from exhaustion, and fell asleep. Once he did, Mama and the woman were able to talk to each other the way people do on trains. It turned out that she too was from the East and that Papa had once worked for her father administering the country estate he owned. I was even born there. I did not find out what happened to the rest of the woman's family because it was not a subject that could be discussed in 1943 in a crowded train compartment. The family, Belgian Jews with a French name, had bought the land in the 1920s and had planned to run a giant farm growing I don't know what. It could not have worked out very well, first because the Russians do not like the rich and second because the Germans do not like the Jews.

We had to change trains in Kielce and wait and wait. After sitting for so long, I decided to take a walk along the platform to an area where some freight trains were standing. I had already turned and was on my way back when a Hitler Youth suddenly appeared at my side. He must have been hiding somewhere between cars—guarding them perhaps—and thought that I had been sent by the resistance to sabotage the railroads. He screamed, pushed me around and was about to hit me when Mama came running from the station full speed cursing the boy in German. Whatever she said to him made him return to where he had come from like a frightened dog with its tail between its legs. Mama knows how to make a scene and is quite good at it. When she was finished with him, she berated me for having once again done something I was not supposed to do, like taking a walk along the platform of a railroad station. A short time later our train arrived, and we boarded it in a hurry.

Now I am at Papa's, exploring. Our room had once been a study. It has a couch for Papa, and I sleep on two stuffed chairs. The apartment is vast, but I can't find out how vast because I have to keep to the left after entering it through the front door. As I pass through the long hallway, on my left is a room, which may once have been the servants' quarters, but is now occupied by a mother and daughter. They will be lending me books. Next comes the kitchen and then the bathroom. At the end of the hallway there is a door to a vast dining room from which I can enter the study Papa has rented for my visit. That is my place. The rest of the apartment, where the bedrooms and a living room are, is a mystery. All of it belongs to a tiny woman whose husband, a professor, and her only son have been arrested. She has been trying to find out what happened to them or perhaps she already had the final word before I arrived, but was not yet ready to accept it. Papa tells me to stay out of her way and I do because I am afraid of the crazy look in her eyes. Besides, she does not care for me. Once, when we came back up after spending some time in the cellar during an air raid, I said "good night" to her in the hallway. The look she gave me made me shrink almost to nothing. "You are confused," she told me. Was it wrong for me to joke about it being a good night?

The apartment building is on a famous street. What it is so famous for, I do not know. Too much history to keep track of. At its far end, on the other side of the Holy Cross Square, is the Ministry of Defense which was in ruins when we passed through this city in the first year of the war. I do not know if it has been rebuilt, because Papa does not take me in that direction. Too many bad memories, I suppose. When I stick my head out of the window and look to the left, I can see the sunset at the end of the street. It always glows yellow and makes the buildings look as if they were on fire. I like that view though it makes me feel a little bit sad. I would like to follow the sun and end up in some magical place, but even if I tried, I would soon be drowning in blackness.

There are books in our room, even an encyclopedia which probably has the description of how babies are made. I tried to look it up but did not get very far since I didn't know under what letter it would be listed. Papa goes to work. Where and what the job is, he does not tell me. Most of the time I am alone and not allowed to roam the streets on my own because, being new to the city, I could get lost. One man comes to see Papa, a friendly man who talks to me as if I were a grown-up. He comes because he has done something wrong and, now Papa, having once been a judge, has to decide how wrong it was. The men talk in the dining room so that I won't know what they are talking about. Thanks to him I have a real job now that I get paid for. Stacks of paper, gray and rough, already cut to the right size and shape so that each sheet can be glued together to make a small envelope. Gluing is my job. I like to be useful and help Papa pay for my upkeep. He must be spending a fortune on the great meal the house servant cooks for us on weekdays: noodles with fried onions and a sprinkling of cottage cheese. As much as I like being with Papa—he reads to me every night as if I were still a little girl—something about my stay here does not feel right. Is it because it is going to end soon or because Papa is trying too hard to make this place into a real home for me? Everything seems set up as if on stage for a show, even the delicious meals. What will he be eating when I am gone? Where will he move to?

The study is nice. For the books it has cabinets with glass doors, for writing a desk, for sitting a few chairs, for sleeping a couch for Papa and the two armchairs that make my bed. The servant is in charge of setting us up for the night. She is a pleasant woman. I wish I could spend more time with her and find out if she has any stories to tell, but I am afraid to hang out in the kitchen because of the landlady with the crazy eyes and unkempt hair. She would tell me, in her own superior way, that I am unwelcome in her kitchen.

Papa and I take the train when we go to visit Papa's cousin, Uncle Ted, who lives with his wife and daughter in a wood cabin in a pine forest. The girl is supposed to be someone I can play with, but since she is a very well-behaved little girl, five years younger than I, we have nothing in common. She is not interesting. Papa likes their one-room cabin because he can spend a night there when he is between apartments and has no other place to go. On our second visit to Uncle Ted's, a young man jumped out of the train as it was pulling into the station. We hurried past his body, so that I would not see how hurt or dead he was. On that day the little girl and I had something to talk about. When we were leaving, she insisted on coming with us to the station so that I could show her the spot on the platform where I had last seen the man. Well, some six hours later, he was still there covered with flies.

And then there is also Uncle Kot. Occasionally he spends a night with us in the study. When he does, he gets to sleep on my two armchairs with a coffee table squeezed between them, so that he can stretch out. Then I have to sleep on a collection of wooden chairs that don't stay in place when I turn. When this happens, I end up on the floor.

Uncle Kot is not Papa's brother but a cousin. He can't spend more than a single night in one place because he is so important that the Gestapo is constantly on his trail. He and Papa talk in whispers and I can rarely hear them. I am sure they have something important to discuss and it is better for me not to know what it is. Only after he gets into his makeshift bed, which is close to mine, can I hear clearly his grunts and sighs of relief and what he has to say about the apartments he sleeps in. He speaks of unbelievably rich homes, of soft beds with down comforters and embroidered linen, fresh and white. Bliss, real bliss after a day of hard work, but it does not last. The moment he turns off the lights and is about to fall asleep, they are out to get him, the bloodthirsty bedbugs. That they are infesting such luxurious homes is beyond belief, but they are, and it would be rude of Uncle Kot to tell the kind people who are risking their lives by giving him shelter for the night how infested their beds are. Refined and high class, they may not even know anything about bedbugs which seem to prefer to feed on the poor. Uncle Kot is thankful for being able to sleep at Papa's and not having blood sucked out of him.

I met Uncle Kot a long time ago, when I was eight years old. I am twelve now. He arrived at our apartment in Wilno with another man when it was already getting dark. I can still see them waiting to be let in after Papa had opened the door. They had just escaped from a POW camp and needed a place to stay. Somewhere along the way, between the camp and our apartment, they were able to obtain false papers and civilian clothes. I saw Papa hesitate for a moment—what would happen to us if they get caught?—but he had to let them in even though they would have to sleep with us in one room because our other two rooms had been rented out to three new policemen. With two beds along one wall and a couch between them, there was enough sleeping space for the five of us. That is how I met Uncle Kot and Papa's other cousin Mietek who is an army colonel.

Uncle Mietek was always in a good mood. The couch was his and he spent a lot of time on it telling stories and laughing. He was sure that everything was going to turn out for the best, though nothing in the news should have made him think so. Papa, in contrast, thought that we were all sinking and would soon reach the bottom with a one-way ticket to Siberia. Uncle Kot's view was somewhere in between: brave men would save us all and one of the brave, daring men would be Uncle Kot himself.

For both men I was an irritating fly they could not just swat away. I tried my best to stay invisible though it was not easy because we were all squashed into that one room. Uncle Mietek did not pay any attention to me, and I liked him for that. Uncle Kot, though, began to pick on me. The dirty plates, glasses, and papers left on chairs and the table were all my fault. One day he even told me to clean up the desk at which I was sitting. Yes, the desk was messy, but the mess was not all mine. He saw how involved I was in writing and decided that it was a good time to let me know that I should do some cleaning. I told him that I was in the midst of writing a poem and that the idea I had at the moment could simply disappear if I went to the kitchen with the dirty dishes. That made him laugh. He did not believe that I was clever enough to write poems. Yes, I had been struggling because I did not want it to be too much like the poem I had just read in an old magazine. "Don't you think you would be more inspired if you were sitting at a clean desk?" he asked me. It was his way of making fun of me. His other demand was for water which I had to bring him from the kitchen where he was afraid to go because of our other tenants, the new policemen, who were not supposed to know that someone was living with us. Once I spit into the glass while carrying it, but my spittle did not mix with the water and I had to go back into the kitchen and dump it out. Next time I just stuck my tongue into the glass and because it did not show I told Uncle Kot what I had done. Perhaps he would think that I was only joking but he did not. He ordered me to take it back, dump it out, rinse the glass and fill it with clean water.

Even before spring arrived, the two uncles began to make plans for an escape. The only way to get from Wilno to Warszawa was through the "green border" because once the war had started there was no other way to travel. Listening to their talk was more exciting than reading an adventure story. I could see them stumbling in the dark through fields and forests, crawling under barbed wire fences, hiding during the day wherever they could find a place to hide. How to carry their money or other valuables which they would need for food and bribes was a big problem without a solution. I listened carefully: a hollowed-out stick might work until they were ordered by soldiers or bandits to throw it away. That their treasures might end up in a ditch and go to waste made me feel like crying. And then there were the border guards ready to use their guns. Uncle Mietek had to tell Uncle Kot how to avoid getting shot while running across a field. Just do what rabbits do when chased by a dog. Uncle Mietek had experience.

They left Wilno at the end of April when it was still too cold to sleep outdoors. Would they find some barns for shelter, I wondered. Later I learned that somewhere along the way they got caught and put in jail. I don't know the details of how and when they got out, but it may have had something to do with the German attack on Russia, when prison wardens changed. They were still far from Warszawa then, and wandering through the countryside did not become any safer. Uncle Kot was wounded and found refuge in the home of a doctor who had a daughter. That is how he ended up with a son and a wife whom he was going to marry after the war, because he could not do it correctly as long as he was on the run.

Papa took me to meet the family, the woman and her son. They live in a pine forest in a villa that is all white, inside and out. A spot of light between black trees and no other house in sight. The soil around it is sand, like on a beach—except for the pine needles and cones that go crunch crunch under my feet. A strange kind of place it is, at once peaceful and threatening, perhaps because it comes in black and white with a touch of yellow, the colors of my nightmares. A hallway divides the villa in two: the right side belongs to Uncle Kot's wife, the left to someone she does not trust. Uncle Kot drops in on her every now and then because he wants to see his son.

The room has hardly any furniture: a bed, a table, some chairs, a trunk, and a stove. It reminds me of the hospital I once stayed in for a long time. The crib is in the center of the room, the baby standing in it holding on to the railing and grinning at us with a toothless smile. Uncle Kot thinks that his is the brightest, most beautiful baby ever born and predicts a great future for him. After the war, yes after the war, the child will get the best education possible. For all I know, he may be right—I don't have any experience with babies. But as long as Uncle Kot is preoccupied with his son, there is little chance that he will pick on me the way he used to when we were all living in one room back home. I am careful not to do something stupid that will attract his attention. We have lunch, the standard fare of potatoes and sour milk topped by a rare piece of poppyseed cake. The baby begins to fuss—all the attention must have worn him out—and while everyone is trying to keep him happy, I can examine the room. There is not much to see. On the window sill I spot a white saucer filled with water, the cap of a toadstool floating on it but no dead flies. I look for some to catch so that I can watch them die a slow death, but there are not any. They may all be outside enjoying the sunny weather. I would like to join them and catch some. But I have to stay in because of the neighbor who may be an informer.

Uncle Kot is not Papa's only relative in Warszawa. His brother Stan lives here too and so does another cousin, Uncle Kot's sister. We visit them, but only once, and so I don't have a chance to find out what they are like. The aunt is in bed very sick. Her bed is the only furniture in a very large room that does not smell good. She dies before I go back to Kraków, and Papa feels very bad that he did not see her more often before she died. I guess he was busy with me and it makes me feel guilty. We do not visit Uncle Mietek even though he too lives in Warszawa. When I ask why, Papa says "Don't ever expect to get anything in return after doing someone a favor." What does he mean by that? In a way it feels good that Papa has a family; his family is also mine. When I see my friend Runia again, I'll be able to brag that I too have relatives. I don't have to tell her that mine are not as good as hers. Her relatives live in palaces and castles, while mine live in almost empty rooms.

Now that I am about to leave—Mama will be picking me up in a few days—I am taking a good look at my stay with Papa and can't get rid of the feeling that I have let him down. He wanted to show me off to his relatives, but unfortunately, neither pretty nor clever and without any social graces, I am not a child Papa can be proud of. And so, in a way, it feels good to be going back to Mama who does not expect anything from me. What I'll miss most from my stay here is being read to as if I were still a little girl.

I am back with Mama, putting the final touches on this report on my stay in Warszawa. I have just received a letter from Papa. Right after I left, he moved to a different location and is giving me his new address. Uncle Kot has been arrested, he writes. It happened when he was visiting his son at the villa. He could have escaped if the neighbors had warned him when they saw the police van arrive. He could have run into the woods behind the villa. Now, no one knows where he is.

19

A Dinner

Coming out of the building, take a left towards the center of the city, another left after crossing the avenue of trees, and then a right. Now I am looking at a map, trying to find out where the three turns should have taken me to. But the street that haunts me is no longer there. What could have happened to it? Does it exist only in my imagination? Many years have passed since I saw it for the last time.

The edge of the old city, a high stone wall on one side of the street, a garden hiding behind it. In spring and summer, I could smell its flowers, mostly lilacs and jasmine. By fall errant branches would drape over the wall until someone came by to cut them off. I was told that the garden belonged to a convent which was somewhere down the street where the stone wall ended. The houses on the other side were not more than two stories high: white paint, black tile roofs, small windows, and gates large enough for a carriage to pass through into the depths of cobbled courtyards and back alleys where one could almost feel safe. Once upon a time horses must have been kept on the ground floor and their grooms lived above them. A charming row of houses, even though they no longer smelled of manure.

A girl I knew from school lived in one of them, in a vast room whose only windows faced the courtyard. I did not get a chance to find out how large the apartment was or how many families were living in it, because one day she no longer wanted to see me. Someone must have told her that I do not come from a good family. Or perhaps she had found out on her own that I was also visiting her neighbors who were not the right kind of people to visit. They were foreigners, but very nice and I liked them: a couple without children living in a vast room whose windows faced the street. My mother's special tenant Mykola used to go there to talk about the war, and I would often come along to play with the couple's dog. I tried not to listen to the conversations Mykola and the host were having, but one day the two men must have had some kind of a disagreement, probably over who was going to win the war and when, so we stopped going there. It did not come to blows, at least not in my presence, because our host was not the type to get into a fist fight, though brawling was one of Mykola's specialties. That is how my visits to the dog ended and I lost another friend.

There was more to these houses than the two vast rooms on the second floor I had been to. There was also a first floor and even a cellar where people must have lived, because once—it was cold, so maybe December 1943—my mother and Mykola took me down some stairs, and we ended up in a maze of nightmarish corridors. We made so many turns that I would not have been able to get out of there on my own. "Everything is going to be all right," I was told. "We are on our way to a wonderful dinner." It had to be an extraordinary occasion, because we were out after the curfew hour. I was twelve years old and not used to being out so late at night when the curfew made the streets scary. Mykola must have gotten a special permit to stay out so late or perhaps he did not even need one.

The room we finally entered had a low ceiling and, at one end, a narrow window so high up that I would not have been able to look out of it to see which way it faced. Not that it mattered. I was stuck deep down in the innards of a house, having no idea how I could escape from it. The dinner table was set and glittering, covered with a white tablecloth and dizzying amounts of food. What was it all about? It was always better not to know. Had I asked, no one would have answered. Our host was a small skinny man with dark hair and quick eyes, the hostess a big blond woman fatter than any I had seen in my life so far. I sat between Mykola and my mother on one side of the table, the couple was sitting on the other side, a wall of history behind them. The objects hanging on that wall were so interesting that I was not able to devote my full attention to the food until I was offered some sprats, a delicacy I knew from before the war. There were other fine foods on the table: meats, sausage, beets with horseradish, hot potatoes with butter, pickled mushrooms, and pickled cucumbers. Quite a sight it was. Nevertheless, I was very much distracted by the hangings on the wall opposite me: swords, sabers, knives, daggers, parts of armor, strange helmets, and medals. Pictures and plaques, here and there, were breaking the monotony of the strange wall décor. A museum, I suppose now, but since I had never been to a museum, I was not then capable of making such a comparison. I ate looking at the wall, while the grownups ate and drank, raising toasts every now and then to a successful year of their business partnership. After a few of these toasts, it began to dawn on me what the celebration was all about.

When the eating was finally slowing down, our hosts noticed how fascinated I was by their strange collection of weapons. And so, without me asking, the man began to recite the weapons' history—how old some of them were and where they had come from: Turkey, Damascus, the eastern steppes, and even India and China. Whenever I went out with my mother, I always tried to stay in the background so that when she did something terribly embarrassing or stupid, the blame for it would not rub off on me. But here I was in an overheated underground room—it had a big tile stove in one corner and enough coal to make it hot—and I was being talked to as if I were a grownup. Were Mykola and my mother listening to what our host was telling me? I don't know, because my eyes were either on our host or on his collection. After getting up from his chair, he stood at the wall pointing to different ornaments and giving them names. It looked as if he really liked to talk about his collection and was very proud of it. His wife, if she was his wife, would smile at me as if she wanted to express her gratitude for my interest in her husband's weapons. It seemed that I was making them both happy. I would have preferred to remain unnoticed and not be talked to as if I were a person of some importance.

I had been trying for a while now to figure out what the business partnership was about and was beginning to make some sense out of it without knowing or understanding all the facts. Mykola would go east and bring back some goods that had to be sold, the kind of stuff that only rich people owned, and my mother would find buyers for them. She was good at it because she looked like a lady. Earlier, in the summer, a distinguished looking man from the East had delivered a truckload of goods to our apartment. A crew of boys brought the packages upstairs into our hallway while I watched bliss spread over Mykola's face. He was very proud of having been able to connect with such a successful business tycoon and tried to invite him for drinks and dinner, but the man left in a hurry, as soon as the stash had been unloaded. One could never be careful enough. The loot had to be divided up and gotten rid of quickly because it was dangerous to keep it around.

And that was when my mother entered this business venture: she was able to find another trustworthy and reliable tycoon, none other than the collector of weapons, who was willing to buy up what Mykola had to offer. For me, the trail ended right there. I was well aware that a new class of people was coming up, the nouveaux riches who were making money off the war. The family of one of my schoolmates fit into that category, but I had no idea where the pretty things that were getting into their apartment were coming from. I called them "stolen goods," but they may have been gifts received in exchange for favors. The stuff Mykola was bringing from the East, had it been stolen? It was very confusing. Stolen from someone who was no longer alive and had no family? Who had the right to inherit what the once rich had to leave behind? Did shipping it off to the West mean saving the valuable things from destruction by troops who did not know what fancy tablecloths and fine china were for? Was it wrong to admire the objects on our hosts' wall?

This unwanted adult attention, trying to figure out what it all meant, and the big meal, made me sweat. I was beginning to feel sick or maybe just very, very sleepy. Going out into the cold was going to make me feel better. And it did.

20

A Christmas Story

It happened just before Christmas of 1943, I am sure of that, because in 1944 there was no Christmas. By November, I did not even leave our apartment, and when I happened to look out of the window, I could only see an occasional woman hurrying in the street below, probably in search of food. Those bundled-up figures seemed to be hugging the walls of the houses as if trying to make sure that, when necessary, they would be able to disappear in a doorway with minimum delay. No celebrations in 1944, no Christmas trees, and, of course, no school. God must have left the city way before that.

In 1943, though, we had classes held in the Barans' apartment, which was a marvel of design. Its architect must have been a clairvoyant who had foreseen the war. It was on the ground floor, had a rear exit and a window in the entry hall, near the front door, that one could jump out of without being seen by someone at the front or rear exit. Even though there were only five of us, all girls—because anything greater than five was a crowd and crowds attracted attention—we never came or left as a group and rather trickled in and out one by one. Our school year began with a geography lesson, the geography of escape routes. We learned it well.

The two windows of our classroom faced the street. We avoided going near them just to make sure that no one saw that there were so many of us in the room. As an escape route they were useless. The window in the hallway, on the other hand, was a possibility. I tried it out once with Runia, and we ended up climbing the stairs of the building all the way to the top floor. After waiting there for a little while, we came down slowly, trying to look dumb and innocent. And we probably did. Looking dumb was not too difficult for us, as we were not the stars of the class. The choice route of escape, though, was through the back door into the yard and then over fences into other yards and a maze of alleys. We did have to leave the apartment that way a couple of times, but I never learned what would have happened if we had not. Once the word had spread of roundups and the foul mood the authorities were in, our teachers did not come for lessons, and we, too, either did not show up or were dismissed empty-handed.

We used to sit around a large table in the one room of the Barans' apartment we were allowed to enter, and then we tried to listen to what the teachers had to say. Of course, there were no books and no blackboard. We did have pencils and enough paper to take notes, but since no one wanted to get caught with evidence of participating in an illegal activity, we did not write down much of anything. Still, Ruta, a hard-working girl and the oldest, was able to learn her lessons well. Hanka Baran tried to, but it did not show. To the rest of us, being a grind seemed indecent, so we were just getting by without even trying.

Ruta had an excuse for outshining us all. Being a Protestant, she could not help working hard, even in the company of some lazy Catholics. Her outlandish religion must have instilled in her, along with some heretical notions, an enviable sense of responsibility. Hanka's goal was to climb out of her social class by becoming a professional. She hoped to accomplish this with hard work. As for the rest of us, well, we just did not care enough, at least not then.

I listened to the teachers, but what I heard most of the time was nothing more than a buzz of words. Only when it was about to be transformed into something I found interesting, meaningful, or challenging, did I begin to pay attention. It happened, for instance, when an old teacher read to us in his hoarse voice an excerpt from a Polish classic about the futility of prayer. Spellbound, I listened to the discussion that followed and even took part in it. The heat it generated seemed to warm up the room. The arguments stopped short of denying the existence of God, at least of one created in the image of man, but my excitement over the discovery that a few more steps would prove that my doubts were justified and that He did not exist was fair compensation for the hours of boredom I had been subjected to. Unfortunately, this particular teacher, who quickly became my favorite, died halfway through the school year and was replaced by another old man who either failed to show up for class or would arrive late and drunk. So, instead of trying to absorb what the teachers had to offer, I studied the changing indoor scenery, the only kind I could see from where I was sitting.

The room was spacious and long, with windows at one end, a door at the other and bare walls in between. In fall, when our classes began, a table, solid and heavy, and a set of sturdy chairs were the only pieces of furniture gracing it. But before long, miracles began to happen: first a grand piano appeared near the windows, followed by a couple of stuffed chairs and next to them some small, dainty tables whose curved legs made me think of rickets. Something new to look at and admire while wondering where the hell all this stuff could be coming from. After all, the year was 1943, the war was on and behind every sale or purchase there was a crime or a tragedy. Every time a new piece of furniture appeared, my friend Runia and I would exchange glances that meant: "Here we go again." It was not worth our time to talk about it—it was a way of life—though I did wonder sometimes if Hanka was ashamed of what her father was doing. I would have been.

A cabinet with gleaming glass doors was a masterpiece and for a while even a mystery. It had been placed along the long wall, bare until then, and just stood there: black, shiny, and expectant. That it happened to be empty intrigued me, and I spent a good amount of class time trying to imagine what kind of treasures it would receive some day. Books, I thought, would not feel at home with the Barans. They were not a bookish family. Crystal was more likely: glasses arranged in neat rows according to their shape and size: some for vodka, some for wine, and some for whatever else people were in the habit of drinking. An even better bet was a set of fine china. I thought the Barans would go for the kind with tiny pink flowers, curly leaves, and gold rims that I must have seen somewhere.

But I was wrong. One day, when we arrived for class, we found the cabinet filled with books. Identical in size, they were bound in green leather with gold letters embossed onto their spines that looked as if they were brand new, had just been put there and had never been opened. Their titles were of forbidden classics, books of great value at a time when printing presses were churning out only newspapers filled with propaganda. Gold on green, green on black, in smooth rows behind shiny glass in a locked cabinet. I was jealous.

Rozmaryna, Runia, and I came from refugee families; Ruta and Hanka were locals. Each family had to cope in its own way with what fate or God was meting out, and for some of us it meant nothing more than not drowning in His largess. Ruta's family was intact: father, mother and a sister. They lived in a large apartment in the ancient part of the city, near the castle, probably sharing it with either real or phantom tenants, as everyone was entitled to only a certain amount of square footage of living space. The few times I had to call on Ruta, always on some kind of business, I had the feeling that the room she took me into was being buried under layers of dust. I never saw her parents but knew that they were always there behind some closed door, whimpering from time to time. When Ruta heard them, she would go in to find out what they needed. Sometimes it would be only a glass of water. Once, through the door she did not fully close, I caught sight of a man standing at the far end of the room. It must have been Ruta's father, the man who saw to it that she did her lessons.

Rozmaryna had five siblings. Originally her family was from the western part of the country, but between the two wars they had the good or bad fortune to inherit an estate in the East. When peasants, using the opportunity of the war's outbreak, threatened to do them in with pitchforks, the family fled west where weapons were less primitive and therefore deemed more humane. Like many well-connected and once rich families, they managed to land on their feet in an apartment at the edge of an off-limits neighborhood. Sometimes Runia and I were invited there for civilized games and polite conversation. Though I liked those visits, especially when Runia was misbehaving, I was so awed by the beauty of Rozmaryna's family and the unstrained orderliness of their lives that I would just tense up into a ball of nothing. Their home was like an art gallery or some kind of unknown sanctuary. Rozmaryna's father did not work—I knew that landowners rarely did—and her three brothers, all of them old enough to be in trouble, somehow managed to avoid arrest. It was remarkable. I thought they owed their good luck to their Tatar cheekbones, blond hair, blue eyes, and dusky skin. Yes, they were beautiful, each and every one of them.

Runia and I were the class pariahs with many strikes against us. That we had been friends for years helped us carry that dubious load. Her father was safe in a POW camp of the kind that admitted Red Cross inspections, and she lived with her mother in one room of a three-room apartment that had to be shared with an aunt and some strangers. The apartment was in a dilapidated building next to a dilapidated palace that was, in some sense, owned by the aunt. A very good life, I thought, with relatives nearby and a mother who liked to read and had a real job in a hospital lab. Their room, though rarely cluttered, looked dirty because soot from the coal that was used for heating hung over the city during winters and was finding its way indoors. Runia's mother, born a countess, had an inherited excuse for not knowing how to cook or scrub floors and was not about to waste time learning. After all, the war was not going to last forever.

In contrast, the apartment my mother shared with Mykola, a man, who was not my father, and a slew of questionable tenants, was clean, if one ignored the bedbug stains on its walls and the giant cockroaches in the kitchen. By 1943, it felt like my actual father had been gone for years, but I was still telling people who were rude enough to pry, that he would be coming back any day and that the man they were so curious about, a rather uncouth character, was only a tenant. My mother had found the black market to be her calling and became dedicated to it. It did not matter that her dealings kept us in constant suspense and danger, making our lives seem at times surreal. Yet, it was thanks to my mother's black marketeering that there was more food at my home than at Runia's, though more of very little never adds up to a lot. Most people did not eat well then, and it showed on some more than on others. And so it was in our small group: Ruta with her sunken chest did not look healthy and neither did Runia, with legs like matchsticks and a bloodless face. Rozmaryna, though skinny, looked perfect, just like her sisters and brothers. Somehow, they must have been getting by. Hanka had to have had enough to eat. As for me, I could not really tell whether I looked starved or not without being able to look at myself from a distance. Most days I had bread and potatoes to eat.

Runia was always hungry, ravenously hungry. I ought to know because we were almost inseparable for three years, when hunger, greater or lesser, was a way of life. She talked about food passionately and almost constantly, the way starving people are in the habit of doing, as I later learned. She devoured everything she was entitled to and more, but of course always within limits. Once, while working on a piece of cheese that belonged to her aunt, cutting off paper-thin slices, so as to create the illusion that the cheese was not really shrinking, we suddenly discovered that its insides were already taken over by fat, white maggots. We did not eat maggots, so at this point we left the rest of the cheese to the aunt. Nice girls that we were and from good homes, we stole mostly from Runia's relatives—we would have stolen from mine too if I'd had any close by.

While passing through some home on an errand, Runia was always on the lookout for sugar bowls and pots of lard that were often left on tables for the next meal. When she spotted them, her eyes would light up and a smile would appear on her lips. If it was sugar she was after, she would quickly stick her finger in her mouth to get it wet and then, even more quickly, thrust it into the sugar as if she were shooing away a fly. A very natural gesture it was, and in summer we had plenty of flies. Dipping dirty fingers into pots of lard and sugar bowls was nothing to brag about, but before the arrival of the front parted us, we pulled off some heists we could be proud of.

The Christmas tree may have been Runia's greatest success.

That the Barans had a right to a Christmas tree was unquestionable, but that they set it up in the classroom before our classes ended was unfortunate and in bad taste. The tree was a spruce: graceful, well filled out, and very tall. It was decorated with candy and a few pieces of tinsel. Obviously, a work in progress: bulbs, candles, and garlands were going to come later or at least so I figured. Christmas was still a week away.

Runia's face began to glow at the sight of the tree and of what it had to offer; her eyes lit up and that familiar knowing smile appeared on her lips. There were no decorations behind which the candy could hide, only those near the top were safe. Pure cruelty, I thought. Would Runia be able to resist the temptation? Something bad was going to happen, but I didn't know exactly what and could do nothing but wait.

Mr. Baran worked for the housing authority in a town overflowing with all kinds of refugees. They came in waves from the north, east, and west while some of the town's inhabitants were being carted away to places of no return. One did not have to be very bright to deduce that graft, heartbreak and ruthlessness were all a part of his job, that one had to be an SOB to hold it, and that everything the Barans owned was in some way tainted by the misfortunes of the people who found themselves stranded in the gangster land of which our town was the capital. Mr. Baran looked imposing— tall, straight, and very well-dressed. While other men made an effort to look insignificant so as not to attract the attention of authorities, he, with his confident carriage, a dark suit, and a white shirt, seemed to flaunt the power the devil had endowed him with. That his hair and skin were dark did not seem to affect his career. I saw Mr. Baran a few times when he wandered into our classroom, probably by mistake, and was looking at us puzzled, as if trying to figure out how he got there and why.

Ah, the tree of Eden, lush with forbidden fruit, the star on its top almost touching the ceiling. What a beautiful sight it is. Runia keeps eyeing it hungrily, while fate, with its perverted sense of humor, is looking for a way to push her over the edge. The teacher is late. Probably drunk, he may have lost his way or been arrested. As we are waiting, the temptation keeps growing and so does the suspense. Ruta, the only one of us four allowed to touch the piano—Hanka was of course allowed, too—tries to break the spell by playing some Christmas carols. Some day she will make music her career. We can't sing because a chorus might give us away. Since I can't carry a tune, it is just as well. Rozmaryna is sitting in one of the new stuffed chairs, the only one of us who dares to. There is something special about everything she does—even sitting—which is at once relaxed and disciplined, as if she owned her perch. And she has a perfectly natural way of looking down at everyone with a disdainful, little smile. I once saw our grade school teachers cower under her smiling gaze when she, Runia, and I got caught climbing the fence while trying to escape from school. Rozmaryna speaks little and thus makes me try to guess what she is thinking. Sometimes I catch a look in her eyes that seems to tell me that she may not be thinking at all. A lucky girl and so beautiful!

Runia walks restlessly between the tree, the piano, and the table where she should be sitting if she were good. She stops every now and then to fondle a piece of candy. They are of the best kind, the "Little Cows," soft and creamy. They melt in one's mouth and can be eaten fast, very fast. As for me, I am not doing much of anything, the nobody that I am, and have not even moved from my hard chair near the table. Waiting and watching, I suppose, just like Hanka. She, too, must sense that sooner or later something will have to give. On and off I look at her while she is still fussing over some papers on the table, as if reviewing the lesson for the day. The poor girl is probably worried and embarrassed. I would be too with a tree like that. The time may have come to dismiss the class, and Hanka leaves the room to check with her mother who, with her uncanny instincts, is always able to make the right decision. Runia uses this opportunity to swipe some candy off the tree and makes us laugh.

"Yes, you can go home," Hanka tells us when she returns. "And you are allowed to have some candy before leaving."

Runia responds with a yip which sounds like some kind of an Indian war cry—or what I imagine one to be. It is her way of letting us know that we should join her in the offensive.

Runia takes one candy, two, three...

Ruta, whose manners always put me to shame, takes one, probably only for the sake of politeness. She can really control herself. When Rozmaryna finally takes hers, she manages to make it look as if she were doing the Barans a favor. She rolls the candy between her fingers studying the print on its wrapper. I go for mine with a feeling of resentment and shame: I want the candy, but I hate that it comes from the Barans. As for Runia, it seems that something has gone haywire in her brain, and she makes the candy disappear one by one, even going so far as to fill her pockets. She laughs between mouthfuls, that inimitable laughter of hers, which she sometimes tries to stifle by squeezing her nostrils together when it begins to sound too obscene. Is it possible to get drunk on sugar and milk? Drunk or not, Runia is having a hell of a good time while letting herself go with abandon. Ruta looks on smiling indulgently, though just witnessing such gluttony must make her feel like a sinner. Her religion is less tolerant than ours in cases of overindulgence. Rozmaryna with her air of superiority seems amused by the spectacle and watches it with disdain. And I? I do nothing to save Runia, in fact I may be egging her on with a smile. She deserves the candy, if not all of it, and, in some way, justice is being carried out.

"Enough, enough..." Hanka begs. "Please don't eat them all." She is on the verge of tears, yet she does not run to her mother to squeal. A nice girl, a really nice girl, yet we don't think much of her, and she probably knows it. "It's okay..." Runia mumbles in response, no longer in full control of her tongue. "Your father can get more. I know he can. He can get anything he wants..." Her words poke and stab. They must be hurting Hanka, when they hurt even me. Yet we all know that they are true. It seems that every truth has a painful underside, or we would not be spending so much time feeling bad about this or that. No one is able to get up and leave, not even Ruta who always knows what is right. Spellbound, we watch Runia violate the Christmas tree and all the rules of good behavior. There is something heroic about what she is doing. When we leave, the tree is almost bare except for a few candies near the top below the star. To get to them Runia would need to climb onto a chair and to do that would be undignified.

I meet Runia outside and walk her home, afraid that after having eaten so much candy she may get sick or stumble or get lost. Nothing seems wrong with her: she looks pleased. The gray world of the street is outlined in black. I no longer see details of the scenery as we walk on gray pavement, between gray buildings, under a gray, fleecy sky. The corners of houses are black and so are their eaves. The crazy man in his gray, tattered clothes is standing in front of the kiosk. As always, we walk faster while passing him because he is in the habit of exposing himself to girls.

Our class met once more before the Christmas recess. We found the tree exactly as we had left it. The Barans had had enough sense not to replace the candy before we disappeared for two weeks. As usual, I was unable to listen to the droning voice of the teacher and instead studied the limp pieces of twisted string that had once supported the candy: a multitude of tiny nooses quivering in the air under the branches of a desolate tree. It was a sad sight that captured the spirit of the time and place.

After class, Hanka's mother wanted to talk to Runia in the privacy of her kitchen. I waited in the classroom, worried that the moment of reckoning had arrived. How could I help her get out of the mess she was in? Of course, I had no idea how, because running away was the only thing I was good at. Mrs. Baran's words must have been few but weighty. In no time, Runia came back looking embarrassed, angry, and contrite, if it is possible to have all these emotions showing up on one's face at the same time. Poor girl, I thought, she must have just gone through the wringer. But Mrs. Baran had said almost nothing—she did not even mention the candy—instead, she made Runia take home three packages she had ready for her in the kitchen. Not much of a penance, I thought, everything considered. I helped Runia carry them and figure out by poking, squeezing, and sniffing that they contained flour, sugar, and lard. Only then did I realize what Runia was suspecting all along: a wild card had been thrown into the game making the mess even deeper. Something was wrong, terribly wrong, and Runia, who rarely cried, was almost in tears. Now she would have to tell her mother about the candy and lose her respect, which was the worst punishment she could possibly receive. Then her mother would have to decide what to do with the gift which was growing heavier with every step we took. Dumping it somewhere was on par with cheating and a sin besides. We considered doing it, but were not corrupt enough to carry it out. As for running away, it was not even an option.

The next day Runia stopped by to let me know what had happened to the food. She looked pleased, but I could tell that this time she had indeed been through the wringer. Yes, she had had to tell her mother about the tree or Mrs. Baran's gift would have made no sense. Had she eaten too much candy? Not really or she would have gotten sick. The real issue was not the candy, but the damn gift. It sent her mother into a rage, a kind that Runia had never seen before. It was a matter of "Who do they think we are?" and "Who do they think they are!" It was immediately clear to me what she meant. Runia had had to take the food back with a note saying, "Thank you very much for the food, but please give it to someone in need."

21
Letter to Józefina

If we ran into each other somewhere, and if I were able to recognize you, it's I who would ask this time, "Don't you recognize me?"

I don't think you would—many years have passed since we last saw each other. Still, I am sure that you would remember how, once upon a time, you caught up to me on an empty street in Kraków. It was early morning, New Year's Day 1944. You called my name. I turned around and saw a stranger. "Don't you recognize me?" you asked. No, I did not. And you had to introduce yourself, "It's me, Józefina." If I had not still looked puzzled, you would not have added, "You don't recognize me, because I am so well dressed." Yes, you were very well dressed, but no longer as big as I remembered you: you had shrunk. Later, much later, I thought that perhaps you looked so small because I had grown bigger since I had last seen you, months earlier. But that couldn't have been it, since I was still wearing the old coat I had inherited from Heniuś, without it getting any smaller. With the shortage of food, we children were not growing much. It was not the fancy clothes that made me look at you in disbelief, but rather your tiny face and your small stature. If it really is Józefina, I thought, something must have happened to her.

You were so proud of your new clothes that you began to point them out piece by piece while we were standing on that cold, empty street. "Have a good look at what I have now: a winter coat, a dress, a hat, silk stockings, shoes, and even underwear. All this is quality stuff that makes me look like a lady." I knew that when you were working for Mama, your dress was a rag, your shoes shackles, and the winter coat you wore not actually yours. As for underwear, we did not talk about it, but you may or may not have had some hidden in the bundle you kept on top of the coal bin.

Once you had me admire all your clothing except what you had under your dress, we began to walk side by side as we both were heading in the same direction, you to catch a streetcar to somewhere, I to a church on the other side of the main square. You may have been surprised that I was up so early on a winter morning and so I had to remind you that it was my birthday and the beginning of a new year and that going to church might put me on the good side of God, if He had a good side. Which I rather doubted, but still, I had to hedge my bets.

All this took place many years ago and so, before continuing with this letter, I am going to remind you how our paths had crossed and when. You may no longer remember, but I still do, I'm sure, even though some of my memories of those days are beginning to fade. You began to work for Mama in May of 1941, right after we had moved into an apartment that was almost ours. Do you remember all those strange tenants who came and went and never stayed for long? You had to do the cleaning, run errands, stay away from men, go shopping on the black market, and listen to Mama berate you for not getting the best deal for what you had been told to buy. On your day off, if you had one, you took me to the zoo, not just once but at least twice. I was sure then that you enjoyed seeing the animals as much as I did, especially the monkeys. Now I think that you were being nice and probably would have preferred to stay home to rest or to run after some worthless man.

In the short time we spent together on that winter morning in 1944, I did not get a chance to thank you for everything you had done for me during the two years you worked for Mama. Perhaps it was not a matter of chance. More likely, thanking you was not even on my mind then. I was not yet old enough to know better. Getting a pair of gloves for Papa when he came to visit me after a long absence was just one of your many heroic acts. You thought very highly of him, didn't you? You told me that he was a real gentleman and that after meeting him you understood why I was waiting for the day he would come to get me. He never did. I was aware in those days that many people thought highly of you, too: our nice neighbor from next door, my friend Runia's mother, the countess, and also Papa, who told me that you were the moral backbone of an immoral household. He hoped that you would stay around as long as I needed you. The nice neighbor disappeared one day, Papa was arrested and died in a camp, the countess survived the war, and if this letter ever reaches you, you will know that so did I.

After being a part of our infamous household, you became a servant for one of those German families that was trying to avoid being blown up by moving to the nice, new section of our town, into apartments with real bathrooms and no pests. Do you still remember? That happened in March of 1943. Of course, I did not want you to leave, but because I knew that you would be much better off working for them than for Mama—more money and more food—I did not cry very much and let you go with my blessing. Besides, you assured me that I would be able to visit you. And I did, once, or at least I tried to. Now I am no longer sure if the visit actually transpired or if it was only a dream. Perhaps you know. I rang the bell and you opened the door. From the hallway, which I did not enter, I could see a part of the kitchen and a woman standing in it with her back to us. That must have been "die Frau." Before she had a chance to turn and see me, you said, "not now" and closed the door in my face. I ran down the stairs as fast as I could. Why do I keep thinking that she asked you who it was and you answered, "just a beggar"? Did you go into the kitchen, the front door still open, and come out with a piece of bread for me? After that one visit—real or imaginary—I did not want to try again. Die Frau did not want us to meet.

Let us find our way back to the day you caught up to me on the empty street. The pavement was dry, the sky gray, and there was a promise of snow in the air. My life had not changed much, and so I had little to report. Obviously, Papa had not yet come to get me, Runia was still my best friend, and Mama was doing her usual business on the black market. She knew where to get vodka that was safe to drink and had reliable clients who needed it on their way to the eastern front. You, on the other hand, had nine months' worth of news and not enough time to tell me all of it, even though we walked slowly because the day was not cold enough to make us hurry.

Your great job had come to an end when, as one says, the writing appeared on the wall with the approach of the front and the family needed to return to German bombs and rubble. They had been good to you, you told me: enough to eat and even enough money to buy some clothes. It was clear that while working for them you had to look presentable, not like a beggar dressed in rags. And so, in a way, you felt bad when die Frau with her two children had to leave, even though it meant that the end of the war was approaching. All of it made perfect sense to me: nothing you were doing or feeling was wrong in my eyes, and I was proud of you. I wish you had not told me the rest of the story. "They cared for me," you said, "and der Herr got me a new job in the kitchen of an officers' club. There, the pay was so good that I was able to buy the clothes I am wearing and many more. As you can see, I am a lady now." Officers' club? The words sounded as ominous as an air raid siren, not just one that warns, but a full alert. They sent a chill down my spine. I did not know how to ask, "Did you or didn't you do it?" because I still did not really know what the "it" was. I knew the word "slut" and that it was bad, but what it really meant was still a mystery to me.

I was just turning thirteen, old enough to be very confused by the many versions of "it" that I had heard by then. My enlightenment should have started with the rabbits, when I was seven years old. To get baby rabbits, I was told, a papa rabbit had to stay in the mama rabbit's cage for a while. It worked: our mama rabbit got her baby rabbits that way. I was not yet interested enough to find out more. If that had any connection with people, I did not care then. Three years later, right after we had moved into the apartment you got to know so well, the janitor's youngest daughter asked me, on my first appearance in the courtyard of the building, if I knew where babies come from. I must have looked puzzled, because she grabbed me by the shoulders, put her mouth to my ear and began to recite some kind of a poem made up of words I had seen written on park benches and walls, but whose meaning I did not know. By the time her spittle was running down my neck I was not any wiser. You knew the girl, her three sisters, her drunken father, and the hardworking wife he used to beat up until the courtyard was exploding from her screams. Do you remember them still? How they lived in one tiny black room? Later, after you had already left, I heard rumors that all the girls in that family were in the business of "it." They, too, were making enough money to buy nice clothes.

At some point, while you were still working for Mama, I began to recognize "it" in the eyes of men when I was running into the park or entering a streetcar. The young ones would joke, laugh, and try to take advantage of the close quarters and touch. The old ones would sometimes unbutton their pants to show off whatever they had there. All that used to scare me out of my wits.

And then there was supposed to be "love," which was not the same as "it." Runia and I talked about these subjects to try to figure out the difference between the two. From what we observed, we concluded that "love" did not exist, whereas "it" did. We were so confused that she finally turned to her mother for help and was told that "love" did exist, despite our doubts, and that "it" combined with "love" was beautiful. This answer did not make us any wiser.

So, turning thirteen that day we collided, my knowledge of the facts of life was not much to brag about. I knew that to have a baby, a couple had to do something. Your parents had had eight children, so they must have done it eight times and lived in misery ever after—just like all the couples in our apartment building. Perhaps it was different for Runia's mother, because she was a countess. From your days in Mama's employ, I feel like I remember that you either did not know much or what you knew was wrong. Even I, as dumb as I was at the age of eleven, knew that something was not adding up when you told me that my Mama is a virgin, because she only has one man at a time.

When we reached the Planty, you had to go to the right, toward the railroad station, I straight ahead across the Old Market to the one church I went to, because it had no paintings on its walls. I found beauty in its columns and arches. Since, by then, you had not yet told me everything I wanted to know, I decided to give up on the church and stay with you until you got on your tram to somewhere. It took a while before you told me where you were going, because you first had to tell me about your work in the officers' club. What I remember of that part of the conversation and can still picture in my mind's eye is a tiny kitchen and you chopping up cabbage and peeling tons of potatoes that had to be boiled. No mention of anyone helping you or if meat came with the meal. Steam pouring out of giant pots and the kitchen getting so hot that you undressed down to your slip. While the stuff was boiling, you had to go out into the courtyard to get rid of the peelings and you did it wearing only that slip, even though it was damn cold outside. While you were telling me this, I began to wonder if some men came into the kitchen to pinch any part of your body that they could put their hands on. I could imagine it happening and had a good reason for my imagining. You may no longer remember how, while still working for Mama, you used to run from the kitchen into the front room so that you could look at men singing while they marched down the street three floors below. Sometimes I watched them with you and felt guilty when I did. Their songs sounded better than the rattle of trucks on their way to the front and were almost a pleasant diversion. Most of the time they were actually just Hitler Youth: black pants, brownish jackets, and white knee socks, their voices not as deep as those of soldiers, their steps not as loud. And then, one day while watching marchers pass our house, you said "These are old enough to have hair around their assholes." I had already learned in my early childhood not to repeat obscenities, but in our unrefined household, no one scolded me for cursing, and I became quite good at it. I was surprised, perhaps even shocked, to hear you use an obscene word to refer to a body part that should not be talked about and had many nicer names you could have used. What were you thinking while you watched them? Was there more to your interest than just their songs? On that New Year's day of our chance meeting, while you were telling me about your life after you had stopped working for Mama, unwelcome thoughts kept creeping into my mind: the janitor's daughters, the fancy clothes, yours and theirs, the Hitler Youth and their songs, and what you were seeing while listening to them and finally you, stripped down to your slip in the officers' club kitchen. I did not know what to make of it all. You had been my hero, Józefina, and people I cared for thought that I was lucky to have you.

Now what? Was I supposed to think that you were like the janitor's daughters? You may want to know that right there and then, while walking towards the railroad station on that winter morning, I decided that you were still as good as you had been while working for Mama. No, you could not have done "it," whatever the "it" was, and no one was going to speak badly of you, I reassured myself.

I remember that when tiny snowflakes began to whirl in the air, you told me how you came down with pneumonia because, sweating and wearing only a slip, you kept going out into the freezing cold to dump those potato peels. You were sick, very sick, sick enough to end up in the hospital, where the doctors told you that it was not just pneumonia but actually TB, too. The dreaded disease of those days! By the time yours was discovered, it was already at an advanced stage. When you shared that, I burst into tears.

I am writing you all this, because you may no longer remember what happened so many years ago. And maybe I'm not sure of all the details. Maybe I don't have all the facts straight. You see, my memory is not as good as it once was. The TB hospital you were in then, how far was it from the city? Could a streetcar take you there or did you have to take the train? I must have known that once. But now I can't remember. You were getting tired and we sat down on a bench near a streetcar stop, the Planty behind us. That is where you told me about your life at the hospital. How everyone liked you, not just the patients but also the doctors. You were able to make them laugh. Yes, Józefina, once upon a time I also found you hilarious. What you had to say in a few words about the strange events happening around us made me laugh. That you were able to make people laugh even in the hospital meant that you were very good at it, and I felt proud of you. We agreed to meet on a Sunday morning in two weeks, on that bench at some specified time which I no longer remember.

The snow began coming down in bigger flakes and was soon going to erase the grayness of the pavement. It was not good for your health to keep sitting on a bench outdoors in the middle of winter. You had already let one tram go by and you got up when we saw the next one approaching. That is when you said to me, "The doctors tell me that I will not live through another hemorrhage." Licketysplit, before I had the time to break into sobs again, you were already in the tram waving to me. I wonder, Józefina, did you see me wave back at you?

I waved for a long time, but the snow was getting thicker and made the tram disappear too soon.

I want you to know that I did go to that bench on the Sunday we were supposed to meet and then again for several Sundays after that—just in case I had gotten the dates mixed up. You did not come, and you may well be wondering why I did not go to the hospital to look for you. I am wondering about it myself. I've been wondering ever since that day...

First of all, I did not know how to get there. I could have asked but did not. Then, I was afraid that once I got there, I would not be let in because I was not yet old enough to enter a place that was such a well-known pesthole. You yourself called it that. And finally, I simply did not want to learn if you had suffered that next and last hemorrhage after sitting outside on a cold winter day talking to me. I preferred to think that you were alive and making other patients laugh. That would have been a happy ending. That was the happy ending I wanted to make real by not going to the hospital.

A few months later, some people in the city were beginning to look for a safe place they could flee to. The front was approaching Kraków. Runia was whisked away to some secret location early in the summer, and I was left without a friend. In the fall, I too had to leave, though I would rather have stayed. I couldn't think of a way to get in touch with you. So now, after so many years, I am finally trying to.

Dear Józefina, if this letter reaches you, let us arrange a meeting on that bench, halfway between the main post office and the railroad station. I will finally ask you what you were doing at the officers' club. Since it no longer matters how you answer, we will have a good laugh.

22

The Sled

Winter of 1943–1944 was famous for the cold that was making history. It was cold enough to kill or to freeze off the limbs of those stuck in the trenches. We talked about it but had no sympathy. Someone in town, a friend of a friend, had bought from a soldier a pair of officer boots at a bargain price. They were wrapped in newspaper with only their tips showing. It was an illegal transaction and had to be done in a hurry. The buyer wondered why the boots were so heavy and thought that they came with wooden lasts to keep them in shape. When he got home and unwrapped the package, he found frozen legs inside. I kept wondering how that could have happened. Do frozen bones break easily or did the legs have to be chopped off? And the man to whom the boots had belonged, was he still alive but legless? The buyer did not know how to handle such rare goods and eventually threw the package over the fence into the cemetery where my friend Runia and I liked to hang out in summer. It landed on the steps of the morgue, at least that is what people said.

One of Runia's relatives—she had a lot of helpful relatives—offered to lend her a sled for a couple of days, the exact day of delivery undecided. Sleds were in short supply because they were not on the list of items a refugee family would take along while fleeing, at least not at that time, and so only a local family would have one. Runia had the right kind of relatives: they were local, had a sled, and were willing to share it with needy children. And that meant Runia and, because of her, I, had to be included.

As soon as she learned of the promise, we began to search for a hill. We went to nearby parks, the ones we were still allowed to enter, but found only one spot where the path had enough slope for a slide. The hills surrounding the city we could see only from a distance. They were there to look at but not to go to because they were either guarded or too far away. Yes, someday we will take a long trip to see them from close up, we promised ourselves. It was going to be an adventure, but we were not yet ready for it.

While we were waiting for the sled—someone was keeping it for too long— the snow began to melt and so did our hopes for a good slide. The fluffy, soft stuff, so beautiful when still fresh and not yet blackened by soot, was beginning to turn into a gray mess and soon black water was whirling through the gutters into the drains. We fretted and even cried. How could God be so cruel and do this to us? After all, we were not always bad. It would take a miracle to have enough snow come down before we had to return the sled, and so there was nothing else left for us to do but pray. Only God was in charge of miracles. Since Runia believed that He was on her side because nothing really bad had yet happened to her family, her prayers were humble and fawning. "Please, dear God, let it snow..." I, on the other hand, after already having lost so much, could afford to be insolent and taunted Him with "Can't You be nice for a change and let us have some fun?" He either did not listen or was confused, because on the eastern front both sides were praying for a thaw and the mud that would follow. He, the All-Powerful, was not powerful enough to give in to all the prayers, theirs and ours, and make the East warm and let our town have some snow. That was my way of thinking.

The hours I had spent sledding were the highlights of my life. On my first attempt at the age of five, I managed to run into a barbed wire fence and watched drops of blood from my cheek land on the pure white snow. In Oszmiana on another hill right behind our house, it was so short and so steep that halfway down the slope and only for a moment the sled would fly through the air like a rocket. Having grown older and wiser I was afraid to try it, and instead watched Henius and some boys from the village below do it over and over again. It was a pretty sight: the gray misty air and snow so clean and fluffy. Everyone who made it all the way to the bottom without a spill was a hero. The last act took place in Wilno on a hill, referred to as the Mountain, across the street from where we lived when the war was already on. The sledding track was steep, icy, and crowded. Ancient women would stop for a little while to watch children go flying by on their sleds but had nothing good to say about what they saw. "Heads get split on the ice... One child got killed here..." Later, in the summer, the same women would tell me that if I didn't wear a hat I would die of heatstroke. I did not even get sick. We had to flee before something so terrible happened to me, and, of course, the sled had to be left behind, Mama's gift to the shoemaker's son, the little pisser, to make up for the years of oppression we had inflicted on the poor.

Sunday, the last day we were allowed to keep the still unused sled, the town froze during the night. Filled with hope, we set out for the one place in the park with a wide walkway that had some slope to it. Perhaps there would be some patches of ice on it, the remnants of the melted snow, and by steering cleverly from one patch to another, even if it meant going over dirt between them, we might end up at the bottom. On our way there, we had to carry the sled through the eerily empty streets. On Sunday mornings in winter even the faithful prefer to stay home.

We had been right about finding some ice on the slope. We were right too about the patches, which we named the islands of good hope. Sitting on the sled on top of what we imagined to be a hill, we surveyed the scenery. Right behind us was a cross path that came out of a churchyard and led to a street that always looked so dark to me that I used to take detours to avoid it. Yes, our path was studded with ice patches, and it also had deep ruts we could get stuck in. Steering through that mess would take real know-how and neither of us believed that Runia, who had the honor of being at the helm, would be able to pull it off. As for me, I did not even want to try, loser that I was. We were doomed. Even the ice patch mixed with dirt on which the sled was resting was not slippery enough for a takeoff. It would take a miracle to get us moving. Runia was near tears. I was angry because, if we ended up carrying the sled down the hill, God would have been amused. He was probably laughing at us already.

We had to decide. Should I get off, push and run, and then try to jump back on the sled? Or should we just walk down the hill in defeat? As we were sitting there contemplating our next move, we heard what we later called "the voice in the wilderness," though I did not know what that phrase meant. Was God talking to Jesus or was it the other way around? What were they saying to each other? We were not in a wilderness and God did not talk. "Do you girls need a push?" a man asked. There he was behind us bending down, his hands already on the seat of the sled! A very handsome man, unbelievably well-dressed and smiling. A woman was standing next to him. She was dressed in black, had a pretty face, and she, too, was smiling the way mothers smile when their little sons are about to do something cute. "Yes, yes, please, do give us a push…" and he did.

I wish I could say that we took off flying, perhaps we did for a few feet. When the sled was about to stall, we used our feet to give it a push and that made us look as if we were walking downhill sitting down. It could not have been a pretty sight and the grating sounds the metal blades were making on the dirt were not music. We gave up the struggle before reaching the bottom and turned around to have a look at the top of the hill. No one was there. The couple that had come out of the churchyard and crossed our path had disappeared on Dark Scary Street.

We just stayed there, sitting on the sled, in the cold, immersed in deep thoughts and silence, trying to figure out what had just happened. Finally, Runia asked what we were both wondering, "Were they real?" I did not know how to answer. They had to be, but I had my doubts. In the two years we had been roaming through the city, why hadn't we run into a couple like that one? Perhaps we were always in the wrong place at the wrong time. The couples we saw on park benches were disgusting: a sweaty red-faced man putting his hands on a girl's forbidden parts, the girl egging him on with her giggles and hugs, spittle spilling out of their mouths during the long kisses. Occasionally, when the pairs were completely lost in their games, we talked about throwing a stone at them just to see if they would notice. But all these men, when their hands were not crawling all over a girl, had mean faces. We were afraid of them.

Our couple, in contrast, was special. They did not rub against each other, and they looked like movie stars. Not that we knew much about movies: before the war there was Shirley Temple, and once the war broke out, there was nothing. Sometimes, when passing a movie theater, we would give a quick glance at the beautiful people whose pictures were pasted on the wall next to the entrance. We never stopped to have a better look at them because it was something one was not supposed to do. Buying a ticket meant supporting the war and supporting the war was treason. Besides, a movie theater was a dangerous place where acid sometimes got dumped from the balcony on the people below. Still, without knowing anything about movies, we both came up with the idea that, in another life, the couple would have been movie stars.

We saw them only for a moment but still long enough to see that they were well dressed and did not look worried. If they were hungry, it did not show. Had we run into anyone like them, in the street or on a trolley, we would have taken notice. All in all, people did not look good and neither did we in our worn-out coats. Runia was always famished. That I was not did not make me pretty. We did not stand out in any way: we were just like other ordinary people. We too had to be alert to dangers, avoid street raids, corpses, lice, and the dirty old men who tried to swallow us with their greasy stares. Why wasn't our couple afraid of taking a walk, wearing their good clothes and looking happy? It was safer to be like everyone else and avoid attracting attention. What was making them so brave? How could they be sure that nothing would happen to them? Did it mean that they were collaborators? If they were, they would have known that a bullet was already waiting for them and that would have made them look worried. I did not share my ugly thoughts with Runia because they could have raised doubts in her mind and destroyed her dreams. "What do you think is making them so radiant and happy?" I asked.

"It's love."

That is what she said, and she may have been right.

23

The Watch

It's strange that one often remembers the insignificant incidents of one's life better than the important events, as if words overheard in passing take on new meaning as they age.

Time: probably winter of 1943–1944, because Józefina was no longer living with us, but it no longer matters, since all the war winters were brutal.

Place: a Polish city where we were living then as refugees.

Protagonist: I am twelve or thirteen years old.

Setting: the building we live in is on one of the main streets. It starts at the city's center and heads east. Our apartment, which we share with strangers who never stay for long, has a kitchen and four rooms, one of which is ours most of the time. It's the nicest room of the four. Its two windows face south, and it has a view into an unkempt courtyard whose crowning glory is a lone linden tree.

Exposition: This story is about a wristwatch that was given to me in the fall of 1940 to compensate for everything I had lost in one year due to war. To make up for whatever toys I had had that had to be left behind. No money to waste on new ones, not when Papa could no longer work. Mama, being practical, had decided that a watch would make an excellent gift for me, even though I did not ask for one. A scooter was my dream, but for that I did not dare ask. Inexpensive German watches were flooding the city then. Getting one could be a good investment, and Mama was already planning to resell it some day at a profit. In the meantime, she was letting me wear it if I promised to take good care of it. True, a German watch was not as good as a Swiss one, the best of the best. Nevertheless, Germany's reputation for making high quality gadgets, like the Leica camera, was good, or at least so I heard.

Christmas of 1938 had been the last Christmas. And that there were no Christmases after that one, made it seem even more special. That year I had received a teddy bear which, two years later, I was allowed to take with me when we fled. A picture of a child clutching a teddy bear is heartrending, especially when there is blood and rubble in the background.

Almost exactly two years later, I was given the watch. It looked and felt new. Its face glowed in the dark. I was proud of it; it made me feel grown-up. I didn't know any children I could show it off to because, when I received it, I was not going to school. To match the bad times, the watch stopped working after a few weeks. Mama tried to get it repaired, but the watchmaker she took it to made fun of it and told her that it needed two stones: one to set it on and one to hit it with. It was definitely a poor investment, but Mama remained hopeful. She put the watch into the box of potential valuables, the kind of stuff she kept for the "black hour." Occasionally, she would take it out of its hiding place and try to get it repaired by some master watchmaker she happened to hear about. Indeed, some were masters, because they were able to fix it! Once fixed, the watch would run perfectly for a few weeks and then stop again. While it worked, Mama tried to sell it and would not let me wear it. The moment the right buyer appeared, the watch had to be available for showing.

***

The story can now begin:

I am painting red poppies on gray paper that is like a blotter, since it makes the watercolors spread until the flowers look like strange, shapeless droppings. It is not all my fault that the petals have smudged edges. Perhaps with the right paper I would be able to do a little bit better. How nice it would be if I had a book to read instead of working on art I am not good at. It's very cold outside and in. I am wearing my winter coat. Mama enters the room, a soldier walks in behind her. There is nothing unusual about Mama bringing strange people into the apartment. She runs an illegal business. They are her customers, and she sells them schnapps or tobacco, if she has any to sell, or lets them spend a night in one of the rooms if they are on the run. Schnapps is in great demand but in short supply. It turns out that a war cannot be fought without it. The man has dark hair, a white face, and gray eyes. His coat is unbuttoned, and he is carrying a package under his arm. Where did Mama pick him up? Did he trust her? Was he afraid to follow the lure? From the few words of German I recognize, I piece together a story. After a brief furlough in Munich, where his parents own a dry goods store, he is once again on his way to the front, leaving tonight or tomorrow. And the front is iced-over hell. If a bullet does not get you, the cold will. He knows, because he has been there. Mama is sympathetic and tries to calm down this terrified young man who is on the verge of tears. His mouth twitches every time the accursed words are mentioned. Ach, die Front, die Kälte, die Russen... I have no idea what Mama can say to him to ease his fears: Don't worry, everything will turn out all right? Ha, ha, ha...What nonsense that would be! His voice is soft, not the kind that would bark out orders. Mama is indeed doing something for him; she is listening and seems to care. That she offers him a tiny glass of schnapps may mean that she feels sorry for him, but then again, Mama is quite good at pretending, so I cannot be sure if her feelings are genuine.

What the hell is it all about, the back and forth that continues between the two? I look and listen without getting up from the table, the gray paper with the runny red poppies spread in front of me. Nothing to be proud of. All of a sudden, it becomes clear to me: it's about that damn watch of mine. The deal must have been made already in the street or someone has sent this man to Mama. So, it will be the watch for the package, and she knows what's in it. The watch comes out of its hiding place, a box behind a meager row of books. I hope that it is not working, that it is taking another break, but unfortunately, it's ticking. A great watch made in Germany, not in some God-forsaken country of Eastern Europe. He is pleased that a piece of home is catching up to him. Mama gets for it two pieces of cloth: a flannel large enough to line a jacket and some kind of flowery cotton fabric that, one day, would be turned into a scanty nightgown. The deal is closed to his and her satisfaction. As he is ready to leave, Mama tells him that someday she may end up in Munich. Will it happen? I wonder. He gives Mama his address. Fate or God willing, they may meet again.

When Mama does something I don't approve of, I mostly keep my mouth shut. Who am I to tell her what to do or not do? She does what she thinks is right. I have no influence over her. But, sometimes, just sometimes, one accusing silent glare from me hits her harder than words would. What I have just witnessed upsets me so much that I can't restrain myself from blurting out: "How could you do it? You sold him a watch that is not going to run for more than three weeks." Perhaps one hard look without the words would have made a stronger impression on her, because, unrepentant, she retorts, "Well, that is long enough. He is not going to last longer than that."

I run out of the room into the kitchen where I can shed a few tears without anyone watching. It is Mama's dishonesty that bothers me. I have caught her in the act, so to speak. Now I have proof of what I have suspected: Mama is a crook. She has let me down once again. My tears are for her and not for the man who, like the watch, is only going to last a few more weeks. Or do I feel sorry for him and am afraid to admit it to myself? Wishing that an enemy soldier stays alive—isn't that treason? The headlines in the newspaper brag about the number of Russians killed. I did not know any of them. And the Germans? They were dying too, but the newspapers do not brag about their deaths. When rumors of German casualties trickle into town, people celebrate. 1812, once again!

The soldier who ended up with my watch was not just a number, but rather someone I saw up close. He was real. He was scared. Was I supposed to feel sorry for him? Was it okay to feel sorry for him?

Mama ended up being right. We did pass through Munich one day, soon after the war had ended. We had no place to stay and took a tram to the address the soldier had given her, but something went wrong. A deserted street lined with apartment buildings no one seemed to be living in though they still had glass in their windows that, like in a dream, reflected some eerie warning lights. Perhaps the tram failed to stop in the right place. Perhaps we were on the wrong street or had the wrong number. The dusk began to feel threatening. There were secrets behind every façade, yet no signs of life. We went to the end of the line and then back to the city to spend the night at what was left of the railway station. While looking for it at curfew time, we were picked up by the American Military Police and taken to a refugee camp. That we did not have to face the family of the unknown soldier made me happy.

I hope that he survived the war and returned to his family, that his house is still standing in the bombed-out city and that my watch is still running. I would like to let him know that he is remembered.

24

Typhus

While walking towards the Main Square on a sunny morning in August of 1944, I could not help noticing that something had changed overnight. Had some secret news reached the city that was spreading through the crowd? Instead of moving on with a purpose, to get to where they were going, people would stop briefly to exchange a few words with each other, smile, and sometimes even shake hands. What I was seeing was a flood of happy faces glowing in the sun and because it was such a rare sight in those days, I began to wonder what it was all about. By the afternoon I had learned that the eastern front had crossed the border and was heading our way. The Russians of course were in the lead, but the English troops were right behind them giving out chocolate. Yes, I did hear it right. So, that morning, people must have been spreading the good news and celebrating the end of the war and the arrival of chocolate.

It's November now and the front has not arrived yet. When I look out of the window, the few people I see hurry like rats along the walls of the apartment buildings and disappear in the nearest holes. I don't go out anymore—it's not safe—but Aunt Kamila does. If she did not, we would have nothing to eat.

Aunt Kamila is new. When people began to leave town last summer, Mama could no longer find anyone willing to share our apartment with us and the rooms, once so full of life, were filling up with cobwebs, dust, and bad vibes. The cockroaches were moving out, we joked, and perhaps even the bed bugs. It occurred to Mama—she is always praised for her resourcefulness—that, thanks to the Uprising, some of Papa's relatives may have ended up in camps, waiting to be released to a welcoming family. She was right: she found them, fished them out of a lice-ridden place, and offered them two rooms in our apartment. They are very nice people, and now that I have someone to stay with, I no longer have to go with Mama on her smuggling trips. We are one big happy family; we laugh a lot.

Kamila is Uncle Ted's wife and Ted is Papa's second cousin. Because of a limp, he is the only one of five brothers to have survived the war, so far. That must be what people mean when they talk about "God's mysterious ways." Ted and Kamila have a sweet little daughter Marysia, who is five years younger than I. The poor girl has nightmares because the family was stuck in the city when it was being turned into dust and rubble during the Uprising.

The larger of the two rooms is now theirs, the smaller one is occupied by Justyna—who may or may not be married to one of Papa's brothers, Uncle Stan. Her dark hair is thick and long, her eyes are almost black, and she can sing "Reve ta stohne Dnipr shyrokyi…" It has become my favorite song, though its language is not mine. Justyna got separated from Stan during the Uprising and has been looking for him ever since. Mama found out what happened to him, but is keeping it a secret. It is better for Justyna not to know that he is now living with a woman who got him out of the camp.

Mama and I share the smallest room, which, because of Mama's travels, is mine most of the time. Sometimes, when I am alone at night, I hear footsteps in the apartment next door, though no one is living there, at least not during the day. Once upon a time it belonged to an old couple and their son who cared about me. The couple moved in with relatives in the country or died, their son disappeared.

Aunt Kamila goes out to look for food, Uncle Ted tells stories about life under the tsar, the Great War, the Revolution, and the escape from the Bolsheviks across the Dniester in a leaky boat. Since gas has been turned off, Kamila does all the cooking on a hotplate in their room. It helps us to keep warm. She boils potatoes, sauerkraut, and an occasional piece of meat we can laugh at. "What animal does it come from?" we try to guess. "Horse, dog, cat, or a very old man?" Once Kamila came back from shopping with something which was supposed to be a great bargain and looked like meat, but after many hours of boiling was still as hard as a rock and its broth had a strange flavor. We could not eat it.

The only person in town Ted and Kamila know is the woman who took them in for a few nights when they were out in the street at curfew time looking for the camp they had been assigned to. They would have stayed with her had the woman not been a drug addict. I don't know what it means, but it must be something bad, because people talk about drug addicts in whispers. It seems that only doctors can get at the stuff needed to become an addict. The woman had once been a doctor but no longer is. I do not know if she still has a husband, but she does have an eighteen-year-old son who drops in on us with the latest news from England, which, sadly, never mentions the chocolate I heard about in August. He wears a black coat and a black cap and is always in such a big hurry that he cannot stand still and keeps moving while staying in place. He carries a handgun under his coat—I really saw it—and his job is to shoot collaborators point-blank. He must be quite good at it. I don't know what to think of him: is he a hero or just an ordinary killer? Whatever he is, Ted and Kamila look relieved when they see him leave. His name is Jurek.

When "higher learning" became illegal after the outbreak of the war, Uncle Ted, who had been a teacher of French, was forced to switch professions and became a manufacturer. He opened up a factory—yes, a factory—in the tiny one room cottage the family was living in then. It is lost now because of the Uprising, but Kamila is doing her best to connect with the right people and restart the production of perfume which even now is in great demand. She is as clever and persistent as Mama because supplies began to arrive: a few bottles of vodka, lots of dainty vials—empty except for the few that hold the mysterious scents—and finally spools of narrow ribbons, red or pink. They are brought in by men or women who are in a great hurry, can see even what is behind them, know the safe buildings, doorways, and alleys and where and when the next roundup will take place. The same people come to pick up the finished product. Uncle Ted who does not go out anymore considers them great business partners.

In the month of November, dusk, night, and the curfew arrive early and make the town disappear under the blackout. Often, just when it is time to turn on the light, the electricity goes off for several hours and no one knows when it will come on again. The one candle Kamila keeps hidden from the rest of us is reserved for emergencies. We make fun of it by calling it sacred and claiming that it is sprinkled with holy water. The blessing might make it multiply and one day there may be two candles in the hiding place instead of one. That kind of a joke originated in the camp, where a louse would not dare to cross the boundaries of the floor space allotted to each family, as long as they were marked off with holy water.

In a black room we all go to bed to nap or to talk. Uncle Ted's stories are the best. Sometimes, when Justyna happens to be home, she sings her Dnieper song and when she does, even Ted stops talking and listens. The Dnieper must mean more to him than just a raging river.

Because of the great demand for perfumes, Ted's new factory—risen from the ashes, we joke—is doing well. If it were not for the shortage of ingredients and the difficulties with the deliveries, it could increase its production. At least that is Uncle Ted's claim. I don't even try to figure out the finances behind it. With what kind of money does he get paid? Is it the same money that can't buy us any food or coal? None of it is my concern. What matters now is that we no longer have to go to bed when the electricity is turned off; instead, we sit around the big table and work on the production by candlelight. Kamila adds water to the vodka and, without spilling a drop, fills the pretty vials. Ted, in whose nose we trust, is in charge of the fragrance. He mixes this and that, dabs the top of his hand with a sample, and takes a deep whiff of whatever is there. An "ah" means approval, a shake of the head a "no." When Ted is pleased with his creation, be it lilac, lily of the valley or some French name, he puts a few drops of it into each vial that is already filled with the mixture of vodka and water. The final touches are left to Marysia and me: the dainty glass corks, the ribbons, and sometimes even labels. It makes me feel good to be able to help and be part of a team. We get along and we laugh. The flame of the candle flickers and so do its reflections in the multitude of glass vials lining the table. It's a sight as pretty as a lit-up Christmas tree or a graveyard on All Souls Day. That there is such a high demand for perfume puzzles me. Don't women use perfume when they go dancing? With the frontline already knocking on the door, is anyone dancing nowadays? Or are people in a great need of perfume because in a town almost under siege there is no warm water for a bath? When I ask Uncle Ted about it, he laughs.

Because the retreating troops don't want to be stabbed in the back, a gigantic roundup targeting men is supposed to take place. Jurek, the killer, drops in to warn Ted that even men with a limp will not be safe. Kamila is on the verge of tears—there is no place to hide—and Marysia says that Jurek came with the bad news because he wanted to have a look at me. This is nonsense of course, but what can one expect from an eight-year-old?

Mama is on one of her trips; she has been gone for over a month now. Will she come back to take me away? The time is running out. I would rather stay with Ted and Kamila, but the decision is not up to me. Mama does come back to pick me up, and she does it right when the roundups are about to begin.

She and I are packing our stuff when the stairwell fills up with the sound of boots. Because in the dark it's a long way to the third floor, Mama has enough time to set the stage for the visit. She gives orders. Ted is going to play sick and climbs into bed in his tattered underwear. I have never seen him so naked. Marysia is the sleeping beauty on the couch, her golden hair spread over the pillow. The light is at its dimmest; we do our best to save electricity. Kamila's part is of a worried wife sitting at the bedside of her beloved husband who may be on the verge of dying. She has to sprinkle water on his face to make him look feverish.

When they start kicking the door, Mama rushes to open it. There are two of them, carrying guns and wearing helmets; "Männer, Männer, ..." they shout. "Yes, there is a man here," Mama answers sweetly, "but he is very sick. You can come in and have a look." One of them follows Mama, the other waits at the door. Eager to watch a promising performance, I follow them into the sickroom.

He goes up to the bed, studies Ted's face, and even lifts the covers by a little bit. Not to give himself away, Ted is keeping his eyes closed. Convinced that the man is too sick to be dragged out of bed, the soldier heads for the door with Mama at his heels. "We are afraid it is typhus. You better wash your hands," she whispers. If he has seen the old posters "Żydzi, wszy, tyfus plamisty" or "Juden, Läuse, Flecktyphus," he must be scared. She takes him to the kitchen sink whose surface is still sparsely dotted with what used to be white enamel. Now the dots are gray, the background is black iron with touches of rust. I rarely go into the kitchen, but when I do, I am afraid to look into the sink because it may be filled with the city's sewage. Mama has a new piece of soap ready for him and even a fresh white towel. Does he know how we children joke about our soap that is filled with air bubbles? He leans his gun against the wall and washes his hands carefully. Vielen Dank, vielen Dank! He is in a hurry: still so many stairs to climb, so many doors to kick. I think that he would rather be in his faraway home than in a pesthole like ours. That he is leaving without a catch must be disappointing.

Mama has to tell me how we are going to leave town. It's not going to be simple. Even to get to the railroad station, we will have to take side streets and alleys where we are less likely to run into someone interested in our bags. Of course, we must get to the station before the curfew and, once there, stay in the waiting room until a mystery man picks us up. We may not get picked up before midnight, and there is always the danger of a roundup. If all goes as planned, we will follow the man and his lamp across innumerable tracks all the way to where the freight trains are waiting for something to happen. The one we will be boarding has two passenger cars; it will be leaving before morning to wherever Mama is taking me. When controls come, I am supposed to play a deaf mute.

I'll hide my story behind the drawer of the dresser in my room. It will lie flat against the wall, in a space too narrow for bulky treasures. Either I'll collect it one day or Marysia will find it while snooping around. If she does, Ted and Kamila will know how happy I was for the six weeks I stayed with them.

25

Justyna

The last time I saw Aunt Justyna was on a late afternoon in mid-December of 1944, when Mama had returned to Kraków to take me to a safe place. The front was approaching the city, and it was time to leave. No place we could get to was safe for us, but there was always hope, "the mother of the stupid," as it was called then. The family gathered in Justyna's room to wish us a good trip without having any idea where we were going. It was better not to know, just in case something happened to us on the way there. Mama assured them that we would be back as soon as the war was over. Knowing that Mama rarely told the truth, I had my doubts that we would and that made me feel like crying. But I did not cry.

Once in the street on our way to the railroad station, we did not hurry. Mama, always very careful, did not want to give anyone the impression that we were running away from something instead of just strolling through the park to get some fresh air. In those days people did not go out to enjoy scenery, but rather only in search of food or coal, and so the streets must have been empty. Our pace had to be just right, neither too slow nor too fast. To avoid running into checkpoints, Mama was taking strange detours into side streets and alleys. We were lucky to reach the railroad station just before the curfew.

I expected that we would spend the night sleeping in the waiting room, but we did not. Had I asked, Mama would have told me to leave her alone, because it was always better for me not to know if something was not going according to plan. When it got very dark—it may already have been the middle of the night—a railroad man came into the waiting room. Seeing him, Mama perked up. Without getting anywhere close to Mama, he nodded in her direction, a sign that we should follow him, and we did. The stranded travelers must have been watching us leave, wondering what the hell was going on. A train they would be allowed to board could not be departing this late at night. So embarrassed was I to see Mama being singled out, that I kept my eyes down. Something was not adding up, and I was sure that people were wondering about it.

We followed the meager light of the man's lamp, the kind designed for blackouts. As long as we were walking along the platform, it was easy, but once the platform ended and we had started to cross many tracks, we stumbled over rails and ties. Not knowing where to put one's foot down made even Mama groan. Well, at least she was not wearing high heels. At what must have been the far end of the station, a train was waiting for us. "That is it," the man mumbled. Mama slipped something into his hand as we boarded.

Was the train empty? Since we did not trip over anyone as we walked through the passage, it may have been. There was no one in the compartment we entered. We would have it all to ourselves. I wasn't sure if that was good or bad. I stretched out on a wooden bench and immediately fell asleep. At some point during the night, the train must had taken off. When I woke up in broad daylight, it was standing in a forest wedged between two hills, waiting for something to happen. A woman ran by our compartment pausing only to let us know that planes are in the area and may strafe our train. "Get off and run into the woods," was her advice. We did get off, but the snow next to the tracks was so deep that we immediately got stuck in it and then had to spend some time just lying in the ditch next to the tracks worrying that the train could leave without us. I stared at the tops of the evergreens, dusted with snow and sparkling in the sunlight. When a whistle blew, we hurried back to the train that was going to continue on its journey to a safe place.

The first time I met Justyna had been four and a half years earlier, soon after our arrival in Warszawa. We had no place to stay, when Maria from back home took us into her daughter's home—only until we could find a room of our own. Refugees were not welcome. Papa did not want to become a burden to people who were not family and began to visit his relatives to see what "possibilities" they had to offer. I quickly learned that something "possible" almost never was. Trying to be funny, he called these visits his "pilgrimages." Mama was not amused.

Papa's uncle, the saintly doctor famous for treating the poor for free, was the best "possibility," because he owned a house near Warszawa, a real house that I had heard a lot about, because it had been bought with money won in a lottery. I imagined a beautiful villa with white stucco walls and a red tile roof, big enough to fit us all. I don't know how Papa was imagining it. He did not take me with him when he went to call on his famous uncle, and so I did not get a chance to see what Papa saw, but seeing it put Papa into an even blacker mood than he was already in. The house was nothing more than a one-room wood cabin with a well and an outhouse in the yard. The two youngest of the doctor's ten children were also living in it, because someone was needed to pump and carry water into the cabin. Papa, angry and sad, explained to me what damage the Great Revolution had done to our once wealthy family, that was still poor though there'd been twenty intervening years of peace. And now we were on the run again.

That the doctor had supplied Papa with so many cousins did not help our situation. Two of his sons had already died in this war; Uncle Kot was in jail, either a Russian or a German one, and the fourth son, Uncle Ted, was as poor as his father. The six daughters, still unmarried, lived in rented rooms, barely earning anything as teachers or nurses. Since none of them could do anything for us, Papa had to turn to his brother Stan, who was not any better off than the rest of the family, but was a closer relation. Uncle Stan had an apartment in a house on the Old Town Market Square. A very historic location, I was told. I knew by then that "historic location" meant that once upon a time something terrible had happened there. The more "historic" the place, the more horrible the events.

That is where I met Stan's wife Justyna.

As I understood it at the age of nine, a man and a woman who lived together had to be husband and wife, and that meant "be married." Did that mean that they had to have a piece of paper with official stamps and signatures on it, sort of like a birth certificate or a visa? I was aware that important papers can get lost in wars and revolutions. When a man and a woman living together were not married to each other, people talked about them in whispers only, so that children would not know what was being said. That was the case with the doctor back home in Oszmiana, whose wife and daughter lived in Wilno, while another woman was living with him in our little town. I had overheard enough about it to know that people were busy wondering how it all was going to end.

Stan's apartment had a tiny kitchen and an almost empty room large enough for at least two more beds because it had hardly any furniture. Papa and Stan may have been negotiating such a possibility, while Justyna was entertaining me with questions. What was I reading? What did I like to do? Did I have any friends? Stuff like that. She was being very kind. While we were talking, I could have a good look at her from close-up: the almost black eyes, the darkest I had ever seen, the waist-long black hair, thick, heavy, and streaked with white. She may have been beautiful once and even then, but with my limited experience I could not yet pass judgment on human beauty. Justyna intrigued me. She was different.

Stan, on the other hand, did not look good. A silly man, ancient and bald, he had a head as round and shiny as a volleyball. I was not impressed. From the way he was smiling at Papa, I could tell that moving in with him was actually not a "possibility." As the oldest of three brothers, he had been in charge of the landed estate, while the other two studied law in Kyiv. He may not have been very good at management, because, according to what Uncle Ted told me later, Stan was unable to make his own decisions. When and what he planted depended on what the neighboring estates were doing.

Since there was nothing for us in Warszawa, Kraków began to look like a town with "possibilities," and we moved there in late summer of 1940, once Mama had wrangled us a permit to "resettle."

I saw Justyna again three years later in the summer of 1943 when I was visiting Papa in Warszawa for a few weeks. That is when I discovered that she could sing and that interesting photographs were hanging on the walls of her rooms, photographs I had not noticed before. Since I could not even carry a tune, her singing sounded wonderful to me, the words of her song mysterious and fascinating. Rages and groans the wide Dnieper, a fierce wind is blowing, or "Reve ta stohne Dnipr shyrokyi, serdytyi viter zavyva." The words were close enough to Polish for me to understand them. The name of the river was familiar, the Dnieper far, far away in the east. Did Justyna come from there, and was being from there what made her look so striking? Was there a connection between the photographs and her song? Pictures of Stan in uniform, a group of soldiers sitting around a bonfire or just standing at the edge of some forest, holding their rifles and almost smiling. No fields strewn with twisted bodies and dead horses with bloated bellies. Perhaps a war had two sides: one side was picnics and songs, the other a slaughterhouse. Who fought whom and where? Was there more than one war with the Revolution sandwiched between the two? Too many countries, too many battles and too many dead. I was getting lost in history. Our war was much simpler. I always knew who was fighting whom and where.

One photograph caught my eye because it was hanging in the foyer, near the entrance, all by itself, and low enough for me to have a good look at it. "Who is this man?" I asked Justyna. "It's your Papa," she answered. I did not believe her. Papa in uniform? Did he really look so dashing when he was young? Had he, once upon a time, been a soldier? If he was, what war was *he* fighting in? On whose side? Why had I never seen this picture of him? Someday I was going to find out.

I saw Justyna again in the fall of 1944, a time so historic that its only colors were black and dark gray. The Uprising was over, Warszawa in ruins, its people either dead or scattered. That picture of the man in uniform got buried in the rubble of the Old Town Market Square, and I was never going to find out who that man really was. Mama began to search for Papa's relatives to offer them shelter so that we would still have our old apartment if we returned after the war. Survivors of the Uprising who were too old, too young or too crippled for forced labor, were waiting in camps to be placed with whoever was willing to take them in. From one of these camps, Mama managed to fish out Uncle Ted, his wife and daughter. Aunt Justyna was harder to find because she was not "in the books" under our family name. Stan, on the other hand, being a man and single besides, had already left the camp by then and was settled in the servant's room in the apartment of an old family barely touched by the war. One could almost say that he was hiding there from Justyna. Mama managed to find him, though. At thirteen I already had a vague idea what that could be adding up to. Mama tried to convince him to join us in our large apartment, but he would not budge. And why would he when the servant's room came with a maid who was young and very pretty?

That is how we ended up living in the three rooms of our four-room apartment that had once been so crowded. Ted, Kamila, Justyna, Marysia, I, and Mama—when she happened to be passing through town. The vast room facing the backyard with its lone linden tree stood empty, the kitchen was abandoned.

Justyna could not be happy without Stan. Since we had to pass through her room, she had no way to hide her feelings from the rest of us. I saw her eyes grow darker and shinier, her face grayer and sadder, her hair whiter. When not lying curled up on her couch feigning sleep, she would mend clothes, rummage through her bundles, or visit a soup kitchen. Sometimes, when asked, she would sing her song for me. Reve ta stohne Dnipr shyrokyi… The wide Dnieper rages and groans.

Slowly, I was learning Justyna's story, not from her, but from what the grown-ups were saying to each other when she would go out. Just like in great patriotic novels—I had read Sienkiewicz by then—a handsome young officer, whatever his uniform, happens to end up on some landed estate where his soldiers set up a camp. The owner of the estate has a beautiful daughter who is waiting for her great love to arrive and take her away. That is how it worked out for Runia's father and mother, and she was very proud of it. So romantic… In Stan's case, it was not the daughter who was waiting for him, but the wife of the owner—and she already had children. That Justyna had done it with Stan was beyond my understanding. Did Stan have all his hair then? I could not even imagine how it all played out. Did they leave on horseback with his soldiers riding behind them and the husband in pursuit?

Uncle Stan was "lucky": the Revolution separated him from his wife and children, and probably he did not even try to reunite with them. For him, his family no longer existed. He was a free man. Justyna, on the other hand, was not so lucky. Her husband and his estate were on our side of the border, records had not been destroyed or lost, and the man was very angry. That is why she could not use our family name.

Some twenty years later, as soon as it became possible, I went back to see what had happened to the apartment that had been ours for almost four years during some very historic times. Ted and Kamila were still there, in the room that became theirs after the Uprising. Strangers were living in the other three rooms, strangers who did not always get along. Having one's own apartment was everyone's wish and dream. Our old furniture was gone. After the war, a woman, young and alone, claimed it as hers and took it away to sell. That helped us get rid of the bedbugs, Kamila was pleased to point out.

I did not care about the bedbugs. I wanted to know what had happened to Justyna.

One year after I had seen her for the last time, she had died of breast cancer in that pass-through room of hers where we had once said goodbye to each other. Ted and Kamila had to take care of her while she was ill and dying, while my poor little cousin watched. The death was grim. Did Stan come to see her before she died? I was afraid to ask. The answer could have been either a yes or a no and in either case it was going to hurt. Justyna's last stand, her way of expressing her opinion of the new order, was the dumping of the contents of her bedpan from the third story window onto the heads of militiamen who, at that moment, happened to be walking on the street below. Ted beamed when he was telling me that it was a perfect hit, though, by then, Justyna could barely stand up on her own. They came to arrest her, but Kamila was able to convince them that the poor woman was no longer in control of her senses. Perhaps she was not.

The linden tree, which in July used to fill the courtyard and float up to our floor with the sweet scent of its blossoms, had been cut down, even its stump was gone. Soon there will be no one left who knows that there was once a tree growing on that spot. I could not leave the apartment without taking a look at the blue lightbulb in the lavatory, a relic from the days of blackouts. Ted called it a miracle that would last for eternity and insisted that I see it for myself. Indeed, there it was: deep blue with light stripes where someone must have scratched off the paint. The lavatory, filthy and ancient, was not the kind of a place where one could enjoy the scenery, and yet, even in that setting, the lowly bulb had the aura of a war monument. "I'll show you that it still works," Kamila said, pulling the switch. And it did. For an instant. A light, a flicker, a sizzle, as if something inside it was getting fried, a ball of very bright white light, a pop, and finally a dead bulb, its insides coated with black soot.

26

Mrs. Kraus

Dear Mrs. Kraus,

You do not know who I am, we have never met. So, I must first introduce myself: I am a thirteen-year-old girl living with my mother and her male friend in your apartment without your permission, not that you would have been able to give it to us. I'll try to explain how it happened, but before I do, I want to assure you that we will be moving out in a few weeks, and once the war is over you will be able to move back in, provided you are still alive.

You may be wondering who brought us to your apartment. If I knew who that man was and what he did for a living, I might be able to figure out who was helping my mother and how we ended up at your place. You may want to know what he looked like: a white face, as if he'd lived his whole life indoors, dark hair, and a black suit. No, he was not wearing a black leather coat. His wide middle made up for his short stature. He moved quickly while emptying your closets and throwing everything onto a pile on the floor of the foyer. Since I know only a few words of his language, I understood very little of what he was saying. You were a widow, I learned, and crazy besides. At some point he looked at me and said, "She should be going to school." To say something so stupid, he must have been the crazy one. What school? Did he know that I could not speak Czech? How much did he know about us?

Your apartment is very nice. I really appreciate it. Five years ago, I lived in one similar to yours. The outbreak of the war put us in motion, from a beautiful town in the asshole of Europe, as that area is called by some, to this famous center of culture. Nowhere along the way did I sleep in an apartment as nice as yours and that means a lot because I have stayed in so many different places. You may want to know that the pile of your clothing on the floor of the foyer was no longer there when we moved in.

I take the streetcar to the center and walk around the Old Town. Everything here is oversize and grandiose: the castle, the churches, the river and its bridges, the main boulevard and the fancy apartment buildings that line its side streets. The last town I lived in had all of the above, but everything was smaller, as if built for children. There, every landmark came with its own story that I heard again and again until it became a part of me. Here, too, there must be stories, but no one can tell them to me.

What were you like when you were still living here? I am not asking what you are like now because once they took you away you stopped being who you had been here. I keep snooping around your apartment for clues, and so far have come up with only one photograph of a handsome mustachioed man who was probably your husband. That it was taken in Sarajevo explains the Turkish decor of your apartment. You must have had other photographs, but either they were thrown out when your apartment was being looted of its real valuables or you took them with you when you had to leave. I took ours and carry them in my knapsack. If you were here, I would show them to you. Someone has told me that people, when they have to flee, take with them pictures of their "once upon a time" life so that they can be certain that it was not just a dream. The trouble is that photographs can't be exchanged for a loaf of bread.

Your phonograph and records have been a great pleasure for me. We never had a phonograph, not even before the war, because Papa did not like music. Later, we probably had no money for something that could not easily be carried when one is on the run. I keep listening to your records. When the phonograph broke down the other day, my mother managed to find someone who was able to fix it. Since people here are not kindly disposed towards those who don't speak their language, finding someone willing to repair it was another one of Mama's great accomplishments. My favorite records, which must have been yours too, are *Der Zigeunerbaron*, *Light Cavalry Overture*, and *La Campanella*. I play them over and over again. Can you hear music where you are?

Your beautiful apartment may be small, but I think it would be perfect for one or two people. There are three of us living in it now, so I sleep on a cot in the kitchen, Mama and her friend on the couch in the main room. That is how we staked out our space. Up until now I was not supposed to know that Mama and the man slept in the same bed. That they do is no longer a secret and we have no neighbors who would care. When not touring the city, I spend most of my time in the main room listening to music, writing letters to my friend, letters that will not be mailed, or trying to read two books in two different languages, neither of which I understand. With no one to talk to, I am often just plain bored. Did someone steal most of your books? I know a lot about looted apartments because I have lived in one. When we moved into yours, only the heavy furniture and some books were still here.

***

I have been away for a while, Mrs. Kraus. Did you miss me? My mother took me back to where we had come from: a very long train ride, bombs on the way, blackouts for most of the evening, people afraid to go out even when they have to in search of food. My aunt did our shopping. She was the only one brave enough to leave the apartment. I wish I could have stayed there, but my mother wouldn't let me. She is not yet ready to give me up—though, every time she leaves me here alone for several days, I wonder what is on her mind. With three different sets of identity papers, all of them false, what mess would I end up in if she disappeared completely?

Do you know your neighbor? I do not. The janitor told us that an ancient man lives next door. He never goes out, and a housekeeper takes care of him. I see her sometimes on the balcony when she puts out the garbage. She never looks at me, not even with a quick glance. If she did, I would try to give her a little smile or even a nod, but it is obvious that she does not want to have anything to do with me. So, when she comes out, I go in. Now, after my mother, her besotted friend, and I got into a fight late one evening, the woman must be thinking that we are true barbarians. The noise we made was not pretty.

I am giving up on one of your books, the one in German, because, after trying to guess the meaning of words connecting those I recognize, I still cannot make any sense out of the first paragraph. Well, maybe I'll try again one day—unless time runs out. It has been much easier for me to decipher the book about clairvoyants and supernatural events, thanks to the similarity of our Slavic languages. I am trying to find the location of the psychic events that took place in your city. Mozart's haunted house, the traffic circle where someone fell under a streetcar as predicted, and that church, the famous church you must know about. No one can tell me what really happened there. Perhaps no one knows. People slow down when walking past it. I think that must be how they express their respect for those who died there.

Of course, I don't believe in the occult—or at least I am not supposed to. But that does not keep me from wishing that my brother would visit me one night, even though I would be terribly afraid of his ghost.

Once upon a time at a dinner party, when the good times were already slipping away, one of the guests insisted on looking at Papa's palm to see what the fates had in store for him. That done, he had the nerve to tell Papa that he would not survive the war. Did I ever cry! According to the palmist, Mama was going to end up on the other side of the ocean where people do not die in camps. I did not want to know what was going to happen to me and ran out of the room. What about you, Mrs. Kraus? Did you go to any of the seances described in the book to find out how much longer you are going to live? I wish we could meet in your apartment and have a talk. I am sure you have some interesting stories to tell.

You may be wondering what the three of us are doing here. Waiting, I suppose. Waiting for the front to approach from the east and, when it comes too close for comfort, we will resume our trip to the West which, at the moment, is not yet ready to receive us. When Mama is working on her business of smuggling tobacco across the border, I am left alone in your apartment, sometimes for days. Her friend is gone then, too, but I doubt that he is traveling with Mama. He is not brave enough for that. Since it is not safe for me to wander the streets when Mama is away—what would I say if stopped by police?—I do not go out, not even to the bakery. No, I am not starving, but after a few days of eating nothing but stale bread, I have to agree that whoever said "Man cannot live by bread alone…" was right.

When Mama and her friend are not away on business, we sometimes go to a restaurant for lunch. A famous place you probably know: it's on an island near the bridge. It has a vast dining hall waiting for the privileged to arrive for a sumptuous evening meal. At noon the place is empty except for one big table near a window where a group of men, twelve at the most, gather to eat dumplings and talk about changing the course of history and liberating the East. Powerless dreamers, they are. I always sit across the table from a man who listens to what the others are saying but says very little himself.

If you are no longer alive, you may be able to see what is happening in your apartment. Some people claim that the spirits of the recently deceased linger in their favorite rooms before settling down for eternal rest, which can be either heaven or hell. If this is the case, then you probably know that I have been snooping around in your closets and drawers, not that there is much left in them. I must have been terribly bored when I began to rummage in the small drawers of the kitchen cabinet where people store odds and ends, the kind of stuff they may need one day but, in the meantime, do not know what to do with. One drawer contained a baby bottle. What could a baby bottle be doing among your belongings? As far as I know, you never had children and at your age you were not going to have them. The man who brought us here, the one in the black suit, assured Mama that you had to be taken to a safe place because you were old and muddled in the head. Perhaps you were, and that would explain the baby bottle. Intrigued, I took it out of the drawer and was holding it when Mama yelled "Put it back! You don't have to touch everything here!" I am sure that had I taken out scissors or a roll of string, she would have said nothing. It is the bottle that set her off, and I have been trying to figure out why. Perhaps you can explain. I know that you have a doll, sometimes I even play with it, but many homes without children keep dolls for decoration because even grown-ups like to look at a doll's deep blue eyes that open and close and its beautiful porcelain face. But a baby bottle? I can't figure it out.

I would like to let you know what happened here the other day in case you are not aware of it. I was sitting at the desk in your living room writing a letter to my friend Runia, while Mama and her friend were having lunch on the island in the company of plotters, dreamers, and spies. I assure you that Mama is none of the above. She joins them so that she can get a hot meal without having to cook it herself. I stayed home because, without any new ideas, the meetings are becoming stale and boring. Besides, Mama promised to bring me back a serving of dumplings. I was surprised to hear the front door open before it was time for them to return. Mama entered the room, a tall man in a black coat behind her. Her friend, the coward, stayed in the foyer where, so close to the entrance door, he could slip out easily. I wish you could see how proudly Mama can walk. The more frightened she is, the more assured is her gait. This time she was really scared, and if her gait was not enough of a warning, her eyes, wide open for a moment, were alerting me that she did not know what was going to happen and that whatever it was going to be did not look good. Halfway across the room Mama stopped and let the man pass. He was heading straight for the desk and me while Mama watched. Was I scared, you may wonder. No, I wasn't. There was not enough time to be. When in danger I tell myself that I should just watch and not become a part of what is happening. Perhaps no one can see me then, especially if I do not move.

The man in the black coat wants to open the middle drawer of the desk, but I am in the way. I do not get off the chair, but I do lean back to give him space. If I stand up, I will miss out on seeing what is in the drawer or what he will do with what he finds there. He seems to know where he should be looking. And there it is, in plain view resting on top of some papers, one of Mama's three false passports, the most fake of them all. Not a single entry in it is correct and that it looks brand-new because it is only used on special occasions, also makes it suspect. The man picks it up, reads the fairytale data entered into it, puts it back into the drawer at the far end—where it should have been—and walks out of the apartment shaking his head. Mama is so upset that she has to lie down and rest. She may be trying to make sense of what has just happened. I think that if I could somehow explain this strange event, I would know how we got here and why. Will I ever be able to find out what is going on? Living in a strange city without any friends to turn to is like being stranded in a desert without any landmarks to navigate by. Yes, I am lost.

***

Big news here: Friday, 13 February, Prague was bombed. Did you hear about it? Were you able to watch the fires at night, black hills dotted with clusters of white flames? In the morning a bomb landed in the no man's land behind your house. Except for some broken glass, the building was not damaged. In the past, when air raid warnings started and stopped, Mama and I did not pay much attention to them, thanks to our "it can't happen here" attitude. This time, as soon as we heard the whistling, we ran down to the shelter packed with people who were crying and praying. Unused as they are to the niceties of war, they were scared and that did not feel or look good. To avoid witnessing their suffering, we stayed in the hallway until the end of the raid. I, too, am afraid of bombs—they make my teeth chatter—but I would never create a scene. At dusk we listened to distant explosions that were turning another city into rubble and watched the glow of a distant fire spread over the sky.

Does this mean that the front is approaching?

***

In case you have not noticed, I have been sick, so sick that I'm coughing up my innards. Mama says that, if it were safe, she would take me to a doctor as I am sick enough to see one. But a trip to the doctor may expose our illegal status and God knows what else. Besides, it is very cold outside, and I am running a fever. I am using anise liqueur as a cough syrup and already drank up a bottle of it. I like it, it tastes very good.

Sick or not I'll be leaving soon. Mama has rented a flatbed truck which we will share with another couple. If nothing goes wrong on the way, it will drop us off at the border where we may have to wait until it is safe to cross it. Would it be better to stay here longer? Once the war heats up again, renting a truck may become impossible, and then we may get stuck here until it's too late. Mama always operates on hunches and psychic insights. She may even have consulted a fortuneteller about this. Her guts are telling her that we should leave now, even though I am sick. Death has not shown up in the cards, at least not yet, and so we will be leaving in a few days, perhaps even tomorrow.

***

I won't be writing to you anymore. This is my last letter. I'll leave it in your desk in the back of the drawer where, according to the man in the black coat, private or secret papers should be kept. If you come back, you will find it there, and, intrigued by my foreign writing, you may even ask someone to translate it for you. That is how you will learn what happened in your apartment after you were taken away. I want you to know that Mama took good care of it. Nothing got broken or damaged, at least not by us. The looting was done before we moved in. I am taking with me a photograph of your great room and will keep it as a souvenir so that years later I'll know that your apartment existed, that it was not just a dream. Mama, who is very practical, may be taking some knick-knacks which, unlike the photograph, probably have some value and could be exchanged for a loaf of bread when the need arises.

Thank you very much for your hospitality and for listening to me when I was home alone at night. Even if you survive, I doubt that we will meet. Good luck to you, Mrs. Kraus.

27

The Picture Album, Part Two

The summer of 1944 brought change: the front was approaching from the east, though when it would arrive at our door was anybody's guess. Runia was whisked out of town to a safe place that had no address. In my nightmares, I kept looking for her, but every time I was about to find her, I could no longer see what was ahead of me. My other friends were not leaving, at least not yet, but they were either turning away from me or unable to fill the void left by Runia's disappearance. It was a sad summer. Even the man who was teaching me arithmetic had to stop giving lessons because it had become too dangerous. As for Mykola, there was no doubt that he would have to flee and that Mama would have to come along to show him the way. My fate was sealed unless Papa came back in time to save me.

In August Mykola started getting ready for his journey to the West by piling up in his room what he would have to bring along. As bulky as it was, the album could not be left behind, and so it lay on the desk exposed to my dirty fingers. When Mykola was away on "business"—tying up loose ends—I would sneak into his room and leaf through the album, while, in the street three floors below, the war was dragging on with its trucks, horse-drawn carts, and soldiers. If they were still singing their marching songs, I did not hear them, but I did hear them curse at their stalled trucks that were running on wood. Zum Teufel...

The picture postcards in the album were not like other images I was hooked on: no sleighs, horses, or wolves. Just a lot of naked bodies. Old men showing off their muscles and hair, women exposing their tits, and girls with flowers growing between their legs. And, of course, the fat Baby Jesus with his dick always showing so that he would not be mistaken for a girl. In the Garden of Eden, the place of eternal summer, Adam and Eve only needed a couple of fig leaves to keep themselves warm. Quite a world it must have been, despite the snakes. Had I been smarter, I would have been able to deduce what the great artists had on their minds while painting. It was a long way from the nudes to what "it" takes to make a baby, the "it" being the part that is always left out by adults to kids. Was I stupid not to see the connection between "it" and the flowers growing out of a girl's crotch? I would have a peek at the album whenever I had a chance. It could hardly matter anymore if my fingers were dirty or not. Things lose their value when one is about to flee. One day Mykola put the album into his valise, and we set out on our odyssey.

Trains standing in a forest—better under the trees than in a field—waiting for the Tiefflieger to pass, towns on fire or encircled by smoke, railroad stations turned into piles of rubble and dust, and the gaping remains of windows staring at me like empty eye sockets in the slices of walls that should have fallen down during bombing. Travel is a good learning experience, I heard people say before the war. Culture and history, history and culture. The countryside is pretty. The train empty—except for one time when a man and a woman moved into our compartment: he German, she Czech, one of them going to beautiful Prague, one getting off earlier, they told my mother. Yet after a few hours they got off in some God-forsaken town that was still enveloped in dust. The landscape came in various shades of gray: the street, long and straight, lined with piles of rubble, the station a heap of gray dust not high enough to obstruct the view of the couple walking hand in hand in the middle of the otherwise deserted street towards its distant, blackish end. I was puzzled. Why would they get off among the ruins? I expected them to turn into a side street, but when the train started up again, they were still walking straight ahead. Perhaps there were no side streets left or they were blocked off by the rubble.

We arrived in Prague well in time for the bombing of Dresden, and so I learned that Dresden actually existed and was not just a collection of postcards with fascinating pictures. First came the rumble of explosions that could be heard even in the air raid shelter. They kept coming without a break but were too far away to make my teeth chatter and not loud enough to make people scream. Everyone in the crowded shelter seemed to be waiting patiently for the show to end. Did anyone know what was happening? Perhaps someone somewhere had a clandestine radio and was receiving news of which town was being bombed. When the all-clear alarm sounded, I followed the crowd into the street. Perhaps once out of the shelter, people would be able to figure out what had been getting the hit. The sky to the north was glowing red and distant explosions could be heard. The few buildings on the black hill were still burning white from the morning air raid. It was a beautiful sight. What people were talking about, I mostly couldn't understand, but I did hear the word "Dresden."

We did not stay in Prague for long, just long enough to give me a chance to see the many faces of the Moldau that even on calm sunny days looked threatening to me. At their best her waters looked as if they were on fire, at their worst they were a dark churning brew waiting for prey. Only once did I feel myself under the river's spell. Standing on the Charles Bridge, I wondered if it would be better to jump or continue my trip into the unknown where finding friends seemed sure to be impossible.

Otherwise, life in Prague was good, almost luxurious: we lived in an apartment belonging to a Mrs. Kraus and had enough to eat. Mrs. Kraus had been taken somewhere and we were her uninvited guests. I wished she were still around for company and even wrote her a long letter of apology explaining our reasons for the intrusion. I left it in the middle drawer of her stately desk, just in case she happened to return.

Mama and I left Prague on top of an open truck on a very cold day at the end of February; our traveling companions were a couple heading for Munich. The woman was German, the man Ukrainian. Before we parted at the Czech border, where we had to wait for Mykola to catch up with us—or Mama's false passport was not yet good enough to enter Germany—they stole our bundle of food. Besides, I was either really sick with pneumonia or Mama wanted everyone to believe that I was, since, she argued to anyone who would listen, a sick child has to stay in a hotel and not in overcrowded refugee barracks.

Towards the end of April, Mykola finally did catch up with us. His train ride between Prague and Pilsen had been hell and somewhere along the way all of Mykola's luggage was lost, including his Dresden album. Pilsen was a bottleneck where a bridge was being bombed every day, making it difficult for refugees to cross the river and escape. Somehow Mykola managed to hitchhike to where we were stranded. That it was such hard going had made him into a hero.

And the album? What had happened to it exactly, I wondered. Did someone pick it up and give it a good home? Was it destroyed by a bomb? I had no way to learn its fate.

The next part of our journey was done on foot and on horse drawn cart; it began on a snowy afternoon and ended in the early morning. That travel was not a good learning experience: all I learned was that I had outgrown my shoes and that blisters hurt like hell. The scenery that rushed by the train window towards where I had come from often moved me to tears, be it hills bald or wooded, or a piece of land as flat as a tabletop that would have looked boring were it not for an occasional tree or a clump of trees placed just right to break up the monotony. The rivers the train crossed and the towns it passed were silent about their history, and no fellow traveler would have been able to enlighten me because we had no language in common. I was missing another year of school and wished that instead of heading west into the unknown, I could have stayed behind with the photo album, found Runia, and learned some algebra.

28

Peace

A war is a time of great expectations and so is one's childhood. In war the great expectation is about survival. In childhood it is about believing that something wonderful is hiding just around the corner even though nothing wonderful can be there.

Around my corner in early spring 1945 was a bombed-out railroad station, dark, cold, and empty, and without a single bench to sit on. A fleeing ambulance dropped us off there and the "us" was not even family. That was where we were supposed to wait for the others to arrive on a horse-drawn wagon. My mother was going to be among the others, I was sure of that, unless, of course, something happened on the way. The night looked exceptionally promising: fog, sleet, rain—even bombers did not fly in that kind of weather. We let the child stretch out on the surviving ticket counter and then had to keep watch so that she did not fall off. It is possible to sleep while standing up and we did, even though we had promised each other that we would not. The child stayed put while we slept.

I was fourteen years old then, in some ways street smart, in some ways stupid. My mother did arrive—I was right about that—and found one room for the eleven of us in an empty hotel across the street from the railway station after threatening to kick in the door that no one would open. All the rooms were occupied, the owner claimed. They were not: the guests had already fled after changing into civilian clothes. Coming back was not in their plans.

That is how we were welcomed into Furth: outsiders, strangers, aliens, foreigners, or simply those damn refugees. It was a beautiful place, but before I could appreciate its beauty, we starved and hid in the cellar when rockets descended on the ruins of the railroad station. Such a waste. The war's end had to be right around the corner. And it finally really was. From the one window of the long hallway, I saw them arrive in their jeeps, dragging the losers' flag along the ground. The sky was cloudless and deep blue, bluer than any sky I had seen up until then. It made me feel like crying at a time when I should have been happy. The street was empty. It took a few days before people felt safe enough to go outside. There was no fighting. White sheets of surrender fluttered from all the windows.

A collection of red-tile roofs, sand-colored stucco houses, a vast town square surrounded by buildings a couple of stories high and a farm near the railroad station with an ox and a cow. Did that count as a village or a small town? I'll call it a village. What I found most interesting were the hills with their ever-changing moods: all black or black sprinkled with white or hiding behind the tatters of drifting mist or disappearing altogether behind a gray wall of fog. And sometimes, when the weather was right, with the sun coming out after a rain, they glowed as if on fire. That was all that I could see from the window of the room I was living in after getting thrown out of the hotel. For a change of scenery, I would climb a steep street on the other side of the village—the cemetery on the left, the Protestant church, a TB clinic, and a nunnery on the right, at its end, at the very top, some kind of a war memorial surrounded by briars. Seen from there, the sky looked immense. At harvest time the checkered fields in the valley below were as bright as the sun. That is where the border was.

Yes, the countryside was beautiful, and since I had nothing better to do—no friends and few books—I feasted on it every day, even in miserable weather. Of course, the village was not dead, people were living in it. They went about their business quietly, probably just looking for food, which was in very short supply then. Some of them must have been refugees but not foreigners and therefore much better off than I who did not speak their language. No one seemed to pay any attention to me. My ignorance made me feel safe: no one was going to harm me while I wandered through fields and forests even when I too was looking for mushrooms and berries, the common good to which, according to some rule, everyone was entitled.

I was curious about the locals. What did they do in their homes behind closed doors? Would they invite me in if I knew how to speak German? I did not think they would. Yet, it was comforting to see that the streets were not empty and that the passersby were ordinary-looking people going about their business in an orderly fashion. No crowds milling around the way they do when something is about to happen, no lines at the stores that had damn little to sell, no pockmarks on their houses, no tottering drunks. I knew that in war a deserted street means trouble. But in this little town people were out walking as if nothing was about to happen.

And that meant peace, for a change.

29

A Night in Regensburg

This is the third letter I am writing to you, dear Runia. The first two I wrote in Prague after some air attacks on the city. I wanted to let you know what a real air raid feels like and that it was wrong for us to have thrown lit matches onto the hay of the crèche on the table that time, pretending that we were bombing Berlin. It made us laugh, though, didn't it? When your mother found out, she told you that we should not have been playing with matches—she was right since we did have to douse a small fire. I remember her saying, too, that making a game out of killing people was despicable, even when the people were Germans. I guess she was right about that, too.

I hope you are doing well and getting enough to eat and that no one got killed where you were staying at the end of the war. The letters I am writing to you now will not be mailed because having contact with the West may endanger you and your family. Perhaps someday when we see each other again, I'll be able to turn them over to you.

You are probably wondering where I am and if I am still alive. You don't even know that I am now living in a German village near the Czech border. Perhaps at some other time I'll write more about my life here. For the moment I'll stick to one recent incident that should give you some idea of what I am going through.

When we came here the trains were not running. After Mama had been taken to the hospital in a nearby town, I had to walk some thirty kilometers—fifteen there and fifteen back—to visit her, all in one day along the railroad tracks. Some hike it was. When I got back, my feet were covered with blisters and I could barely stand up. Now I can go there by a rickety train that often just stops moving, but it sure beats walking.

We have been here for over a year now. Mama has been looking for a way out. That is why we make so many trips by train. On the way to Munich we pass through towns whose names won't mean anything to you: Schwandorf, Passau, Landshut, Straubing, Regensburg. I wish you were here so that we could travel together, but I know that will not happen. You will go your way, while I go mine.

Railroads have not yet recovered from the war. Trains come to a halt in the middle of nowhere and stand there for what seems like hours. Even the conductors don't know why. Perhaps tracks have to be repaired up ahead or a train from the opposite direction has to pass. On our way to Munich, we often miss connections because of delays and have to spend the night sleeping in the waiting room of some station that looks and feels like a pile of rubble. There is still a curfew here, and we don't want to be caught wandering through a bombed-out town after dark. The countryside is beautiful: hills, forests, fields of different colors, wildflowers along the tracks and the famous Danube river. Do you still remember the funny story of how Strauss was inspired to compose the Blue Danube Waltz? You would want to know that the Danube I see from train windows is either brown or gray, never blue.

When we first started traveling, the trains were empty. The locals were not going anywhere because everything they needed was within their reach. Can you imagine being able to stay in one place because you have everything you need? When refugees finally got their identification papers, true or false, though, they began to travel. Some of them may be searching for friends or relatives who could have ended up at some camp and do not yet know how to get around. Others are transporting black market goods from one place to another. Cigarettes and vodka or vodka and cigarettes in exchange for food, just like during the war. Remember?

Refugees are interesting. When they fill a train compartment I am in, I can watch them and listen to their different languages and accents. The Hungarian fascists look very good; they must have been rich once. The Ukrainian collaborators look like peasants; if they were once wealthy, it does not show. Then there are the survivors whom the war did not treat well. Our compatriots, you know. Whether coming from a KZ or forced labor, they're not a very pleasant bunch. The Russians are here, too, terrified that without forged papers, they will be forced to return—and we know what that means... That is why so many kill themselves before being put on the train. It happened near where we are living now. They stabbed themselves to death with knives. That leaves the famous Balts. They're here, but I don't run into them on our trips. Perhaps they travel in limousines provided to them by the Americans as a reward for their good behavior during the war. The SS, remember? There is no justice. I wish you could come here to see it for yourself.

Something unusual happened to Mama and me on our recent trip to Munich and, since you used to ask me for letters when you were sent to the country in the summers, I am now trying to make up for not having written much then.

As the train we were on was heading towards Regensburg, our compartment filled rapidly until all the seats were occupied. The passengers were refugees except for one, who was a genuine German of Bavarian variety: he wore Lederhosen, a sleeveless jacket, and a hat adorned with a tuft of animal hair. A big fellow and so talkative that soon everyone in the compartment was speaking German out of politeness and having a very good time. In all my traveling, I have never seen anything like it. Normally, the locals and foreign refugees do not mix well. To talk about the Americans was safe, because no one here is very fond of them, though they can be terribly funny. They speak as if a hot potato is stuck in their mouth, and they seem to think that every country in Europe is the same. Pure ignorance and no culture, they even put their feet on the table while eating, don't know how to use a knife at meals, chew gum like sheep chew their cuds, and think that they can get anything and everything for a piece of chocolate. I still don't know German well enough to understand every word that was being said, but it must have been very funny because the compartment was bursting with laughter and glee. Just before Regensburg there is the Walhalla, a white speck on a green hill with the Danube below. Probably you do not know what Walhalla is, and neither do I, really. It's a monument to something; it looks majestic and beautiful when the sun is shining on it just right. On my travels I see people rush to the window to have a look at it, but have yet to hear someone say anything helpful about it.

The train was late, connections missed, the curfew coming. Which refugee camp is the best to spend a night in? How far away is it? Can it be reached before dusk? Is it any better than the waiting room of a bombed-out railroad station? For Mama and me, the station was the best possible choice until the Bavarian specimen said to her, "You don't look like the kind who should be spending the night in a waiting room." Had I been allowed to open my mouth, I would have told him that we are used to it and that we do it all the time. "I can put you up in my apartment," he said in the voice men use to order women around. "No, no, we will be fine," Mama answered, smiling sweetly and looking at me for agreement. She must have seen how scared I was, but did not give a damn. Did anyone from the train see us follow the man into an empty street lined with rubble and ghosts of apartment buildings? I was too embarrassed to turn around to look.

Dusk was setting in and with the curfew on its heels, we had to hurry. The man was walking very fast, and Mama, who does not run, could barely keep up with him. The streets were empty, the ruined houses dark. I was giving up hope that we would ever get to one that was not in ruins, but we did after so many turns that I would no longer have known how to retrace our steps back to the station where we had to be in the early morning. A house suddenly appeared, and it was still in one piece! We entered it in such a hurry that I did not even get a chance to see if it was pockmarked or not. We climbed a few flights of stairs, passing many doors on the way. Were people living behind them in silence? I wondered. He rang a bell—why doesn't he have a key?—and a woman opened the door. She turned out to be his wife. "We have guests here for the night. They need dinner and a bed." I expected her to scream "Get them out of here!" but instead she just said "Yes, I see… Dinner is almost ready"—as if she had been expecting us. Short and broad but not fat, she would not look distinguished even if she were dressed up. Clothes can make Mama look like a queen, but they would not be able to do much for this woman whose calm face lacked spark. Had I not been so damn scared, I would have liked her.

The room we entered was out of a fairytale: its walls were covered with shelves, the shelves were covered with beer mugs of different sizes, shapes and colors. It was a collection of fancy pottery fit for a museum. To please its owner, Mama had to admire them properly. "How beautiful… How beautiful!" she kept saying. I know that she likes pretty things however useless, but I don't think that beer mugs are actually on her list.

The dinner was just like it is supposed to be: a big table in the center of the room decorated with the mugs, a white table cloth, china, silver cutlery, and real food: potatoes, mushrooms, salad, and even some pork, all to be washed down with beer. Pure magic. Your mouth must be watering at the description unless you are getting enough to eat now. Mama and the man talked, his wife had little to say. They agreed that Russia should not have won the war. If not Russia, then who? Does it mean that Germany should have won? It does not make sense. Mama made sure that he knew whom we were going to visit: a well-known family with a villa near Munich. I have been there already and found it to be a very sad place because the wife's best friend is her husband's mistress. I now sort of know what that means.

Though hungry, I was afraid to eat not because I did not want the couple to see my bad table manners—in the past too many of my meals had been served on pieces of newspaper—but because the food could have been poisoned. Only one bad mushroom would be needed for that. Wedged as I was between two crazies, I had good reason to be worried. Who in his right mind would invite a completely strange stranger to spend the night in his home? Mama, too, could not have been in her right mind when she accepted the invitation. Yet I had to eat up whatever was on my plate, even the mushrooms, because it would have been very rude and stupid to turn down a meal of such high quality. Every time I looked up from my plate, I saw the beer mugs staring at me.

What kind of sleeping arrangements could I dream up? There was a couch near the window and a closed door to what I thought was a bedroom. Was the couple hiding something behind it? A torture chamber, perhaps? It turned out to be just another room with an alcove and in the alcove, there was a giant bed with fresh linen. The host told Mama that the bed would be ours for the night. Mama insisted that we would be fine on a couch with a blanket and a pillow. We should not be taking over his and his wife's bed. It just was not right. Where were they going to sleep then? On the couches, he said. I did not get a chance to get a good look at the room with the alcove because it was poorly lit. If there was a couch in it, I did not notice it.

And that is how Mama and I ended up in a bed so strange that I could not fall asleep. I listened to the sounds our hosts were making: their footsteps, their whispers, the squeaking of springs. They had done their best to be quiet, to let us sleep so that we would not know when something bad was about to happen. How stupid it was of Mama to get us into this mess! She fell asleep as soon as she lay down, so I had to stay awake, keep watch and try to figure out where all the little sounds were coming from. By early morning, when it was already getting light, I was too exhausted to keep worrying and fell asleep.

During breakfast, eaten in a hurry, the man wrote down his address on a tiny piece of paper which he gave to Mama. Any time you pass through Regensburg and need a place to stay, you can come here. Oh my God, I thought, don't let it happen again. Then he walked us to the street that led directly to the station, even though there were many twists and turns before we reached it. The air was misty either from the dampness of the night or from the dust of the ruins. All of it was gray.

The way trains get stuck in some town between Munich and the village we live in cannot be avoided. Now that we have the address of a strange man whose name we don't even know, Mama prefers to get stuck in Regensburg, while I keep hoping that it will be in some other town. It all depends on which route the train will have to take the day we set out on our journey. What I wish for hardly ever happens. I've even tried to wish for the opposite of what I really want, but that does not work either. The Fates can't be fooled. And so, on our way back from Munich, we got stuck in Regensburg whereas any other town would have been fine with me. Mama was pleased: she was sure that we would have a bed to sleep in.

At first it was easy: the exit from the station faced the street, the one on which we had been left off a few days earlier, and that was the street we took straight towards what must have been the center of town. First a right turn, then a left followed by another right, I stopped keeping track of the turns when I realized that we were lost. We may have been walking in circles, yet Mama was still pretending that she knew the way. Having an address scribbled in pencil on a tiny piece of paper was not going to be of much help when there were no street signs, no lights and no one to ask because it was getting dark, and the curfew was coming.

Do you remember the times when, to beat curfew, we had to run for our lives? You, in particular, had a very close call one evening and it took you a few days to recover from the exertion. But we always knew where we were, where we were going, and what building we could slip into when necessary. Here I knew nothing. A bombed-out town makes a strange landscape:

no landmarks, no colors to steer by because rubble comes only in different shades of gray. As one wanders through the ruins at dusk, one begins to think that someone may still be living in a cellar deep under the ground. It's like being surrounded by spooks and ghosts. Even Mama finally had to admit that we were lost. Not that she said anything, but I could see that she looked worried. Spending the night outdoors sleeping on stone seemed even scarier than the apartment of the strange couple. As for me, though no longer afraid of them, I did not want to sleep in their bed again, eat their dinner or look at their beer mug collection because it was a gift we had no right to and Mama should not have accepted. Out of pride I preferred to go hungry and sleep on a pile of rubble.

We were still walking, trying to decipher the numbers on the houses that had them, when a jeep pulled up in front of us. You probably do not know what a jeep is. It is an American army car that, with its top off, looks like a small truck. Like all American equipment, it is supposed to be the best of the best because it sticks to the road when driven at high speed. There were four of them inside: the driver and three others sitting on benches, guns between their legs. Military police. Even Mama had no idea what their habits were—we had always managed to stay out of their way, so far. One of them understood a little bit of German, and Mama was able to convince him that we were just lost and did not plan to blow up anything because everything had been blown up already. They were going to take us somewhere but did not say where. Most likely it would be a jail. We got into their jeep, and I had a good, long look at them from up-close. They were able to talk with gum in their mouth and were making strange popping sounds while chewing. Their voices were loud, and they laughed a lot. I had no idea what they were laughing about, but it could have been us, the big fish they had caught that evening.

No, they did not take us to jail but to a DP camp. Have you already learned that DP stands for displaced person? Someone can be referred to as "just a DP," as if DPs are not quite human. The camp was not the kind of place Mama would have chosen to spend the night in. She is really picky. We slept on straw in a large room which was home to some Polish women who were neither kind nor friendly. Where are you from? How did you get here? These are the questions people ask under the circumstances. To answer them Mama has to invent stories. When we began to feel itchy after lying down, she asked the woman who had settled near us for the night if there were any lice in the straw. No, there are not any, she told us, because there was enough DDT in the straw to kill a whole army.

I hope you now have a picture of my life here. You would probably like to see all those different people from different countries. When I watch them board the train, I try to guess where they come from. If you were here, Runia, we could do it together and see which one of us is better at it.

30

Evhen

Driven by her rich imagination and ready to do the unexpected, my mother may have saved the Ravich family. At the end of February 1945, she and I had arrived in the Czech border town Domažlice where we had to wait for a propitious day to continue our journey west. During the two months we were holed up in that godforsaken place, I had to play sick so that we could stay in a hotel instead of in an overcrowded refugee camp where, according to the hotel owner, we belonged. To keep me in place, a kind Czech doctor was willing to provide my mother with certificates that I was suffering from pneumonia, pleurisy, possibly tuberculosis, and whatever else my mother could think of. Yes, I was sick then but not that sick. Mykola who had stayed in Prague to fight the Bolsheviks until the very end, joined us in the middle of April after a harrowing trip during which he had lost all his luggage including the Dresden picture album that had been given to him by the elegant Jewish lady whose thread factory he was in charge of expropriating. Mykola really needed my mother to help him navigate the way forward. In Pilsen the refugees escaping the East had to cross a bridge which was under almost constant bombardment; among them, according to Mykola, was a wonderful Ukrainian family that deserved being saved. And that is what my mother did: she hired a farmer with a horse drawn cart and headed for Pilsen to find the Ravich family. They must have stood out in some way, because she did find them and brought them to Domažlice. A few days after their arrival they joined us on the next leg of our odyssey. Together we set out for the Bavarian border on foot because the horse drawn cart hired by my mother and paid for with smuggled tobacco was meant for our bundles and the very old. That no one checked our papers when we finally arrived at the entrance to paradise implied that even the SS were on the run at that point. During the following two weeks, I was a lucky witness to the unraveling of a great empire. It was a privilege to have the Ravich family for company when one potato, one onion, and a lot of water went into the making of soup for ten. Yes, Mykola had been right, I had to admit, the family was wonderful.

There were seven of them: the patriarch, his daughter Zoya, and her husband Alexander, all of them physicians, and his widowed daughter-in-law with her mother and two children. The old doctor talked to me about medicine, his son-in-law used a scalpel to divide a potato between us, and the grandson—he had a head start on the language—gave me my first English lessons. Unfortunately, they did not stay at the border for long and moved on to Regensburg where the newly founded DP camp in the Ganghofersiedlung was waiting for them. My very brief intellectual life ended with their departure. For the next four years my broken family continued living in the village because according to my mother's hunch, that was the correct strategy, and perhaps it was.

The Ravich family shared with me rumors that a Polish school was going to open up at their camp in Regensburg, and that if it did and if I were given a chance to attend it, they could offer me a bed to sleep in. Was it a payback for my mother's good deed of saving them? Did they make the offer because they thought I was worth saving? It did not even occur to me to ask.

In the spring of 1946, the school became a reality, as real as a meteor lighting up the sky and fizzling out moments later. After staying open for about two months, it succumbed to the demands of realpolitik: Poles were encouraged to return to Poland—the encouragement meant closing their schools—while citizens of countries that had collaborated with the Nazis were welcomed to the Free World with open arms. The other Polish pupils were a sad lot, just like me. Most of them were on their own; their fathers and brothers lost in the war. After the closing of the school, they returned to Poland. I would have also if my mother did not need me to help her stay out of trouble.

The teachers, too, were a sad lot, as most of them were alumni of concentration camps. I had no idea what they had done in their previous lives, but very likely it was not teaching. The school even had a principal, a mysterious man who according to rumors had once been a famous academic. He had a booming voice and occasionally came to class to teach English by making us memorize and sing "My Bonnie lies over the ocean, my Bonnie lies over the sea..." So awed was I by the man that, even I, who in real life could not carry a tune, sang along the best I could or pretended to. Once, I overheard him say to someone that nobody in the camp is what he claims to be. This statement left me intrigued. Did people need to molt every so often like snakes? Or did they just do it after a war to get rid of their past?

What did I learn during the two months I had the opportunity to learn? A lot or nothing? Thanks to the books provided by the government in exile, I was given a chance to follow the peregrinations of my compatriots from the Gulags along the great Russian rivers through the Middle East to the Free World that did not want them. Quite a journey it must have been, covering a lot of territory. Overhearing my classmates talk about their last places of residence, I learned to recite the names of German concentration camps, a skill that was not on the list of prerequisites to enter college in the US where I ended up. My history lessons suffered from a gap of several hundred years, as if not much had happened between ancient times and the Thirty Years War. And there was also the matter of math! Two years earlier I had had my last contact with it when, to make my father happy, I promised myself to become a model pupil and began to take arithmetic lessons from an old man who was teaching "in hiding." That promise of mine made me plunge into the mysteries and acrobatics of multi-layered fractions with so much enthusiasm that I became quite good at handling them. Even the professor was impressed. Unfortunately, my father was arrested before I had a chance to let him know how smart I was. Euclidean geometry was going to come after fractions and after geometry algebra, but by fall of 1944 it had become too dangerous to give lessons, even in hiding. Two years later I was supposed to be solving quadratic equations when I still did not know how to play around with symbols.

By the time I arrived to attend school as a guest of the Ravich family, the daughter-in-law had left for another camp and the three remaining members of the family were living in a large room meant to house seven. What a luxury that was! The news about the empty beds and the linen must have spread through the grapevine, and the Ukrainians traveling in search of their relatives and friends knew where they could spend a night. As a reminder that the room was not just an ordinary dormitory, a big table and chairs graced its center, to be used for meals, conversation, homework, and playing solitaire. When not doing any of the above at the big table, I was in school or exploring the neighborhood or sleeping in my own bed. And yes, I did try to find among my classmates someone to replace the friend I had lost, but the chasm between Runia and the kids who had been through the wringer was too great to allow any real bonds to develop.

In the spring 1946, the camp was the safest place I could imagine, simply because I did not know any better. It was beautiful, besides. The Ravich house was located at the bottom of a rise. The street it was on was not straight but curved for a better fit into the side of a hill and that made it stand out among the other streets. The complex had a gate across the main entrance so that the incoming trucks could be checked. But if one stepped out of a house, one could just keep going into the fields or follow the Danube into Regensburg.

By summer of 1946, the camp was in a state of flux. Still, even I, with my limited experience, could see that the Ukrainian section where the Ravich family resided consisted of the educated class that, between the two wars, had lived in Czechoslovakia and had done very well there. I was lucky to have been able to join such a distinguished group of people and take advantage of their good will. One of these people was Evhen, the poet—who, as it turned out, knew math and was willing to tutor me. At the end of our algebra sessions, he said to Zoya, "She sure catches on fast, much faster than the other kids I am teaching." I knew which kids he meant. I used to see them pass in front of the Ravich house on their way home from their school which met every day except on Sundays. Sometimes they would stand on the sidewalk talking. When I passed them, they never looked my way. That I may have been better at math than they did not console me. I would have rather traded "having caught on fast" for a life in families like theirs.

After my school had closed, I continued to hang out at the camp the way teenagers nowadays hang out at shopping malls. By then I had met some people I could relate to: a Polish-American couple who lived in a villa thanks to their American connections, a *Volksdeutsche* family whose background I could not fathom however hard I tried, and finally a Jewish couple who, for some unknown reason, was still pretending to be Christian. I listened to the Volksdeutsche, explored the city with the Jewish Poles, and sometimes babysat for the Americans. All of them were mongrels, just like me. They provided me with a bed when the Ravich beds happened to be occupied. I did not get to know any real Poles; those I ran into were unfriendly.

The best way to get from the camp to the railroad station or into town was along the banks of the Danube: the river on one side and the wilderness of a brushy rise on the other. I had been warned that the path was dangerous after dark, yet the warnings did not keep me from taking it when I had promised to spend a night with the *Volksdeutsche*, the Sauers, after they had moved to the city for a little while. I did it for Mrs. Sauer's stories about life in the Poland I was too young to really know even though I was living there.

The Danube near the camp was not a Viennese blue, but at its worst a churning brown, at its best a shimmering silver. I liked to look at its moody waters and soon, during my visits to Regensburg, my walks along its bank turned into a daily habit. Evhen, too, must have been unable to resist the river's charms, because soon we were running into each other at its edge. And we talked and talked and whatever we talked about was much more interesting than the algebra that had originally brought us together.

First came the rivers we both knew, Wisła and Vltava. The Dnieper I had never seen, so it belonged to Evhen and he recited the poem "Reve ta stohne Dnipr shyrokyi..." that had turned into a song that I used to beg Aunt Justyna to sing for me. It had been her river until she was stupid enough to run away with a colonel stationed on her husband's estate during the Polish-Soviet War. She had left her children behind, never to see them again, and the caddish colonel abandoned her when she needed him the most. Her story connected me with the mighty Dnieper, which like her heart raged and moaned, and created a bond between the river, Evhen, and me.

As we walked along the shimmering Danube, Evhen talked to me as if I were a grownup. Somewhere along the way he introduced me to Marx, whom he criticized for leaving the middle class out of his theories. His views of Trotsky were similar to my father's: Trotsky's revolution would have been an improvement on Lenin's. On the eve of the arrival of the Soviet troops in Wilno, I had watched my father burn some books in the kitchen stove, Trotsky's masterwork among them. The chimney was not drawing well, their pages curled slowly before turning brown, and it took a long time for them to turn to ashes. I was eight years old then and well-informed for my age, but inexperienced enough to start worrying that the Bolsheviks with their NKVD or GPU were already on their way to our door to look for the remains of Trotsky in the kitchen stove. Their tanks arrived on our street at pink dawn of the next day; it took some seven months before the NKVD or whatever its name came pounding on our door. I thought that Evhen enjoyed listening to my version of history.

We talked also about the lesser rivers. His was Synyukha, mine was Oszmianka. Did I tell him how frightened I was of raging waters, like those flowing under the Charles Bridge on a particularly bad day in February 1945? Did I even mention the bridge to him? When he talked, I listened and kept my hurts to myself. Now I don't even remember what I told him about my father and Mykola. Did I say that my father would come to get me as soon he was allowed to leave Poland? At that time, I wanted it to happen so badly that I believed that it would, and so I was not lying. As for Mykola, I don't remember ever talking to Evhen about him. What could I have said to explain his existence, the way I used to once upon a time—that he was only a tenant in the room the three of us shared? The two men could have little to say to each other.

In response to my prodding, Evhen told me about his life. He was born in the Ukraine in a town between Odessa and Kyiv, the two cities that were also my father's territory. Yet my father was Polish, Evhen Ukrainian. After the Revolution and the two little-known wars that followed it, both men ended up in what had become Eastern Poland, Evhen as a prisoner of war, my father in search of a new career. After his release from the POW camp, Evhen joined the Ukrainian intellectual elite on their trek to the West, where Czechoslovakia let them open an institution of higher learning that gave Evhen a chance to become an engineer specializing in hydrodynamics. Hydrodynamics brought him to the water filter system of Warszawa where my father, then on the run, was living briefly in a villa on a street appropriately named Filtrowa that was frequently bombed because of its proximity to the city's water supply. He was even wounded there during a night air raid. In the summer of 1943, when I was visiting him, my father showed me that villa; it looked enchanted, embedded as it was in lush exotic greenery. I liked to imagine that he and I were going to live there after the war, while my mother and Mykola would, like the Bonnie of the song, end up over the ocean and the sea. Snippets from my past kept our conversation going.

Besides, to be polite I had to say something, though it was never as interesting as what Evhen had to tell me.

It seemed that at the Ganghofersiedlung, he was known not as an engineer but as a poet. When our paths happened to cross at the Ravich residence, even I was able to notice that other guests treated him with awe, though he did not seem to interact much with them. I had learned a few Polish poems by heart as a child and, though they told stories and were not just about moods, my interest in poetry did not last. And so, as we walked and talked, I preferred to listen to the story of his life than to any poems I would not have understood.

Evhen did not seem to hesitate to tell me what I thought should have been secrets. Once upon a time, he was married to Zoya and their marriage ended in divorce. Being short on social graces, I asked him why. That divorces do not happen in good families I already knew from Poland. According to the Church, marriage was for life and divorce was impossible. My understanding of the subject was hazy and my interest in it minimal, even when I got wind of my parents' divorce that Mykola kept insisting on, so that he could marry my mother. Had he already dumped his wife and daughter by then? I did not even try to find out, so uninterested was I in the mess the grownups were concocting as they argued about fleeing the country.

Evhen was the epitome of a gentleman. When I asked him about his divorce, he did not hesitate to explain. He wanted to have children and once it had been medically confirmed that Zoya could not have any, they divorced. Evhen left for Warszawa and its water filters, while she stayed in Prague and married Alexander, a Greek physician from Odessa, who looked like a scarecrow dressed in a floppy oversize suit. He was short and flat as a board and had a big nose. I liked him, good man that he was. He used to tease me and make me laugh. Compared to Alexander, Evhen may have been handsome, but if he was, I did not give it much thought. At that point in my life, I was more interested in men's brains than their looks, especially when they were as old as my father. Some fifteen years after the divorce, the Raviches and Evhen were still a happy family and it was natural for Evhen, who must have lived on the same street in the Siedlung though I did not know where, to stop at the Raviches for brief visits just to ask them how they were doing.

Did he get the child he wanted? I could not stop wondering. Since he was not telling me on his own, I had to ask. Yes, he did have a son with a Czech woman who was living in Prague. I was puzzled. Why weren't they together? It did not make sense that, after wanting a child so badly, he was not taking care of it. Perhaps he was not even married to the child's mother or she was married to someone else. I was after Evhen's secrets, but even my carefully worded questions were not getting me anywhere and I had to give up. Perhaps his son's mother could not leave her country or Evhen did not want them to follow him into exile?

All in all, it was a good summer, the summer of 1946. I spent most of it at the camp, taking long walks with people who were kind to me. Regensburg was rising from the ashes and its parks were coming back to life. Even at its angriest, the Danube was lovely, always there waiting for Evhen and me. I have absolutely no recollection how I got my food at the camp, a sign that I was not starving.

In the fall, I went back to Furth, the village where my mother, Mykola, and I stayed cooped up on the farm. A cozy place it was, with one room for everything. Water had to be brought in from the outside in a pail, whereas the outhouse could be conveniently entered from inside the house. With not much else to do, Mykola was suffering from an overload of ideas about getting rich or just making a living. With the help of his enterprising Ukrainian friends, he built an illegal vodka still next to our stove. It made for quite a sight. On the evening when Mykola's venture was embarking on its maiden voyage, we watched its mysterious parts spring into action: the basin of slops and the tangle of pipes and tubes that soon were filling up with ominous bubbles in search of an exit. It seemed that the process had to be slowed down, but the wood in our stove was burning too well and turning it off was impossible. Warned by the hissing and bubbling emanating from the still, my mother insisted that it be disconnected before the contraption exploded and we ended up burned and in jail. Worse yet, the villagers would be amused by our predicament and curse "die verdammten Ausländer." I had to admit that sometimes my mother was capable of good judgment.

The winter of 1946–1947 was very cold, perhaps as cold as the famous ones of 1942 and 1943. I started taking German lessons from a man who lived with his wife in the attic of a villa on a hill. To get there I had to walk east into the wind that carried love all the way from Russia. My teacher, who had lost an arm on the eastern front and was a refugee, called it the Russian revenge. That winter I helped Mykola cut logs with a long saw for two hands. We got along well while doing it. I was not strong enough to use an axe to split the cut-up logs; for Mykola they were not a challenge.

By spring 1947 my mother must have become tired of my whining about school and found me tutors in the town where the school, not mine yet, was located, about an hour away by train from the village. I had four months to learn what I should have learned in two or three years. Swim or sink was my choice. I was given a month to show if I was capable of keeping afloat. If I was not, an expulsion would follow and make me earn another feather in my list of academic accomplishments.

The summer of 1947 was not good. I worked hard but got no encouragement. My two tutors probably did not know what the gaps in my education were, and I was not able to tell them. Often, I had time to kill between lessons and would waste hours sitting in the waiting room of the railroad station. In the summer of 1946, the bits of intellectual life I had had the chance to participate in at the camp kept me well nourished; in 1947, with all the catching up I had to do, trips to Regensburg had turned into a luxury I could no longer afford. Besides, on my brief visits there, I could sense that the camp had changed. The Ravich family was still there, but because of ill health, its patriarch was living in the hospital. The Polish Jewish couple had moved back to Munich where they had a room. Mrs. Sauer died minutes after having eaten a dinner as a guest of a Belarusian couple who had arrived at the camp a few days before this important event and then disappeared after cleaning up the mess the unfortunate woman could not help leaving behind. Being Soviet citizens, the couple had no right to the camp and how they got in and out remained a mystery. The case was closed and except for Mr. Sauer, who was recovering from shock at the home of one of his German relatives, no one seemed to care. Perhaps Mykola had been right: the camp was crawling with Soviet agents ready to assassinate great Ukrainian patriots like him. I distrusted Mykola's pronouncements because they often turned out to be wrong. His belief that the Soviets were determined to get rid of him was in my opinion delusional. He was not important enough to be worth the trouble. But I could have been wrong.

The Polish Americans were the first in my group of acquaintances to leave for the States. I inherited their dog, a Dachshund named Moritz. Having him as companion compensated a bit for the loss of the camp as my security blanket.

My mother liked to play the hostess, even at a time when entertaining seemed impossible. She would meet people on the train, mostly men, and invite them over for a homemade midafternoon dinner. Her need for company must have been so great that she could not resist doing something that was crazy even by the standards of those muddled times. Most of our guests were from the Balkans, well-educated older men. A few were young Poles in search of a woman to hook up with. Sometimes I worried that my mother would sell me to the highest bidder. Fortunately, none of the boys was interested in me. All of the above would have been of little importance if it did not interfere with my ability to make sense out of Evhen's sudden appearance on the scene. I should have been wondering why he came. Did my mother invite him? If so, why? As I had suspected, he and Mykola had little to say to each other. Their brief exchanges I had overheard in the past smoldered, crackled, and steamed the way unseasoned wood does before dying out in the stove. Perhaps Evhen wanted to have a look at the beautiful village I used to talk about on our walks along the Danube? I would have to show him around because my mother was not a fan of outings, and Mykola preferred to hang out at the soccer field.

First, I showed Evhen the street that led up the hill towards the Czech border. It had charm because of the old chestnut trees lining it on one side. For me they were a sign of stability. The war had bypassed them and now they were going to last for another century, providing shade to the Lutheran church, the TB sanatorium, and the nunnery, all symbols of an orderly life. On the other side of the street was the crowded cemetery that looked gaudy in summer with all the red and pink flowers on its graves. It looked so cheery that it reminded me of a country fair. It came with a morgue where bodies were sometimes displayed. The five-year-old granddaughter of our landlady told me proudly that her mother took her there to have a look at the man who had hanged himself. They wanted to see if there were red scars around his neck. Of course, I had to share this story with Evhen and let him know how I was spying on the natives. The favorite of my attention was a girl, probably not much older than I, who in foul weather used to walk with her dog in the middle of the street, kicking stones in anger. She definitely had style.

On top of the hill, where the row of chestnut trees ended, there was some kind of monument hidden in brambles and brush. I never found out what it was dedicated to or what its shape was. If it were just a grave that had escaped the cemetery, I did not want to desecrate it with my presence. It may have had some meaning to the natives, and, besides, the thicket it rested in looked impenetrable.

A few steps beyond this mysterious structure one could look down into the valley below, which, before harvest on sunny days in August, was a giant bowl filled with gold. The Czech border snaked its way through it, though I didn't know its exact path. On lucky days after a rain, a full rainbow would come to rest briefly over the valley, dipping its feet in the golden wheat. When Evhen and I were on our way to view this enchanting sight and see the deep blue of a cloudless sky highlighted by the gleaming yellows of the grains, he started talking to me about Rilke. While still in Poland, I had learned the names of great German poets Goethe, Schiller, and Heine. Two years later my German teacher, who had lost an arm on the eastern front, told me that Lessing should replace Heine on the list, because Heine's poetry was worthless. Perhaps it was, but I was too ignorant to pass judgment on Heine or my teacher's opinion. The only German poem that stuck with me was Goethe's "Der Erlkönig," in a Polish translation. "Wer reitet so spät durch Nacht und Wind…?" Now, decades later, I can still see the place where I first heard it: an unpaved country road lined with straggly young trees. There, inspired by the setting, my friend Runia's erudite mother, who had invited me to come along on their outing, began to recite the poem. The trees must have been alders, the evil spirit was the alder king, and because of the twists and turns my life was going through then, my father would not have been able to save me. Listening to the poem, I realized that I was doomed.

Rilke? I had never even heard his name. As we were climbing the hill, Evhen recited one of Rilke's poems to me, in German. A short poem it was, and its first lines did not make an impression on me, but its ending did: "Wer jetzt kein Haus hat, baut sich keines mehr …" Evhen has no home and will not build one… I too had no home, and with all my losses weighing so heavily on me, I may not be able to build one. Though still young, I felt once again that I was doomed. Doomed to the exile of being blown in the wind like the autumn leaves in the poem.

Evhen never talked to me of his own work as a poet. Had he ever said something of importance about it, I would have noticed and remembered. Rilke's poem had given him ideas how to express the pains of an exile, and he had been trying to put them down on paper, he told me that day. It had not been easy.

I did not keep track of Evhen's visits to the village: I did not miss him when he was not there and was glad to see him arrive. Now I regret not having paid more attention to his comings and goings and to his brief exchanges with my mother and Mykola. Perhaps if I had, I would have been able to get some insight into what happened in the woods on Evhen's final visit to the village.

A multitude of paths leading to and through the forested hills made the area ideal for long, leisurely walks. My favorite path was a logging road sheltered by a hill on one side and a sprinkling of trees and a creek on the other. It was easy to get to from where we lived, and, though it lacked spectacular vistas, it provided me with the daily opportunity to commune with nature. If one got off the road and climbed the hill, an outcrop would suddenly come into view: too high and too smooth to climb, five rocks stood next to each other to form a vertical gray wall spiked at the top. A church with five steeples? A fort? I thought of it as a castle that only I could enter. Indeed, it could be accessed from the other side if one did not mind braving boulders, briars, and brush that shielded the outcrop behind. The view from the top depended on the weather and the time of the day. It was most intense early in the morning when dew sparkled on the meadow below, and the sky was a cloudless deep blue. On days like that, the red tile roofs had sharp edges, the railroad station was in focus, and the trees on the hill against which the building was resting were black. That day we got to my castle in the afternoon when a grayish haze was filling the air.

"Follow me," I called out to Evhen as I climbed. "I will in a moment," he answered.

Evhen did not follow me.

Another moment passed.

"Where are you?" I called out to him.

He did not answer.

I should have shouted, but shouting in a foreign language might have disturbed the sensibilities of the natives who could have been within earshot. I climbed down as quickly as possible, no longer paying any attention to the briars. Having made sure that he had not fallen from one of the boulders, I ran from one nearby tree to another to see if Evhen was hiding behind one of them. Of course, he was too serious a man to play hide and seek with me. Perhaps he had to answer the call of nature in a country where men regularly pissed in the street. I had never seen him stay behind for that purpose and thought that he was too cultured to do it, even in the privacy of the forest. Or perhaps he had something urgent to say to my mother or Mykola and went back to say it. Nothing I could think of made sense, and, hoping to find an explanation for what had happened, I ran to the farm as fast as I could. Only my mother and Mykola were there, not Evhen. As soon as I entered the room, I could tell that something was afoot and whatever it was did not seem promising. Their faces were red, their eyes shiny, and there were traces of spittle around their mouths, as if they had been hissing.

"I lost Evhen in the woods," I called out crying. "Did he come here?"

"Yes, he stopped by on his way to the station."

"Did he say anything?"

They squirmed around looking for a lie, but were unable to come up with one on such short notice. "You won't be able to see him again," Mykola finally announced.

There was no time to ask why or start an argument. I ran to the station hoping that Evhen would still be there waiting for a train, but he was not. He must have taken off on foot in an unknown direction. Having nowhere else to go, I sat down on a bench near the ticket counter—the very same one that had welcomed me to the village in the middle of the night two years earlier—trying to make sense of the events. I tried then and, in a way, tried again and again when I had time for such idle thoughts. The best explanation I could come up with was that Mykola had followed us, and, while I was standing on the outcrop taking in the view, dragged Evhen out of the woods so quietly that I did not hear even a peep. Why Mykola had done it remained a question. Had I asked my mother, she would have answered with a lie or with "someday you will understand." As for Mykola, at least he did not lie, but I was sure he would tell me how hopelessly stupid I am, perhaps even retarded. Then his eyes would light up and he would break into laughter. Was he amused by my stupidity, or by what, according to my mother, I would understand someday?

Had I somehow offended Evhen and it was my fault that he left? I should have made an effort to find out, travelled again to Regensburg, and talked to Zoya or Alexander who may have been able to solve the mystery. Perhaps, on the other hand, they knew nothing about the incident in the woods and to spare Evhen and myself the embarrassment, it was better to keep them in the dark. I felt guilty and ashamed of being the cause of Evhen's contact with Mykola. The start of the school year saved me from my futile search for an answer. I had to study hard to keep afloat and let fate take care of the unresolved issue.

When I learned that Evhen had left Germany for the safety of New York City, I was surprised. In what kind of a place did he end up living until he died? A tiny room with sweating walls and cockroaches hiding in the kitchenette, just like the apartment I was living in at that time but in a different city? "Wer jetzt kein Haus hat, baut sich keines mehr..." For me life in America meant the loss of a cultural identity that I would not be able to replace. I don't know what it meant to Evhen. It seems that through all the trials and tribulations of exile he was able to keep his sense of identity. He was much older than I when he left his native country and, being brilliant, he had absorbed its culture by then. I, in contrast, was of mixed parentage, a child of refugees, and myself a refugee at a young age. To my sense of it, Evhen was lucky, and I was not.

I did see Evhen one more time, at Alexander's funeral ten years later, in the beautiful America where pursuit of happiness is guaranteed by the constitution. Some of the people who came to pay their last respects to Alexander I had run into in that other life, that life at the camp. The day was hot and humid. After getting up at dawn to make the train, I felt tired by noon. Former neighbors of the Ravich family invited me to lunch at their home in a giant apartment building in the slums of Newark. As drops of sweat were pouring down our faces—the fan was not of much help—my host, once a professor of chemistry, was telling me that life is good. He had a job, a wife, and no children about whose education he would have to worry. I nodded in agreement, while thinking of the airy rooms at the camp and the cool breezes blowing between the rows of red-roofed white houses.

During the funeral services in the church, I cried not just for Alexander, but also for the loss of my Ukrainian connection. At some point, it occurred to me that I should not be crying so much for someone who was not a relative. People may begin to wonder. But I could not control my tears. After the funeral, group photographs were taken. Evhen is in one of the two polaroids I was given as a memento of this important event. He and I are standing at the opposite ends of a row, four women between him and me. Our eyes met for a moment. That was our chance to exchange some words, but fate interfered. The group was breaking up in a hurry and, before I found my bearings in the crowd, a woman asked me if we could share a taxi to the station, a ride neither of us could afford on her own. Only a few trains were running in the direction she was going, and she needed to get there fast. When the taxi driver objected to our miserly tip, we had to search our pockets for coins. During the ride she had asked me about my connection to the group we had left behind, because it was obvious that I did not belong. I mentioned Alexander, Zoya, the chemist and his wife, and finally Evhen.

"He is a great man," she said with awe.

Did I already know this or realize it only then?

31

School

Slowly, I was learning the local language by listening: no dictionary, no grammar book, and at first no one to practice on. I had to guess the meaning of words from the context in which they occurred, right or wrong. My best classrooms were the trains I took to visit refugees in other towns. Sitting in a train compartment on trips that were inevitably long, because railroad lines had been among war's favorite targets and had to be repaired, made people sociable and talkative. Often, they had something interesting to say and some even volunteered to help me. At first, the only books I had access to were romances which, for a small fee, my mother was able to borrow somewhere. But when one of my traveling companions, a woman who lived in a nearby village, saw what I was reading, she offered to lend me real literature, so that I would not waste my mind on reading rubbish. The first two books she lent me were Meyer's novellas *Das Amulett* and *Gustav Adolfs Page*. I was impressed.

One day, something unexpected happened: I had friends. Well, perhaps not exactly friends, but kids my age I could talk to. I was no longer alone, sick of my own company. This change came at a price: I was permitted to attend a school on a trial basis, a school in which I would be the only foreigner. Put into a class appropriate for my age despite my poor academic background—missing several years of school, often not studying hard enough—I was given two months to prove myself. If I did not, well then... I hated to think about it.

It was not easy. I knew some algebra but no geometry. If I knew any history, it was of the wrong kind. And the language itself was not the one I had learned in the cradle, and I could not compete in it with the rest of the class. There were no books to study from. We had to listen to the teachers and take notes that had to be deciphered after school. I had no one at home to help me with that. Some students were able to take better notes because of their knowledge of stenography, and I was learning the rudiments of it from them. What I had to learn and absorb to make up for years of neglect, when learning was almost illegal, was endless. I just plodded along, doing the best I could without fretting or losing sleep over not being able to keep up with the rest of the class.

The school was in another town, Cham, some twenty kilometers from Furth, so I had to take the train there. That meant getting up at five in the morning and spending one hour traveling in railroad cars whose windows had been blown out by bombs. Soot in spring and fall, snow and cold in winter. From the station, the path to the school was straight, long and steep: up a hill which was the town's park with giant trees, past the Catholic church, an old people's home, and a historic cemetery with the unmarked graves of nameless prisoners who were all shot in March 1945 when they could no longer walk. After the trial period, I was allowed to stay at the school only because I was good at Latin, I assumed.

My school was no place for romance and getting caught at it would probably have meant expulsion. Yet, something must have happened in its halls of innocence, because one day the principal everyone was afraid of came into our classroom with the announcement: "All of you had better cut it out. The wives for you boys are still in kindergarten, the husbands for the girls are at the university." I, the stranger lacking any smarts in such matters, had no idea what he was talking about. Did someone get caught at kissing? I did not ask because it was still "them" versus "me," an abyss between us, that after years of war and brainwashing, I could not cross. Simply put, this was not my business and whatever business it was, I was not a part of it. My conscience was clear. Besides, I thought to myself, if men were so important to the girls in my class, they were in for a disappointment. Didn't they notice that the prospects of getting one looked bleak?

The principal was a good man, feared and respected. Since my fate was in his hands, I dreaded to talk to him lest he discover that my command of the language was not up to his standards. The man had lost his only son in the war, and even I, a stranger, could sense that he would never get over this loss. He was an angry man. "Be nice to him," a teacher once told my class. "He is a war casualty."

We did not talk about the war. And though we were hungry, we did not talk about food. The refugee kids were hungrier than the locals: one could tell by just looking at us. We were fed oatmeal for lunch. It did not even occur to me at that time that someone in the class could be talking about sex, though, perhaps the crude boys, the ones who were failing in their studies, did. Dull as they were, I avoided their company. If anyone in class had tried to pick on me, the outsider, it would have been one of them. That I did not learn any dirty words in my new language is one proof that I was not involved in conversations about sex. Did hunger help keep my fellow refugees' speech clean? I don't know. We did not talk about clothes either, as if we had already forgotten what people wear in normal times. Three dresses made into one to get rid of the holes, jackets with a multitude of patches, and trousers, shiny and threadbare at the seat, were staples of our postwar refugee couture, cleaned by hanging them out to air.

What innocent topics did we stick to, then? I remember discussing the play *Joan of Arc* with a friend of mine, the one who, I suspected, still admired Hitler, though since we never talked about politics, I could not be sure. Besides, I reasoned then, she was entitled to her views as much as I was entitled to mine. What could Joan have done after the fighting was over, we wondered. She would have had to get married or become a nun. Getting burned at the stake saved her from a dull life or perhaps even abuse and paved her way to sainthood. Joan's death was not a tragedy—we agreed on that. She was a lucky girl.

Some of the students in my class were very good at reciting poetry, be it in Latin or old German. They could get the rhythm right, whereas I could not. I explained it to myself by deciding that those poems were not written by someone sitting on a cloud up in the sky, but rather were sprung from the local soil, were a part of the scenery and, in a sense, belonged to the boys and girls reciting them. A Roman wall was right around the corner. The landscapes described were the same I could see, and the wisdoms they contained understandable and soothing. I was relieved that at least no one around me was saying, "He's a great poet, but you are too dumb to fathom the greatness of his poetry."

Those were the days...

Yes, truly! They were the happiest days of my life. I was learning things, had some people to talk to, and was respected for being able to keep my head above water. And yet, the writing was already on the wall, and I knew it. Those days were going to come to an end, and what was around the corner did not look good. Refugees had to be resettled or sent back to where they had come from. I had been put into the pipeline that would eventually lead to resettlement, and one day sooner or later I would have to leave unless something broke down along the way. Did I hope that it would? If it did, would I have been allowed to stay? I did not belong, neither here nor there, had been only a guest, my hosts were very nice, but guests do not stay forever. By not joining them for a class photograph taken at an excursion and not signing up for a course in dancing, I was trying to let my classmates know that I was aware of being an intruder and that they did not have to worry that I might overstay my welcome. Did they even notice what I was trying to tell them by my actions? Probably not, but my view of what they thought of me then changes with my moods now.

I also made friends in the village where my mother's reputation was not the best. One of them was the protestant minister's daughter. They too were refugees. She had very long braids, thick and blond, and was a year behind me in school in a class in which Greek was taught in addition to Latin. We began to talk to each other on the train, yet I was never invited to the rectory where her family lived. The other two were not friends but kind men who cared. One of them was the village doctor, a local from an old family, the other a refugee priest to whom I went for help when hopelessly stuck on the translation of some Latin sentences. Sometimes we would talk briefly about the important issues of the times, and while I was spewing out my venom against the church, he listened and often agreed with me. He held some unorthodox views for which he had been reprimanded by his superiors. I did not go to church, and, for me, the fat parish priest was the embodiment of what was wrong with religion: the farmers in his parish were trying to get on the good side of God by giving his servant an oversupply of food in a time of famine. I still wished to meet the girl who walked with her dog in the middle of the road when the weather was foul.

It was winter when my turn came to enter the pipeline that would lead me to paradise. By then my documents, real or fake, had to be in order and they were, because, for a fee, someone had been willing to testify under oath as having been present at my birth. So then came the train trips to the town where a regional center of the refugee organization that was handling the resettlements was located. Once there, I had to wait in a long line of applicants for my turn to be deloused, as no one was allowed to enter the holy site without having been anointed with DDT. Inside, the authorities poked and pried into the past and present of the powerless. All that was taking weeks and did not leave much time for attending school just when the class was getting its first exposure to calculus. No notes, no books, and no one to help me out, I was getting hopelessly behind and probably would not be able to catch up. Staying could mean giving up school, leaving would mean the same. And the decision was not up to me. What a time it became. Black or deep gray, rimmed with black—and I don't mean just the snow. As hard as I tried, I could not find a way out of this mess. Realizing that the war was over, and I was no longer a child, though too dumb and not yet old enough to strike out on my own, put an end to my time of great expectations.

And yet? I must have still been capable of dreaming.

Some civic organization in the village decided to offer an evening class in stenography, and I jumped at the opportunity. Once I mastered this skill, I would be able to take better notes in class and have more time for the drudgery of catching up. Besides, the notes for missed classes I would have had to copy from other students were often written in steno that I was unable to decipher, and so I was doing myself a great favor by taking the course. It was a spot of sunshine on a bleak landscape.

The class met in the basement of a building I would not be able to find if I went back there now. What I remember is not the building, but the path I had to take to get to it, the path to the village square. I remember too that when all the seats had been taken, people had to stand in the aisle and along the walls. The mood was festive; the women looked happy as they waved to connect with others they knew. I listened to the hum of their voices and tried to find a familiar face but did not recognize anyone. It was a very well-behaved crowd: they all settled down the moment the teacher entered the room. I learned something in that one hour of class and even got a manual I could dip into when lost. I was pleased. I was just reaching the door in the midst of the crowd when I recognized... the girl who walked in the middle of the road! She must have spoken to me first because I would not have dared. For a few minutes we talked to each other as if we had been friends for years. And I was able to speak to her like a native, flawlessly and fast. At the regular school, in the company of students who were aiming high, I felt like I was constantly under scrutiny. People wince at errors in grammar or pronunciation, and I hated to make mistakes. Whereas with her, I didn't even think of that. I could see how excited and happy she was over our meeting. Was she able to see that I was too? At the next class we were going to arrange to get together and practice what we were learning.

Except there was no next class—not for me. No more stenography instruction. No catching up to my level at the school in Cham. I had to leave the country two days later.

32

EH

I have your address. I found it on the internet. Since no one else with your name is listed, it is very likely the place where you are now living after your stint in Brazil. So, I could end up at your door one day, though of course I won't, not only because you will not remember me, but also because I don't want to see what a long life, however good, could have done to you. I prefer to keep you in my memory as the youngest, the smartest, and the most mature boy in the class. Decent and good at everything, you even dared to criticize Goethe. That such a mundane activity as the cooking of oatmeal makes me think of you is not flattering. Once upon a time you did not need to be flattered: you knew your worth and accepted praise with grace and humility. You were not one to show off. Did that change? I hope not.

What agency or organization do we have to thank for the oatmeal we lunched on five days a week and for the tasty wafers on Wednesdays? Was it the Marshall Plan? Courtesy of Quaker Oats? The Quakers? I don't think anyone knew the difference. The boys from the upper classes took turns dragging the giant pot up the hill, from the kitchen where it had been cooked to our school, where we, our tin cups in hand, lined up in the hallway to receive our share of the slop. When out of luck, one would end up with a cupful of lumps the size of golf balls, and when in luck, with a rare piece of some exotic fruit that had a way of settling in the slime at the bottom of the pot where it preferred to stay.

On the day hell broke loose, four boys from our class were entrusted with the delivery of our midday meal, and you were one of them. What happened? Some or all of the oatmeal got spilled on the way, a crime worthy of a death sentence. The principal, a good man everyone was afraid of, burst into our classroom to question the offenders. After hearing out the incoherent narrative of the other three, who must have been scared out of their wits, he turned to you: "From you, EH, I expect to hear a report that makes sense." Yes, though you were the youngest and excelled at boyish pranks, you could, even under pressure, collect your thoughts and string them into a coherent and logical account of events. I could see that you were flattered and at the same time embarrassed by being singled out: a trace of a smile on your lips and then a long, deep breath. You had to be careful about what you said. After all, you could not betray your classmates. "Yes, there was some horsing around on the way up, but not more than in the past… The path was slippery because of ice and snow… We should have been more careful, but it is difficult to see a patch of ice, under a layer of snow, however thin." Your poise and calm impressed me. I think the principal was so angry because for a few of the students who did not get any oatmeal that day, there would be no other meal.

Do you still remember the incident with the priest? In that case, too, the principal wanted to hear your story because it would have been the one closest to the truth. The priest had arrived early for our religion class, and the Protestant students were late to leave the room. They may have been held up by something they had no control over. Do you still remember what it was? It does not really matter, of course. The few infidels in the class, you being one of them, collected their stuff in a big hurry and with the hurry came the noise that sent the priest over the edge. It is hard to pack one's bags in a rush. He should have known that. And then, suddenly, there we all were, the few Protestants and the rest Catholics, facing a raging man, his face red, with sparks in his eyes. He started screaming. I was ashamed to watch the performance, perhaps even worried that that puny, little man might become violent. No one liked him. Religion was not an inspiring subject, not like the plays and the poetry we read, and the priest was not the inspiring kind. Students did not respect him, yet mostly they were not mean to him. They must have felt that he was too weak for their pranks and would not have been able to shake them off the way a strong man would.

How did the principal learn about the incident? You may have told your minister about it who then complained to the principal, and an investigation ensued. Again, the principal came into our classroom to question the students, seeming more upset than angry. No one in the class tried to defend the priest. Some of us must have felt sorry for a man who had made such a spectacle of himself. Perhaps you did too. When your turn came to testify, you were not as calm as the day you explained about the oatmeal. You had a cause and had to see to it that such incidents would not happen again. Some kind of a truce was reached between the class and the priest whom, after all was said and done, we did pity.

I knew that you were a German refugee living with your family in one of the small towns surrounding Cham. You had an older sister who was a year ahead of you in school. Not a pretty girl—but who am I to judge? Was she as smart as you? I tried to find out without asking anyone and had to conclude that she may have been smart and yet, did not stand out the way you did. You also had a father at a time when having one was rare: German fathers were either in some POW camp or missing in action or dead or too decrepit to count. Do you remember the railroad station we had to rush to at the end of the school day? When the train was late, we drank beer in its waiting room. No other beer ever tasted so good to me on a hot afternoon. It was at the station that I saw your father for the first and only time—just after you and he had run into each other unexpectedly. Was it on the day he came to town to let the principal know that you would be leaving school? You two looked so happy to find each other that I had to stop and watch until you separated. I doubt that you saw me staring: your eyes were on your father who seemed delighted to have run into you. A big, strong man with light-colored hair wearing a green Loden coat unbuttoned and the kind of boots men put on for hunting in the woods. Was this the man to whom you owed your wisdom, I wondered. Did he teach you everything you knew?

You had the courage to read to the class "The Tell-Tale Heart" instead of one of the standard classics that the teacher would have preferred. It was not a very appropriate time for peddling the works of the victors, but the students did not care: the story was a hit. It helped that you could read very well. I can still hear the pounding heart and feel the suspense.

There was also music. How did you learn so much about it when you did not seem particularly interested in it, at least not like the class musician Heinrich for whom music became a career? I don't remember our music teacher. Was he someone who just came in occasionally to make sure that the great musical heritage of your country was not forgotten? One day he played on the piano a few bars from some work for the students to identify. I, who couldn't even carry a simple tune, was, of course, the lesson's idiot, but did not feel bad about it, as there was no chance that I would ever grasp the rudiments of sound and rhythm. I enjoyed the class to which silence was my only contribution and admired the students who tried to guess and managed to come up with the right answers. It was suspense followed by excitement. That Heinrich was the best at this game was not surprising, but that you were not far behind him made my respect for you skyrocket. How can anyone be so good at everything? As some kind of a reward, the teacher played something easy, a few lines from one of Strauss's waltzes. Heinrich tried to guess its name and so did some of the other students, but no one was getting it. Was it so difficult because Strauss had composed hundreds of waltzes that all sounded the same, at least to me? Silence, the teacher waiting, the class running out of ideas when you called out "Wein, Weib und Gesang," making everyone cheer. Then you patted yourself on the shoulder for winning the jackpot.

Were you good in mathematics too? I never heard you professing great love for it. The guy crazy about it was Volkmar. Do you remember him? His seat was across the aisle from mine, so I was able to study his dirty, tattered clothes and see how unhealthy he looked with his red-rimmed eyes full of puss, and a paunchy middle. An epitome of neglect and an example of what happens when a family falls on hard times. He was a refugee, too, and lived with his mother and two brothers in a nearby village. His father had been killed on the eastern front. One day some lucky students in the class were presented with a gift of extra food, unlabeled mystery cans that some aid organization must have dug up in an abandoned bunker. Volkmar got one—I think we all knew he was the most deserving—and, with a jackknife, began to drill a hole in it during class. It was not easy. Sitting across the aisle from him, I had a good view of what he was doing. I was as much interested in the contents of the can as he was. His efforts paid off finally because he spent the rest of the class sticking his jackknife into the hole and licking off whatever was coating the blade. The "whatever" was some kind of a fruit jam. Volkmar was trying hard to keep out of the teacher's view, with the guy sitting in front of him providing the cover, because even at a time of such ubiquitous hunger, eating during class was not an acceptable behavior. As involved as Volkmar was in fishing out bits of jam from the can, he did look at me once and smiled. Even then I had enough insight to think that the smile was not for me but for the sweetness on his tongue. Have you ever thought as I have how lucky we were that in those days sugar was good for us? And so was chewing on a piece of side bacon until almost nothing was left of it.

To take on Goethe, the greatest of the greatest, was an act of courage, especially when the class was immersed in reading some of his works and had to admire the man not only for his writing but also for being someone who could do no wrong. And, of course, young as we were then, we needed heroic figures to inspire us. Was it *Die Leiden des jungen Werther* or one of Goethe's innumerable love poems that made you ask in an excited voice, "If he loved his Lotte so much, how could he love so many other women?" Your question made the teacher smile because he either did not know how to answer it without insulting the great poet or found your naiveté amusing. Though so incredibly clever, you were a dreamer who at the age of fifteen still wanted to believe in Goethe's fairytales.

You did not look like your father, your sister did, with her flat, rectangular face, a prominent jaw, a slightly turned-up nose—strong and handsome for a man, coarse for a girl. Your face was far from flat, your nose was big and hooked, your chin receding, your head had the shape of an egg, a tuft of unruly reddish blond hair on top, and you did not have the bulk of your father or sister, though that probably changed when food became more plentiful. I wish I could have seen you in your prime.

I often wondered what life would have been like for me had I been as clever as you and had had your poise and self-assurance. I did my best to stay afloat in school without a family for support and could not do more than that. My ambition was survival. You can't possibly remember—probably you never gave a second thought to this incident—how you came up to me to ask for the names of the two American observatories. Mount Wilson, I answered and then got stuck on the second one, Mount Palomar, that you also could not remember. I was so flattered by your faith in me, for thinking that I may know more than the other kids in our class, that my search for the name ended up in a black hole of my brain. And though I was unable to deliver that day, you made me feel proud. I am thanking you now for making me happy then.

As I understood it, no dating was allowed in school, and, as far as I could tell, there was none. No long glances for me to notice, no giggling or jokes for me to overhear. Being a foreigner from a country at odds with yours, I felt like my only viable position was to be an observer of the workings of a social group, not a participant in it. I did not want anyone to even consider saying, "Who does she think she is?" To see you with a girl one day surprised me. Do you remember her? The American everyone wanted to have a look at, as if she were some exotic animal in a zoo. As a student in one of the lower grades, she was probably only twelve years old. The single time I saw her I happened to be in town on a beautiful day in late June just before the beginning of the summer vacation. I had some time to kill before getting on the train and decided to take a walk to the old town square. In those days I walked just for the sake of walking and enjoyed every moment of it. I was on the bridge when you two were trying to cross the river below by stepping from stone to stone. It was a crazy undertaking. Do you still remember it? Was it your idea or hers? I could watch you unseen, since all your attention was on the rocks and on how to keep the girl and yourself from slipping into the water. You had to hold her hand or her arm and even her body when you both ended up on the same rock. Quite a dance it was. The girl was very pretty and still only a child, short black curls around her face, wearing a beautiful dress, and white socks, and shiny black shoes on her feet. Dressed like that she did not fit into this town. Walking in the street, she would have attracted attention. You, on the other hand, were wearing your only jacket which was threadbare in places, its sleeves patched with leather. The typical post-war chic. How did the two of you manage to connect? Did you ask her for a date or did someone suggest that you give her a tour of the historic sites? Did she stay in school? Once the novelty wore off, she was no longer making a buzz, and I stopped hearing about her.

In February of the following year, you left school, and our class mourned for you. First your family moved to the Rheinland, waiting there for a while before being shipped off to Brazil, where your engineer father was going to run an automobile plant. I left school a couple of months after you did and ended up in a hell of a place. I am mentioning it only so that you know how my writing is affected by that experience. A few years later, on one of my postwar pilgrimages to our school town, I learned that you had studied

"Maschinenbau" and become a mechanical engineer instead of an academic. Our class teacher told me that he had run into you, your sister, and your parents in a theater in Munich. Every few years your family was entitled to a trip back to Germany all expenses paid. That was the last time I heard anything about you.

And then I stopped going back to our old school town.

It was too painful.

33

The Girl from Furth

It must happen, maybe even often, that a connection unexpectedly occurs between two people, a connection in this case that lasted for only a few minutes but that has stayed in my memory for what seems like forever. This connection hurts, like a wound that refuses to heal. To stop the pain, if it can be stopped, I have decided to reconnect to you by writing you this letter. And should that not work, at least it will give me a chance to finish the conversation we started so many years ago.

Because you may no longer remember me, I should introduce myself first: I am the refugee girl who arrived in your village at the end of the war. An Ausländerin, a DP—always said with a sneer. I was once even called the foreign cripple. Foreign? Yes. Cripple? No. That is how it is when one isn't among one's own. To avoid encountering the natives and hurting their sensibilities, I did not go into the village, but rather took walks through the woods behind your house. Yet we did not run into each other there. I no longer remember when I began to notice you. I only remember why. You had a dog, a big one, and when the foul weather was keeping people indoors, you two walked in the middle of the road because it was all yours then. You would throw sticks for the dog. The way you threw them made me think that they were meant to hurt someone, though certainly not the dog. You were out walking when it was blowing snow or raining so hard that water would run across the road making it into a creek. Sometimes, when you did not have a stick to throw, you would kick an icy snowball or a rock that happened to be in your way, and you did it as if that kick was meant for someone you wanted to hurt. You must have been angry, I thought, but of course had no idea why. Had you known that I was watching you from behind the gray picket fence, trying to blend into it, perhaps you would not have kicked so hard. War should have made me angry—losing a home, a father, a brother, and friends; being on the move for years and ending up where I was not welcome, with a mother who was prone to irrational behavior and, at times, had to be watched like a child. But instead of kicking anything at all, I stayed behind fences, took solitary walks in the woods, and just like you developed a penchant for going out in foul weather. Braving the eastern winds, I would trudge up the hill in deep snow to the one-armed veteran who was helping me learn German. A walk to remember, much easier on the way down when the wind was on my back. Did you know them? He and his wife lived in the attic of that solitary villa and were refugees, like I, except that they were not foreign. Not being an Ausländer was a tremendous advantage in the scheme of postwar life—and it turns out it still is.

When you were walking in the middle of the road while I was hanging out at the fence, the distance between us was too great to see what kind of a face you had. Your hair was dark and in that heavy coat of yours you looked bigger than I, and older. The house you used to head for was set back from the road to make room for the rows of logs stacked up in front of it, ready to be shipped by rail from the station conveniently located almost at the door to the lumberyard. For a long time, I did not know your connection to the house: were you a part of the owner's family or merely a servant? But no servant would dare walk in the middle of the road—not even in bad weather—throw sticks in anger or kick ice balls and rocks. So, I decided, you had to be a part of the family.

I was learning about you little by little. It seems that our landlady, the owner of the farmhouse where we were lucky enough to have a room to live in, found your behavior rather odd. While picking up some food from her kitchen—potatoes and nettles paid for with cigarettes—I overheard her talk to some woman about you. Not wanting to let an opportunity to learn more German pass, I always listened carefully to what the natives had to say, though I never felt certain if I was understanding them correctly. Gossip or not, I learned that you and the doctor's daughter were the richest girls in town, and if men of suitable age had not been in very short supply after the bloody war, and if you had not been a little bit off your rocker, you would have been surrounded by suitors. Yes, they would be lining up at your door. Impressive. You were going to inherit the lumberyard and needed a man to run it. If what I overheard was true, I wondered how you felt about it. Homeless as I was, I had no door for suitors to line up at and that was fine with me. What I was wishing for then was being able to get into the German school. As for my inheritance, if any, the Revolution had already taken care of it before I was born.

Did you by any chance have an older brother who was supposed to take over the business after coming back from the eastern front? If you did, that could have been the reason for your anger and your need to walk in the middle of the road kicking stones. I did not hear anyone talk about him. He either did not exist or people were too respectful to speak about the war dead and summed up the losses with the words "Ach, Russland." Shot, frozen to death, or taken prisoner.

Why weren't you in school, I wondered. Eventually I learned that you had spent some time at a boarding school in a nearby town, an institution run by nuns where rebellious girls were taught how to behave. It must have cost your parents a fortune to keep you there and what a waste of money it was because even the good nuns could not tame you. That, according to our landlady, was a disgrace. Good for you, I thought. There is no glory in being pushed around. And your dog? He could not be with you while you were serving your time there. Poor dog. I felt sorry for him. He, too, owned the road you were walking on, but it was not his without you.

By this point, if you are actually reading this letter, you may be wondering why I am writing it. There are some questions I would like to ask you, and I would also like to let you know how I felt about our meeting when it finally happened.

I did get into the school and survived the six-week-long trial period. If I had not, I would have been thrown out, like a piece of garbage. And had I been thrown out, I would be, still to this day, suffering from shame. Once I had made it, I could proudly take the train to Cham on a student pass, climb the hill to the school, from which one could overlook the valley, end up in a classroom that had its share of German refugee children, and listen to them recite Goethe's poems. It was not easy to stay afloat: after missing years of schooling, I was behind in all subjects. There were no books—I had to reinvent geometry to keep up in trigonometry—and students had to use stenography to take notes in class because to remember all the details of the lectures was impossible, at least for me. Yet, those were the happiest times of my life. I had friends, refugee girls with names like Brigitte, Eva Maria, and Ulrike, and was even invited sometimes to their humble homes. And I had earned the respect and the support of my classmates, even of those who were local. They seemed to like me, and so I liked myself. Still, I was very careful not to step out of my territory or threaten to become one of them or lay claims to what they were entitled to.

While attending school, I did not see you often. How could I, when I had to leave the village before sunrise and return after sunset, every day of the week except Sunday? Were you aware that I was going to school, to a gymnasium at that? Besides me, three other students from the village attended my school in Cham: the daughter of the Protestant minister—she was younger than I—and the von Perger young men, one of them so handsome that I was too embarrassed to look at him when we faced each other briefly on the train. Did you know them? They, too, were refugees: the girl lived in the manse, the young men in a mysterious mansion in the forest behind the railroad station. I did not dare to climb the hill to have a peek at it, though I was curious.

In those days I was a dreamer or why else would I have signed up for a stenography class offered by the wise elders of the village? My classmates had learned about it when the school opened up after the war, but I was not there at that time. To miss a chance to catch up, to fill in the void, I found my way to the community center in the village square where someone was going to talk about the virtues of stenography. Germany was to become a normal country and would need secretaries to take dictation. The lessons were free, the manual was not, though well worth the investment.

That evening in the middle of March, there were remains of icy snow on the ground and the air was freezing cold. I had arrived early to make sure that I found my bearings in a building I had not been to before. The large room, filled with rows of chairs, was almost empty when I arrived but began to fill as soon as I had found a seat. For me it was an unusual sight: so many locals stuffed into what once may have been an air raid shelter, some standing along the walls, some even sitting on the floor. And there were men in the crowd, older men, not boys. With all those bodies heating up the room, people began taking off their coats and, without a place to hang them, dropping them on the floor. None of the air raid shelters I had been to were as untidy or stuffy. Finally, someone opened the door to the outside so that we could breathe again.

Do you remember all that? The heat, the crowd, its enthusiasm for stenography? Why do I still remember so well a room I had sat in for a single hour, my mind on the problems I had been facing? The proceedings for my departure had already been set into motion and that meant taking a train to Amberg where the authorities would look into every crevice of my body to see if I was fit for export. Sometimes I even had to stay there overnight to be available for examination before sunrise. I got jabbed and shoved and had DDT sprayed around my face and into my underpants—all that, while my fellow students were sitting in a classroom, learning calculus. It was not at all clear that after getting so far behind I would be able to catch up on my own: a tragedy in the making that my departure would solve. But I did not want to leave and was hoping that some doctor would find a spot on my lungs that would make me unfit for departure. A touch of consumption would do the trick and I would be able to go back to school, and once I did, stenography would help me catch up. These are the thoughts that brought me to the community center. Yes, it would take a miracle, but I could still end up among my kind classmates and try to reinvent calculus. Belief in better tomorrows is the privilege of the young, and I was practically still a child then.

Yes, there would be a test a month or so later and if we did well on it, we would earn a certificate. To find someone to practice with would help; it was almost necessary. The meeting over, the crowd began to move towards the exit, the bottleneck we had entered through, though there must have been another way out, a door that remained closed. To get into the cellar, we had climbed down a flight of narrow stairs and now, before being able to step onto the street, we had to climb them. The progress was slow, but I was in no hurry. To have a better look at my classmates I lingered in the crowd, hoping to find a familiar face, and finding none—not even yours, because I had previously seen you only from a distance. I knew that your hair was dark and that in winter you wore a bulky coat, ochre in color. Without the dog I couldn't recognize you.

And then it suddenly happened: as I was just standing there, not far from the exit, letting people pass in front of me, you stopped next to me and said clearly, "I know who you are. We should meet for practice." You did not say that you knew that I was the girl who had been watching you from behind the picket fence. I want to thank you for that. I preferred to think that you knew of me, because I was the only Ausländerin in Furth to have made it all the way to the Gymnasium in Cham. You seemed very happy to have me standing next to you: your face was glowing, your eyes sparkling. True, we had been sitting in an overheated room. But even I, who never expected good luck to be on my side, was convinced that having connected with me was the cause of your excitement. What I was seeing in your face was real. I could trust you and be just as happy as you were. We started making plans where and when to meet. The community center had a small reading room, an ideal place for practicing shorthand in winter. Once spring arrived, we could go into the woods and, on warm, sunny days, sit on tree stumps or logs. And there, you would tell me about yourself, what was making you so angry that you had to kick stones that were in your way. I really wanted to know. And I might have told you about myself, just a little bit, because the story of my broken family was a secret that I was not yet willing to share with anyone. Had you learned about it, you might not have wanted to become my friend. And to have found a friend among the natives of the village was making me very happy and proud at that moment.

I am now writing to you to apologize for not having been able to meet you for practice. Perhaps I should have gone to your house and told you about the change of plans, but I did not want to get you in trouble with your parents, since to have become friends with an Ausländerin was nothing to be proud of.

A few days after our first and only meeting, I was taking an endless train to the north, knowing full well that I would never get over the pain of leaving.

34

Father Zeisel

I am finally answering a letter I should have answered many years ago. The letter you wrote to me in 1949. Ashamed as I felt by your accusations, I did not know how to respond to them. Some years later, when I was passing through the town where we had met, I tried to look you up and explain, but you were no longer there. You had moved to another part of the country and to try to find you in a faraway place would have been too much of an effort.

Since you may no longer remember me because so many years have passed since we last saw each other, I will have to reintroduce myself. I am the girl you met on the train and later helped with some schoolwork. Thank you for having been so kind. I would go up to your mansard room and knock on its door—there was no way to let you know in advance that I was coming—and when you were in, you would help me translate some convoluted Latin sentences. Once you even dictated to me a brief biography of Jesus I needed for my religion class, facts I more or less knew, but you put them in a nice order, and I got the highest grade for it.

I loved the street you lived on. When I had no time to go into the forest and had to settle for a short walk in town, that was the street I would take to get a view of the valley below: up a hill, past a church, a TB hospital and your house where the nuns who took care of the sick lived; old, giant trees lined your side of the street, across from it was the cemetery, crowded but peaceful.

On trains, people talked. Stuffed as they were into a compartment with nothing to do, they amused themselves with tales of what they had to leave behind, true or false, and tried to learn what ideas were floating around about the future of refugees that the East had disgorged. In those days I was spending a lot of time on different trains: to get to school and back or to visit some camp where I had friends or to deliver goods my mother was black-marketeering in. I was too young and too insignificant to participate in the conversations of adult travelers. Overhearing what they had to say was my forte. Occasionally someone addressed me and that is how I learned about you. A very nice man... speaks German, Hungarian, and Slovak... a refugee... a priest... I was curious, and to check you out, I sat down in the compartment where you and a group of refugees were sitting. I had to hear first-hand what you had say. That is how we met.

We kept running into each other on the train and sometimes we talked. You listened to people as if what they were saying was of great interest to you though you did not always agree with them. All were entitled to their own opinions, and the opinions expressed on trains were as diverse as the people expressing them. Soon you knew why I had to commute and began to talk to me about my schoolwork. That I was a foreigner, the one and only, attending a local school was an anomaly in those days because of recent history. The wounds of war don't heal overnight. "If you need any help with Latin, you can come to see me." Latin was my favorite subject because I could beat my classmates at it, but sometimes I could not pull off a good translation of the text from one foreign language into another just as foreign, and so I began to go to you for occasional help.

What would people think now of our meetings? A sixteen-year-old girl visiting a priest in his bedroom? Did the nuns keep an eye on you and me? Or did they eavesdrop on our conversations? It never occurred to me that there could be something improper about my visits. I may have been dumb and unenlightened, but my instincts were good or I would not have survived a life in the streets. I could tell lascivious looks when I saw them long before I had any understanding of what they meant. In your room, I felt safe.

It was not all Latin, though. Sometimes we talked about politics, world events, religion or school, but never about my mother. Speaking to you about her could have saved me some grief later on. When I was only four years old, I already noticed that, at times, she was "not quite like other people." At that age, with my limited grasp of concepts and vocabulary, that was the only way I could describe her personality. I was not sophisticated enough to use the word "normal," and so if not normal then crazy... but I was not yet ready to call her that. Even now, despite being older and hopefully wiser, I still have no idea what was wrong with her. On the day I lost my father—I was barely ten years old then—I saw clearly what my life with my mother would be like. Yes, she was going to see to it that I would not starve—after all she did love me in her own way—and to do that she had to avoid risky adventures that would endanger her and me. In a sense we were each other's keepers. I tried my best to make her look good and often lied to cover up her transgressions. Had you asked me about her, I might have told you the truth, the truth as I knew it anyway. But you never asked and thus saved me from betraying her.

When we talked, my attacks on the Catholic church did not disturb you. Why was the Protestant church helping my Protestant classmates, while the Catholic church did nothing for the Catholic students? Why was the parish priest growing so fat on food contributions from his parishioners while refugee children were starving? And on and on... I had plenty to complain about. You listened and sometimes even agreed. In those days I was not yet willing to take on God, at least not publicly. If He existed, His punishment might be so severe that it could push me over the edge, and I was not quite ready for that. I had to protect myself, because, after all, it was not kindness that had made God so famous. You once told me—I remember it very well—that a number of times you had been reprimanded by your superiors for spending too much time in the company of sinners who needed a priest to talk to. Who were the sinners, I wondered. Were they women of ill repute—I still was not quite sure what that meant—or was it someone like me, ordinary and harmless? I was afraid to ask you for an explanation.

Politics and world events were other endless topics, though at that time the great powers were taking a rest before starting another war, and the next apocalypse was not yet on the horizon. So, we must have talked mainly about the losses we had suffered in the war that left us without a home to return to. One day, after a particularly sad exchange about my past, the uncertain future and what was happening in-between, you put your arms around me and said, "It's a cursed inheritance your country got from the war in exchange for the land in the east..." I knew that it was going to become a disputed piece of real estate and began to cry. So did you. Do you remember? How long did we stand there near the table in the middle of your white room crying? That you kept holding me in your arms convinced the wary me that you did indeed want to ease the pain, yours and mine. Only now do I realize how much that gesture meant to me then.

Many years later I met someone on a train, between Marseilles and Paris, who looked like you: similar build and face, dark hair, dark skin, lively brown eyes, your smile and your animated way of talking and probably the same age as you, had time been standing still. A Doppelgänger, perhaps, if there is such a thing. He was a physicist, either Swiss or French, a handsome man. Seeing him brought back the memories of our time together. Remembering you felt good.

I left school in March 1949 and emigrated with my mother to the land of milk and honey where streets are paved with gold. I did not want to leave, but staying was not an option. After arriving in that garden of Eden, I sent you a letter which you probably did not like because it was full of complaints. Ridiculed for my braids, fingers pointed at me as if I were some kind of a scarecrow, learning, even before getting through customs, that schools were not going to be free—why the hell did I expect that they would be?—at least I was not going to sleep under a bridge because a job and a room were already waiting for me. It was a long trip from the boat to the town that was going to welcome us with open arms. Waiting rooms with glaring lights, trains without bullet holes. At transfers, grinning ladies, their faces crusted with make-up, were making sure that I got on the right train and had something to eat. A hot dog, unnaturally red, a donut, and a soda. It was April and spring had arrived unusually early. The train had to cross the great river and keep going through its floodplain like a boat. I remember the water, pink at sunrise, on both sides of the tracks. The sight was so bewitching that my old fear of drowning didn't surface. As we got closer to our destination, the landscape did begin to look frightening: an endless snow-covered flatland with no tree in sight. I did not yet know that the state tree was the telephone pole.

You answered, but your letter did not assuage my fears for the future. I was not going to fit in without changing myself into someone else, and I either was not able to do that or did not want to. In my response to you I took up the nuns in whose care I had ended up. For a country founded on the premise "dog eat dog," they were not overly wicked, but their smugness and hypocrisy were monumental. Though I'd been raised on slogans like "Edel sei der Mensch, hilfreich und gut...," I was no longer so naive as to believe that such sentiments were true. Still, I was stupid enough to expect that God's servants, even when unable to subscribe to some high moral principles, would at least follow the Ten Commandments—which these did not.

Your second letter, the one I am finally answering, began with the news: "After you two left, your mother became the talk of the village... She had claimed to be a countess..." Etc... etc... My face began to burn, my hands shook, and I either did not read to the end or was too upset to follow the list of her transgressions. I stuck it between the pages of one of the books lying on the table and rushed off to work. To reread it later was my plan, except that in the evening, when I finally had the time to look at it, the letter was gone. Only my mother could have taken it. She liked to rummage through my stuff for secrets and stole things sometimes.

After she died, I looked for that last letter of yours among her papers, even though I did not expect to find it. To make sure that it would never fall into the wrong hands, she must have burned it in a hurry. I couldn't blame her for that. Asking about it when she was still alive would have been pointless. "Letter? What letter? I don't know what you are talking about." And she would have looked at me confused, as if she really did not have the slightest idea what letter I was referring to.

I could have responded to your letter by claiming that gossip was just gossip, none of it true, or by admitting that the stories she had made up for a rapt audience were indeed lies, however harmless. The latter would have been a betrayal, and since I was not yet ready for that, I chose silence. Besides, since I no longer had your letter, only part of its contents in my mind—and that hazy—it would have been difficult to address its charges. Did you ever wonder why I gave up on you just when I was in such great need of moral support?

Some years later, while visiting Germany and passing through the village whose beauty I could not resist, I stopped at the nunnery and asked for you. By then I was ready to admit, "Yes, my mother was a liar, sometimes even a thief. Lying and stealing helped her survive two wars and became her second nature. Often some stranger would plant an idea in her mind, some kind of an evil seed that she would nurture until it developed into a big lie."

Once, I heard her tell someone, "We had a visa for England... We should have fled..." at which that someone then asked if she were an English spy. She did not say "Yes," and neither did she say "No." Instead, she smiled the kind of smile that is no more than a quiver in the corner of one's mouth. It meant that she liked the idea, because otherwise I would not have heard her later confiding to someone that, "During the war I worked for the British."

Is there truth in any of this, you might have wanted to ask me, if I had delivered my little speech to you. Eventually, I was able to ascertain that the year the war broke out, we did not have a visa for England, but we did have a piece of paper from the British consulate stating that some documents needed for one had been filed and validated. When we finally fled Wilno, it definitely was not to England, but rather from that frying pan into the fire of German-occupied Poland. We managed it at the very last moment just before the closing of the borders. I can't blame my mother for not having wanted to leave a place that still felt like home.

The German village, for a short time yours and mine, was filled with post-card charms: red-roofed houses nestled in a hollow surrounded by forests and misty hills. I who had felt myself to be the village pariah back then, hoped to just slip in for a visit unnoticed. You were the only person I wanted to see. When passing the farm where my mother and I had once lived, I hastened my pace and tried to look the other way. The farmer's family could have recognized me—after all, they saw me daily for almost four years—but fortunately, the only person I saw near the fence to their garden was a girl, about nine years old and just the right age to be the daughter of the farmer's wife and the French POW who had helped her run the farm and more, while her husband was stuck on the eastern front and eventually taken prisoner. He survived and was on his way home when his poor wife tried to find a solution to her unbelievably long pregnancy. She turned to my mother for help. My mother, who had a talent for taking charge in times of crisis, found a refugee doctor from the Balkans of all places, who tried to induce labor in the attic room we lived in then. I was sent into the woods for the day and had no idea what was going on. The procedure did not work. Was this one of the pieces of gossip you wrote to me about? Do you count it as one of my mother's transgressions? Do I?

I don't think I do.

The only person who may have recognized me was the woman I talked to briefly when I inquired about you at the house where we used to meet. She was not a nun, but rather some kind of a servant. You had moved to a town on the Bodensee, she told me. Should I have asked her for your address? I wanted to let you know that I still remembered you and missed our Latin lessons.

While I stood at the door undecided, she was looking at me as if I were a ghost or had arrived from another planet. "You must have come from America," I heard her say when I was leaving, and my back was already turned to her. I did not have to answer and did not want to. How could she tell? Did she remember me or did she notice that I was wearing sneakers that were not yet in fashion in the village?

I hope that you had a good life and no regrets about having sent me that letter.

35

Mama

It's about the silverware set you bought me a long time ago when I was young and newly married. It was not something I needed or wanted, but it was a part of your tradition: the dowry that you thought you owed me even when you had to buy it on the installment plan. It was a sacrifice I did not fully appreciate then. Now I do. For some sixty years the set was well taken care of and used only for company. I preferred to use the cheap flatware, the Woolworth variety, which was more in line with my values and lifestyle. So, the silverware was as good as new when, at the end of my life, I have had to start getting rid of my belongings. A man came to the house—a dealer, an auctioneer or a pawnbroker or whatever else creatures of that kind are called—and descended on my belongings the way a vulture descends on a corpse.

It was before my trip to the hospital that I last wrote a story. With my mind so befuddled by my stay there, I am afraid to give it a try. Even typing has become more difficult, let alone thinking. But without writing, I get even more depressed than I should be. It's not over facing death; rather, it's the waiting for some new symptoms to appear—a burp, a fart, a feeling of nausea, however slight, a touch of pain in the abdomen—and wondering if they will lead to another trip to hell.

So, here I go. I write. I could call this "Econ 101." Or "The End." But I'm calling it "Mama." Afterall, you're the one who taught me most of what I know about economics. And I don't really know when the end will come.

***

At what age did I begin to grasp the value of money? It must have happened in the third year of my life because, before I turned four, we moved to a small town at the border and by then I had already lived through my experience with Grandma and her bag of gold. Moving from town to town helped me keep track of years and sometimes even months. Thus, I know that it must have happened while I was still three years old and that it was not one of those eureka moments but more of a slow realization that some things in life are free and some have to be paid for. It cost money to stay alive, whereas to soak up the beauty of a city cost nothing. The sight of the hills, trees, and flowers often moved me to tears. So did the majesty of some of the buildings in town: the white walls of the cathedral shining in the sun and even the crumbling remains of a castle. And then there were two rivers to look at, the big and the little: one that raged black or rippled silver, one that trickled soothingly between rocks and water weeds.

One day Grandma arrived, an event Mama had been preparing us for. She was not like the welcoming grandma from *Little Red Riding Hood*, but rather an evil woman who would force Mama, who already had two small children to take care of, to work even harder than she already had to. Worst of all, she would order Mama around and Mama preferred ordering to being ordered. The two women would end up fighting and our apartment did not have enough room for that. From what I overheard, I gathered that Papa tried to convince Mama to be nice, to let Grandma come, and to see if peace was possible. After all, Grandma, the selfish woman, owned a bag of gold, and the possibility existed that she would share some of it with us. I had not yet had enough experience in my life to have an opinion.

Grandma was a small, dried-up woman dressed in black, and she did have a bag of something that she always kept near her. She would take it with her when out for a stroll or a visit and kept it under the bed when asleep. I never saw its contents, so I can't say now if it was gold or not. Heniuś and I did our best to dissuade Grandma from staying with us. He, being four years older than I, was way ahead of me in experience and inventiveness. It was his idea to cover Grandma's feet with pots and pans when she was trying to take a nap on the cot in the kitchen and had asked us for a blanket. Yes, it may have been cruel, but we were only doing our best to help Mama, and it worked. One day the bag of gold was gone, and so was our Grandma. I wish I could say that we lived happily ever after.

It took me at least another year to begin to understand what being poor meant and why we were so terribly poor. It all had to do with the War and the Revolution I knew nothing about until we moved to the next town, where a kind neighbor and mother of five grown children did her best to enlighten me about the bloodletting humanity was so addicted to. Napoleon was her hero because he wanted to get rid of the Russians. She even gave me the impression that she had seen him riding through the fields on his white horse.

For Papa's family, first came the War and then the Revolution, which was worse than the War. To avoid being dismembered by the angry peasants, Grandpa and Grandma had to flee from their estate, leaving everything but the bag of gold behind. First, they went to Odessa and then to Constantinople. Grandpa died from a broken heart somewhere along the way, while Grandma continued to Poland where her three sons had already fled. One of them would have to take her in and provide her with a home; the choice was up to her. The oldest son had no family nor an apartment of his own. Her youngest son, my Papa, was still at the university trying to get a license to practice law in a foreign country. If we had more space than just a kitchen to live in, I was not aware of it. The middle son was best off: he had a job and a family. He even sent us photographs of his children sitting on tricycles and fancy rocking horses with hairy manes and tails. His apartment was big enough to fit another person in. Mama was glad to be rid of Grandma, but not of the gold. She said that Papa's brother was doing it for the money and that a part of it should have gone to us. At the time I thought that Mama was right.

A few years later, I learned from a former neighbor that Grandma was a charming woman, clever and lively for her age. She had even done what few people would have dared to do: when a fire broke out in the family mansion, she threw her children into a snow drift from a second story window, before jumping to safety herself. No one got hurt. When robbers came to steal her jewels, she distracted them by dancing on the dining room table until servants arrived to save her. I don't think that even Mama, who could be very brave, would have been able to pull off anything like that. Many years later, I met the cousin whose family had taken Grandma in and provided her with a loving home until she died during the war in my cousin's arms. I will never know what happened to the bag of gold, but I do know that that family stayed together—unlike mine—and its children were well educated.

When we moved from the city to a small town at the border, I still did not understand the value of money. What I really cared about didn't cost anything: the endless field at the edge of town, the red berries of the rowan trees lining our street, the hill behind our house and the stories it came with. Then there were other people's gardens with flowers, strawberries, and currant and raspberry bushes, and the smell of horses, and the feel of their hair and skin. Peasant cottages were more beautiful than the crumbling castle in the city. The cottages had two rooms—one for the cow, one for the people—and hollyhocks grew along their walls. We hardly had any furniture, but neither did the people we visited.

Mama liked to dress up in fancy clothes. She looked like a queen in the dress she had to rent for a ball. That it was not truly hers upset her. "I have nothing to wear," she kept saying. I already knew from Cinderella that one needed a fancy dress for a ball and even golden slippers. That Mama had neither meant that we were poor.

We had to move again because moving from place to place was a part of Papa's job. The town we moved to was even more beautiful than the town we had moved from, and it was not sitting right on the border. "It will be safer here," Papa said, but he was wrong. Our new apartment was in the courthouse, except that it was not new and had to be fixed up first. Two rooms, the living and the dining, were for entertaining guests. Papa found somewhere a pile of broken-down furniture and had it carefully restored to suit his tastes. The wood was oiled walnut, the upholstery grayish blue velvet. And to make sure that people thought that we had class, or whatever it was called, he told the admiring guests that we had inherited it from some distant relatives. The other three rooms had nothing more in them than beds and some tables and chairs; I liked them in their emptiness because they resembled the rooms I was used to.

Now that we were living in an apartment people could admire, Mama set out to get some decent clothes for Papa and herself: winter coats with fur collars and linings and the kind of fine wool fabric that was going to last forever. Mama wanted to get herself a Persian fur coat, but had no money left. "Someday I will get one," she promised. "We are coming up in this world." Yes, we were. Even I could see that. Perhaps someday we would be able to buy a peasant cottage or better yet, return to the estate of Papa's family where, according to Papa, the scent of mock orange was sweeter and stronger than anywhere else.

The good days had to come to an end because nothing lasts forever. People had been talking about another war breaking out and, as if to harden us for what was about to come, Heniuś died, and I got sick. I was still in the hospital when we moved back to the city, but by the time I was discharged, the air raid sirens were going on and off, windowpanes had been decorated with white paper tape, and we were given one gas mask for the three of us. I had no idea what we were supposed to do with it. Suddenly, like in an epiphany, the meaning and importance of a bag of gold became clear to me: soon Papa would have no job and we would starve.

Some of our furniture must have already been sold before we had moved to the city, because our apartment, as small as it was, would have only one pretty room and two others with beds only. It was no longer safe to be rich. There was little fighting when the troops arrived. After they had finished looting the stores, life almost went back to normal, and people began to go out again in search of bread. But even I, still a child and not very bright, could smell fear in the air. Even the young men, once so cheeky, avoided attracting attention. When Papa would have to stop working, we were doomed.

I kept track of what was happening. At first, when it was still possible, Mama would take me for lunch to a soup kitchen, but to give people the impression that life was back to normal, it was closed down after a few weeks. Chocolate was no longer sold in the grocery store next door because chocolate did not grow nearby, but the hard candy was still there, in a jar on the counter, as colorful as before. Mama stopped caring if I was anemic or not and was no longer forcing me to eat boiled spinach. That was one of the war's good sides. I was not going to get the doll promised to me after Heniuś had died, because dolls had disappeared once the department store had been looted and shuttered. And my dress, so short as to be obscene, was not going to be replaced.

When refugees began to arrive in the city—some from the west, some from the east—Mama managed to rent one of our rooms to a mother and daughter duo who, after their flight from somewhere, had been counting on their rich relatives to provide them with lodging. Unfortunately, at the beginning of the war, the rich, who must have been in a state of denial, were not yet ready for such a sacrifice. It was only after the arrival of the troops, that they began to look for people with whom they could share their empty rooms. We lost our tenants when their own family was ready to welcome them. It was my first lesson in what it meant to be rich. It made me think of Grandma, the Revolution, and her bag of gold.

Papa and his friends kept talking about fleeing, but every time they tried to find a place to flee to, it turned out to be a dead end. Going east was not an option, going west was. In fact, people who had come from the west were trying to get back to where they had come from. If it sounds very confusing, it was! It was not easy to decide where it was safer. One country was accepting refugees for thirty thousand dollars a piece, but no one Papa knew would admit to having that kind of money. And besides, getting to the border was no longer possible without some kind of a false passport and connections. I realized that sometimes—but not always—being rich helped.

"Currency" was a new word I had to learn because there was going to be a currency exchange. It meant that the money we had was going to be replaced by different money, which looked almost like the old—silver coins except smaller—because now, without having to move, we were going to live in a different country and that new country was smaller than the old one, its size reflected in the coins. The rate of exchange—another new concept—was not meant to be fair and would make us even poorer.

It was almost certain that if we did not flee, we would end up in Siberia. The reports from there were not good: icy weather, wind and snow, and almost nothing to eat. Some strange new words entered my vocabulary: "liquidation" and "being resourceful." We had to liquidate first, and, to do it right, one had to be resourceful. Liquidating meant getting rid of whatever other people were willing to buy and giving away the rest. "Resourceful" was a cross between helping oneself and becoming a crook. Mama was resourceful, Papa was not. He was good as a judge, but once the war broke out, he was good for nothing. Mama had managed to rent two of our rooms to three new policemen who had been released from jail. We had to share our room with Papa's two cousins who had escaped from a POW camp. A day came in spring, when they all moved out, and Mama finally decided that it was not safe for us to stay. That was the start of the big liquidation.

The shoemaker's son got the few toys I still had. His mother had been seen at the May Day parade shouting "Down with the bourgeoisie" and threatening to make it come true with her fist. Our gifts were supposed to buy us time. Next to disappear was the small stuff: the kind that could be carried out in a bag. There were still people in the city who were willing to buy china and silverware, as if parties and entertainment were on their to do lists. I saw Papa leave the apartment carrying a set of dessert plates in a basket. It meant that we would not have any more parties, and that Papa was doing something he must have hated doing. I found it very sad and cried.

Mama began claiming that everything Papa had sold she could have sold for more. He was not good at business, she was. She was resourceful, he was not. Still, even she was not able to sell the furniture that had been so lovingly restored: it went into storage in a dank cellar where mice would nest in the upholstery.

Our suitcases were packed by an expert who had learned how to do it in the army. Mama, being resourceful and charming, managed to get us a permit to leave, so that we did not have to crawl under a barbed wire fence in the middle of the night. We took the train, though crossing borders was nerve-wracking, even for Mama who almost got beaten up at one of them. First, we travelled north, then west, and then south again until we arrived in what was supposed to be paradise. The gold, if any, was carefully hidden in bras, panties, the seams of other clothing, and places I am too embarrassed to mention. That is how we fled from the frying pan into the fire. On the way, we had a chance to spend two days in a free country and even sleep in a hotel. While there, Mama succumbed to a moment of weakness and bought me a navy-blue coat with a checkered white and red trim. It was beautiful and made us look like a good family.

The trip was long, but we did manage to get off the train in a city in which "possibilities" were supposed to exist. "Possibility" was another one of those big, vague words with hidden meanings; it was different from the word "opportunity." "Opportunity" meant something real—if you were lucky, it was there for the taking—whereas "possibility" was something that could be there but perhaps was not and, if it was, it would have been very hard to put one's hands on. Papa called it a "figment of the imagination." We had to move on to another town in search of opportunities and that is how we ended up in Gangsterland where we fell on hard times. The relatives had no room for us. Almost every night we had to find a place to sleep. Most often it was the waiting room of the railroad station. Mama kept chiding Papa for not being able to find any "possibilities," while she, on the other hand, kept unearthing new ones: strange, outlandish ideas that led to nowhere. These were very sad times for Papa and me; we never knew what would happen the next day. Eventually, Mama did find a tiny store licensed to sell paper products, and, if all went well, tobacco. Unfortunately, the permit for selling tobacco did not come through—the bribe for it was too high—and without it, the little store was doomed. Still, Mama, being resourceful, found a solution: the black market and Mykola. At this point, because of Mykola, Papa left and did not take me with him. "If you come with me, you will starve," he said, while I cried and cried. "Mama will see to it that you get enough to eat."

Using the language I had been learning, I put Mykola into the category of "opportunity"—he was there for the taking—but with him came the possibility of getting an apartment. After moving from room to room to escape landladies who did not appreciate Mama, we needed a place where we could live in peace. It took Mama many trips to the housing office before the dream of having an apartment without a landlady became a reality. It had four rooms that had yet to be filled with tenants. It had its share of bedbugs and giant cockroaches that were not about to move out and some vandalized pieces of furniture that, once upon a time, could have had treasures hidden in their stuffing. What it did not have was peace; when the tenants began to move in and out, it turned into a hornet's nest.

The location of the little store was not favorable for business: squeezed as it was between a nondescript church and an equally nondescript building, one could easily pass by it without noticing it. Its windows had no displays because Mama did not have "the capital to buy an inventory." The occasional customers to stop by rarely needed more than some writing paper, an envelope, a notebook, or a pencil. When Mykola turned out not to be resourceful enough to help Mama with her venture into legal commerce, she was forced to embrace the black market and found in it her calling.

I tried not to follow Mama's exploits in business too closely: it would have been too upsetting. Sometimes she had fights with the buyers or sellers. Some even threatened to report her to the police. Sometimes I worried that she was being dishonest, though it could not have been often, because there were times when we did not have money to buy bread. Well, every business has its ups and downs. Her best venture was schnapps, because no soldier in his right mind would head for the eastern front without being drunk. When Hans was passing through town—one could never be sure when—he would buy his supply from Mama. They could trust each other. Mama would take anything for resale: clothes, jewelry, antiques, and even stuff like family heirlooms people could do without. Not all of it was heartless business. During the coldest winter of the century, Mama lent someone a coat she had taken in for resale. It may have been somewhat dishonest or unethical, but the poor woman was freezing and did not have money to buy even a tattered one. In spring, Mama took it back and sold it at a profit because of inflation. The supply of clothing was shrinking. The only new ones were being stitched together from parts of old ones.

In those days only a teddy bear and a few books were truly mine, probably because they had come from home and were not worth much. Mama had told me that the coat she had bought for me in the free country was mine and that so were the watch and the one Mark she had given me as a present. And then she sold all three. I did not care about the watch—it did not work—and I could not do much with the one Mark without knowing how to exchange it, legally or illegally. But I did care about the coat: I wore it to the park and, while sitting there on a bench near the pond, I imagined myself to be a child from a real family. "I have to sell it while it is still as good as new," Mama explained. "Soon you will fit into Heniuś's coat."

Sometimes Mama needed me to make herself look more respectable to a client: to have a little girl in tow inspired trust. All I had to do then was to stand or sit nicely and say nothing: it was a great opportunity to have a look at what other people do to survive. Only once did I see something that made me run for my life. Mama had asked me to take a buyer to an apartment in which there was a man's suit for sale. The neighborhood was a tangle of alleys, tiny, paved courtyards, and dead ends. I had explored it in the past because during a war one is supposed to know possible routes of escape. A woman led me and the buyer into an empty room where a suit was draped over the back of a chair. "There it is," she said and walked out, leaving me alone with the gnomish man. Before I had the time to turn around and look the other way, he pulled down his pants and was standing in the middle of the room half naked, his eyes glazed, his mouth drooling, and his giant thing pointing at me. It was an ugly sight. I ran out of the house and kept running to the center of the city where I would blend into the crowds. Somewhere along the way I began to wonder if he will ever find his way out of the maze I had left him in.

In the fourth year of the war, Mama's business picked up. Until then, it was having its ups and downs, and, though some people seemed to be making fortunes on the black market, Mama was not one of them. She still had dreams of a Persian coat, but every time one was almost within reach, she ran out of money. Mykola was not of much help. Though he was living with Mama, he had a wife and a child to support. Often his ideas on how to make money made even Mama cringe. There was a limit to how far one could go in breaking the law: cheating and petty theft were all right but not robbery. At least that is how I understood her value system.

When bloodbaths became a way of life in the eastern part of the country where many scores had to be settled, Mykola finally found his true calling. He would travel there on his own without getting lost, meet the tycoons who had been able to get their hands on loot, and bring back whatever they could not sell locally or was too big to fit in the lining of one's coat. No gold, just the heirlooms of rich families that Mama would try to sell on commission, pretty things I could look at and admire until they were put out of sight. After all, they were stolen goods, though their owners were no longer alive, and it was safer to keep them hidden, just in case.

At first business was good: in fact, it was so good that Mama was finally able to buy herself a Persian lamb coat that was going to make even her look very respectable. But with the approach of the front, the deliveries began to slow down. By the time they stopped altogether, few people in our city, preoccupied as they were with possible air raids, arrests, and the search for food, seemed interested in buying bulky heirlooms. "We are living on a powder keg," Mama kept saying, while Mykola worried that if he went out into the street, someone would cut his throat. He may have been right. Here, too, scores had to be settled, the way they had been settled in the East. Mykola had to leave, and he needed Mama to show him the way: he was not able to do much on his own. Of course, I had no choice but to come with them and be doomed to a lifetime of wandering. This time around, we were going to leave with a cartload of stuff. What was left over from Mykola's trips to the East was too good to be left behind. And so, the fancy china was taken out of the coal bin and carefully packed into a suitcase. When we got to our destination and hired a fiacre to take us to a hotel, passers-by were pointing their fingers at the overloaded carriage and laughing as if we were a part of a Charlie Chaplin show. The city was not yet used to seeing refugees; we were ahead of schedule.

Five years of working the black market did not make Mama rich, because as soon as we had settled a bit in a stranger's apartment, she turned to smuggling tobacco, a merchandise she had little experience with. We were by then in a different country with a different currency: tobacco instead of vodka. The war, which was supposed to end in August, was dragging on into the fall. And Mama, being terribly brave, was able to make several trips to where we had come from and return with a suitcase or two filled with tobacco. A few times she even took me along, for whatever reason. It was dangerous, not only because she could have been arrested for smuggling, but also because trains were being strafed. I had stopped learning the language of higher finance, either because I was living in a daze or because I had nothing more to learn.

When the front began to catch up to us, we had to flee again, and this time on top of a truck, lugging everything we had brought with us plus a big bag of staple foods in anticipation of famine. The bag was stolen on the way and, indeed, the day the war ended, we had only one potato and one onion to live on. Peace did not kill the black market: it flourished until the currency reform came into effect. We had been through one twice, so I already had some experience. However, this reform was different from the other two because new money had value while the old did not, not the other way around. Economics never stopped being a mystery to me. What happened next may have had something to do with supply and demand: plenty of goods for sale, but no money to buy them. Without the black market, Mama could no longer make a living, and she was not yet ready to let go of what was supposed to save us at the "black hour." That was the time when we began to eat pigeons caught on the windowsill and even had to pawn a gold bracelet. The heirlooms stayed either because they were too bulky to carry around or because no one was interested in buying them. Occasionally she did show them to someone as proof of our illustrious background, and people were appropriately impressed. "We have lost everything but this," she would say wiping the tears from her eyes. Mama was always secretive; she did not tell me about her plans for the heirlooms. Perhaps she just wanted to keep them so that for the rest of her life she would have something beautiful to look at.

Our next move was across the ocean to the land of freedom and pursuit of happiness. I had no idea what was meant by these lofty words and probably neither did Mama because, before our ship docked, she stuffed her gold ring into the most unlikely place on her body, to make sure that the custom officers would not be able to find it. One could never know what kind of aberration can hide under the mantle of capitalism.

What came next was worse than the war in my view. Mykola and Mama parted on the way because we had different sponsors. Good riddance as far as I was concerned. But Mama and I ended up on a treeless, snow-swept plain in a town whose cultural center was the giant Sears store. With that kind of competition, no one was going to buy our secondhand goods, which fortunately, we did not have to sell, as long as we had real jobs. Mama scrubbed the floors in a hospital, I emptied the bed pans.

Scrubbing floors must have been hard on Mama, demeaning for someone who had been able in the recent past to get all dressed up and play the queen. As for me, I did not care, even though what I had to dump out was disgusting and foul. If I could save enough money doing it, I would be able to go back to school. Nothing else mattered. I was still strong then.

The heirlooms were kept in a closet in a locked valise, out of sight, out of mind. Because of their bad history, I did not even want to know that they were there. Though no longer needed to save us from starvation, they must have meant a lot to Mama. One day, when the scrubbing of floors got her down, she showed them to our landlady, who was so impressed that she brought her friends to have a peek. Their oohs and aahs perked Mama up. "That is how we once lived," she told them and she may have even believed it.

We kept moving from apartment to apartment, from town to town, at first Mama and I together, then we parted ways. There was not much money for a decent life, the rents being unbearably high, but she was able to buy some furniture and, with the help of kilims, pictures, and doilies, made any apartment look better than it actually was. Yes, she had a flair for interior decorating. Though she did not speak to me about the state of her finances, I knew that she was trying to keep track of reparations paid out to war refugees and political prisoners. "See," she would say, pointing to some item in a newspaper, "Some people are getting paid for their suffering and getting rich." I had little faith in these reports. Perhaps someone somewhere did get compensated for what he or she had had to live through because of the war, but to collect a reward would have required a lawyer and neither she nor I had money to hire one. I did not try to discourage her from applying—after all, she was entitled to her pipe dreams—but neither did I encourage her, if for no other reason than the poor reputation of lawyers. Sleaze bags, they were called in this country. Besides, I knew damn well that I had no influence over Mama: for her I was still a child and she had to be in control. Twice she even travelled to Europe. I did not ask her why, but she implied that it was for her health and a break from her hard life. I understood that. How had she been able to save enough money for the trip? She dreamt of having a Swiss bank account, the ultimate sign of financial security, and even mentioned that she would open one as soon as she got her mythical war reparations.

When Mama moved, so did her treasures. The gold-rimmed china stayed packed in our best leather valise, too good to be used or displayed. She may still have been showing it to people who had to know how well off we had been in the distant past. "I am all right as long as I still have the china. When I run out of money, I'll sell it," she kept reminding me. And then there was the stamp collection started by Henius, and for a while carried on by me until Mama took it over, just in case there was a real fortune hidden in it. She became so dedicated to stamp collecting, that she started a little business of her own, a business that smelled of the black market. Someone was giving Mama used clothing that she would send to a friend behind the Iron Curtain and was paid for it with postage stamps, lots of them and very pretty because they were being printed for export. It seemed that the donor, whoever it was, was cleaning out the closets. When telling me about her business venture, Mama beamed at the prospect of making a fortune. I did not try to find out if the value of the stamps covered the cost of shipping. I left the arithmetic to Mama. Besides, I did not want to be the bearer of news that could embarrass her.

That one day she would ask me to store her heirloom china in my home surprised me. There were some break-ins in her neighborhood, she told me, and someone could steal her most valuable possessions. She was so afraid of being robbed that she had even bought theft insurance for her heirlooms. It did not make sense, but I obliged. For one whole year the locked leather valise was kept under my bed instead of hers. In the past Mama had scolded me often for not being suspicious enough of people: to her everyone was a potential thief, and I was just a naive fool.

Poor rich country we were living in: a great place for the rich, the pits for the poor. Mama must have been worried—life here had not been as promised—high rents, high health care costs, and wages too low to save for retirement. She was good at making small talk, but there were no cafes she could go to to chat with strangers, the way she used to once upon a time. No more black market and smuggling here, at least not for someone like Mama, a newcomer not exactly brilliant or a big enough crook. She was withering from lack of excitement and from worries about paying rent. Life was hard. When she retired, going to stores to look at fancy clothing and to garage sales to buy trinkets became her hobby. Most of the time, the goods were passed on to me. "I could not resist," she would explain, "it was such a great bargain." I did not mind paying her for them, within reason, because, without any friends to speak of, shopping was not only her source of entertainment, but also a reminder of how strong and brave she had been while immersed in the black market and smuggling. Buying useless stuff was a substitute for the business she had once been devoted to.

I had no idea then how irrational old people can become. I do know that it was not all Mama's fault. When her landlady saw Mama's shortwave radio, she reported her to the FBI for spying for the Russians. We had bought the radio hoping to be able to listen to European stations. It had turned out to be a complete failure and of course a waste of money; we could not even get Canada on it. An agent came to check on Mama's illegal activities and had a good laugh. Still, the landlady was not convinced and served Mama an eviction notice. It was not the first one Mama would get. Sometimes she would move on of her own volition when the apartment turned out not to her liking: some were too cold, some too hot, some had bad neighbors and even worse landladies. One of those women was convinced that standing on the balcony in the middle of the night to catch a breath of fresh air was a sign of mental illness; she would rather keep the apartment empty than rent it to someone who might kill her. The inevitable eviction followed.

The first impression Mama made on people was usually very good. Occasionally, I had a chance to witness a first meeting when she would overflow with smiles and charm. You have a wonderful mother, I would be told. Though I had my doubts, I always nodded in agreement. Even as a young child, I wanted people to think well of her. The trouble is that soon after that first meeting something strange would happen, and people, once so enamored of Mama, no longer wanted to see her. A few times, when the break was sudden and seemed to be final, I asked her if she knew what had caused it. She did not, but the frightened look in her eyes kept me from pursuing the matter: to press her farther would have been cruel.

 I felt sorry for her and also angry at her. Simply put, I just did not know how to deal with her problems. After a call from one of her landlords, an educated man who was not living off the rent, I finally turned to professionals for help, only to be told that I could do nothing: crazies had to admit to being crazy or endanger themselves or others. What I read in the advice columns—Mama, I love you very much but don't do it anymore—had no effect on her. She was insulted. Who was I to tell her what to do or not to do? After a visit from the police, the educated landlord began to question Mama's sanity. She had reported a break-in and a theft of her valise, the one that was resting under my bed. When the police arrived at her apartment to check on her claims, she slammed the door in their face. Such improper behavior prompted them to talk to the landlord who called me with the plea: "Do something about your mother." She had been a nuisance with her complaints about strange odors in her apartment that neither I nor anyone else could smell. Was someone trying to poison her? She may have thought so. The man did not tell me what that "something" was, except that she would have to move out. By then Mama's reputation with the landlords had spread, and those with decent apartments for rent did not want her as a tenant. Some of them even told her that directly. I tried to suggest that she apply for senior citizen housing where rents would be closer to what she could afford. The thought of her moving into one made me shudder, since she would not have gotten along with anyone and soon the entire building would be up in arms against her. Mama may have been aware that that would happen. For her, though, senior housing was not an option for a different reason: I don't want to live where people die, she told me.

 The next call was from a landlady who wanted Mama out of the apartment she had just rented to her. It was urgent. I managed to get a social worker to enter the fray: a defrocked priest, still full of enthusiasm for counseling crazy old ladies. He was married and had a young child he was very proud of. I took him to Mama's current apartment, which I had not seen before. I warned her first that I would be bringing someone who may be able to help her with the latest eviction.

 We were ushered into a living room that looked pleasing: the furniture arranged just right, knickknacks and pictures placed where they seemed to belong; the faux Persian carpet spread over the uneven floor provided a pleasant contrast to the dark green wallpaper. Where did she find the strength to pack and unpack and then to rearrange this and that until she found a perfect fit? The window shades being down, the room was lit by a few small lamps placed in selected spots for maximum effect: just enough light to add to the mystery. At one time Mama had a taste for the sun, whereas, in recent years, she preferred darkness. The strong aroma of a meat stew let one know that there was life beyond the living room and that Mama was still able to cook her own meals. The priest took advantage of the odor to pay her a compliment: delicious, delicious. He was savoring his words and Mama gave him a little smile in appreciation. Unfortunately, after this friendly exchange, the sliver of good feelings disappeared. Mama's eyes widened in panic. "Your landlady called. You have to move out by the end of the month." I, who from the age of nine had done my best to cover up her misdeeds, had dragged another person between us and let him in on a secret that was supposed to stay in the family.

Her eyes filled with hatred and anger as she looked at me. "Aren't you ashamed of yourself?" Yes, I was: it was treason of the highest order. I had betrayed her and the unspoken pact we had lived by.

After she had finished with me, Mama took over the stage and it was her best performance ever. It happened to be a monologue rendered in better English than I was used to hearing from her. Mama had a talent for languages, but English must have come too late in her life for it to sink in properly, especially without formal instruction. Flashing her eyes at me in anger, she was letting the priest know that in her country, before the war, her husband was a judge in the court of appeals, and therefore she knew something about the law, be it Roman or English. There was also the Napoleonic code, according to which people could not be evicted during the winter months, even when they were too poor to pay rent. Yes, Napoleon was a great man. And in this country, one can lose a home on the whim of a landlord, even when one is a model tenant. She is paying her rent on time and being as quiet as a mouse. It's December, a difficult month to find an apartment.

The priest was impressed by Mama's speech and so was I, though I was not sure how much of it was true. When the war broke out Papa was only a district judge, I was sure of that. Of course, that distinction was unimportant almost half a century later.

When Mama had finished her speech, she herded us both towards the door. That was her way of letting us know that she did not need any help, that everything that had to be done, she would do on her own. The good man, the priest, was not giving up so easily, and on our way out, he began to present Mama with a string of "possibilities." He could negotiate with the landlady who might change her mind. Yes, winter was not a good time to move. If negotiations did not work, he would help Mama find an apartment and arrange the moving. In the meantime, she should call him when she felt threatened or smelled odors or heard noises that should not be there. I shuddered at the thought of what this poor man might have to go through; he would break down under the strain. Mama listened and nodded her head in disbelief. Did she think that he was joking? Did his generous offer amuse her? I could never figure out what was on Mama's mind, and I could not at that moment either. She may have needed time to think about the priest's generous offer before saying yes or no. Her last look at me was filled with hatred.

To be sure, I had let her down.

Was it a tragedy or a comedy? I felt like crying because, as far as I could see, nothing good came out of the visit. Mama had won the battle and made a fool of me. Was the priest going to believe anything I had told him about her? When we got to the sidewalk and out of Mama's sight, we stopped for a brief talk. The wintry cold felt good on my burning cheeks. That was when the priest told me what he thought of our foray into Mama's territory. "Wow, what a woman! In all my years of counseling, I have never run into anyone able to invoke the Napoleonic code. What a speech and what class!" Yes, it did seem that, just like in the old days during the war, she pulled off the trick of snowballing the authorities. That she still had the strength for it was amazing. The priest promised to talk to the landlady, and he did. She turned out to be as paranoid and difficult as Mama. "The war must have pushed this woman over the edge," she claimed, "and I am not going to be her next victim." There was no room for negotiations.

So, Mama did move. I never found out how she did it, because after I had betrayed her, she would no longer speak to me and perhaps even ordered the priest not to. He may have helped her settle down in her new place. If he did, I was not supposed to know about it. Though a respite from her complaints felt good—the ringing of the telephone used to send me into panic mode—I did feel guilty about not helping her.

One day she finally called and asked me to take her to the grocery store. It was the end of January by then and the weather was cold and nasty. Naturally, I drove her to the one she wanted to be taken to, a store she had been shopping in before. Already in the car we got into a squabble: she was not planning to buy anything and only wanted to give me her food stamps. Oh my God, food stamps!!! Again, it was my fault. I should have been able to foresee that once our ways had parted and I had stopped giving her a meager monthly support, she would run out of money. The state of her finances had always been off limits to me. She liked secrets and was of course entitled to have them. Sometimes I did wonder how she could afford the relatively expensive apartments she kept renting and abandoning. Still, had I asked her, she would not have told me. She was her own mistress and put me off the track with statements like "When I need money, I'll sell the china and the stamp collection. They are worth a fortune." To suggest that she have them appraised would have been cruel. If she was overestimating their value, what else did she have to keep up her spirits?

I managed to convince her that I could not use her food stamps, that it would be against the law. When caught, we both would get into trouble. If she did not want to let them go to waste, she would have to do the shopping on her own for whatever she needed, and we would divide the loot at her home. For us, because of the war, our daily bread was an object of reverence, too sacred for the trash bin, even when no longer fresh. Mama agreed. After running some twenty minutes worth of errands, I was going to meet her at the bench near the exit. It had to be absolutely clear: I showed her the bench, and we even sat down on it while we talked. Mama was not well-dressed: she was wearing my American coat bought to replace the one I had arrived in, which, made of an old army blanket without a lining, had not been warm enough for the forty below weather where we were living. Mama must have kept it for sentimental reasons; for both of us it was an heirloom from the days of fading dreams. After some thirty years of use, it looked shabby, but a fur coat at the check-out in a grocery store while paying with food stamps would have looked out of place. "Just look at the welfare queen," people would say. Unlike at our last meeting when she had enough strength to put on a great performance for the priest, Mama was not in a fighting mood: she looked worn-out and sad. No mention was made of what had transpired between us, and our relationship seemed to be renewed with a clean slate.

When I came back to pick her up somewhat earlier than promised, the bench was empty. I ran through the aisles looking for her, checked the lavatory, asked the cashiers if they had seen an old lady in a brown coat pass through the check-out, and even asked some of the shoppers. A store with many aisles is not an easy place to look for someone. When I finally became convinced that my search in the store was futile, I went into the parking lot. She may have decided to wait for me outside, I thought. That did not make sense, but there was always the possibility. I ran from car to car to see if she had lost her way into one of them. No luck, and so I drove to her apartment planning to leave her a note explaining why I had given up looking for her. When I rang the bell, she opened the door. "I was not feeling well, so I asked some man to drive me home," she told me, and that was it.

The next time I saw her, she was in the hospital, unable to speak.

If abstractions were my forte, I would now be writing a few words about death. The months I had spent emptying bedpans of the terminally ill were not conducive to the development of deep thinking, but they certainly had a great effect on my view of life, a view that I would rather keep to myself. Mama was afraid of dying—probably almost everyone is—and she expressed her fear by pointing out to me how her very "rational" diet was going to keep her healthy for many, many years, the way the heirlooms and the stamps were going to keep her from running out of money.

Three months after a massive stroke, she choked on the milk she was forced to drink despite my warning that it would make her vomit and that she should not have any. I was at her bedside when an aide was trying to make her take the sip which made Mama gag. I rushed over with a tray to catch anything that could have come up, but she knocked it out of my hand. Her last look at me was filled with anger and hate; it was her way of saying "I need more than that." As a daughter, I had failed her.

I visited her almost every day and saw the terror in her eyes. Was she aware of what had happened to her and that whatever it was might lead to her death? Or was her inability to comprehend the event the cause of the terror? Paralyzed on one side, unable to speak or make sense of anything, surrounded by strangers in a strange place permeated with a mixture of odors, none of them good. The nurses told me that she was cognizant enough to navigate her wheelchair to the nearest bed and through a crack in the curtain watch her neighbor die. They took it for a sign that Mama was getting better.

After her death, whatever she had left behind—the things she had loved so much—had to be taken care of. I did my best to be respectful and kept everything that had been hers: the furniture, the trunks, the valises, and a box of secret documents I had never wanted to see. Was she going to come back from the dead or wherever she was and claim her belongings? Some of the papers had to be looked through, everything else could wait. There were five hundred dollars in her bank account. The landlord refused to return the security deposit because she did not give him two months notice, and the lawyer whom I saw at family services was on the landlord's side and sent me packing, because Mama had reported him to the building inspector for some violation of the building code.

I should be ashamed to admit it, but Mama's death was a relief. Almost instantly, all my anger towards her vanished on its own. I did not even have to work at it. It took a long time, though, before the ringing of the telephone stopped sending me into a panic. I did cry and I did grieve, but my grief was made up of regrets and soul searching. What could I have done through the years to make our relationship better? What did I owe her for keeping me alive when food was scarce? For keeping me alive so that someday she would be able to sell me off to the highest bidder and live in comfort ever after? In that respect I had let her down.

Though we never talked about it—it would have been too painful—she must have known how I felt about losing Papa and a real home because of her. A grudge may start in the head, but settles in the gut, and once there, it cannot be dislodged easily. I had no control over it.

Mama's worldly goods were not her only legacy to me. As the source of my recurrent nightmares, she too became a part of my inheritance and makes me wander through streets and towns I have never been to or no longer remember. Is it her I am looking for? It's getting dark and soon dusk will turn into night. I must hurry but don't know where to. I enter tumble-down houses and shabby apartments with rotting floors, cracked window-panes, and wallpaper coming off in sheets. Worst of all, there are no locks on the entrance door, and Mama, who is so terrified of thieves, won't be able to lock herself in. Yet she is living in one of them in dusty emptiness. Even when I do not see her, I can feel her presence, and that is already scary. Sometimes a gust of wind opens one of the doors, and Mama rushes into the room wearing a white hospital gown. She is clutching its front to her sunken chest to keep herself covered. Her hair is disheveled, her face gray. She would never let herself be seen looking like that. There is terror in her deep-set eyes and hate and anger. I wake up with a jolt before I can ask her what she has been up to.

Now that I am near my own end, I feel that it is my duty to find a good home for the furniture she has left in my care. She would like me to sell it, I am sure of that. Giving it away would be a terrible waste and a lack of respect for Mama and the hard work she had to do to be able to pay for it. Still, it quickly became clear to me that to sell it would cost more than it could be sold for, since someone would have to be hired to move it into a warehouse where it could be displayed. Besides, Mama's furniture is no longer in style, and if no one buys it after a couple of months, it would have to be brought back and the merry-go-round would start again.

I pay a junkman to take it away and while he is here lugging her stuff, I let him lug some of mine: household goods, clothes I no longer fit into, knick-knacks, and mementos, hers and mine. That is how our past goes down the drain. No trace of it will be left.

Before I turn to the valuables which were supposed to save Mama from the poorhouse, I take a look at the documents. None of them is from before the war. That part of our lives has been erased. Only two are from 1939: Henius's death certificate and a frayed sheet of paper with Mama's photo. The English visa, she used to call it. "We could have fled to England, we had the visa," Mama would tell strangers on the train, people who had ended up as homeless refugees in strange countries. "But we did not act fast enough, and then it was too late."

As far as I could make out, that tattered piece of paper was not a visa, but a confirmation that the documents needed for applying for one had been filed. And that is where the story ended, at least for me. Did Mama actually believe that it was a visa and that we would have been able to leave if we had had the money?

From the war years, there are no papers. She must have burnt them before they could get her into trouble. I know for sure that at one point she had three different passports proving three different nationalities. One of them was so utterly false that even Mama would not have been able to live under the weight of such a gigantic lie. 1945 to 1949 were the boom years for documents, partly because of me. I had to have a birth certificate and got one thanks to a woman who was willing to swear before a priest that she had been at my baptism and through a strange coincidence or divine intervention ran into me in the DP camp.

To get support from the government in exile, doled out in cigarettes, Mama needed a document to prove that she was married to Papa, and that Papa had been a judge. I found several copies of such a document among her papers, issued by the association of former lawyers and judges headquartered in Munich. Since all the records from the war years had disappeared, Mama's possible divorce from Papa remained a mystery, partly because I did not want to believe in what I had heard when it was presumably taking place. After all, I was only twelve years old then. Did Mykola push for the divorce? Did he and Mama actually get married? Did he ever divorce his wife? By now no one knows or cares.

The early fifties were the dry years. I don't think Mama could have been totally idle then, but before getting her US citizenship, she had to be on good behavior. During that time, she had some dealings with Mykola. I was aware that occasionally he would send her some money. A payback for their partnership during the war? But I found no records of those gifts. In the late fifties, Mama began to collect news items about war reparations; someone must have been helping her with that. In the early sixties she traveled to Germany and Switzerland. She claimed to have some health issues American doctors could not solve, and she decided to travel to Germany for treatment. It worked: her tonsils were removed, and she managed to charm the doctor who had done the surgery. Yes, Mama had style. There were a few mementos from him among her papers: a letter addressed to the countess, namely Mama, and a copy of his obituary. That is how I learned that he had been a famous professor and the head of a university clinic. I did not read the letter to the countess, because it would have been too embarrassing.

Her second trip included Switzerland and the United Nations. She kept a few records from that visit: a letter from the United Nations Commissioner for Refugees and a copy of a United Nations check for nine hundred dollars, barely enough to pay rent for two months. Sometime after that trip she had told me that she had opened a Swiss bank account, the ultimate symbol of financial security and a topic of conversations at the outbreak of the war. The number—she offered to share it with me—was easy to remember because it consisted only of three digits. I found it, written in ink on a small piece of paper tucked into a letter from a Geneva bank that no longer existed, thanking Mama for her interest in opening an account. That is where that trail ended.

A one-time gift of nine hundred dollars was not a fortune; Mama needed more for her retirement. I can't blame her for trying to make the German government pay for her husband's death, even though when Papa died, she was probably no longer married to him. She must have hired an American lawyer to file the claim—an advertisement for his services was in her files. From the letter of rejection of the claim, written in a refreshing German that I was happy to be reading, I concluded that the application had been so garbled, that it did not make much sense. I hope the lawyer did not charge her too much for his services.

During my youth, Mama's dishonesty and her erratic behavior frightened me because I expected that it would get her into trouble. It was my responsibility to keep her safe. The only weapon I could use against her were the accusing looks I used to give her when I thought that she had gone too far. Since words rarely accompanied those looks, I can't be sure that she got my meaning. Eventually I became somewhat inured to and more tolerant of what I considered her transgressions. Perhaps it was a sign that, after witnessing so much evil in this world, I too was becoming corrupt.

When, among Mama's papers, I came onto the trail of the stolen heirlooms, the fancy china that for a whole year had stayed hidden under my bed, I felt the kind of excitement a sleuth must feel when he is about to identify the perpetrator of a heist. Yes, Mama did buy insurance. The policy was still in her files. There was no copy of a check she would have received had her claim gone through. After the failed report to the police of a break-in, did she try to pull it off again? Did she have a second chance with the help of the insurance agent whom she had wined and dined a few times? She had kept a copy of the UN check, but a corrupt American insurance company whose riches come from fleecing people like Mama, does not have the glamor of the UN, so why immortalize its check? Besides, it may have been safer not to have a record of it. I still have folders for these documents; they are in a box marked for the dump. Should they be shredded first? The stamps have lost their value because people have stopped collecting. Just as I suspected, those from behind the Iron Curtain are worthless. I still don't have buyers for the fancy china. "Who needs dishes like these?" I am told. "What would a dishwasher do to the gold rim?"

Eventually I did find someone willing to buy the stamp collection, mainly because it included some rare German stamps. The two hundred dollars I got for it would not have saved Mama from destitution. Perhaps the heirloom dishes would have if she had sold them some fifty years earlier. Had she tried and failed and the failure gave her the brilliant idea to insure them and then claim that they were stolen in a break-in? Probably it did not work. Mama must have lost her cool when the gum-chewing police came to her door unexpectedly. They should have made an appointment because, to put on a show, Mama always had to work herself into the right mood and that required time and effort.

About to finish my long treatise on economics—the pre-revolutionary bag of gold with a lot of history hidden in it, learning what is free and what has to be paid for, the difference between looting and the spoils of war, devaluation, liquidation, currency reforms, war reparations, supply and demand, the black market ways of doing business, and how the taxes on the poor feed the rich—I find myself asking: If in 1939 we *had* had Grandma's bag of gold and Switzerland *had* welcomed my little family with open arms, would that have kept us intact? I do not know. I do know that I now find myself cheering for Mama.

I hope you were able to pull off the heist, Mama.

That would have been justice.

Afterwords

Afterwords

Mothers and Daughters—and Grandmothers

Joyce Gross

Since my mother's death, I've been prying into her past. While I knew about the major events of her early life in Europe, she usually discouraged me from learning more. If I asked questions she'd sometimes walk away as if she hadn't heard me, tell me that no one is interested—even though I clearly was—get angry and yell, or start to cry.

Even without her here, I feel I need to tiptoe around her. I don't want to risk opening wounds. I still feel ignorant about history when I look at myself through her eyes—which no doubt I am, but that's a bad excuse for not trying to learn. Her frustrations that most people in the US didn't understand what life is like in the midst of a war, nor did they know much history, plus my tending to avoid unnecessary conflict, resulted in my staying at a safe distance from her ruminations about her early life. Only for a while in the 1990s, did she open up more than usual with me about her past.

That a new war started between Russia and Ukraine a month before her death makes Eastern European history loom large again, as does the move towards authoritarianism in the United States. Events that happened in her lifetime, and in her parents', that I thought could never happen again now seem to be happening again. She would not be surprised to learn that, as I write this, war has exploded between Israel and Gaza, as she always anticipated. As much as I have never had to experience the instability and horrors of war and cannot feel the damage from it as viscerally as she did, I was always aware there could be another world war, or some war that would impact me directly. Now more than ever, I feel I've simply been lucky to have avoided such a scenario in my lifetime so far. Other people across the world have not been so lucky. What my mother went through in some ways impacted my life, though after years and decades of a multitude of experiences that shaped each of our lives, it's hard to know exactly what impact her war had on me. I just know that it did. The war was always there in her life, and therefore in mine. My heart sinks with the realization of how many generations of families even since she died have been impacted anew by war.

Whether I'm still tiptoeing around her or not, there's nothing to stop me now from asking questions and, when possible, finding answers about her time in Europe. She left many clues. I began putting them together, like a puzzle. I've been unable to stop.

As a child, I knew that her brother had died from scarlet fever before World War II broke out and was buried in Vilnius, that her father had died in a Nazi concentration camp, and that after the war and spending four years as a refugee in Germany, she and her mother had emigrated to the US. I knew she missed Poland. She often listened to phonograph records of lively war songs with soldiers marching and singing, gun shots, bomb explosions, and terrified screaming. She played the records so often that by the time I was twenty these sounds reminded me of my own childhood, even though I'd never experienced war. My childhood was stable and happy, while hers was not. At the same time, she spoke of her childhood with great happiness and longing, as if her life since leaving Europe had been unpleasant and a failure. She always wished she could go back to Poland to live, go back to a time before life became difficult and so many things went wrong. She also wished passionately that people would end all wars and not start new ones.

In the 1990s, she and I had a few conversations about her family and life before 1949. This was such a rare occurrence that when it happened, I took notes. We were on the telephone, she in Ithaca, New York, me in the Bay Area, California, so she didn't know I was taking notes. She may not have talked if she'd known. I did not ask many questions, because I didn't think she wanted me to; it might expose my ignorance and make her stop talking. The collapse of the Polish communist government in 1989 and Lithuania gaining independence from the Soviet Union in 1990 made it easier for her to visit both Poland and Vilnius, Lithuania.[1] In 1992, for the first time since she was nine years old, she traveled to Vilnius. She remembered the location of her brother's grave, according to her husband Len, my father, who traveled with her. At first, she wasn't sure which cemetery was the right one, but after the taxi driver first stopped at a wrong cemetery, she instinctively knew the second one was the right one and walked straight to the grave, somehow remembering the cemetery's hills and paths after fifty-two years. The grave was marked with a teetering old wood cross and a small metal plaque with the name "Połtowicz" barely legible. The caretaker later confirmed that it was her brother's grave. On a trip she and I took to

---

[1] To my knowledge, my mother visited Poland three times after 1989. She had visited Poland at least three times before that. But it was definitely easier to go to Vilnius after 1990, and the only two times she went were after 1990.

Europe in 1994, she told me more details about her life as she showed me places where she used to live.

During this trip, I was surprised that she lit up with the emotions of a child, a person with her life mostly ahead of her instead of the other way around, an innocent happiness and excitement, different from the way I knew her to be. She felt comfortable and more sure of herself, despite the more than forty-five years that had passed since she had left.

She loved the high school in Cham that she attended while living in Germany. When we went to its location, she was frustrated and disappointed that it no longer looked the same as it had in 1949. While the building was still a school, it had been expanded and altered, so she wasn't able to recognize anything other than its location. While we were walking near the school, she noticed a street named after the man who had been the principal when she was there, a man she had both "feared and respected" ("School").[2] That the school was so different was a disappointment to her, but that the principal of the school had been recognized and was being honored with a street named after him pleased my mother very much and even made her cry.

In Kraków, she took me through the double doors of her old three-story apartment building as if she still lived there. The plaster was falling off the decrepit brick walls. The courtyard on the back side of the apartment was run down and filled with overgrown bushes. My mother pointed out a window on the third floor that was the room where she had lived. Again, even though it had been fifty years since she had lived there, it seemed to me as if she'd never left. Emotionally she was still eleven or twelve, living in the Kraków apartment, waiting to hear from her father, silently watching her mother's performances as she navigated life during the war, or planning a romp with her best friend Runia in the cemetery.

The building owner arrived and began asking questions. A tenant had reported someone taking photos. Because I don't know Polish, I had no idea what the man was saying, but I could tell he wasn't pleased to see us. Still sounding as excited as a twelve-year-old visiting a place of wondrous memories, my mother explained that she used to live in the building. The man asked her if she was Jewish. Despite her telling him that she was not, he proceeded to tell her that his father had bought the building in 1947 when the previous owners weren't making money from it, as if he needed to justify his ownership. He did not have anything more to say, except that he didn't want us to be there.

---

2   From 1945 to 1952, Hans Muggenthaler was headmaster of the Oberrealschule mit Gymnasium Cham. The street in front of the school is now called Dr.-Muggenthaler-Straße.

As we walked away, it dawned on my mother that he must have thought she was Jewish and possibly related to a previous owner of the building. He thought she might claim ownership of the property. It was in the Kazimierz district of Kraków, had had a lot of Jewish people living in it when she moved into one of its apartments, and before the war most likely had been owned by Jews who were later killed. The new communist government probably sold the building to non-Jewish Poles after the war. It surprised my mother that anyone might think that she was Jewish or that her family may have owned a building in Kraków.

When we walked further into the former Jewish district of Kazimierz, I did not feel welcome walking around the streets there either. The film *Schindler's List* had been released the year before, and Spielberg had shot some of it in Kazimierz. The area was run down, some buildings just ruins, really. Grim-looking people looked down at us from second and third story windows. I felt like an unwelcome American tourist, looking at layers of history and barely understanding them. Despite living so close to what before the war had been a largely Jewish district, my mother was unfamiliar with the area. "I had been told not to turn right [towards Podgórze] on leaving our building because, by turning right, I could end up seeing something that would be bad for me to look at" ("Mama"). In comparison, Market Square and Planty Park, which were also close to her apartment, my mother knew very well.

The two docents we met at the Remuh Synagogue and Cemetery were kind and friendly towards us. They were old men, one a survivor of Nazi camps, the other a survivor of Russian Kolyma camps. One of them showed us around the cemetery, explaining how the gravestones were being restored after Nazi destruction. Afterward my mother said she found it odd that she felt more comfortable with these two Jewish men, had more in common with them, than with the Catholic Poles. The Poles in 1994 were not the same as the ones she had been accustomed to in the 1940s. I believe she already knew there was no way to go back to what she had left as a child—too much had changed. This must have been another reminder.

While I didn't say anything during those moments after visiting the cemetery, it was hard not to think over the facts that my mother had married a Jewish man and, that, despite my believing religion to be nothing more than a system humans dreamt up to help themselves find meaning in their lives and to justify the killing of other humans, I am myself half Jewish. Now those thoughts are even more poignant because, after my mother's death, I learned that one set of my Jewish paternal great grandparents lived just twelve miles southwest of Kraków in 1900. My other set of paternal great grandparents lived two hundred miles east of Kraków in Lviv until 1910. All of them must have left to escape antisemitic violence. I can't help but think how random it is that I exist, living in California, working with computers that are now ubiquitous, chasing insects around deserts and mountains with my camera, not religious at all, and having a certain freedom as a woman that was rare fifty or one hundred years ago. I'm the descendent of people who escaped the violence of the Russian Revolution, the pogroms of Eastern Europe, and, during World War II, both the Russian invaders of Poland from the east and the German invaders from the west. I live now in a place where Native Americans once lived, before European settlers killed them. Depressing as the violent tendency of humans is, I'm grateful to have experienced very little of it personally in my life so far, aside from witnessing the trauma left on my mother from the war.

Centuries of violence were visible everywhere during our trip. I was not used to seeing so many memorials to people killed, often murdered in great numbers. I eventually tired of the many monuments showing men who had done some great deed that most likely involved killing a lot of people. In contrast, I did not tire of my mother's stories about her life in Europe; hearing them actually made life there in the 1940s more real to me than seeing the monuments. I'm thankful she wrote down all her stories, because the brief notes I made to record some of them while on our trip lacked many details and the rich colors, sounds, smells, style, and heartfelt experiences contained in her own writing.

Despite or even because of all the wars caused by Poland's invaders over the centuries, my mother was very interested in the country's centuries-old cultural history and wide mix of people. She loved the castles that dot Poland and all of Europe. That her friend Runia's family owned a castle impressed her. One detail that always jarred me, though, was my mother often describing people as "coming from a good family" (or not), as if it was okay to judge a person based on their class and ancestors. I know class is part of European history. I don't know how much of the class system is still evident in Poland today, but now, thirty years after our trip to Poland, I see the class system everywhere throughout the world, even in the US. Sadly, it comes in different flavors of inequality.

In Vilnius, we visited Henius's grave site over which there was the new stone, the result of her trip to Vilnius with my father two years earlier. I was moved to see my grandmother's name on it and the name of the town where I grew up, Ithaca, all the way in Lithuania, in a beautiful though slightly neglected cemetery on a wooded hill, the buildings of the seven-hundred-year-old city below slightly visible through the trees. The gravestone also listed her father's name and the name of the concentration camp where he died, Bergen-Belsen. The spot felt peaceful—a pleasant place to be when one is dead, I thought.

I had visions of carrying a box of my mother's ashes there some year in the future and having her name added to the stone. I think that's where she would be happiest now, with her father, brother, and mother, in a place where they had all been together before her family was torn apart by death and war.

Most of what I learned about Eastern Europe and my mother's life there was not something I often thought about during the several decades between that trip and before her death, and some of it I had forgotten. On visits each year to my parents' home in Ithaca, I wished we could go through photos from her youth, to make sure I would know their details after she died, but I was afraid to stir up whatever emotions would arise for her if I asked. Plus, I never liked thinking about "after she died," as if avoiding thinking about it would prevent it from happening. After her death, I dug up my notes taken during phone calls in the 1990s and from our 1994 trip. I read and listened to history books on World War II and Eastern Europe. I found her photos, brought them to California, and scanned them. While I was able to figure out identities of many people in the photos, the identities of others will remain a mystery.

I also found all her beautiful stories—not one of which she let me read when she was alive, but which she did not destroy before her death. Clearly her life in Europe was in the forefront of her mind her entire life. My mother's stories contained her familiar subtle and often sarcastic humor, her succinct way of letting you know the irony of a situation, and her openness about different belief systems—Catholic, Jewish, parapsychology and superstitions, patriarchy—while at the same time questioning the existence of God and the sanity of humans. My religion is like hers: "I think the park is like a church—sacred and much more beautiful, though. When allowed to stroll through it, I sometimes stop under one of these giant trees, look up, and try to find heaven above its crown" ("Maybe Not a Story").

While I was not surprised that her stories were good, I was surprised at a distinct style she had that I had not known she had, something Irene writes about elsewhere in this book. Bigger surprises included the many details about my grandmother that bring her to life in a way she never had been for me before; that Mykola (my grandmother's lover) has a name and was a lot more involved with my mother's life than I realized; and that my mother had tried to hide their identities, and her own to some extent, in her writing. She had even tried to hide the names of towns where she had lived. She did this despite the fact that she valued historical accuracy and wasn't planning to publish the stories.

I understood and respected her desire for privacy to write. I remember the spiral-bound notebooks stacked on the living room table in the 1980s that she didn't want anyone opening, and I did not open them. Later, she told me about her friendship with Irene after a serendipitous meeting at Moosewood Restaurant. Years later, she showed me an early draft of Irene's essay "A Polish Childhood" and then said not another word about it. Now and then, I looked up Irene's publications and eventually found out that the chapter had been published in *Eastern Europe Unmapped.*

I knew my mother had shared her stories with Irene and had given her permission to do what she wanted with the stories after she died, but I only had a vague idea of what the stories were. I didn't know how many there were or how organized (or not) they were. I wanted to see for myself what I thought. It turned out there were stories on my mother's computer that Irene didn't have, and so many versions of the stories she did have, that it took a while to create any kind of inventory. Thanks to my father Len, there were numerous computer backups from over the years. It was clear that my mother rewrote many of her stories numerous times.

What I could not find were the spiral-bound notebooks from the 1980s. I assume they contained older versions of her stories that she later typed into the computer. Probably it's just as well that she did not keep them, but I wish she had. I did find one notebook that led me to be quite sure she was writing already in the 1970s. Also, she kept several notebooks in which she had written between 1942 and 1945. Aleksandra has been able to decipher my mother's Polish handwriting and discusses points about these stories elsewhere in this book. While I was surprised that the 1940s notebooks, written when she was a young teenager, consisted primarily of fictional stories rather than factual, diary-like writing, all of the writing contained unaltered glimpses into my mother's life at a young age. Stories of a girl living in the woods with her animals align with what I know about my mother; starting each story with "In the Name of God" surprised me but I was grateful to get a few glimpses at what she was taught as a young child. The girl traveling with her horse, pony, and dog to the notorious Pawiak prison to give her grandfather food is a sad and strange twist of reality. Did she know when she was writing this that her father had been in the Pawiak prison? From documents I found, I learned that he had spent three weeks there after his initial arrest, before being sent to Gross-Rosen. That my mother's stories are in Polish—a language I did not learn as a child—somehow drives home the distance she came from her childhood to mine, and the disruptions she had to her life before I was born.

My mother saved copies of all the letters and emails she wrote to Irene. They contained a lot of information about her life in Europe that I didn't otherwise have. I used this information along with my own notes, her stories, and historical facts to make a chronology of events in her life (which eventually became a jointly written timeline for this book). Pursuing my mother's history quickly became like a new hobby, something that helped me adjust to the sadness and disbelief of her being gone. If neither of us had written anything down, if she had not met Irene, I would know much less about her life. I would not have had the history lessons either.

The day my mother died was the first day I actually got hold of one of her stories. It was "Mrs. Kraus," published three months earlier in the volume Irene edited called *On Being Adjacent to Historical Violence*. When I called a friend in Ithaca to tell her about my mother's death, she told me that one of Grażyna's stories had been published, though my mother hadn't shared the actual publication with her yet, and she certainly had not said anything about it to me during our weekly phone or Skype calls. I went online that day and was able to get a digital copy of the book.

That story was the first of many that allowed me to understand how resourceful my grandmother had been during the war. Time after time my grandmother seemed to proactively (and apparently successfully) solve problems in any way possible, whether it was via "her business of smuggling tobacco across the border," acquiring three false passports "the most fake of them all" which nearly got her arrested in Prague, or simply getting a phonograph fixed: "Since people here are not kindly disposed towards those who don't speak their language, finding someone willing to repair [the phonograph] was another one of Mama's great accomplishments." In "Mrs. Kraus," I could sense the confusion, curiosity, hope, stress, and feeling of doom my mother must have felt as a young teenager moving from place to place during the war. It was a window into her childhood and a more vulnerable, secret part of her adult self, rolled up into one narrator. I wanted to read more of her stories. It felt strange to see this very vibrant side of her at the same time that I was trying to get used to the fact that she was dead.

A week after my mother's death, my father Len located and emailed me a copy of the story "Evhen." In it was the name Mykola. This was the first time I'd seen him referred to as something other than "my mother's friend" or "Mr. M." I'm not sure why, but I thought maybe my mother had forgotten his name after all these decades. I knew that she disliked him and that she believed he was partly to blame for her father's death.

A few days later, Len sent me a copy of the stories she had worked on with Irene. It was an older version than what we are presenting in this book, with names of towns where she had lived not included, and Mykola's name not included either. Because the stories are based so much on historical accuracy and my mother's writing was so engaging, I was puzzled by the missing town names and immediately wanted to know what they were, along with details of historical events touched on in the stories or that impacted her—my—family members' lives and trajectories. For example, in "Maybe Not a Story," my mother writes "Papa was transferred for work, and we had to move …. The war placed that town in a different country and a border now separated us from it." Maybe it's not important to know where they moved from or to, but to read a simple description such as a child might write, then see the actual towns and borders on a map and spend a little time learning about the political changes of that era, excited me more than just knowing that her father had to keep moving. With each story that engaged my interest—all her stories did that—I was inspired to learn more about Eastern Europe.

I enjoyed the familiar subtle and irreverent humor in my mother's stories: "The Church of the Holy Cross had a part of its roof missing, so even Jesus could not keep the bombs out" ("The Fortune Teller"). As much as I sometimes cringed at what I felt was her unjustified negativity about her life in the US ("What came next was worse than the war in my view" ["Mama"]), I also laughed at some of her other digs at and pessimism about the future: "As for me, I am afraid to learn about my fate because I can't imagine that there will be anything good in it" ("The Psychic").

My mother was expert at conducting Google searches that led to information about her past and people she used to know in Europe. Would she find humor in the fact that I was googling her maiden name when I discovered Registration of Foreigner records from Furth im Wald, Germany, with her, her mother's, and Mykola's names all listed at the same address each year between 1945 and 1949? The records were on ancestry.com; I had to sign up for an account to see the records in their entirety.[3] Many official records, I learned, contain inconsistencies and typos, these Registration of Foreigner records included. It was clear, though, that Mykola lived with my mother and grandmother throughout their four years in Germany. Those four years plus the four years in Kraków meant he lived with my mother when she was between ten and eighteen years old. Of course she didn't forget his name! After all my sleuthing to figure it out, when I finally arrived in Ithaca three months after my mother's death, I found Mykola's full name among some papers pertaining to my grandmother, exactly as I had already deduced. There was even a note that he was a McCarthyist. My mother and grandmother had clearly been in contact with him after moving to the US. According to his emigration papers which I had found online, he arrived in Bismarck, North Dakota a few months after my mother and grandmother. All three of them lived in Minneapolis at the same time at least briefly. Mykola eventually died in 1972 on the East Coast, though not in New York where my mother and grandmother had been living for quite a while.

My grandmother and Mykola split up after they arrived in the US. Part of the reason for this, my mother told me—or maybe the whole reason—was

---

3   I've since learned that these same records are available online in the Arolsen Archives.

because my mother had told her mother that she, Grażyna, would stop living with her mother if she got back together with Mykola. My mother, eighteen when she made that declaration, was finally old enough to make her own way in the world. Her mother chose her daughter over Mykola—despite their relationship being fraught with anger, with or without Mykola. Perhaps my grandmother thought she needed her daughter more now than she needed Mykola.

It's been a surprise to learn so much about my grandmother from the stories and to learn that she was not exactly what I was led to believe as I was growing up. For example, opening and running "the tiny store which has almost nothing to sell but keeps her out of forced labor" ("Tereska") must have taken some ingenuity that not all people had, and doing so, I assume, would have allowed her to keep a closer eye on her daughter. Possibly getting rid of her husband in exchange for another man who could be of more help to her during the war was another of her strategies to stay alive, even if it broke my mother's heart.

I didn't know until I read the stories that my grandmother had helped save a relative's life by having everyone in the apartment pretend he had typhus when an officer came to take all the men away. Having the gall not only to lie to the officer about Ted being deathly ill but then to follow "at [the soldier's] heels" to the door and whisper to him "We are afraid it is typhus. You better wash your hands" ("Typhus") shows not only her bravery, but also how good she was at playing whatever role was needed during a given emergency. The story continues: "Mama has a new piece of soap ready for him and even a fresh white towel. Does he know how we children joke about our soap that is filled with air bubbles?" The "soap filled with air bubbles," my mother told me once, meant that it had been made from the bodies of murdered Jews. I am not sure whether or not she really believed this. Her including it in a version of this story, however, shows that in her world this was a persistent, widespread belief—for which, though, I learned there is no proof.

My grandmother may not have been able to keep my mother in school for all years of the war and during the difficult years afterward as Europe tried to recover, but she did enable my mother to be in schools for half of those years, even when it was illegal (see, for example, "A Christmas Story"). That my mother got through the war and the years after without being sexually assaulted is another testament to my grandmother's powers to keep my mother safe. Maybe a bit of luck was involved, too, and my mother's own instincts to stay away from unsafe situations. Also, while my mother was hungry at times and food was often scarce, my grandmother seems to have provided enough food throughout the war that my mother was never starving. It's very likely that Mykola helped provide either food or money for food.

When I was growing up, my grandmother lived in downtown Ithaca, and we lived a few miles out of town. She visited us regularly during the first ten years of my life. Sometimes we went to her apartment for dinner. At our house, she enjoyed helping in the garden. I remember little else about her from my first ten years. At some point when she was in her seventies, she became paranoid about odors in her apartment that did not exist and people stealing from her when they were not. My mother tried to reason with her, but it always ended in a shouting match—all in Polish. I didn't know Polish and didn't understand what was being said except that it was unpleasant.

My grandmother developed dementia in her later years, not enough to lose her independence, but enough to make life difficult for those around her. I saw little of her during the last ten years of her life, because my mother was on such bad terms with her that she rarely visited us and we rarely went to her apartment. The last time we did, I remember that my mother was irritated by everything my grandmother said and barely responded to her attempts at conversation.

I believed that my grandmother had done truly horrible things in the 1940s and thought that was the other reason why she and my mother were always fighting. I didn't feel animosity towards her myself. I thought of her as my crazy old grandma who had done bad things long ago. I thought she was still doing terrible things, even though I know now that comparing the behavior of a person with dementia to her younger self trying to survive during a world war is not a fair comparison.

Even having read the stories, I wonder what exactly my grandmother did in Europe that caused so much animosity between her and my mother. She was involved with the black market, but so were most people living in Poland during the war, if they wanted to survive. Even lying was a useful skill, one which my grandmother had. I'm sure she lied to my mother sometimes when she shouldn't have. Perhaps often. My mother hated lies, as do I.

One serious lie of omission is that my grandmother never told my mother that her father had died, even though the paper trail points at her knowing this while they were living in Germany. After my grandmother's death in 1984, she left behind documents dated 1948 stating that she was a widow. Later she tried to get war reparations for her husband's death. My mother never asked her mother if she knew what had happened to her father because she thought her mother would not tell her the truth. In 1957, my mother asked someone to visit the Red Cross in Warsaw to inquire about her father. That's when my mother found out, twelve years after his death, that he had died on 11 January 1945, in Bergen-Belsen.

Perhaps my grandmother can be blamed for my grandfather's death, because her taking a lover caused him to leave his family and, with nothing left to lose, he was more likely to become involved with the Polish resistance and put his life at greater risk. He had already lost his job, he was a member of the hated intelligentsia, he lost his only other child to scarlet fever, and then he lost his wife as well. He felt his only remaining child, my mother, would be more likely to survive if she were with her mother, and he was probably right. My grandmother saw him as someone who "will never learn how to work the black market or how to cheat and lie. He is ... a useless drone" ("The Root Canal"). If he had stayed with his family, would they all have survived the war? If the family had stayed in Wilno and never met Mykola, would they have been sent to Siberia? I've thought many times about "what ifs" like this.

Given all I now know, it seems to me that while Mykola may have been a benefit to my grandmother's survival during the years in Kraków, as the war was ending, he may have become a liability. Ukrainians were not liked by the Poles. It's possible he had been involved with the transfer of stolen items from Polish property in Eastern Poland. Mykola had been too friendly with the Nazis to be liked by the new Polish communist government. Germany may have seemed like a friendlier place for him at the time, and my grandmother helped him to leave by going with him.

I find that I can understand my mother's dislike of Mykola, as a human being and as a participant in the breaking apart of her small family. But it seems that for the rest of her life she also felt shame about him, about what had happened with her family breaking up, and felt that it reflected badly on her. She was too ashamed of and angry about Mykola to use his name or acknowledge his existence. It seems this shame she felt as a child, she carried inside her her whole life. The arrival of Mykola and departure of her father also meant that she lost whatever toe-hold she had had in belonging to a "good family." Her father's family had owned an estate in Transnistria, currently in a disputed part of Moldova, before it was lost in 1920 during one of the skirmishes of the Russian Revolution or its aftermath. Even though the estate was gone eleven years before my mother was born, now her ties to it were further severed, along with her hopes to have people see her as belonging to a more privileged and educated class.

My mother was also ashamed about other aspects of her mother's behavior. That she lied, that she sold goods on the black market, that she wasn't loyal to her husband. This shame and anger dominated my mother's feelings about my grandmother, and it seems there was no other way for her to see my grandmother.

A year and a half before my grandmother died, she came to our house to retrieve coins we had been keeping for her (presumably because she thought they would be stolen from her apartment). I took her into the back yard to show her our animals—the only way I knew how to interact with her and share something we both enjoyed. She liked animals as long as they weren't her own and she didn't have to take care of them. We had dogs, chickens, ducks, goats, and a horse. The horse, Corey, was the center of my world then. During his first and only meeting with my grandmother, when he saw her, her hair neatly rolled up and tucked into its bun the way it always was, he pricked his ears forward and stared at her, eyes big. It was not his usual reaction to people; it was as if he was seeing something he'd never seen before, something from another world. He put his head on her shoulder, gently holding his cheek against hers. The two of them stood still for some moments. My grandmother was radiant afterward and always told me "I will *never* forget..." As for me, I was pleased that Corey had shown such affection toward my grandmother and that it had made her happy. At the same time, I still wonder what he detected about her that I was missing.

Not having the instincts that animals sometimes seem to have, I had no way to know what I was missing. Similarly to how my mother felt, I was more comfortable with animals than with people and at age eighteen didn't have the knowledge or skills to learn anything about my grandmother other than what my mother told me. Nor was I curious. Perhaps my lack of curiosity was also because my mother would likely get angry if I asked my grandmother questions about herself—my mother would not have felt the stories my grandmother told me were accurate. It did not help that my grandmother's English was not very good, and my Polish was nonexistent.

In phone conversations near the end of my grandmother's life she would tell me that she was worried about my mother, that she thought she didn't look good. I was certainly aware that they were fighting all the time and no one looks good when they are angry and shouting. At the time, I did not question my mother aloud about my grandmother's concerns—I felt the rule between mothers and daughters was for the daughters not to ask questions. Now these statements that my grandmother made make me sad. Even if she was driving my mother crazy with her imagined odors and faulty accusations of crimes against her, she did love my mother. As much as my mother did not want to give her mother credit for much of anything before her mother died, my mother's stories now seem to me like a way of crediting her mother for keeping her safe and alive during the war. Even if it was a haphazard team of people keeping my mother alive, a team that included Józefina and Runia, my grandmother was a part of that team.

I knew on my own, without reading it in my mother's stories, that my grandmother was good at putting on appearances. I think this was partly why I didn't relate to her more than I did: maybe with her hair down and her making less of an effort to be a Countess—seeming to live in a world I did not understand—I would have been able to connect with her better. I was more comfortable with people who were happy to run around in the woods and fields with me and my animals. I was living the life I believe my mother wished to have had as a child, though in another country. Like my mother, I also had a hard time connecting with people who did not tell the truth about everything. Even before the complications of my grandmother's dementia, would I have been able to believe stories told to me by my grandmother?

That during my grandmother's life my mother never let go of the anger she felt towards her could not have helped my mother adapt to life in the United States. It's as if the anger and shame about her family seeped into her, always made her ashamed of her mother, ashamed of how they ended up in the United States, ashamed of their past; simultaneously she thought her life in Europe was a lot more interesting than her life in the US. My mother was a woman of many contradictions. She and her mother did not have a lot of good opportunities at the end of the war, when Poland ended up behind the Iron Curtain and Germany became overwhelmed with problems of its own, including trying to find homes for many displaced Germans.

My mother thought people from "broken marriages" were flawed, damaged somehow for the rest of their lives. That she was from such a marriage and that her family had lost everything during the war may have impacted her own sense of self-esteem. She was overly sensitive to criticism, or even potential criticism. Whatever the reason for her sensitivities, it took me a long time to realize that she was not a healthy role model. I wish she had not felt that way, for her own sake and for mine.

It is pure speculation how different my mother's life would have unfolded had she been a boy. I will speculate anyway. Based on my knowledge of her and her comments about gender in her writing, it seems likely she'd have been happier as a boy. She would have had more options available to her as a child and young adult. She may have felt less responsibility for her mother, too. As a boy, she may have had an easier time leaving her mother to her own devices and thus avoiding the complex and constant animosity that they felt towards each other as each tried to "protect" the other. She would have had more options for intellectual pursuit. She would not have been trapped caring for children. If she had been a man in the 1960s and 1970s, his wife would most likely have stayed home with the children while he worked. As it was, by the time she was living in the United States, it was hard to completely overcome setbacks caused by being on the run from the war and the death of her brother and father. I'm convinced that if she had been a man (or had come of age later in the century) and had been able to make better use of her intellectual abilities, she would have felt less frustrated about her life.

In the period between leaving Germany and arriving in Ithaca, my mother spent time in Bismarck, Minneapolis, Chicago, and New Haven. A Catholic organization sponsored my mother's and grandmother's immigration from Germany to North Dakota. My mother spent her first two years in the United States working in a Bismarck hospital, cleaning bedpans, while earning a diploma from Bismarck Junior College. She then earned a Bachelor's degree in mathematics from the University of Minnesota. She told me one reason she studied math is that it was easier for her than a subject requiring a better grasp of the English language than she felt she had. While studying for her master's degree, she met my father who was also a graduate student at the University of Minnesota at the time. She completed her masters and my father completed his PhD, both in mathematics, at the University of Chicago. After that she taught college-level calculus near places my father moved for his career. She did not work outside our home after my brother and I were born.

Having to navigate life in a new language for the second time in four years did not make adjusting to life in the United States any easier. She never felt she mastered English, despite how well she knew it. Living on a different continent also severed ties to people who knew what it was like to lose a parent to the Nazis, lose multiple homes running from people who wanted to arrest or harm you, and live surrounded by the instability, fear, and violence of war. Two friends she made during her years in Europe, Runia and Brigitte, she kept in contact with for the rest of their lives, and, after they passed away, with their adult children. Another friendship I only learned about recently was "Krystyna," a young Polish woman who was working, along with her elder sister, in the hospital in Bismarck. They visited a few times when my mother found herself in Chicago where Krystyna had settled and married, exchanged Christmas cards for years, and it turns out that in a letter to Irene, my mother reported even receiving a phone call from Krystyna as late as 2009. She called it "very interesting," but didn't offer any details why. My mother's sometimes prickly and intimidating personality kept some Americans at a distance or unsure what to think of her. With people she liked, she developed decades-long friendships that were very important to her. These friendships may have lacked the spoken and unspoken knowledge of shared wartime horrors but focused on other important topics: hobbies, children, health, politics, and gossip. Irene is the only person she met during my lifetime who opened the floodgates to her past—the thoughts of which had never stopped bubbling actively in her mind all the decades she lived in the US, with or without friends who had shared her experiences.

Animals were important to both of us. German shepherds were her special love—in her home and daily life; in the hours each day she spent walking with them in the woods behind our house; in the time she spent preparing for and going to tracking tests, agility trials, and obedience trials. In the few photos that exist of her when she was a child, the ones where she is with a dog are the ones where she is smiling. In Ithaca, she bred German shepherds and made quite a few people happy with puppies they got from her. Some of the people became lifelong friends. I was one of the people who received dogs she had bred—three over the decades—and, as she did with the new owners of many other dogs she placed in homes, she gave me much expert advice about training and day-to-day issues that came up.

Most of her friends in the United States trained dogs, too, but when it seemed she might have a story published, she did not want people to know she was the same person who trained dogs, just as she didn't want her friends who trained dogs to know she wrote stories about her life during the war. A sense of low self-esteem either way she looked at her activities? Didn't she know by the time she received a master's degree in mathematics, raised two successful children, learned five languages, and knew more about politics and history than most people, that she was smart and unique? That she did not have to worry any more about what her mother did long ago? After she died and I was looking through her files and books, finding and reading her stories for the first time, a friend she'd known for decades through dog training told me that she knew my mother had a certain book on German shepherds. She probably had had the book at one point, but by the time of her death, all her many books were literature, especially European literature, and history books. I kept quiet about that. I felt I had two mothers, and most people only knew one of them. I mailed myself many of my mother's books and have been reading them in part because they are helping me learn more about her. The more I read, the more I understand her and understand details in the next book I read. I even learned a little Polish so I could at least partially decipher some of the Polish writing, letters, and books she left behind. I hesitate to admit this because I still cannot form any sentences in Polish, at least none longer than two or three words, one of which will probably contain incorrect grammar and hurt my mother's ears if she were still alive.

It's ironic that my mother made such an effort to get rid of her mother's possessions without first asking her children if they might want any of them, for example, my grandmother's German china. My mother had tried but failed to get rid of it. She may have been right about my lack of interest in the dishes. I didn't need my grandmother's china; I prefer cheaper, mismatched dishes that don't upset me when I drop them and they break. However, once I had read about my grandmother requesting that all the dishes be taken to and hidden in my parents' house, then claiming they had been stolen in an effort to get insurance money ("Mama"), I shipped the dishes to my home in California. Later, I discovered an entry in my journal from when I was eighteen years old that my grandmother had told me she planned to give me the dishes when I married. Now that I've read my mother's stories, these are not just dishes, but rather a physical remnant of my grandmother's dreaming and scheming. I'm also aware these dishes might have been part of the loot that Mykola acquired from Eastern Poland where

Ukrainians killed tens of thousands of Poles in 1943–1944 and looted their properties. The dishes may have more history than I wish to know, and all I have to do is open my kitchen cupboard to see it.

I like to think that my mother wrote the stories, especially the story "Mama," in part to acknowledge what her mother did for her to keep her fed and safe during the war. It must have taken extra effort on my mother's part to give her mother credit for doing anything right. I question whether or not my grandmother's last look at my mother could have been "filled with anger and hate" and that she could have been thinking "as a daughter, [Grażyna] had failed her" ("Mama"). More likely, the look in my grandmother's eyes was of terror, as my mother also writes. There's no doubt that my mother was still under the spell of her complicated mother-daughter relationship during those last days, despite my grandmother's paralyzed condition.

Having tiptoed around my mother for the last three years, I've wondered what I'd say to her if she caught me looking into her life.

***

When I Zoom with my father these days, I sometimes imagine that you are still in Ithaca, that you will walk into the room and sit in front of the computer next to him. It doesn't seem possible that you are really gone. So much seems different now, though. Would you know, when you looked at me, how much more I know about you now than I did in March 2022? What would you say to me? Or I to you? Would you be angry? That I read your stories? Read your letters? Thank you for giving me my life, for caring about me in a way no one else ever has or will (even when it irritated me), for leaving such a rich and vivid trail of history, and for teaching me that there is usually more than one way to interpret events that happen around us.

What is Historic? What is Heroic?

Aleksandra Szczepan

I never met Grażyna Gross. I will never recognize her voice in her writing, never remember that very story from an anecdote she would have told me once or a photo she would have shown me, I will never be able to imagine how she made decisions about what to add and what to omit.

Yet, I do understand what she is saying, I do hear her voice. I recognize Polish words and phrases in her writing, with their thick meanings: when she calls her jobless father a "drone," I hear the tenderly ironic alliteration of Polish "truteń." And when she describes how "connections" were essential in Nazi-occupied Kraków, I know very well that she means "znajomości," a social disposition that is still essential in Kraków, where I studied and worked in the twenty-first century. Although I dislike proverbs, they immediately reverberate in my head in Polish when I read in her stories: "Hope is the mother of the stupid" or "Man cannot live by bread alone." But it is not only Grażyna's first language that I speak. I understand where she comes from: I speak her landscape, imagination, and social fabric. I have walked repeatedly every inch of the Planty Park in Kraków that she knew so well. Like her, I read in school "great patriotic novels" and could not memorize the order of Polish medieval kings; likewise, I was raised as a girl in an enduringly patriarchal and class-hierarchic Polish society. I also read fluently her Eastern European dark humor that underpins her narrative with a layer of irony and sometimes crystalizes into witty aphorisms, often blasphemous towards things considered fundamental, such as god, homeland, or gender hierarchy. As in: "It was not kindness that had made God so famous" ("Father Zeisel"). Finally, I find familiar her trajectory: like Grażyna's Mama and Papa, my great grandparents came to Warsaw from places that had changed their names in the twentieth century and are now in Belarus. Like Grażyna's father, my great grandfather was sent from Warsaw in 1944 to Gross-Rosen and then deported to an unknown concentration camp, from which he never came back. Like Grażyna, I sometimes feel out of place as an Eastern European in Western contexts.

In her stories, Grażyna rarely talks about herself: herself as a present self, made by chains of choices and coincidences that brought her to the place and language she is speaking from and in. And this very specific positionality of Grażyna Gross, a contemporary author who narrates herself in the past, will be of my interest here. I am curious about how her voice complicates the trajectories and narratives that are familiar to Western audiences: a refugee going westward after the Second World War from a "God forsaken country of Eastern Europe" ("The Watch"), yet not a Holocaust survivor but an ethnic Pole; an ethnic Pole but ironically addressing the Catholic and patriotic inclinations of her upbringings; an eyewitness to the Holocaust yet rarely conveying this experience; a postwar emigrée to the US, but with a class position much more complex than usual economic migrants from this part of the world: a descendant of a downgraded aristocratic family, educated from scratch in the wartime economy of survival. Grażyna is always "on the run," both as a protagonist and as an auto/biographical narrator, always out of place, contingent but also instinctively contiguous to the places where she happened to be. Her late writings, however, are not the only trace of this experience: as a teenager on the run, Grażyna also wrote stories: in Polish, by hand, in hardcover ruled notebooks, four of which survive into the present in her family archive. I will try to interpret some facets of Grażyna's being on the run by juxtaposing these two chronologically distant instances of life-writing.

Geography of Escape Routes

In the first chapter of *On the Run*, "Maria and Mirek," its child protagonist—whom I will call Grażyna in this essay, however not taking for granted her identity with the author of the stories—decides to do "something heroic." She lives with her parents and brother on the outskirts of the town of Wołożyn in the Eastern Borderlands of interwar Poland, and she is a girl, excluded from boys' games of adventure and gender privilege. She decides to run south through the endless field that spreads behind her house, until she reaches Turkey. "I knew very well where Turkey was, because Henius had an atlas in which all countries appeared in different colors, just like the hard candy in the jar at the Jewish store," she comments. Her geographic imagination, like most kids of the war generation, is shaped by a bird-eye perspective of cartography, commonly available thanks to popular atlases. But Grażyna herself lives in the area of Europe where the borders are much more blurred than edges of sweets "at the Jewish store." Her town lies in *Kresy*, the multiethnic and mostly rural vast terrains on the eastern flanks of Poland that were reassigned state identity repeatedly across the ages, an exemplary case of borderlands.

For centuries under Polish rule, *Kresy* were seized in the late eighteenth century by Tsarist Russia during the partitions of Poland (between Russia, Prussia, and the Habsburg Empire) which made Poland disappear from the map until 1918, the end of the Great War (World War I). Some of these territories then became part of a newly created independent Polish state and started to be a matter of an intensive politics of "polonization," realized through governmental decisions to sell land to Polish owners or to hire almost only Polish clerks in local administrations—such as Grażyna's father working in Wołożyn's court. But this transformation was also perpetrated through means of the press, literature, and art, in which *Kresy* were constructed as an epitome of Polish identity. World War II and the decisions made by the Allies at the Yalta Conference in 1945 changed this landscape again, and *Kresy* were permanently incorporated into the Soviet Ukraine and Belarus, its Polish population forcibly displaced westward, to within the new borders of postwar Poland. Even today, the Eastern Borderlands remain a mythical place in Polish collective memory: a token for both devastating nostalgia and nationalistic resentment. Wołożyn is now Valozhyn in Belarus, and its population has changed almost entirely, not only due to the postwar resettlements: before World War II, it was considered a "Jewish city" and one third of its inhabitants were Jews (2,300 people out of 7,000), almost all of whom died in the Holocaust, primarily in mass executions.

This uncertain status of home geography is expressed repeatedly in *On the Run in Occupied Poland*: "Its names depended on which country owned it, and when and if you were going east or west. Old people called it by one name, the young by another," comments the narrator of "Doctor's Daughter" about Oszmiana (now Ashmyany in Belarus) where Grażyna's family moved in 1937. Not only does the geography around Grażyna change constantly, she is herself permanently on the move. The temporary stability of the interwar period is disrupted by the outbreak of World War II. On 1 September 1939, Nazi Germany attacks from the west; on 17 September, Soviet Russia invades Poland from the east, and the borders in *Kresy* change yet again. Now they divide the USSR and Nazi Germany. These changes put thousands of people on the run. While Polish Jews are *en masse* escaping the Nazi-occupied part of Poland towards the east, the non-Jewish Polish bourgeoisie and intelligentsia from now Soviet-occupied territory are running in the opposite direction, westward, "from that frying pan into the fire of German-occupied Poland" ("Father Zeisel"), in order to avoid mass deportations to Gulag labor camps in Siberia and exile settlements in Central Asia. This is the case of Grażyna's father who, as a civil servant, but also as a landowner before the Russian Revolution in 1917, is likely to be arrested by the NKVD (the Soviet secret police agency). This is why, although "borders were dangerous, even the legal ones" ("The Fortune Teller"), the family decides to move to Warsaw and then Kraków, which are both situated in the Nazi-occupied part of Poland, the General Government. The family moves in July 1940; one year later borders change again when Nazi Germany invades the Soviet Union in Operation Barbarossa (commenced Sunday 22 June 1941).

Kraków seems to give Grażyna's spatial identification a sense of stability: there, she and her mother spent four years—from autumn 1940 until December 1944—and the city itself was not so heavily affected by the war as was, for instance, Warsaw. Yet, its topography was regulated by the conditions of war (and genocide): Kraków's Royal Castle, Wawel, was the headquarters of Hans Frank, the head of the General Government; the whole population of Kraków's Jews, consisting of more than fifty thousand people, was forced to either leave Kraków or to move to the ghetto in the Podgórze District that was created in spring 1941. This is when Grażyna and her mother move to a new apartment at 37 Starowiślna Street, within the traditional Jewish neighborhood Kazimierz, the apartment vacated by a Jewish family that had been forced to move out. Starowiślna Street is a peculiar space in the wartime topography of Kraków. It connects the very center of Kraków, with the picturesque Old City and Royal Castle, to its dark zone: Jewish Kazimierz, plundered by Nazis and their helpers, and Podgórze, the site of the ghetto. However, we will not learn much about Kraków's topography of violence from Grażyna's stories. It comes up explicitly only once, when Mykola takes her to a Jewish thread factory that is being expropriated, located towards the Vistula (Wisła) River, in the part of the city that was usually off-limits to her. "When we came out onto the street," Grażyna narrates in "The Picture Album, Part One," "we turned right instead of left, taking the path always forbidden to me." Gross aptly portrays mechanisms of intimate violence during genocide: formerly shared topography becomes divided along often invisible borders (Kraków Jews were forbidden to enter Main Square and Planty Park), so that those whose lives are not grievable anymore, to use Judith Butler's poignant term,[1] are no longer within sight: humiliated, dispossessed, displaced, deported, killed.[2]

The divisions between Jewish and non-Jewish Kraków are not the only ones that are rendered in Grażyna Gross's stories. Others are those going

---

[1] See Judith Butler, *Frames of War: When is Life Grievable?* (London and New York: Verso, 2016).

[2] See Andrea Löw and Markus Roth, *Juden in Krakau unter deutscher Besatzung 1939–1945* (Göttingen: Wallstein, 2011).

along the lines of social class and belonging. As refugees from the East, Grażyna and her mother experience in Kraków alienation and loneliness: their transient and uncertain status is constantly contrasted with the steady lives of the Kraków bourgeoisie, protected not only by wealth but above all else by being rooted in place. This is why, perhaps, we will not learn from Grażyna's narrative names of streets and exact coordinates: for her, Kraków's topography has a precarious nature, established by flows of movements and ephemeral connections. Kraków is only one of many stops on her way, followed by Prague, Domažlice (the German "Taus"), Regensburg, Furth, and finally the US. "Geography of escape routes," as she calls her spatial disposition ("A Christmas Story"), is the condition of refugeedom: the state of permanently seeking a refuge, a place that would allow one to feel rooted, to feel located, to be at home.

This is why an interesting counterpoint to Grażyna Gross's tales included in this volume are her Polish notebooks, three of which were written during her stay in Prague and Domažlice in 1945 and one probably earlier, in Kraków in 1942. Although created by a child and determined by naïve imagination, perspective, and forms of expression, these handwritten volumes are intriguing sources. Their narrator is far from making an autobiographical pact with her readers, but rather, in a series of (often unfinished) stories and fairytales, she generates autofictions about herself. She also practices the genre that she will master in her adult writing: fictitious letters to people important in her life (such as Runia or her father). Especially Gross's writings from 1942 are striking in this regard: she designs her writing as a diary and addresses her journal as her trusted audience. But she counterfeits her life as a forester's daughter living in a fictional forest somewhere between Central Poland and Belarus, with a flock of domesticated animals, her best friends. In a sense, in her wartime notebooks, Grażyna creates imagined safe spaces and fairytales about belonging and safety, in stark contrast to her real condition of constantly being an outsider on the run. But Grażyna uses the power of writing also to try on possible painful scenarios: in the stories in which she loses her grandpa to Germans, or in the unsent letter to her father (whose fate at the time remains for her unknown) she imagines what she hopes could never come true.

It is worth mentioning that the unstable and troubled space of Eastern Europe, together with its culture and way of life, is a site of strong identification for her, bitter and tender at the same time. The narrator of *On the Run in Occupied Poland* is very much aware of othering and orientalizing images of "the East" by "the West." When, in "Mrs. Kraus," the protagonist identifies herself ironically as coming from the "asshole of Europe," in this vulgar denomination may be heard dismissive stereotypes about Eastern Europe as the "second-hand," "epigonal," or "backward" Europe, deprived of local specifics and diversity, and the also widespread image of Eastern Europe as the "bloodlands" (Timothy Snyder's term),[3] defined only by the violence and conflict that were inflicted on it. For Grażyna, this heritage will delimit her later existence, which in some sense continued to be one of a refugee until the end, but in a much more complex form. On the one hand, her inheritance is the one of the war: "I learned to recite the names of German concentration camps, a skill that was not on the list of prerequisites to enter college in the US where I ended up," she confesses in "Evhen." But, on the other, she inherits rich and diverse cultures, landscapes, forms of identification, in comparison to which the US—devoid of the cultural environment Grażyna was accustomed to—was "worse than the war" ("Mama").

History Will Arrive

Fairytales that Grażyna rehearses in her wartime notebooks are not only a part of childish folklore. They appear frequently in *On the Run in Occupied Poland*, and "omens, ghosts, signs, and seers" ("Henius") have a status of alternative ways to experience and narrate history. "Fairytales were about what one wanted to be true but was not" ("Maria and Mirek"); they are performative narratives that offer an understandable universe. Little Grażyna is raised with fairytales as a default way of interpreting reality. Her nanny Maria "must have known every fairytale," both published—such as Little Red Riding Hood (known by Grażyna probably from the version by the Brothers Grimm, very popular in all of East and Central Europe)—and coming from oral tradition—such as Slavic legends about the "fern flower" that blooms only on the night of the summer solstice, called St. John's Eve or Kupala Night. Fairytales also punctuate the rhythm of her wartime notebooks, as in the case of her story "Memoir of the Spinster Mouse," that tells of a mouse family that takes over the apartment of a certain woman. Here, I hear the echo of an old Polish legend about mice that ate the evil Prince Popiel. But considering her stories composed as an adult, I also interpret it as a metaphor of her permanent condition of living in other people's apartments, surrounded by objects whose history do not concern her own. Fairytales are a method of dealing with uncertain reality, one that Grażyna's mother mastered to perfection, always "operating on hunches and psychic insights" ("Mrs. Kraus"). This specific sensibility makes Grażyna's mother, and subsequently herself, prone to forms of interpreting reality usually considered irrational or inferior, such as "divining the future" by Roma

---

[3] See Timothy Snyder, *Bloodlands: Europe between Hitler and Stalin* (New York: Basic Books, 2010).

women from itinerant communities that frequently visited peripheral locations of the Eastern Borderlands, or psychics and fortune tellers that mother and daughter (and servant) encounter in Kraków. These forms of interpreting reality also allow Grażyna's mother to be open to her intuition that often proves to be beneficial under uncertain conditions of war and historical flux. However questionable her choices might be from the perspective of her daughter's ethics, Mama manages to skillfully navigate this wartime reality and bring her daughter and herself to safer places in the geography of conflict, be it Prague, postwar Germany, or finally, the US.

"When Maria began to run out of fairytales, she would talk about wars," Grażyna states in her first story. The power of storytelling is not reserved to supernatural narratives, it is also a way of training one's imagination to understand the most palpable of experiences and most intimate of identities. History is then, to refer to historian Hayden White, a well-constructed narrative.[4] For Eastern Europe, the most encompassing narrative is the one about war and military conflict: it comes back with a certainty of change of seasons, and when Grażyna is a few years old, according to Maria, "a new war [is] already in the making." War influences the most local environment, such as Blood Creek near Wołożyn, or *krwawnik* (common yarrow; *krew* means "blood" in Polish), the weed that Grażyna mentions, that is a natural medicine that helps stop bleeding. The transcendental order of wars also allows one to foresee the future: when the German army starts losing on the eastern front, people celebrate: "1812, once again!" ("The Watch"). Like the Napoleonic Wars, like winter, the German invasion too shall pass. Portraying war as an inevitable course of events makes peace only a transitory condition, not a part of history with a capital H. When Grażyna's father wants to make sure that she "would not miss what he called 'History'" and see how "History will arrive," he positions her on the balcony to see the Russian tanks entering the streets of Wilno (now Vilnius in Lithuania, "The Shoemaker's Son").

War is not only an inescapable part of reality, it also defines what is the most valuable form of existence in Grażyna's culture. Thus, her imagination is trained to perceive historical events in hierarchical order: the most important are those related to military conflict and the perpetual fight for the Homeland. Even her very name carries traces of this logic since it was used for the first time by Polish Romantic poet Adam Mickiewicz, who bequeathed "Grażyna" (from Lithuanian *graži*, beautiful) on the female protagonist of his 1823 poem that concerns the fight against the medieval order of Teutonic Knights, undertaken by Lithuanians and guided by a mythical female leader. This set of values can be found in her wartime notebooks, for

---

4   See Hayden White, *Metahistory: The Historical Imagination in Nineteenth-Century Europe* (Baltimore, MD: Johns Hopkins University Press, 1973).

instance, in a recollection about Grażyna and her brother Henius browsing together a book called *The Blaze*, which contains reproductions of several series of panels by the Polish Romantic painter Artur Grottger. Those panels portray in an allegorical manner failed Polish insurrections against Tsarist Russia in the nineteenth century, in which the natural (and expected) fate of men is to die for the Homeland and of women to await and mourn their beloved. Grażyna's wartime notebooks record very well her training in Polish patriotic culture: the fables usually open with the invocation "In the Name of God," and portray forests as the hideout for partisans, from 1863 or the 1940s. They evoke images of "the crucified Homeland" that needs to be freed at whatever cost. In the most elaborated variation of the fictional story about a girl living in the woods, the protagonist follows her grandpa—who had been imprisoned in the infamous Warsaw prison Pawiak due to his partisan activities—and embarks with her animals on a lonely journey from the Central Poland forests to the capital. When she arrives, the Warsaw Uprising, that is the actual historical Polish military revolt against Nazi occupation begins (1 August 1944). The girl protagonist traverses Warsaw through underground shelters, and becomes a courier for the Polish Home Army. She compares herself to Jurek Bitschan, the child soldier who fought for the Polish defense of Lwów (now Lviv) in the Polish-Ukrainian War of 1918–1919. Considering that Gross (probably) writes this story in early 1945, just a few months after the Warsaw Uprising, I am astonished by how early the military-heroic narrative about this event—which prevails until now, especially in conservative and right-wing versions of Polish history—was already cemented. The Warsaw Uprising was in fact a real civilian tragedy that caused the death of two hundred thousand Warsaw residents and the expulsion of a further six hundred thousand, and it resulted in the complete destruction of the city.

Yet, *On the Run in Occupied Poland*, written in her adult life, avoids this martyrologic perspective, consistently focusing on the other aspect of the war: the civilian disaster that it causes. The narrator of the stories comments ironically on the real ramifications of history conceived in military terms, as a supernatural order of war and death. "I knew by then that 'historic location' meant that once upon a time something terrible had happened there. The more 'historic' the place, the more horrible the events," Grażyna points out about the topography of Warsaw ("Justyna"). And she continues: "I saw Justyna again in the fall of 1944, a time so historic that its only colors were black and dark gray." The history she was trained to recognize is the one that petrifies into allegories of the "homeland in shackles" and of "sacrificing life for freedom," both motifs omnipresent in her wartime writings. The history that Gross decides to narrate in her stories written as an adult is much more "unspectacular": it is the history of thousands of casualties whose deaths are not legitimized by any higher cause, and thousands of refugees, whose lives have been irreversibly altered. But there is a seed of this perspective already in her wartime writings, when she describes her readings of Grottger's allegorical images. The eleven-year-old Grażyna confesses: "Again, war and haze… But now I live through it for real, not only staring at Grottger's paintings. … How different the house which is burning in reality looks from the one painted as burning. … I saw Grottger's 'Captive,' but a 'roundup' is maybe worse, a man is not a man anymore but a hunted animal." Chaos and violence of a roundup on the streets of Kraków—in which random civilians were arrested and sent to forced labor or concentration camps—are well captured in her adult story "A Boy."

I Only Watch

The hunting metaphors from Grażyna's notebooks quoted above evoke the key civilian tragedy from the period, namely the Holocaust. Is it the History with a capital H? Grażyna's life story is adjacent to the history of Polish Jews, 90 percent of whom did not survive World War II, yet their fates rarely appear explicitly in her writing. Jews are "part of the scenery" ("Maria and Mirek") of her childhood in the Eastern Borderlands[5] and are the protagonists of antisemitic tales offered by Maria, the nanny. In Kraków, the fates of its Jewish residents appear in Grażyna's laconic statement: "We are waiting for a Jewish apartment to be vacated, so that we can move in and take a bath" ("The Root Canal"). Soon, Mykola, who works for the Germans as a *Treuhänder*,—a trustee handling confiscated Jewish property, a "profession" reserved mostly for local Germans but exercised also by Ukrainians who enjoyed privileges under Nazi rule[6]—takes Grażyna for a trip to the forbidden side of their street, where she is to witness "a piece of history" ("The Picture Album, Part One"). The historical event he means is the liquidation of a Jewish thread factory which the narrator depicts in generous detail. "Was she thinking about the trip to the camp, the camp, and finally death of a special kind?" Grażyna ponders about the Jewish owner of the factory, Mrs. Goldweber. The almost dispassionate way in which Jewish fates appear in *On the Run* may cause unease, but it also might be interpreted as a

---

5   Both Wołożyn and Oszmiana had large Jewish populations and both have their *yizker-bikher*, memorial books, written by the survivors and published after the war.

6   See Paweł Markiewicz, *Unlikely Allies: Nazi German and Ukrainian Nationalist Collaboration in the General Government During World War II* (West Lafayette, IN: Purdue University Press, 2021).

conscious decision of a skillful storyteller rendering the common attitude—or perhaps a viewpoint—of the time.

The narrator of the stories indicates her positionality very clearly, albeit in passing, as an observer. "When in danger I tell myself that I should just watch and not become a part of what is happening. Perhaps no one can see me then, especially if I do not move," Grażyna explains in her letter to Mrs. Kraus. In another story she states: "I only watch what is happening around me" ("The Ring"). To watch means to not cast judgment but also to not engage, to not take responsibility for one's own possibility to act. What is the agency of a child, however? Is she an eyewitness? a gawker? a bystander? She is a representative of the 1.5 generation of the neighbors (rather than the victims), to adapt Susan Rubin Suleiman's category: a child that witnessed the genocide and experienced the war, whose formation was deeply influenced by the events she went through, but who recognized this experience as fundamental only later.[7] Gross decides to honestly depict the consciousness of a child observer during the war and genocide, and the most evident order that her child narrator notices is the rule of wartime economy, in which bare lives (to recall Giorgio Agamben's term) become a commodity like anything else.[8] Grażyna observes and notes in a crude manner: they are waiting for "a Jewish apartment to be vacated" (the passive voice is of the utmost importance here) "so that [they] can move in and take a bath." In other words, she is aware of how the lives of her mother and herself become more valuable than those of the former Jewish owners of the apartment they take over and how Jewish property, even that of mostly personal and intimate value (as the picture album that Mykola gets—or maybe takes?—from Mrs. Goldweber), becomes worthless and ready for reappropriation. The distinct world of the wartime economy may be grasped in the changes of language accurately recorded by Grażyna: people become elements of the logic of "possibility" and "opportunity" ("Mama") rather than of solidarity and community. Finally, I would suggest, in this ostensibly indifferent voice, Gross manages to stay fair towards her readers and herself. Her wartime notebooks contain a few statements that may represent a trace of the antisemitic milieu she grew up in. Her postwar stories do not mimic prejudice she might have been prone to, but rather try to convey how children in prewar Poland became acquainted with antisemitic sentiments: through her nanny's fables about bad Jews ("Maria and Mirek") and through cruel indifference to Jewish fates.

---

[7] Susan Rubin Suleiman, "The 1.5 Generation: Thinking About Child Survivors and the Holocaust," *American Imago* 59, no. 3 (2002): 277–95.

[8] Giorgio Agamben, *Homo Sacer: Sovereign Power and Bare Life* (Stanford, CA: Stanford University Press, 1998).

Grażyna's special disposition to observe and record needs to be contextualized. The most recurrent self-description of the narrator is the one of self-deprecation and belittlement, she is never clever nor pretty enough. At the same time, she outlines very precisely what objective elements define her position: namely social class, gender, and ethnicity. One of the most banal and mysterious descriptions of class in *On the Run in Occupied Poland* is the following: to be "(from) a good family." At the beginning of her narrated biography, Grażyna may seem to possess this ephemeral quality of being from a good home, but with the war she quickly loses it. In Soviet-occupied Wilno, she is a stranger from the destitute upper class ("As for my inheritance, if any, the Revolution had already taken care of it before I was born," she notes in "Mama"). Yet, she is also a street kid, "the dumb girl from some crumbling village" ("The Shoemaker's Son"). Moreover, her family cannot be considered a "good" one anymore when her father leaves and her mother engages in a romantic relationship with her "prize tenant" ("The Psychic"), Ukrainian Mykola. Thus, she is both: "a bourgeois leech" under communist rule, and a "class pariah" in bourgeois Kraków. And this very condition of being in-between, her double class attribution, seems to be the source of her extraordinary sensitivity to social class subtleties.

It is worth mentioning that social class in the Eastern European context concerns much more than economic capital: it is habitus, to use Pierre Bourdieu's term,[9] a complex disposition, a set of habits, skills, language, and esthetic choices that allow "distinction" from those one does not want to identify with and from those one desires to be taken for. The most fluent in this quicksand of class affiliation is Grażyna's mother. Waleria successfully performs being a "countess" if the situation demands it; she also pays extra attention to training her daughter in proper class belonging, for instance, sending her to a school where she will be able to strike up valuable "connections," despite her dire economic state. For Grażyna, this double attribution is a source of suffering rather than social flexibility: she detests her mother's various "transgressions" and constantly feels looked down upon. But again, it is also a source of remarkable perceptiveness. Grażyna scolds "the nouveaux riches who were making money off the war" ("A Dinner"), appreciates those who are "real gentlemen," and admires her sister-in-dispossession, Runia, who shares her condition of being "at the bottom of the [school] class" ("Tereska"). Runia retains the status of a "good home" as the presumably eventual heiress of a palace in Kraków. So, her act of unabashed consumption of sweets at the home of the newly-rich Barans enchants Grażyna with its class bravado: "Spellbound, we watch Runia violate the Christmas

---

9 Pierre Bourdieu, *Distinction: A Social Critique of the Judgement of Taste*, trans. Richard Nice (Cambridge, MA: Harvard University Press, 1984).

tree and all the rules of good behavior. There is something heroic about what she is doing" ("A Christmas Story"). There is also a trace of Gross's class sensitivity in her wartime notebooks, for instance, in a story featuring girls from disparate social backgrounds: a city girl whose mother works in a factory, a peasant's daughter, and one from a noble family, who together come to realize the differences that define their lives. Interestingly, the child narrator of the notebooks makes a remark about the difficulties in mimicking a "peasant accent."

Ultimately, we need to note that social class never goes unattended: in the case of Grażyna, it intersects with her gender and her ethnic belonging. The narrator of *On the Run in Occupied Poland* is very much aware of the limitations that being a girl casts upon her: she is subjected to greater scrutiny regarding personal freedoms and social expectations. At the same time, she realizes that gender saves her from the deadly order of war, since she is not expected to die in combat: "To decide which of the two evils was worse—becoming a girl or getting killed in a war—was not easy" ("Maria and Mirek"). But class in the Eastern European context is also intertwined with ethnicity, especially with regard to Polish-Ukrainian intersections. Grażyna's father comes from a family of Polish nobility in the Eastern Borderlands that constituted a colonial power abusing the local Ukrainian population under the system of serfdom that was not very distinct from slavery. Although serfdom officially ended in 1861, its legacies were still abiding in the early twentieth century, and during the 1917 Russian Revolution many estates of Polish gentry were sacked by Ukrainian peasants. The resentment and class disdain towards Ukrainians were still enduring among Poles in the interwar period. The instances of Ukrainian collaboration with Nazi power (in the hope of regaining independence from Soviet reign) and then the ethnic cleansing perpetrated on Polish neighbors by Ukrainian nationalists in Volhynia and eastern Galicia in 1943 and 1944 only reinforced these sentiments. Grażyna expresses her aversion to Mykola often in class-related terms: apart from his shady activities, he behaves like a philistine "who picks his nose in public and spits in the street" ("The Root Canal").

In this context, an interesting coda for Grażyna's class struggles are her postwar stories based at the DP camp, the Ganghofersiedlung, a meeting point for people whose state of refugeedom allowed them to ignore their various differences. It is enough to mention that Grażyna herself befriends a Polish Jewish couple, a Ukrainian family, and Polish *Volksdeutsche*, namely people of German origin who were reestablished as Germans by the Nazi regime during the war. On the train, she meets both survivors from concentration camps and Nazi collaborators. Perhaps only this temporary utopia of refugees—rootless, poor, struggling with language but full of hope—offers the chance for classless solidarity. And in this specific habitat, Grażyna is happy: suddenly she has a clean slate, she "is" what she is able to learn and to share.

What is Heroic?

"As the saying goes, heroic deeds don't grow on trees, except during a war," comments the child narrator of the first story in *On the Run in Occupied Poland*. The heroic is inscribed in the military, nationalistic, and masculine orders of war. Although focused on a war period, stories from *On the Run in Occupied Poland* purposely subvert this perspective. Runia is being heroic when she eats all the candy on a Christmas tree in a sudden acknowledgment of her own hunger; Grażyna does something heroic when she transgresses gender boundaries and decides to see what is outside the town when she is a little girl. In a way, Grażyna's mother, who "had a talent for taking charge in times of crisis" ("Father Zeisel"), is heroic in her relentless resilience. However troubled, Gross's stories are a tribute to Mama's "trying faces" and "being on the run" as civilian ways of survival under the conditions of war. Or perhaps a lesson we and she can take from this writing is that the concept of the heroic is a part of vocabulary that may, finally, be abandoned for the sake of kindness and solidarity. By narrating her wartime childhood from her refugee perspective, always displaced in her nationality, language, social class, gender, and geography, Grażyna portrays the war not as a narrative of victory and sacrifice, but of civilian experiences of attempting to survive. This angle is crucial in our contemporary moment when we seem to have passed the point in which "the great powers were taking a rest before starting another war, and the next apocalypse was not yet on the horizon" ("Father Zeisel").

My Friend the Writer

Irene Kacandes

The stories that make up *On the Run in Occupied Poland* grip me in a way that I cannot fully account for. When I read them—something I have done dozens of times—I find myself in a certain uneasy mood. I am living through World War II in Central Europe, even though I was born in the United States in 1958. This essay is my attempt to explain to myself and to anyone who cares to read this why I get so tangled in them.

Grażyna

To be sure, when I read these stories, I hear the voice of my friend again. It's very distinctive to my ear. In some stories I hear the innocent child subjected to forces she cannot control. In others, the mature adult, sometimes sad, sometimes embittered, more than once sarcastic.

There's no obvious reason why Grażyna Gross and I should have become friends, but we did. She was what a lot of people might call "a difficult person." I wasn't oblivious to her thorny sides, yet, realizing that she accepted me as a person in her life made me feel special. The age difference just didn't seem to matter—she was two and a half years older than my mother. In an essay where I tried to describe our relationship once before—an essay Grażyna heavily redacted to make it harder for any reader to figure out whom I was talking about—I called it "gratuitous": we didn't owe each other anything.[1] We wrote to each other when we felt like it and had the time, and didn't when we didn't; we shared what we felt like sharing. At some point I wanted more of her, though. More of her history. Was some sign of affection unrealistic? I got little of the former and the barest of hints of the latter while she was alive. Thanks to her daughter Joyce reaching out

---

[1] Irene Kacandes, "A Polish Childhood," in *Eastern Europe Unmapped: Beyond Borders and Peripheries*, eds. Irene Kacandes and Yuliya Komska (New York: Berghahn Books, 2017), 248–68.

to me after her death in March 2022, I did eventually learn much more of Grażyna's history, partly through documents and photos Joyce had found and catalogued, and also through pieces of Grażyna's writing that I had not yet seen (these are mainly, though not exclusively, the longer, later chapters of what you've just read). I learned even more when Aleksandra joined this editing team and shared what was in Grażyna's Polish wartime notebooks.

Grażyna and I had met in a restaurant completely by chance when I had come to Ithaca, New York in spring 2002 to give a lecture at Cornell University. We were both eating lunch by ourselves at tables next to each other in the famed Moosewood Restaurant. I noticed she was buried in a book. I couldn't resist glancing at the cover: *Die Glut*, a novel. I hadn't heard of it and assumed that if she were reading in German, she might only speak German, so I addressed her in German. She seemed surprised, but responded, and the conversation took off. She wasn't German, she explained, but rather Polish. She'd gone to school in Germany and enjoyed reading in that language, even a book like this which was a translation of a novel by the prolific Hungarian author Sándor Márai. She asked what I was doing in Ithaca and before the meal was over, I boldly asked for her address. She gave it to me. I read *Die Glut*. In German. I wrote to her. She responded.

For years, we sent each other letters by regular mail. At some point, we started punctuating them with email. Like our first conversation, we mostly shared about books or films or current events. I often sent her the actual copies of books I had just finished reading that I thought she would find worthwhile. Eventually, Grażyna started including in her letters short texts she'd written—vignettes about her experiences in occupied Poland and East Central Europe during the mid-twentieth-century catastrophes. The Holocaust, or what I prefer to call the Nazi Judeocide, was my academic area of expertise. I knew more about what had transpired in Poland during the war than your average person on the street. Grażyna liked that I could follow her without requiring historical context or translation of German words she occasionally used. I, in turn, was hooked by learning what she had experienced as a non-Jewish child during that period—almost all my previous knowledge about wartime Poland coming from or being about Jewish lives. I was reminded of my own attitude in the presence of Grażyna and her storytelling when I read the line in "Evhen": "I thought that Evhen enjoyed listening to my version of history." I never met Evhen, but I believe that. I know I enjoyed listening to her. "Evhen," by the way, was the last story she ever sent me, and we exchanged thoughts about it in several long emails. We were emailing with one another quite regularly in the last years of her life, the very last exchange taking place two weeks before she died—though I did not know that she was dying and couldn't really have guessed because she didn't express anything more dramatic than many other times when she would tell me she was about to croak.

My father, almost exactly one year older than Grażyna, had been trapped as a child in Fascist-occupied Greece during World War II. I had started researching his experiences around the same time I was getting to know Grażyna, that is, in the early 2000s. I eventually turned my research on my paternal family into a book that Grażyna read in draft. She found it "interesting." I dared propose to her that she and I do some kind of similar book using her life and her writing as a basis. She rejected that idea, but eventually agreed to try to rewrite and collate her texts into a story cycle. She didn't want to call it a memoir and not even a paramemoir, which is the generic category I invented to describe *Daddy's War*, the book about my father and which is what I am calling this volume you are reading.[2] I think Grażyna's resistance at the time was both to the idea that her life warranted a memoir and perhaps even more importantly that she needed to protect certain individuals, starting with her mother, but extending certainly to her best friend Runia and her family. If something got published, it needed to be received as fiction, she insisted. I didn't quite get the logic of this since her mother, but also the few others she named to me, were no longer alive. But I was determined to get her writing an airing even if it had to be by publishing what I considered autobiographical vignettes as fictional stories.

I can still see the two of us at her dining room table at the house on Ellis Hollow Road where she had lived for decades and where I had already visited her and her husband Len. By the time of this, our third in-person encounter, we'd known each other for about sixteen years. Work took center stage. I'd have one story in front of me and she usually another, hers one that I had already made some pencil marks onto with suggested edits. As she read through my suggestions, she'd either let them be or would pick up her head and ask me what I thought of a different phrasing or word choice. I'd respond. She'd nod or make a new suggestion and then mark the change. She seemed to genuinely enjoy this way of being together. To me, she seemed happy as we worked. I love editing, and since I hadn't experienced Grażyna that often in a joyous mood, I was happy that she was happy.

I didn't remember well my efforts to publish what we put together as a fictional story collection at that time until I looked up the correspondence in

---

2   Irene Kacandes, *Daddy's War: Greek American Stories; A Paramemoir* (Lincoln: University of Nebraska Press, 2009; published in paperback in 2012). Using the polyvalence of the Greek prefix "para," I count as paramemoir something that goes beyond memoir, that may stand as a substitute for one, that includes the voices and lives of more than one person. See also Irene Kacandes, "Paramemoir," in *Experimental Life Writing Today*, eds. Vanessa Guignery and Wojciech Drąg (London: Bloomsbury, 2025), 55–70.

preparation for this current project to publish Grażyna's writing. It turns out that I had tried harder than I had remembered. A big shot literary agent's attention was attracted enough by the sample story and my cover letter for her to request the whole manuscript (as it was constituted at that time). The agent ultimately decided that she didn't know how to market this kind of fiction—especially short stories—by an unknown author to the famous presses she normally pitched to, but she thanked me for sharing the manuscript with her. I tried other agents and other publishers with similar results: "stories by unknowns" were just not in demand... I felt partial victory when—after originally refusing—Grażyna agreed to let me publish "Mrs. Kraus" in an anthology that I was putting together with others during the Covid lockdown, a volume that we decided to call *On Being Adjacent to Historical Violence*, and that appeared in early 2022.[3] Again, Grażyna insisted that her writing appear as fiction, and in the brief biographies on contributors that appear in the back of such books, she was identified as a writer of short fiction. Whatever the label, Grażyna did get to see her writing in print before she died. I sensed that that was satisfying to her. It certainly was to me, and I did not remember until getting ready to write this reflection, how frequently we were in communication in this period despite her increasing ill health.

The decision to publish Grażyna's writing now as a memoir kernel of a paramemoir was taken carefully and with the permission of Grażyna's family, and as you can see elsewhere in this book, with the active participation of her adult daughter, Joyce Gross. One factor in taking this decision was certainly the point that I began these comments with: these vignettes grab me, transport me, have never left my consciousness. I could say—picking up on a feature of Grażyna's childhood—that they have actually haunted me with their poignancy and also maybe with a touch of reproach for not having finished what I started. The fact that the stories drew in Joyce—who had not read them prior to her mother's death—and then Aleksandra, a Polish scholar I had met recently and immediately admired, also contributed to my determination to push forward by revealing them as the autobiographical writing that they certainly are and in a new format, with new episodes that provide better chronological coherence. My two collaborators would have perspectives that seemed invaluable to me in terms of creating an overall text that featured Grażyna's writing and offered additional information that could allow strangers to appreciate the unique contribution to history of Grażyna's experiences. Another factor was certainly all the additional material—letters, photos, documents, and, as already mentioned, some writing unknown to me—that Joyce Gross found after her mother's death, studied herself, and then shared

---

3   *On Being Adjacent to Historical Violence*, ed. Irene Kacandes (Berlin: De Gruyter, 2022). "Mrs. Kraus" appears on pages 393–8.

with me and a bit later with Aleksandra. This paratextual material—things "around" the main text—offers a fuller picture of Grażyna's experiences that I think transform a string of arresting anecdotes into a mostly painful account of growing up without a home. That Grażyna experienced herself as an outsider refugee becomes particularly apparent through this larger set of materials, as does the fact that what she wrote recounts her own experiences.

Moving a bit further away from the personal, when a society is in crisis, it's not always the everyday that gets recorded. Some of the specific details that are included in Grażyna's account offer concrete historical information about things like underground schooling, the black market, liquidations of various kinds, and housing in Nazi-occupied Poland. Could it be the most persuasive reason for publication that the topics of refugeedom and specifically refugees from war zones are only becoming more relevant to a huge swath of the world's population today? Sharing a reflective account of what it feels like to be on the move, indeed often literally on the run, could be supportive to those who have had similar experiences and enlightening to those who have not. The process of figuring out how to proceed once we decided to work together as a threesome was deeply rewarding for me. Our video conferences to discuss various issues created delightful echoes for me of Grażyna and me at her dining room table. Emails we would exchange or remarks we wrote into the margins of drafts of this text were methods of carrying out our own friendships and also extending our relationships to Grażyna.

For many reasons, then, I became determined that there *would* be a trace of Grażyna and her mother's past, contrary to what Grażyna predicted in "Mama." And we pushed forward with this volume.

Grażyna's Writing as Writing

Many of us know that Anne Frank aspired to be a writer. Particularly after the announcement she heard on a clandestine radio broadcast during her time in hiding that the Dutch government in exile planned to collect (after the war) writing that recounted people's experiences during the war and Nazi occupation of the Netherlands, Anne thought of her diary as something that others would want to read, and she began to rewrite it accordingly. Though she herself did not survive the war and never saw publication of her work, over thirty million copies of her diary have been sold.[4] Many "real" writers have praised the quality of what the young Anne Frank produced and have

---

4   For more information, see https://annefrank.com/about-afc/about-anne-frank/.

offered the judgment that she had the seeds that make for a successful professional writer (see, for instance, Francine Prose's assessment).[5]

Grażyna was two years younger than Anne Frank. For a short while during the war, she kept a kind of journal that might be considered a diary, but its nature was quite different than Frank's to record daily what was going on directly around her, and with two others notebooks that survived the war period, we should probably count all of these pages as the child's attempt to create a safer, fictional world for herself.[6] Within Grażyna's late adult writing, that is, what she still wanted to call "stories" that we have presented here in *On the Run in Occupied Poland* as memoir, we get a glimpse of the child Grażyna writing during the war, though not of the notebooks just mentioned. The narrator of *On the Run in Occupied Poland* describes the child in Wilno trying to write a poem, an activity that Uncle Kot teases her about ("Uncle Kot"). She and Józefina concoct a story at the end of their long simultaneous illness that the child Grażyna writes down and illustrates—a neighbor and his friend even think it a masterpiece, though the authors ridicule that opinion.[7] And, of course, the child writing letters is mentioned within the adult writing, and some of the segments presented in *On the Run in Occupied Poland* themselves constitute letters.

From my conversations over the years with Grażyna, it became clear to me that, in contrast to Anne Frank, she had trouble thinking of herself as a writer. She did take a few writing classes at Cornell University but reported to me that what she produced there was "awful." It was a long, slow campaign I waged that she consider her writing otherwise. No matter her self-evaluation, the fact remains that Grażyna Gross wrote over many years and produced a lot. To cite just one example, the versions of "Józefina" are so numerous and long that they fill scores of pages. I still remember sitting on the huge bed of the bed and breakfast room I was staying in during what turned out to be my last visit and having sheets of just this story spread all over it. How will I ever untangle it, I wondered. It seems to me that Grażyna was trying to get her writing to a certain narrative truth right up to almost the day of her death.[8] Once we decided to embed her writing into a paramemoir and once I had reread our correspondence, new stories, more drafts, some statements she made to another scholar, I realized how many

---

5   See Francine Prose, *Anne Frank: The Book, the Life, the Afterlife* (New York: Atlantic, 2010).
6   For more on what that "diary" and other notebooks are like, see Aleksandra's essay.
7   This story has not been located in Grażyna's posthumous papers.
8   See Donald P. Spence, *Narrative Truth and Historical Truth: Meaning and Interpretation in Psychoanalysis* (New York: W. W. Norton and Company, 1982).

choices she had been making about tone, style, form. The straightforward way she occasionally wrote to me in letters about the facts of her life, for example, differs enormously from the way the course of her life is presented in the series of tales you have read. Whether Grażyna thought of herself as a writer or not, she was working in a writerly way.

As a scholar of narrative, storytelling, and life writing, I want to share a few thoughts about what Grażyna Gross produced. One of the basic observations we specialists in narrative theory make about how first-person narratives—whether fictional or factual—work, concerns the view on what is being recounted. Sometimes the individual "I" who is writing or narrating is very close to the "I" whose experiences are being recorded at a certain moment, and sometimes the writing I and the experiencing I are very far apart. To put this second situation otherwise, it's obvious that the person doing the writing knows a lot more than the younger self they're writing about knows. Perhaps this distinction is clearer if you think about the situation of a traditional autobiography: an old man—and it often is a man—recounts his life from birth to childhood to young adulthood to middle adulthood, eventually catching up to where he finds himself now. When he's narrating the parts about his childhood, his adult self might point out all the foolishness or immaturity or mistakes: the writing I is "far" from the experiencing I he is describing at that moment—not only in calendar time but also in maturity and attitude. Toward the end of such a traditional scheme, those two I's are presumably closer together and in greater harmony philosophically, affectively, or ethically, as well as chronologically. One other point to note is that even the writing I is a persona that a "real person," an autobiographer, takes up. We create a certain image of ourselves as we write about ourselves at no matter what age or at no matter what moment in time.

Though I can date the time of writing of hardly any of the stories included in this volume, to my knowledge and Joyce's, the stories were written and rewritten when Grażyna was a mature adult. So, her biological age at the time of writing is very much more advanced than the age of her younger self in the various episodes. What is important to me here is that as narrator of her own life, she experimented with different distances to her accounts. I was pulled in very quickly by—and admire enormously in terms of the skill required—Grażyna's stories where the distance between the narrating self and the experiencing self is almost imperceptible even if chronologically they are far apart. In other words, I was convinced by how Grażyna depicts her younger self, especially relating the thoughts and logic of a child. Already in the first tale ("Maria and Mirek"), Grażyna doesn't just "report" that she was afraid of the geese or laugh at why a young child might be afraid of them, rather she reproduces what seems like a plausible train of thought that a child might have had because of encountering vicious geese: wondering whether the geese bothered boys too; then observing that she hadn't seen any boys having to go to the store and therefore encounter the mean animals on their way there; and then the complaint about boys not even being asked to go to the store: "as if boys always had something more important to do!" Between the train of logic and the diction, the actual words used, we can practically imagine that this is what the child is thinking as she walks that scary path between home and store. A similarly striking moment occurs just a little further along when she reports being inside the store on a day when the door into the Jewish family's apartment is ajar. Given the antisemitic tales that her nanny Maria had been feeding her, the reported thoughts when she spots the (presumably Catholic Polish) servant girl seem believable for a young child to think: "Did she know what could happen to her? Wasn't she afraid?" Of course, what also draws us in is that this child has superior powers of observation and from a very young age seems to have always tested what adults said against what she herself actually witnessed: "there were barrels in the store: one with herring, one with sauerkraut, and one with pickles. I did not see one studded with nails." In this manner, and without directly challenging the antisemitism of people her child-self relied on for her own well-being, she signals her skepticism that Jews could engage—were engaging—in such murderous actions as her caretaker maintained.

There are lots of marvelous turns of phrase rendering a child's point of view. In reporting the events of the day of her brother's funeral, for example, the family arrives at a "hole in the ground in which he is supposed to stay forever" ("Heniuś"). Much of the convincing—and often humorous—rendering of a child's inner world has to do with sex, which is usually referred to as an "it" that she doesn't understand. After Grażyna's father has left because of her mother's relationship with Mykola, the child picks up clearly on the landlady's hostility. But she's not quite sure if that hostility is directed at her or at her mother. She asks herself: "What is the difference between 'a slut' and 'a daughter of a slut'?" ("The Root Canal"). I'm not sure I have read many accounts in fiction or non-fiction where the writer can represent so convincingly and memorably a child's mind. I admire the writer in this respect also for *not* adding many things that she figured out later and that the adult writer knew as she was drafting. An example of this to my mind is almost hidden in what is a very dramatic episode in any case, that of the child's father returning briefly to Kraków. Grażyna only includes observations that the child would have perceived, not the (adult) conclusions to be drawn, when she narrates that her mother stays in bed, and Józefina says she has to do that or she will bleed to death. The narrating I stays close to the experiencing I by concluding that Józefina just doesn't know how to explain what's actually going on.⁹

As for my own adult predilections and as someone who knew this author as an adult, I am also drawn to passages in which the adult narrator is clearly speaking as an adult. Whereas it seems feasible that the landlady could have been muttering something about sluts, I hear the cynical, irreverent adult Grażyna I knew using words like "tit" and "dick" in the description of the religious art works in the huge picture album that Mykola receives—Aleksandra has suggested perhaps "takes"—from Mrs. Goldweber, the elderly lady in the thread and yarn warehouse: "Old men showing off their muscles and hair, women exposing their tits, and girls with flowers growing between their legs. And, of course, the fat Baby Jesus with his dick always showing so that he would not be mistaken for a girl. In the Garden of Eden, the place of eternal summer, Adam and Eve only needed a couple of fig leaves to keep themselves warm" ("The Picture Album, Part Two").

Readers will also have noticed passages when the narrator is speaking most explicitly in her adult voice, from and about her adult world. She reflects at the beginning of "EH":

> I have your address. I found it on the internet. Since no one else with your name is listed, it is very likely the place where you are now living after your stint in Brazil. So, I could end up at your door one day, though of course I won't, not only because you will not remember me, but also because I don't want to see what a long life, however good, could have done to you. I prefer to keep you in my memory as the youngest, the smartest, and the most mature boy in the class.

Grażyna often told me about her searches on the internet for people and places she had known during her childhood and adolescence. She was quite a good researcher and through her efforts she "found" many people she had once interacted with. The caution she expresses in the passage just quoted about not trying to follow up in real time with any of them though, seems born of an actual experience when she located the beautiful Rozmaryna during a 1992 visit to Warsaw and discovered her former classmate strangely unwilling to remember that they knew one another: "I am a stranger to her; even the memory of Renata [Runia] does not bring us together" ("Rozmaryna," unpublished fragment in the Gross family's

---

9   The hints to Waleria having had a miscarriage or an abortion during the war as here or towards its end, as in her strong reactions to the baby bottle Grażyna finds at Mrs. Kraus's, with what I consider a follow up hint of Waleria's stay in a hospital not long after (in "Night in Regensburg") remain inconclusive, and I respect Grażyna's decision to leave it that way in the public record.

possession). Still, the writer's decision to open this segment with mention of how she "found" EH, constitutes one of many references in *On the Run* to the time of writing, not to the timeframe of the storyworld itself. In doing so, Grażyna foregrounds the act of writing and draws attention to the "writing I" as opposed to the "experiencing I" of the past. Another way to put this is that she also makes her elderly adult self a part of the whole sequence.

The opening of the segment "Letter to an Unknown Man" can perhaps solidify the points I've been making about adult selves and childhood selves that are so prominent in Grażyna's writing. She opens this chapter with:

> If this message could get to you somehow, it would probably, as people say here, make your day. If there are days where you are. You did not leave a forwarding address, so I cannot mail it to you. Besides, I no longer remember your name. It is possible that I never really knew it, or I may have heard it, but it never sunk in. You did stick with me, though, and that's all that matters at this moment. I wish I could still believe in the superstitions and tall tales I was exposed to in my childhood, but I gave that up a long time ago. So, as far as I am concerned, there is no way of reaching you. Still, in case I am wrong, and the superstitions are right, I will go ahead and try to explain why you have been on my mind for so many years. It certainly was not love at first sight or something equally silly.

Her label of the phrase "make your day" as something "people say here" foregrounds, in a different way from the previous example, the place and time from which she is writing. Words like "here" and "at this moment" are referred to by linguists as "deictics," words that by their nature refer to the act of enunciation, to the situation of the saying rather than the representing or describing of something out there. Grażyna's wish that "I could still believe in the superstitions and tall tales I was exposed to in my childhood" brings into relief the two timeframes as well as the ultimately majority retrospective thrust of *On the Run in Occupied Poland*.

The Magical Second Person Pronoun

There's one other technique evident in the previously quoted passage that is crucial to the magic that Grażyna is conjuring for herself and us through her writing, and that's the use of the second person pronoun, the "you." Addressing someone who's not actually there is referred to by rhetoricians as "apostrophizing." One of my favorite literary theorists, Barbara Johnson, demonstrated how use of the second person necessarily *resuscitates*.[10] An "I" can breathe life into someone or something, can create a relationship through the act of uttering "you." I wrote a whole book about this, though it's not part of my scholarly work that I remember discussing with Grażyna.[11] She figured it out all on her own. Further, each of us can be addressed as "you," so when we hear this word, we respond on some level, even as we quickly or more slowly realize that whoever is uttering this particular "you"—for instance, a writer—cannot actually and specifically mean us.

By addressing the Unknown Man or Józefina or Runia or the Boy or the Girl from Furth, or even Mrs. Kraus—someone she never actually saw—with "you," Grażyna allows herself to be in relation to them, even if it is "just" rhetorically.[12] And her reasons for these resuscitations seem profound to me. Most obviously, she puts herself into, she creates (!) an interpersonal relationship. And being in relationships, having friends, is paramount to this young lonely refugee child. Her search for friends is ubiquitous in almost all episodes. Another reason that the writer uses apostrophe is to do things that she neglected to do then and seems to feel guilty about, for example, explaining to Józefina that she did actually go to the arranged meeting spot at the arranged time, but she did not go to the hospital to try to find her when Józefina did not appear. By writing that segment in the second person and by suspending it in the second person, Grażyna keeps Józefina alive in a certain fashion anyway.

Doing something good for herself, however, is not all that these gestures are accomplishing. The resuscitator-narrator also wants to do something for those she is addressing. These apostrophes, or letters as she calls them, can be considered ethical gestures. She wants the unknown man to learn that he was not just hunted and executed, but rather was noticed and thus "known" on some level by someone, if only by her, as her poor opinion of herself would have it. She remembers him.[13] Grażyna and the White Russian may only have seen each other for moments, but she has never forgotten him; she sees him still. To take it to the extreme, she gives him life through her rhetorical resuscitation of him. The communists in wartime may have killed him.

---

10   Barbara Johnson, "Apostrophe, Animation, and Abortion," in *A World of Difference* (Baltimore, MD: Johns Hopkins University Press, 1987), 184–99.

11   Irene Kacandes, *Talk Fiction: Literature and the Talk Explosion* (Lincoln: University of Nebraska Press, 2001).

12   The use of apostrophe in "A Boy" is particularly accomplished, since it embeds Grażyna's attempt at the time to create relationship by addressing the boy with advice about how to escape, and it also places the reader into the dramatic scene in the manner of the historical present I discuss below.

13   The question "do you remember me?" and its implicit answer "of course I remember you!" could be considered a subtext of this book.

But she brings him back to life at her writing table. To return to the other example mentioned above, Grażyna wants Józefina to learn not only that she *did* go to the agreed meeting place at the agreed to time, but also that she ultimately decides that Józefina remains her hero, even if she did do "it." By talking "to" her, she communicates this to the woman who did so much for her in her childhood vulnerability that she considers her her "hero." To take yet another example, she wants Runia to experience Grażyna's current life in Germany, to laugh together again—something she seems to worry about as soon as she begins to understand that Runia is behind the Iron Curtain, even if neither of them had that terminology then. Grażyna wants to undo the harm to Mrs. Kraus by turning her into a real person again with a past and a present, to rescue her from being dismissed as a "crazy" to be carted off and obliterated.

Though he gets there a different way, intellectually speaking, from Barbara Johnson, the relationship that necessarily inheres between an "I" and a "you," is something that caused the French linguist Émile Benveniste to insist that these pronouns stand for "persons" in a way that so-called third-person pronouns cannot.[14] The great German Jewish philosopher Martin Buber talked about recognition of subjectivity that comes about when one addresses another as "you/thou."[15] In my own work I have used the power of the act of the I/you exchange to think about co-witnessing to another's trauma.[16] Grażyna's desire to learn what is eating away at the young woman in Furth by creating a connection to her using "you" constitutes for me such an act of co-witnessing. Grażyna has chosen to notice someone else, to notice her distress; she wants to learn about it, to listen to her—to be her co-witness in my terminology. In Grażyna's words, when the two young women found the right place in the woods to practice their stenography, "there, you would tell me about yourself, what was making you so angry that you had to kick stones that were in your way. I really wanted to know" ("The Girl from Furth"). And here's the reciprocity of the I/you relationship: "And I might have told you about myself, just a little bit, because the story of my broken family was a secret that I was not yet willing to share with anyone." For one brief moment, this enunciation, this writing, this reaching out to the past in a way that reanimates so profoundly allows her to imagine a moment of healing for herself.

---

14 Émile Benveniste, *Problems in General Linguistics*, vol. 1., trans M. E. Meek (Coral Gables: University of Miami Press, 1971).

15 Martin Buber, *Ich und Du* (Cologne: Hegner, 1955; original publication 1923).

16 I have written about this in a number of publications, most recently in "My Mouth, Your Story: On Co-Witnessing," in *The Routledge Companion to Narrative Theory*, eds. Paul Dawson and Maria Mäkelä (London: Routledge, 2023), 193–204.

Alas, the war has done a lot of damage. And the girl Grażyna was by the end of that war could not really imagine such a reciprocal friendship working out: "Had you learned about it, you might not have wanted to become my friend." I would point out further, that this is another great example of the author being able to think her way back to her younger self: This particular logic shows how deeply, perhaps we might even need to say "permanently" marked Grażyna was by the earlier break-up of her nuclear family.

There are many other aspects of Grażyna's writing that I admire and don't have space to discuss here. But I do want to mention her power of description, especially of nature where she draws not only on sight, but also on smell and sound and even touch. Consider this last when she describes her childhood self in Wilno appreciating the feel of different levels of moisture in the sand with which she wanted to build sandcastles ("The Shoemaker's Son"). Readers probably have their own favorites, but I am struck by the many vivid descriptions of the area around Furth in all different kinds of weather. And I can almost smell the blossoming linden tree in the courtyard in Kraków.

I can't resist mentioning also Grażyna's good writerly sense for when to shift into the present tense for dramatic effect. There's a great example of the "historical present" in "Mrs. Kraus," when Grażyna narrates the time her mother unexpectedly came home early with a man in a black coat behind her. Just when the man was about to reach the desk at which the child Grażyna is sitting, the narrating I switches into the present tense. I quote below several lines so you can remember how the narrating I moves from (past tense) recounting, to a generalization about herself and how she behaves, back to the action but in the present tense:

> Halfway across the room Mama stopped and let the man pass. He was heading straight for the desk and me while Mama watched. Was I scared, you may wonder [IK: this "you" is her addressee Mrs. Kraus]. No, I wasn't. There was not enough time to be. When in danger I tell myself that I should just watch and not become a part of what is happening. Perhaps no one can see me then, especially if I do not move.

> The man in the black coat wants to open the middle drawer of the desk, but I am in the way. I do not get off the chair, but I do lean back to give him space. If I stand up, I will miss out on seeing what is in the drawer or what he will do with what he finds there. He seems to know where he should be looking. And there it is, in plain view resting on top of some papers, one of Mama's three false passports, the most fake of them all. Not a single entry in it is correct and that it looks brand-new because it is only used on special occasions, also makes it suspect.

By saying "the man wants," "I am in the way," "I do not get off the chair," and "there it is," *we* are right there in this dramatic—and dangerous—situation with the experiencing I.

Grażyna recounts some very distressing situations in a way that makes them unforgettable not just because of what happened but also because of her skill in narrating and structuring the scene. Consider the child on her way to the bookstore through an ice tunnel suddenly spotting the death notice for her brother Henius, or the two girlfriends trying to make their way down the sloshy hill in the park on the late winter day when they finally receive the sled and get a push from a mysterious handsome man or, perhaps most memorable of all, Runia's raiding of the Barans' Christmas tree candy. Some objects become symbols that reveal much about the time and place, like the strings that were once holding the now-consumed candies as "nooses" or the blue light in the communal toilet of the apartment building that seems to have kept working for decades and yet precisely by having the status of immortality bestowed on it, then flickers, sizzles, pops and finally reveals itself as "a dead bulb its insides coated with black soot" ("Justyna").

Jews and Poles and Ukrainians and Germans... and German

There's one more topic that I feel I need to share from the perspective of someone who knew Grażyna: her sense of her own identity and her concomitant attitude toward different ethnic groups. I could write a whole essay on this subject but will limit myself to what I hope are a few suggestive remarks that can be weighed by readers along with the episodes themselves and the comments by Joyce Gross and Aleksandra Szczepan that also touch on this topic.

War is ugly, and having lived through one on the ground, Grażyna was certainly aware that it does not bring out the best in folks (to borrow some of her sarcasm). She became a convinced pacifist, and every conflict that reared its violent head in the period in which we knew one another was something we discussed and lamented. Grażyna was also extraordinarily observant, brutally honest, and sensitive to suffering. This first, I would say, caused her to notice (and hate) exploitation, this second brought her to recognition of her own prejudices for the Poles and against the Ukrainian wartime collaborators, and this last surfaced her deep caring about individuals she actually got to know no matter what their background (think of her fascination with Mrs. Goldweber; her love for "Cinderella," Józefina, the Raviches; or her concern for the German soldier her mother sells her watch to).

In the previous essay, Aleksandra explained that *Kresy*, the area where Grażyna spent the early years of her life, were multiethnic. I would add that in notes and in correspondence, Grażyna commented numerous times on this multiethnicity, especially of Oszmiana, the identity of her father's friends there, and how people of such different backgrounds got along. "EP" [Eastern Poland] became a code for not only the lost borderlands where she had once lived, but for a whole lost, multiethnic way of life. Most of the research she did about EP did not enter the stories you have read. Grażyna chose, I believe very consciously, not to share it. What she considered her home, EP, was nearest to the core of her own identity, and since it was lost—simply did not exist any more—there was a way in which her own Polishness also disappeared.[17]

Despite her acute awareness of her refugee status and of "not being from here," Grażyna developed a love for the German language while she was living in Furth and especially in going to school in Cham in the immediate postwar years. Perhaps it was the background of the cessation of war that allowed her to fall in love with German. Perhaps it was her nearly superhuman and successful efforts to learn it mostly on her own. Perhaps it was the extent to which it allowed her to finally go to school and have a peer group. Whatever it was, this love went deep. I laughed out loud when I first read in "Mama" that she found the bureaucratic German of the letter rejecting her mother's application for reparations "refreshing." I suppose the fact that I too fell in love with the language of those who had caused so much suffering to my own family during World War II explains why it was understandable to me that Grażyna had also. I don't know if I would have said anything to a solitary diner next to me in a strange town if she hadn't been reading a book in German. But I'm grateful she was and that I did.

Though, ultimately, I will be the first to make clear that this writing remains that of an amateur, I want to be Grażyna Gross's Max Brod for at least one reason that Max Brod must have wanted to play Max Brod for his friend Franz Kafka. Grażyna's writing reveals pain—deep human pain caused by those who are determined to acquire money and exercise power, to protect and get ahead themselves at the expense of others, who don't even see that there exist others who are on the run and suffering because of them.

---

17 A very small hint of what was closest to her heart occurs in "The Shoemaker's Son," where the narrator is commenting on her experience of the beginning of the war: "We had moved to Wilno only a few weeks earlier, and almost everyone here was a stranger to me. On the other hand, when I heard that someone from the little town we had come from had been dragged out of bed in the middle of the night and taken to no one knew where, it hurt me so much that soon I stopped listening."

Writing helped Grażyna stave off some of her own pain and depression. In a few prefaces to segments she was writing or rewriting shortly before her death, Grażyna expresses an almost existential *need* to write. In a note to the sequence that became "Mama" in what you have just read, for example, Grażyna reported in 2019:

> It was before my trip to the hospital that I wrote last. With my mind so befuddled by my stay there, I am afraid to give it a try; even typing has become more difficult, let alone thinking. But without writing I get even more depressed than I should be. It's not over facing death but waiting for some new symptoms to appear—a burp, a fart, a feeling of nausea, however slight, a touch of pain in the abdomen—and wondering if they will lead to another trip to hell.

I hope we can agree that the effort Grażyna then made despite how she was feeling, an effort that succeeded in producing "Mama" and more, resulted in a gift to us. Perhaps we can also agree that Grażyna was talented and honest enough to render in her writing not just her own childhood suffering but also that of many others. Preserving representation of that pain through publication seems to me like, if not justice, then at least some kind of counterbalance to that suffering.

At the end of "Mama," Grażyna wonders if having had her paternal grandmother's gold at their disposal in 1939 could have saved her little family. She answers her own question with "I don't know." Would Grażyna approve of this volume? I'll give the same answer: I don't know. I felt a pinch every time I made an editorial change. But like Grażyna's apostrophes to some friends and strangers, some far away and others probably long gone, I hope this volume and my role in it mark that Grażyna and those others really were here.

I miss her. And I wish her well, "wherever you are."

Appendices

Timeline

N.B. Entries in plain type relate events in Grażyna Gross's or her family's lives. Entries in italics concern larger political or public events.

22 September 1886 or 1888 (probably 1886)
Birth of Henryk Połtowicz, Grażyna's father (documents have both years), presumably on family estate in Oknica, Transnistria (then Russia's partition of Polish-Lithuanian Commonwealth, now Ocnița in disputed border territory of current Ukraine and Moldova)

21 March 1900
Birth of Waleria Orzyszyńska, Grażyna's mother in Czernowitz (then part of the Austro-Hungarian Empire; now Chernivtsi, Ukraine)

11 November 1918
End of World War I and restoration of Poland's sovereignty after 123 years of partitions

1920, 1922
Polish-Soviet War and Polish occupation of Vilnius resulting in annexation in 1922

1920
Połtowicz family loses estate due to new borders resulting from Russian Revolution and after skirmishes

1925?
Henryk and Waleria marry

1927
Henryk Piotr Połtowicz (Henius) born to Henryk and Waleria; location unknown

1 January 1931
Grażyna born to Henryk and Waleria in Sarny (then Poland, now Ukraine)

April 1931–1934
Połtowicz family lives in Wilno (then Poland, now Vilnius in Lithuania) where Henryk studies for additional law degree

1934–1937
Połtowicz family lives in Wołożyn (then Poland, now Valozhyn in Belarus) where Henryk receives a post

1937–1939
Połtowicz family lives in Oszmiana (then Poland, now Ashmyany in Belarus) where Henryk is a district judge

March 1939
Henryk Piotr (Henius, Grażyna's older brother) dies in Children's Hospital of Wilno of scarlet fever after contracting strep throat

August 1939
Grażyna contracts meningitis; taken to same hospital where her brother Henius had died; Grażyna survives; no record of exact date she leaves hospital but prior to 18 September 1939

August or September 1939
Połtowicz family moves back to Wilno (no record of month)

24 August 1939
Non-aggression pact between Nazi Germany and the Soviet Union (Molotov-Ribbentrop Pact) signed, with a secret protocol establishing Soviet and German spheres of influence across Eastern Europe

1 September 1939
Germany invades Poland from the west

3 September 1939
Great Britain and France declare war on Germany

17 September 1939
Soviet Union invades Poland from the east

18–19 September 1939
Battle of Wilno between Poland and Soviet Union;
Grażyna watches Soviet troops enter city from apartment balcony

27–28 October 1939
Lithuanian troops enter Wilno after Lithuania has been granted the city by the Soviet Union

1939, 1940
Polish government in exile established first in Paris, then in London

10 May 1940
Germany invades France

Late June 1940
Grażyna and her parents leave Wilno by train; as an adult, Grażyna considers this the moment she and her parents become "refugees"

July 1940
Grażyna and her parents arrive in Warsaw via Kaunus and East Prussia; no record exact date

September 1940
Grażyna and her parents move to Kraków

January 1941
Grażyna's father Henryk returns to Warsaw alone

May 1941
Grażyna, Waleria, and Mykola move to apartment at 37 Starowiślna Street, Kraków; Józefina starts to work for Waleria

Summer 1941
Grażyna starts attending the Ursuline school for girls located at 3 Starowiślna Street, not far from her apartment building; meets Runia there

22 June 1941
Nazi Germany invades the Soviet Union (code name "Operation Barbarossa")

7 December 1941
Bombing of Pearl Harbor; the US enters the war the next day

20 January 1942
Wannsee Conference, secret meeting of German leaders during which the systematic murder of European Jews is planned

2 February 1943
German Sixth Army surrenders at Stalingrad, which is considered a turning point of World War II and the beginning of the end of the Third Reich

13–16 March 1943
German SS and police liquidate the Jewish ghetto in Kraków

March 1943
Józefina stops working for Waleria to work for a German family

19 April–16 May 1943
Warsaw Ghetto Uprising

July 1943
Grażyna visits her father in Warsaw for three weeks

27 May 1944
Henryk is arrested by Germans in Warsaw and sent to Pawiak prison

6 June 1944
D-Day: Allied troops land at Normandy, France

15 June 1944
Henryk is transferred to Gross-Rosen; camp medical records indicate time spent in August in infirmary with heart problems

1 August–2 October 1944
Warsaw Uprising

26 November, 6 December, 22 December 1944 (dates from postmarks)
Henryk (or a proxy) writes postcards to Grażyna in Kraków from Gross-Rosen

December 1944
Grażyna, Waleria, and Mykola depart from Kraków; arrive in Prague

11 January 1945
Henryk dies in Bergen-Belsen at the age of fifty-eight; not clear when or how he was transferred there from Gross-Rosen (presumably after postcard of 22 December, so whether by death march or by train, the transfer seems connected to his death); neither Waleria nor Grażyna has this information until later

18 January 1945
Red Army enters Kraków; the speed of their arrival foils German plans to destroy the city before departing

4–11 February 1945
Allied leaders meet in Yalta and, among other plans for the end of the war, give control of Eastern Europe to the Soviet Union; considered most fateful meeting for future of Eastern Europe

13 February 1945
70th Motorized Infantry Brigade of Red Army liberates Gross-Rosen

14–15 February 1945
Allied bombing of Dresden; (mistaken) bombing of Prague by American pilots

Late February 1945
Grażyna contracts pneumonia; exact date unclear; Grażyna and Waleria depart Prague; arrive in Czech border town of Domažlice

April 1945
Waleria rents horse cart; she, Grażyna, and other refugees cross border into Germany

15 April 1945
Bergen-Belsen liberated by 11th Armoured Division of British Army

18 April 1945
Cham, Germany bombed

Late April 1945–Spring 1949
Waleria and Grażyna arrive in Cham; Waleria rents a room at Hierstedder farm in nearby Furth im Wald; not clear when Mykola arrives. All three registered at the farm (address with local authorities: 197 Postgartenweg, Furth im Wald)

30 April 1945
Hitler commits suicide in Berlin bunker; Goebbels next day

7, 8 May 1945
Nazi Germany signs surrender agreements; first signing by Jodl in Reims, France; second by Keitel in Karlshorst (eastern Berlin)

6, 9 August 1945
US drops atomic bombs on Hiroshima and Nagasaki

10 August 1945
Waleria files cards with A.E.F. (Allied Expeditionary Forces) for herself and Grażyna as DPs wishing to go to Canada. She gives her last name as the hyphenated "Mykolajenko-Poltowicz" and indicates on her card that her first husband "[is] in CC Gross-Rosen [daet]"

2 September 1945
Japan surrenders on the USS Missouri, ending the war in the Pacific

1946–Spring 1949
Spring 1946 Grażyna moves in with Ravich family in Regensburg so she can attend Polish school (only open for two months); Grażyna teaches herself German; in 1947 accepted into Oberrealschule/Gymnasium in Cham originally on provisional basis; attends by commuting from Furth until departure with her mother for the US in March 1949

April 1949
Grażyna and Waleria arrive in Bismark, North Dakota, USA; both work in local hospital where Grażyna meets two Polish sisters; keeps up friendship with younger of two, Krystyna, until at least 2009

May 1951
Grażyna receives degree from Bismark Junior College; Waleria and Grażyna move to Minneapolis

May 1953
Grażyna receives BS in Mathematics from University of Minnesota

Fall 1953
Grażyna enrolls in graduate school at University of Minnesota

Fall 1954
Leonard Gross transfers to graduate school at University of Minnesota

Spring 1955
Grażyna and Leonard (Len) meet in a graduate seminar

September 1955
Grażyna travels to Europe to visit her German friend Brigitte from Cham schooldays; they vacation together in Switzerland

Fall 1955
Grażyna and Len move to Chicago

17 March 1956
Grażyna and Len marry

Spring 1957
Grażyna earns MS in mathematics from University of Chicago where Len is working on his doctorate

1957
Grażyna finds out where and when her father died (Bergen-Belsen, 11 January 1945) by asking a family friend to consult with the Red Cross in Warsaw

1957–1960
Len accepts three-year position teaching mathematics at Yale University; couple moves to New Haven; Len continues work on his PhD at a distance, earning it in 1958

July 1960
Grażyna and Len buy their first home in Ithaca, NY, where Len has received a teaching position at Cornell University

August 1961
Grażyna visits Poland for the first time since leaving in late 1944

November 1963
Joyce Gross is born in Boston, MA, where Len is spending his sabbatical

November 1965
Mark Gross is born in Ithaca, NY

October 1966
Grażyna and Len buy a house on Ellis Hollow Road, Ithaca, which has more land than previous home

1969, 1970, 1975
Gross family takes a trip to Poland in 1969; Grażyna returns alone in 1970 to hike; family returns again in 1975

15 February 1984
Waleria Połtowicz is found lying on kitchen floor of her apartment in downtown Ithaca after having a stroke; is taken to hospital

21 May 1984
Waleria Połtowicz passes away at age eighty-four

4 June 1989
End of communist rule in Poland

11 March 1990
Lithuania gains independence from the USSR

1991
Grażyna travels to visit her son and daughter-in-law in Paris and then all three travel to Poland

26 December 1991
Dissolution of the Soviet Union

1992
Grażyna and Len travel to Vilnius; Grażyna's first visit since leaving with her parents in 1940; she is able to locate her brother's grave

1994
Grażyna and Joyce return to Europe and travel to most of the towns where Grażyna had lived

April 2002
Grażyna meets Irene Kacandes at the Moosewood Restaurant in Ithaca, NY while they are lunching at adjacent tables; twenty-year correspondence and friendship with two additional in-person visits in 2015 and 2018

2018
Grażyna and Len sell the house on Ellis Hollow Road and move to Kendal, also in Ithaca, NY

January 2022
Grażyna reads published version of her story "Mrs. Kraus" in the volume *On Being Adjacent to Historical Violence*, edited by Irene and published by De Gruyter

25 March 2022
Grażyna dies

Notes to the Tales

N.B. The information below is organized by chapter, stating first time and location when known, and then any additional relevant information about something in the chapter in the order in which it appears there.

Chapter One: Maria and Mirek

Time: earliest memories to summer 1937; location: mainly Wołożyn

Wilno is the Polish name of Vilnius, current capital of Lithuania and its largest city. After World War I and the Polish-Soviet War, it was annexed to Poland in 1922. Statistics vary depending on source, but according to the Polish census of 1931, almost two thirds of the city's inhabitants identified as Polish and one third as Jewish, with a minority identifying as Russian or Lithuanian.

Wołożyn, now Valozhyn in Belarus, was before 1939 a small town in eastern Poland. One third of its population was Jewish. Its yeshiva established in 1807 was a model for later similar schools in the region.

During the Napoleonic Wars (1803–1815), French Emperor Napoleon I created the Duchy of Warszawa, which comprised the ethnically Polish lands ceded to France by Prussia and Austria. A French client state, it was the first attempt to re-establish Poland as a sovereign state after the eighteenth-century partitions between Austria, Prussia, and Russia.

Grażyna may be referring to yellow yarrow, a plant which is native to Central and Eastern Europe and can be used to staunch bleeding.

Child Grażyna has been fed the antisemitic lie that Jews used Christian blood for their own ritualistic purposes. For more on "blood libel" see Alan Dundes, ed., *The Blood Libel Legend: A Casebook in Anti-Semitic Folklore* (Madison: University of Wisconsin Press, 1991).

Chapter Two: Henius

Time: late summer 1937 to late summer 1939; location: mainly Oszmiana; also Wilno

Oszmiana, now Ashmyany in Belarus, was before 1939 a small town in eastern Poland with a significant Jewish population. It lies in the basin of the Ashmyanka River.

Grażyna is referring to the Italo-Ethiopian War. Mussolini used some border skirmishes as an excuse to invade Ethiopia in early October 1935.

Chapter Three: Maybe Not a Story

Time: mainly summer 1939; location: Oszmiana, an estate near Oszmiana, and a lake district, possibly Troki (now Trakai, Lithuania)

After the Soviet invasion of Poland on 17 September 1939, Oszmiana fell under Soviet rule (as per the Ribbentrop-Molotov pact dividing Poland between Nazi Germany and Soviet Russia, signed in Moscow on 23 August 1939). Wilno became a part of the Soviet-controlled Lithuanian Republic on 25 October 1939, and was subsequently incorporated into the USSR on 15 June 1940.

Chapter Four: Letter to an Unknown Man

Time: September–October 1939; location: mainly Wilno

Under the Soviet occupation of what had been eastern Poland, the judiciary became one of the most targeted groups, together with other civil servants, forest workers, university professors, and landowners, who had been given or sold state land in the Eastern Borderlands ceded to Poland by the Polish-Soviet Riga Peace Treaty of 1921. Approximately 800,000 Polish citizens were arrested between 1940 and 1941 and sent in four waves of deportations to the Gulag labor camps and exile settlements in remote areas of the Soviet Union. The arrests usually happened at night. People were deported by train in cattle cars.

White Russian émigrés were Russians who left the territory of the former Russian Empire in the wake of the Russian Revolution (1917) and Russian Civil War (1917–1923), and who were in opposition to the revolutionary communist Bolsheviks (Reds).

Chapter Five: The Shoemaker's Son

Time: 1939–1940; location: mainly Wilno

By mentioning eagles and flags, the author signals that at least some of the books she and the shoemaker's son find in the street were dangerous and discarded because they related to Poland; a crowned white eagle is on the Polish coat of arms that was incorporated into the flag of the Second Polish Republic.

Chapter Six: The Doctor's Daughter

Time: mainly mid-1940 with flashback to years in Oszmiana (1937–1939) and to attending one party during the even earlier years in Wołożyn; location: mainly Wilno and also Oszmiana

Oszmiana had its territorial affiliation changed several times in early twentieth century. After partitions of Poland in 1795, it belonged to the Russian Empire until the end of World War I, when it fell under Polish jurisdiction. After a brief change of government due to the Polish-Soviet War when it belonged to Lithuania, it came back to Poland by the Peace of Riga (18 March 1921). It was called Oshmyany in Russian, Ašmena in Lithuanian, Oszmiana in Polish, Oshminah in Yiddish, and Ashmyany in Belarusian The intricate history of Oszmiana is a good example of the character of *Kresy*, the multiethnic Eastern European borderlands. In several notes that did not make it into this or other chapters, Grażyna emphasized how multicultural Oszmiana was, something that she believed minimized her sense of Polish nationalism.

The narrator Grażyna makes an allusion to two classics of children's literature: *Anne of Green Gables* by Lucy Maud Montgomery (1908) and *The Secret Garden* by Frances Hodgson Burnett (serialized 1910–1911 and then published as a book). By writing "I liked to think," she assigns knowledge of those books to her own childhood.

Chapter Seven: The Fortune Teller

Time: mainly summer 1940; location: in transit from Wilno to Warsaw; and in Warsaw

The Eye of the Prophet (in the original *Oko Proroka*) is a novel by Władysław Łoziński from 1897. The plot takes place in the seventeenth century and tells the story of Hanusz and his expedition to Turkey to find his missing father. He discovers a rare diamond called "eye of the prophet."

Kraków, a historic Polish city, became the capital of the "General Government," a German zone of occupation established on 26 October 1939, after the invasion of Poland by Nazi Germany. Hans Frank was the General Governor from its establishment to its collapse on 19 January 1945.

Chapter Eight: The Root Canal

Time: mainly fall 1940; location: mainly Kraków

Grażyna refers to international travel documents that were issued to stateless refugees by the League of Nations between 1922 and 1938. They quickly became known as "Nansen passports," after the Norwegian who promoted them, Fridtjof Nansen.

Residents of Poland were fleeing or being deported in both directions, east and west, in the early months of the war. After the German invasion of Poland on 1 September 1939, approximately 250,000–300,000 Jewish Poles escaped eastward, fearing the Nazi violence that had already been inflicted on Jewish populations in Germany. After the attack of the Soviet Union from the east on 17 September, the territory of prewar Poland was divided between Nazi Germany and the USSR roughly along the Bug river. Many Poles decided to move from the Soviet-occupied territories westward in fear of repressions.

Chapter Nine: The Day Papa Left

Time: mainly late 1940 to early 1941; location: mainly Kraków

A trumpeter plays a five-note Polish bugle call (*hejnał*) every hour from the highest tower of Kraków, Saint Mary's Basilica (Kościół Mariacki). The tradition can be traced at least as far back as the fourteenth century.

Chapter Ten: Tereska

Time: early to mid-1941; location: Kraków

The youth branch of the Nazi party was set up in Germany as early as 1922. It received the name "Hitler Jugend" several years later. As a paramilitary organization for boys, uniforms, marching, singing martial songs, and other types of physical activities were prevalent. Many types of Nazi paramilitary activities would have been taking place in Kraków during the time of Grażyna's residence there.

Ola Gum is a Czech brand of condom that was available in Kraków at the time.

Walter von Brauchitsch (1881–1948) was not only a general in the Wehrmacht, he was Feldmarschall (Field Marshall) and then Oberbefehlshaber (Commander-in-Chief) for the first two years of the war. It is unclear why Tereska had developed such an admiration for him.

Grażyna probably has in mind Józef Piłsudski and Edward Rydz-Śmigły. Piłsudski (1867–1935) was Marshal of Poland and its political leader after Poland regained its independence in 1918 until his death, and is considered a father of the Second Polish Republic. Rydz-Śmigły (1886–1941) was also Marshal of Poland and Inspector General of the Polish Armed Forces at the start of World War II. Due to lack of help from the Western Allies and the attack of the Soviet Union, Rydz-Śmigły ordered a retreat towards Romania where he was interned on 18 September 1939.

Wilhelm "Willi" Messerschmitt (1898–1978) was the name of an aircraft designer, then the name given to a major supplier for fighter aircraft of various models that also had Messerschmitt as part of their names.

The other names Tereska uses refer to plane manufacturers and specific bombers and fighters the German Luftwaffe was using at that stage in the war.

Chapter Eleven: The Picture Album, Part One

Time: summer 1941; location: Kraków

Grażyna's mention of "the beginning of another war" presumably refers to Germany's declaration of war on the Soviet Union of 22 June 1941, the start of Operation Barbarossa.

Grażyna and her mother Waleria take over a Jewish flat in the Kazimierz district after Kraków's Jews are forcibly displaced. Mykola is presented as a tenant. Approximately 32,000 people had been resettled outside of Kraków, after the head of the General Government, Hans Frank, issued the order of 18 May 1940. Remaining Kraków Jews were moved to the ghetto created in March 1941 in the impoverished district of Podgórze, across the Vistula river.

Ukrainians were a significant group among those who ran westward after the Soviet Union's invasion of Poland, given persecutions against Ukrainians and the human-made famine in the Soviet Ukraine in the early 1930s, known as the Holodomor. Under German rule, Ukrainians were treated preferentially over Jews and Poles. Kraków became one of the main Ukrainian centers: Ukrainian political parties and charities operated, and there were schools, banks and bookstores in the "Ukrainian quarter" near the Planty Park. Ukrainians also helped the German administration and military forces, since Ukrainian nationalists hoped that collaboration with the Nazi regime would enable them to re-establish an independent state. Many Ukrainians went back to Ukraine after the German invasion of the Soviet Union on 22 June 1941. For more information see Andrzej Chwalba, *Okupacyjny Kraków* (Kraków: Wydawnictwo Literackie, 2011).

Among her posthumous papers were found several different descriptions of these particular "ancient" neighbors, in all of which Grażyna emphasizes how kind to her their adult son was.

The center of black-market activities in wartime Kraków was Plac Żydowski, Jewish Square, at Szeroka Street in the Jewish district Kazimierz, a five-minute walk from 37 Starowiślna Street where Grażyna lived.

Mykola worked as a *Treuhänder*, a trustee handling confiscated Jewish property. Trustee Offices (*Treuhandstellen*) were a tool of Nazi civil anti-Jewish measures that aimed at expropriating the Jewish population and exploiting former Jewish businesses and property. See Paweł Markiewicz, *Unlikely Allies: Nazi German and Ukrainian Nationalist Collaboration in the General Government During World War II* (West Lafayette, IN: Purdue University Press, 2021).

The actual name of the woman who owns the thread and yarn warehouse was not remembered by Grażyna. In a surviving note she writes that she made up a name for her.

The majority of Kraków's Jewish population was deported to Bełżec extermination camp and killed there. The two biggest deportation waves happened in June and October 1942.

Grażyna seems to have been the keeper of this envelope with the photographs (and a few documents) that survived the war; some are reproduced in this book.

Chapter Twelve: Half-Boarders

Time: mainly fall 1941 with some information about earlier periods; location: mainly Kraków and specifically the Ursuline school.

See also figures 17 and 18, Grażyna and Runia in school photos.

Janek first appears in the segment "Henius"; he was one of two brothers who kept Grażyna distracted while her own brother was very ill and in the hospital. From other notes of Grażyna's, it appears that the two had more than just a friendship, even though they were both very young. They may have said to each other, as many children do, that they loved each other and promised to marry when they were older. The war and Grażyna's family put these plans into the back of her head, and though she mentions Janek here as her savior, it seems that the adult Grażyna doubted whether her memory with regard to him and their "love" was reliable or fabricated by her then or at a later time.

It appears that initial approval of a member of Grażyna's family, Uncle Kot, opened at least some social doors for Grażyna, even though the courtship between Kot and Rozmaryna did not lead to marriage.

Grażyna may have meant Władysław Raczkiewicz (1885–1947), a Polish politician, lawyer, diplomat, and President of Poland-in-exile. Until 1945, he was the internationally recognized Polish head of state, and the Polish government-in-exile was recognized as the continuation of the Polish government of 1939. He did not have a son.

The Ludwik and Anna Helcel House for the Poor was funded in 1890, thanks to the testament and endowment of Anna Helcel née Treutler von Traubenberg, a Kraków philanthropist and the wife of mayor Ludwik Edward Helcel. The institution is still in operation.

Chapter Thirteen: Józefina's Mistress

Time: unspecified references to Józefina's childhood and time working for and fleeing eastward with wealthy family from western Poland in 1939; also after she starts working for Waleria in spring 1941; location: western Poland, unspecified; and Kraków

Following the invasion of Poland at the beginning of World War II, nearly a quarter of the entire territory of the Second Polish Republic was annexed by Nazi Germany and placed directly under German civil administration; the biggest annexed territories were Danzig-West Prussia and Wartheland. The rest of Nazi-occupied Poland was renamed as the General Government district. Many businesses as well as other types of properties were expropriated and hundreds of thousands of former residents were forced to move east.

By labelling Józefina a "displaced person" as opposed to a refugee like herself, Grażyna seems to want to label her as one of the mass of Poles expelled from those western Polish terrains annexed to the Reich (probably specifically from what became Reichsgau Wartheland). The designation of "DP" was given to millions of displaced persons more commonly at the *end* of the war. In describing the postwar period, Grażyna will further distinguish between those German speakers or ethnic Germans living in Eastern Europe who fled the Red Army or were expelled from the terrains that after World War II were ceded to Poland, and those like herself who ended up in Germany, but had no connection to the language or the ethnicity.

Chapter Fourteen: The Psychic

Time: winter late 1941 or early 1942, with brief flashback to Połtowicz family arrival in Kraków and rental of store in 1940; location: Kraków

The story Józefina and Grażyna make up during their simultaneous illness does not seem to have survived the war, though several notebooks with Grażyna's writing did (see Fig. 37, 38). The neighbor who compliments the writers on the story is the kindly adult son of an elderly couple Grażyna describes multiple times in several pieces of writing including in the chapter "The Picture Album, Part One." Grażyna refers to him elsewhere as her "savior" and "guardian angel," along with Janek and Józefina.

Chapter Fifteen: The Gloves

Time: winter 1941–1942; location: Kraków

RGO stands for Rada Główna Opiekuńcza (Central Welfare Council), a Polish charitable organization, operating between February 1940 and

January 1945 in Kraków, financed by the Polish government-in-exile, with German donations from taxes and international aid.

Chapter Sixteen: The Ring

Time: end of summer 1942 or 1943; location: Kraków

The literal English translation of "Kleider machen Leute" is "Clothes make people," though the phrase is usually translated as "Clothes make the man." A common saying in German, it is also the title of a well-known story by Gottfried Keller (1819–1890) first published in 1874 that Grażyna probably read at some point, possibly postwar during her schooling in Cham.

Błonia Park is a vast meadow directly adjacent to the historic center of Kraków, a site of official parades and a local recreation area.

Montelupich prison has been located on Montelupich Street since the early twentieth century. It was used by the Gestapo during World War II. It is still in operation.

Chapter Seventeen: A Boy

Time: winter 1942–1943, possibly March 1943; location: Kraków

Chapter Eighteen: Uncle Kot

Time: mostly summer 1943, with flashback to earlier encounters with Uncle Kot and Uncle Mietek in late 1939–1940; location: mostly Warsaw and environs, with references to Wilno in the flashback

The Warsaw Ghetto Uprising started on 19 April 1943 as an act of resistance to Nazi Germany's final effort to transport the remaining ghetto population to the Majdanek and Treblinka extermination camps. It ended on 16 May 1943. On the night of 12–13 May 1943, there was area bombardment of Warsaw undertaken by Russian aircraft. Although the main goal was the destruction of German war facilities, the biggest losses were inflicted on the civilian population.

Grażyna's explanation of who the people in their train compartment on the way to Warsaw are is astounding, since it seems improbable that Jews were traveling in a train as Jews in summer 1943 and equally improbable that they would have revealed their identity to Grażyna's mother if they were Jews traveling with false identification. Jews were immediately persecuted if discovered or reported to the authorities. Perhaps discovery of the past personal connection in eastern Poland caused the woman to lower her guard with Waleria.

Kielce is a city in south-central Poland, in the Świętokrzyskie region. Many of the stories that child Grażyna composed during the war are set in this area.

Holy Cross Church is a baroque Roman Catholic church located in Warsaw on Krakowskie Przedmieście Street where it merges with Nowy Świat Street. The author means the adjacent area near the Staszic Palace. The church was partially destroyed in September 1939, which is mentioned by Grażyna in "The Fortune Teller."

Irene Kacandes has a very vivid memory of Grażyna recounting to her this scene of her witnessing a man consulting her father on a legal matter. No written variation of it beyond the one here has been located.

Chapter Nineteen: A Dinner

Time: opens with reflections of the adult narrator, that is time of writing in the 2000s; most of episode takes place in late 1943, with brief flashback to summer 1943; location: Kraków

It may be that they go to Sarego Street which was called the "Ukrainian Quarter" during the war.

Chapter Twenty: A Christmas Story

Time: mostly just before Christmas 1943 with some explanations of the schoolgirls' backgrounds; location: Kraków

Grażyna is referring almost certainly to Jan Kochanowski (1530–1584), "Lament XI":

What man did his own goodness e'er advance

Or piety preserve from evil chance?

Knowing Nazi belief in the superiority of the "Aryan race," that among other characteristics was supposed to have light-colored hair, blue eyes, and light skin, Grażyna assesses that somehow Mr. Baran's "career" under the Nazis was not disadvantaged by his (dark) coloring.

Chapter Twenty-One: Letter to Józefina

Time: January 1944, though with a flashback to 1941 when Józefina started working for Waleria and written from perspective of narrator as adult, that is, decades later than the time recounted; location: Kraków

This is the story that a surviving note of Grażyna's identifies as the first one she wrote as an adult. How important the segment, the events recounted, and the person of Józefina were to her as a child and as an adult is indicated in part by the numerous extant drafts of this "Letter," amounting to scores of pages.

Chapter Twenty-Two: The Sled

Time: winter of 1943–1944; probably in 1944 as there has already been a major thaw; location: Kraków

Neither of the girls remembers that the "voice in the wilderness," a quotation from the prophet Isaiah, refers to John the Baptist as calling for repentance in preparation for the arrival of the Christ. This reflects their lack of interest in whatever Christian education they were receiving—apparent in many other passages in the overall text as well. Nonetheless, evoking the divine in any manner indicates how important the salvaging by this stranger of this sleigh ride was to them.

Chapter Twenty-Three: The Watch

Grażyna herself spells out the main setting at the beginning of this segment:

"Time: probably winter of 1943–1944, because Józefina was no longer living with us, but it no longer matters, since all the war winters were brutal.

Place: a Polish city where we were living then as refugees."

There is a flashback to 1938 when she received a teddy bear for Christmas after her illness.

The phrase "Ach, die Front, die Kälte, die Russen…" translates to: Oh, the front, the cold, the Russians…

Chapter Twenty-Four: Typhus

Time: August, November 1944; location: Kraków

The Warsaw Uprising was organized by the Polish underground resistance (Polish Home Army) to liberate Warsaw from German occupation. It started on 1 August 1944 and ended on 2 October 1944. Circa 200,000 civilians died due to German reprisals and another 600,000 were displaced. Up to 40,000 refugees from Warsaw came to Kraków in its wake.

Justyna is singing in Ukrainian. "The Mighty Dnieper Roars" (Реве́ та сто́гне Дніпр широ́кий, Reve ta stohne Dnipr shyrokyi) is a song composed by Danylo Kryzhanivskyi to the poem by Taras Shevchenko, describing the landscape of the Dnieper river (in Ukrainian: Dnipr; in Polish: Dniepr). During World War II, it was used as a signature tune of Ukrainian radio and was considered the unofficial anthem of Ukraine. Grażyna includes the first line several times in several different story segments, each time with a slightly different spelling, which may reflect that even though she understood it, she did not actually know Ukrainian very well.

"Żydzi, wszy, tyfus plamisty" or "Juden, Läuse, Flecktyphus," translates to "Jews, lice, typhus."

In an earlier version of this scene, Grażyna included the widely believed myth that the Nazis made soap from the fat of Jews. Presumably she removed it because it is not historically accurate.

Chapter Twenty-Five: Justyna

Time: mostly fall 1944; also flashback to first meeting with Justyna in 1940; and flash forward to Grażyna's visit to Kraków in 1960s; location: Kraków, en route to Prague, Warsaw

Grażyna mentions that by 1944, she has read Henryk Sienkiewicz (1846–1916), a Polish author of historical novels, such as the *Trilogy* series about the seventeenth-century history of Poland and *Quo Vadis*, set in the Roman Empire.

Chapter Twenty-Six: Mrs. Kraus

N.B. To our knowledge, this is the only segment of Grażyna's life-writing that was published in her lifetime. It appeared in an anthology called *On Being Adjacent to Historical Violence*, edited by Irene Kacandes and published by De Gruyter (Berlin) in December 2021. Grażyna received her copy in January 2022, and she and Irene were exchanging emails with her reactions to the volume up until shortly before her death on 25 March 2022.

Time: late 1944 through late February 1945; location: mainly Prague

The musical favorites of Grażyna would have been quite well-known to a general public. *Der Zigeunerbaron* (The Gypsy Baron) is an operetta in three acts by Johann Strauss the Younger that premiered in Vienna in 1885. *Leichte Kavallerie* is an operetta in two acts by Franz von Suppé that also premiered in Vienna (1866). Its overture is better known than the operetta as a whole. "La campanella" is the name by which the third of Franz Liszt's six *Grandes études de Paganini* (1851) is widely known, a particularly challenging piece for the pianist.

Some sources report that American pilots thought they were over Dresden when they bombed Prague and that that bombing was never intentional. The bombing of Dresden first by the RAF and then by the Americans was so fierce that it has been reported that the resulting fire and smoke was seen up to one hundred miles away, so just about all the way to Prague. Grażyna, the adult writer, was very careful with hard facts, so it's uncharacteristic that she insisted on 13 February (rather than 14 February) and in the case of either numerical date, why she remembers it as a Friday. In the year 1945, the thirteenth was a Tuesday and the fourteenth a Wednesday. It may just be that as a day of negative events, it was imprinted on her memory as the bad luck day of Friday the thirteenth.

Chapter Twenty-Seven: The Picture Album, Part Two

Time: summer 1944–late April 1945; location: Kraków, in transit to Prague, and then to Domažlice on the border between Czechoslovakia and Germany

Teufel means literally "devil," but the phrase of the German soldiers Grażyna quotes would be understood as the equivalent of "go to hell."

Tiefflieger is the equivalent of "low flyers," meaning low-flying aircraft (that were especially used for strafing people and anything else on the ground).

Chapter Twenty-Eight: Peace

Time: April 1945, last days of the war; location: Furth im Wald, Germany

The main distinction Grażyna is making here among "refugees" concerns on the one hand ethnic Germans, *Volksdeutsche*, and German citizen-colonists who had been living for centuries or just a few years in Eastern Europe, or Germans from the eastern territories of prewar Germany, newly acquired by Poland with the post-World War II Potsdam Agreement, and, on the other, refugees like herself and her mother who had no ethnic or national connection to Germany but ended up there at war's end. Grażyna expresses numerous times that these two large groups were treated differently by the local populations and that the German-speakers were at an advantage. It is also important to note that many Jews who survived the camps or death marches ended up in Germany at war's end, too, and Grażyna mentions them only very briefly in a few passages, though in other writing she left behind, she does talk about contact with mostly Jewish women survivors, particularly in a hospital where her mother was taken by the American occupying forces.

Chapter Twenty-Nine: A Night in Regensburg

Time: brief mention of spring 1945, mainly one year later; location: southeastern Bavaria, especially path between Furth and Munich with main action in Regensburg

Referring to Furth where she is living as "a German village near the Czech border," is one sign that this is possibly another story (like "Letter to

Józefina") written early in the evolution of this manuscript when Grażyna was determined to disguise places and people.

There are no additional references to how the girls came to this knowledge of how and why Strauss composed the Blue Danube Waltz or why they considered it funny.

"Walhalla" is a neoclassical building high above the Danube at Donaustauf, modeled after the Parthenon. Proposed in 1807 by Crown Prince Ludwig of Bavaria as a memorial to German heroes of various stripes and periods, it was constructed between 1830 and 1842.

Chapter Thirty: Evhen

Time: ranges over many years between 1945 and 1957, though mainly 1946–1947. As for location, in an earlier version of this segment, Grażyna herself wrote a long explanation: "In the mid-thirties, between the two world wars, the Messerschmittwerke built for its employees a state-of-the art housing development on the outskirts of the historic city of Regensburg. Some of the houses were for two families, some for four; all had white stucco walls and red tile roofs. The crowning glory of the Siedlung [housing development] was a giant community center, big enough to provide space for a hospital. The official name of this piece of real estate was the Hermann Goering Siedlung, but by the time I arrived on the scene in the spring of 1946, the less toxic Ganghofer had replaced Hermann Goering. When in 1945, at the end of the war, millions of foreigners, scornfully called DPs, ended up stranded in Germany through no fault of their own, they had to be housed before being sorted out and gotten rid of. This urgent need for temporary housing led to the creation, under the auspices of UNRRA, of DP camps in parts of Germany occupied by the Western Allies. The Ganghofersiedlung became one of them. To me, who later found my way into it in search of a Polish school, it would have been on par with a five-star hotel or, better yet, a vacation colony for the rich." "Evhen" is Ukrainian poet Yevhen Fylymonovych Malaniuk (1897–1968).

The author has already made references to Poles being deported to Siberia, Central Asia, and the far east and north of the Soviet Union (her designations). In 1942, 116,000 Polish citizens (including Polish Jews) sent originally to Soviet Siberia and Central Asia were evacuated to Iran (probably what Grażyna meant by "Middle East"). Four major centers for Polish refugees were Teheran, Isfahan, Ahvaz, and Mashhad. Some of the refugees ended up also in Iraq, Palestine, and Egypt.

Grażyna did an enormous amount of research on the internet about history related to her personal past. About the camp, she wrote in a surviving note:

"Only recently did I learn that in the Little Ukraine of this DP camp, the two great powers were competing with each other in their quest for double agents, potential spies, and assassins."

The term *Volksdeutsche*, ethnic German, applied to individuals with vastly different backgrounds from an array of locations in Eastern Europe where groups of Germans had settled or been settled at one historical point or another. Some did not even speak the German language. During World War II, ethnic Germans throughout Europe enjoyed privileges and benefited financially from Nazi policies. Among the indigenous populations in the Nazi-occupied lands, those who signed the *Volksliste* were considered traitors, and *Volksdeutsche* became a term of ignominy.

The Wisła (Vistula) is the longest river in Poland, with many associations with Polish culture, history, and national identity. The Vltava is the longest river in the Czech Republic. In the 2000s, Grażyna named one of her dogs "Wisla."

The Syniukha is a river in Ukraine, a left tributary of the Southern Bug, the basin of the Black Sea.

The Oszmianka (Belarusian: Ashmyanka) is a river in Belarus, passing through the town of Oszmiana, a left-bank tributary of the Neris (Wilia).

Grażyna did not know for certain until 1957 that her father had died. After requesting of a friend to seek information from the Red Cross in Warsaw, she was able to learn the date and location of his death on 11 January 1945 in Bergen-Belsen.

The phrase *verdammte Ausländer* means "damned foreigners."

Heinrich Heine (1797–1856) was born into a Jewish family and converted to Lutheranism in 1825. His books were banned under Nazism, although his poems persisted in the lyrics of many well-known songs.

Grażyna probably knew the translation by the Polish poet Władysław Syrokomla (*Król olszyn*, 1856) that opens, "Kto jedzie tak późno wśród nocnej zamieci?" However, when she drafted this sequence, she quoted the German original that may have replaced in her memory the text she remembers knowing by heart in Polish.

The line from Rilke that Evhen quotes to Grażyna during their walk in Furth—"Wer jetzt kein Haus hat, baut sich keines mehr…"—means literally: whoever does not have a house now won't be building one anymore.

Presumably Evhen and Grażyna spoke Polish to one another.

Grażyna attended the funeral with her husband Len; he is standing next to Grażyna in the polaroid photo in which Evhen is at the other end of the group of people (reproduced in this book). She does not mention Len here, but he must have been with her during the taxi ride, too.

Chapter Thirty-One: School

Time: mainly 1946–1949; location: Cham and Furth

Das Amulett and *Gustav Adolf Page* are the titles of two novellas by the popular Swiss author Conrad Ferdinand Meyer (1825–1898).

Prisoners from Nazi extermination camps and labor camps were force-marched by the Nazis westward as the Red Army advanced. These death marches constitute a particularly tragic chapter in Nazi persecution since they came so close to liberation. It is noteworthy that Grażyna has the month of March connected to these particular deaths.

Presumably the two girls are discussing Friedrich Schiller's play *Die Jungfrau von Orleans* (The Maid of Orleans, premiered 1801).

Chapter Thirty-Two: EH

Time: 1947–1949 with some filling in of post-schoolyears; segment frame is from narrator's time of writing; location: Cham and environs

EH has the originality to select to read a story by Edgar Allen Poe (1809–1849); the story "The Tell-Tale Heart" was first published in 1843.

The epistolary novel *Die Leiden des jungen Werther* (The Sorrows of Young Werther, 1774) is considered one of the first European blockbusters. It is widely taught and read even today in German-speaking countries.

Chapter Thirty-Three: The Girl from Furth

Time: 1945–1949; location: mainly Furth with some mention of Cham

Ausländerin, which Grażyna uses several times in this story to refer to herself, means literally, someone from outside the country, someone not from here, a foreigner. Perhaps the author reproduces the word in German because she could still hear and feel the sting of this appellation decades later.

The sigh of recognition and empathy "Ach, Russland" could be translated as Alas, Russia.

Chapter Thirty-Four: Father Zeisel

Time: mainly time of writing when Grażyna is looking back on receipt of a letter received in 1949 once Grażyna is already in North Dakota; most events refer to postwar period in Germany; location: mainly Furth

"Edel sei der Mensch, hilfreich und gut..." means: "May man be noble, helpful and good"; the first lines of a poem attributed to Goethe ("Das Göttliche"; the Divine; first published without his permission in 1785 and then by the poet himself in 1789).

"Bodensee" is the German name for Lake Constance which lies some four hundred kilometers to the southwest of Furth.

Chapter Thirty-Five: Mama

Time: this chapter covers the longest time frame of any of the tales, essentially from Grażyna's birth to the present time of her writing; location: essentially all the locations covered in previous stories plus many years in the US

Referring to her paternal grandparents' flight from their ancestral estate in the wake of the Russian Revolution, Grażyna uses the name "Constantinople," modern-day Istanbul, which demonstrates how careful she was about history; the name Istanbul was not officially adopted until 1930.

Grażyna refers to three currency reforms in this chapter, the first presumably of late October 1939, shortly after the Russians ceded Wilno to the Lithuanians. The new rulers declared Polish złoty abolished and ordered all currency to be converted to Lithuanian litas at a 250% devaluation. Later in the chapter, Grażyna refers to having been through two currency reforms before the major one of her postwar period in June establishing the Deutschmark and replacing the Reichsmark and the Rentenmark in the three western zones of occupation. It is not clear which is the second reform.

Due to the impunity of its German occupiers and flourishing corruption, the General Government was also referred to as the "Gangster-Gau" (*Gau* means "district"), with Kraków as its capital in many senses of the word. See Andrea Löw and Markus Roth, *Juden in Krakau unter deutscher Besatzung 1939–1945* (Göttingen: Wallstein, 2011).

Family Photos

Figures 2 through 34 are from the Gross family archive and are used by permission. Figure 35 is used by permission of Jane Walker. Figure 36 is used by permission of Gail Cashen.

Figure 2. Waleria Połtowicz. 1920s.

Figure 3. Waleria Połtowicz. 1920s.

Figure 4. Waleria Połtowicz and her son Heniuś. 1927 or 1928.

Figure 5. Grażyna and cow. Early 1930s.

Figure 6. Maria Połtowicz, Grażyna's paternal grandmother. Date unknown.

Figure 7. Henryk, Heniuś, Waleria, and Grażyna Połtowicz. 1930s, perhaps 1933.

Figure 8. Grażyna's brother Heniuś. 1930s.

Figure 9. Grażyna's father, Henryk Połtowicz. Location and date unknown.

Figure 10. Heniuś's funeral in Wilno. Grażyna, her mother (wearing a black veil), and her father walk behind the horse-drawn carriage. 1939.

Figure 11. Heniuś's burial in Wilno. Grażyna and father Henryk kneeling. 1939.

Figure 12. Henryk, Waleria, and Grażyna after Heniuś's death. 1939.

Figure 13. Grażyna and C. taken during outing. Summer 1939.

Figure 14. Outing in unidentified lake district. Waleria (second from left), C.'s wife (presumed, center rear), Grażyna with dog, C. (far right), and three unknown people. Summer 1939.

Figure 15. Józefina (left) and Grażyna with dog. Planty Park, Kraków; in the background is City Arsenal and Stolarska Tower. 1940s.

Figure 16. Grażyna with dog and Józefina. Market Square, Kraków. Cloth Hall (Polish: Sukiennice) is in the background. 1940s.

Figure 17. Grażyna (third from right, second row), with classmates and teachers at the Ursuline school. Kraków. 1940s.

Figure 18. Grażyna (third from left, first row) and Runia (third from right, first row), with other classmates and teachers at the Ursuline school. Kraków. 1940s.

Figure 19. Grażyna (second from right back) with nine younger children. Possibly in Kraków. 1940s.

Figure 20. Waleria and Grażyna. Presumed in Kraków. 1940s.

Figure 21. Runia (left) and Grażyna. Kraków. 1940s.

Figure 22. Grażyna with dog. Kraków. 1940s.

Figure 23. Grażyna and her father Henryk. 1940s.

Figure 24. Grażyna and her father Henryk. Kraków, Planty Park, near the pond. 1940s.

Figure 25. Photo found in Grażyna's possession that fits description of Mrs. Kraus's apartment and that may be the one Grażyna writes that she took with her when she left Prague.

Figure 26. Waleria Połtowicz. 1950s?

Figure 27. Group photo after Alexander's funeral in the US at which Grażyna (front row second from left) sees Evhen (far right) for the first time since he mysteriously disappeared while they were on a walk in Furth, Germany in the late 1940s. Len Gross, Grażyna's husband (far left front row). Circa 1957.

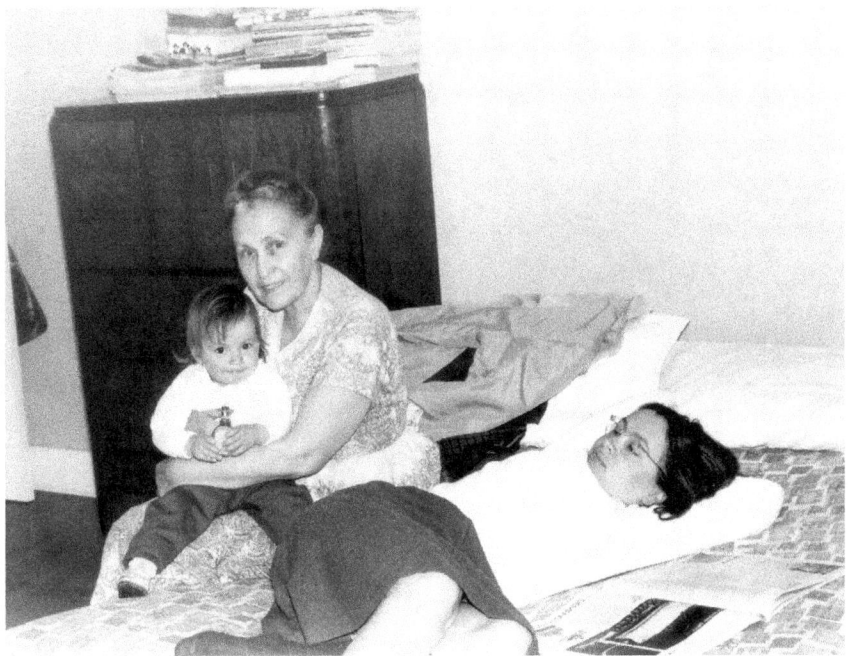

Figure 28. Joyce, Waleria, Grażyna (left to right). Ithaca, NY. 1960s.

Figure 29. Grażyna, her dog Afra, and Afra's puppies. Ithaca, NY. 1960s.

Figure 30. Waleria and Grażyna. Ithaca, NY. 1960s.

Figure 31. Grażyna at an obedience trial with her dog Falka. 1970s.

Figure 32. Joyce, Grażyna, and family goats. Ithaca, NY. 1970s.

Figure 33. Grażyna trying to work at her dining room table. Joyce and her dog Mernia watching. Ithaca, NY. 1979.

Figure 34. Grażyna and Runia, with dog Nelke. Ithaca, NY. 1982.

Figure 35. Len and Grażyna Gross. Date unknown. Photo courtesy of Jane Walker.

Figure 36. Grażyna. 2018. Photo courtesy of Gail Cashen.

Extract from the Polish Notebooks

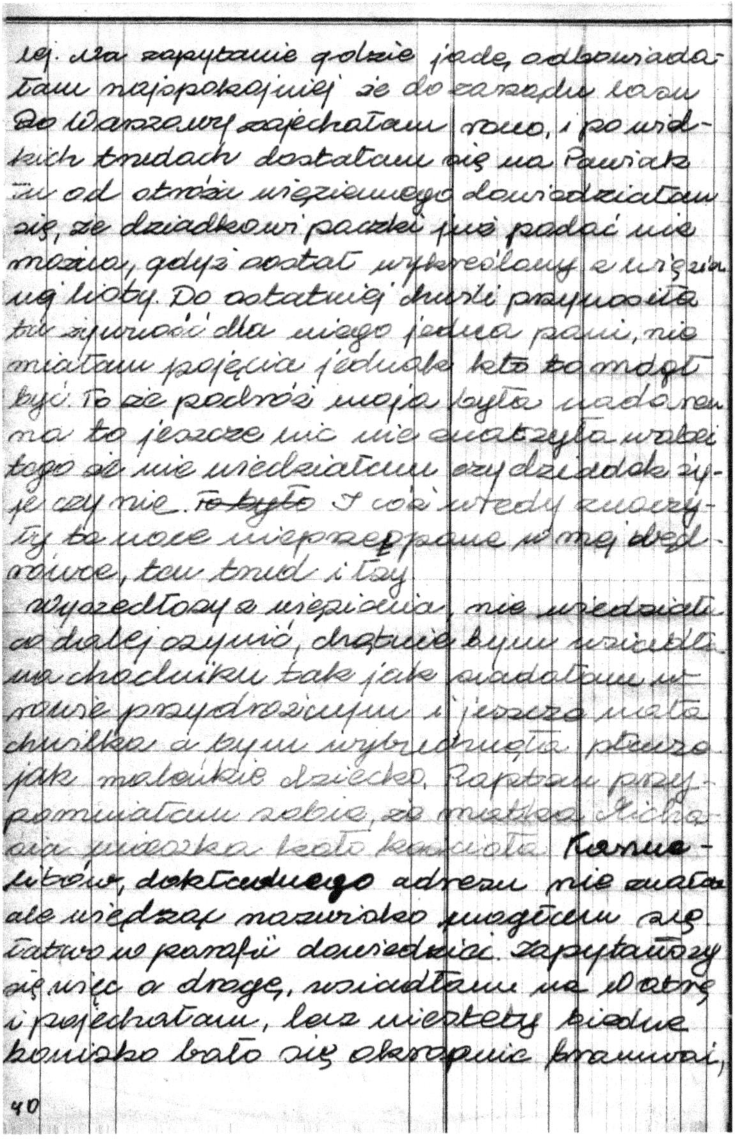

Figure 37. Page from Grażyna's notebook, handwritten in Polish in the 1940s.

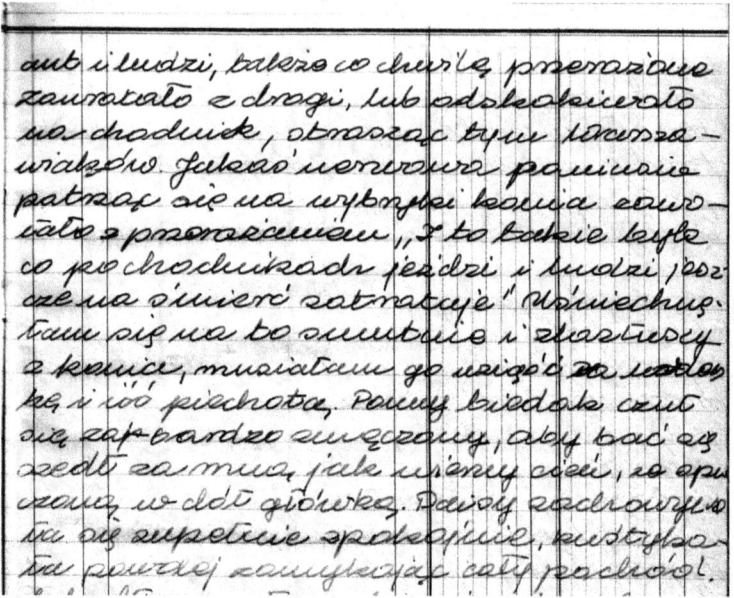

Figure 38. Page from Grażyna's notebook, handwritten in Polish in the 1940s.

[Notebook 1, Part 1, 40–1 (in Gross family archive, used by permission)]

I arrived in Warsaw in the morning and after many troubles I managed to enter the Pawiak prison. Here I learned from the prison guard that I cannot give the package to Grandpa because his name had been removed from the prison's list. Until the last day, the food was delivered for him by one lady, I had no idea however who it might have been. That my travel was futile did not mean much in view of the fact that I did not know if Grandpa was alive or not. What would be the point of my sleepless nights during my journey, all this struggle and tears.

When I left the prison, I did not know what to do. I just wanted to sit down on the pavement like I used to sit in a roadside ditch, and I was a second away from bursting into tears like a little baby. But suddenly I remembered that Michał's mother lives near the Carmelite church. I did not know the exact address but having her name I could inquire at the parish. So I asked for directions and got on Watra [the horse] and left, but sadly my poor horse was so terribly afraid of trams, cars and people that every so often he turned away in fear or jumped on the pavement, scaring Warsovians. Some uptight lady seeing the horse acting up, shouted with terror: "Any old rubbish can ride on pavement, it seems, and trample people to death!" I smiled with sadness hearing that, and I got off the horse. I had to take his bridle and start walking. Poor Panny [the pony] was too tired to be afraid, he followed me like a faithful shadow with his head down. Daisy [the dog] was completely calm, slowly hobbling in the back, closing our parade.

[This section of notebook undated; presumably written in late 1944 or very early 1945; translation Aleksandra Szczepan]

Figure 39. Recto and verso of postcard sent by Henryk Połtowicz
from Gross-Rosen to his daughter Grażyna in Kraków
(in Gross family archive, used by permission).

Card from Henryk Połtowicz at Gross-Rosen to his Daughter

The handwritten parts recto (front side) of the card: include upper-left identifiers for Grażyna's father (Połtowicz Henryk), the camp (Gross-Rosen), and his internment number (2928) with the area of Germany (Silesia) and routing (through Striegau). Right-hand side has Grażyna's name (Połtowicz Grażyna), Krakau (German for Kraków), and the street name and number (Starowislna Nr 37/6). The pre-printed parts of the front side include indications for location of address of sender and receiver, the word for postcard, and a slogan that translates into English as: "The Führer knows only battle, work, and worry. We want to relieve him of the part we can relieve him of." The front side also contains several stamps: upper right: a "traditional" round postmark with the name of the camp (GrossRosen), the date (26.11.44), and routing (through Striegau). On the left side are two stamps, a round one that has "Groß-Rosen" legible in the bottom part with the top illegible, and a rectangular one on top of the round one that reads: "zipcode not to be forgotten." Henryk's date of birth is written very lightly in pencil near the postmark stamp.

Verso (back side) is handwritten horizontally across both halves with a message (in not very correct German) that translates: "Dearest Grażynka! I am well, and hope to soon receive news about your health. For the food package and the 30 Reichsmark I give you great thanks. It tasted good. Greetings and Kisses." It is signed in a different hand: "Henryk Połtowicz." The bottom left corner has a date European style, with the day first (18) then the month (X = October) and the year (44). The upper left has a rectangular stamp with the printed word: "censored" and a dotted line on which appear some letters in pencil that look like a capital S followed possibly by a lower case "u."

Two other similar cards were found with postmarks of 6.12.44 (6 December 44) and 22.12 (22 December, where "44" can't be read, but is assumed). The handwriting in German looks different from the signature in all three cards, and none of the three German texts seems to have been written by the same hand; the signature does appear similar, though almost illegible in the third card postmarked 22.12.

[description and translation Irene Kacandes]

Acknowledgments

All three living contributors to this volume are most grateful to Grażyna Gross for deciding to write down stories from her early life and hanging on to them long enough for us to eventually read them. We thank Sonia Kane, the University of Rochester Press, and the board members of the Rochester Series on East and Central Europe for their interest in this project. Two anonymous external readers gave strong encouragement and helpful suggestions that led to a better and more useful book, we hope. We are also enormously grateful to each other for the time, dedication, and cooperation it took to puzzle through many questions together.

Joyce Gross thanks her father, Len Gross, for helping locate documents related to Grażyna after her death, for backing up Grażyna's computer files, for answering many questions, especially those related to the timeline, and for perfecting the scanning of notebook pages. Joyce also thanks Diane M. Erwin and Lisa Christianson for reading and providing helpful comments on the stories and essays. Joyce thanks Jane Walker for the photo of Grażyna and Len, Gail Cashen for the 2018 portrait of Grażyna, and Cyril N. Alberga for helping Len with scanning.

Irene Kacandes thanks the Department of German Studies at Cornell University for the invitation that brought her to Ithaca where she met Grażyna Gross for the first time. She also thanks her sister Tina Kacandes for introducing her way back when to the original Moosewood Cookbook that eventually made Irene determined so many years later to eat at the Moosewood Restaurant where she met Grażyna. Irene thanks her friends and interlocutors Ann Cvetkovich and Yuliya Komska for their support, knowledge, and creative approaches to the study of Eastern Europe. Grażyna and Len were wonderful and interesting hosts during Irene's subsequent visits to Ithaca. As for Grażyna herself, she made possible the most mysterious friendship Irene has ever had.

Aleksandra Szczepan thanks Robert Kusek, Wojciech Szymański, Karina Jarzyńska, Rasa Stakauskaite, and Agnieszka Haska for help in deciphering Grażyna Gross's literary references and geographic allusions.

Notes on Contributors

Joyce Gross grew up in Ithaca, NY, and has an undergraduate degree in English from Cornell University. She has lived in the Bay Area, California since 1990. She works as a computer programmer with the Berkeley Natural History Museums at the University of California, Berkeley. She has been doing nature photography for twenty-five years and has co-authored a book on California insects.

Irene Kacandes is the Dartmouth Professor Emerita of German Studies and Comparative Literature, Dartmouth College. Author or editor of ten books and author of scores of articles, her interests range from East European studies to German literature to experimental life writing to human mortality. Irene's commitment to the public humanities has led to the creation of a conversation series called "Humanities for Humans," sponsored by the trans-Atlantic non-profits 1014: Space for Ideas and the De Gruyter Foundation. Irene edits the "Interdisciplinary German Cultural Studies" book series at De Gruyter Brill. She enjoys gardening, tennis, and making Greek food. She and her husband Philippe Carrard split their time between Francophone Switzerland and New York.

Aleksandra Szczepan is a postdoctoral researcher at the University of Potsdam, Germany. She holds a PhD in literary studies from the Jagiellonian University in Kraków. She also participated in oral history projects by the US Holocaust Memorial Museum interviewing survivors and eyewitnesses of the Holocaust. Her recent scholarly interests include how popular culture shapes collective memories and how maps drawn by survivors and witnesses can be a form of Holocaust testimony. She likes cycling, birds and plants, cooking, and horror cinema.

Index

Page numbers in bold type refer to illustrations and their captions.

abortion 241n9
Agamben, Giorgio 228
Americans 114, 138, 139, 142, 146, 150, 165, 174–5, 193, 196, 197, 204, 215, 254, 269, 270
Anne of Green Gables 261
antisemitism 2, 228, 240, 259
apostrophe, definition of 242–5
  examples of 19–21, 73–80, 81, 100–6, 137–42, 161–6, 167–71, 172–7, 217, 248
autobiography, *see* first-person narrative

Benveniste, Émile 244
Bergen-Belsen, *see* concentration camps
Bitschan, Jerzy (Jurek) 226
black market 39, 43, 54, 59, 65, 70, 74, 91, 95, 101–2, 112–14, 138, 143, 172, 184–9, 198, 211–12, 237, 263
Bodensee 274
Bolsheviks *see* Russian Revolution
book burning 28, 147
borderlands, *see* Kresy
Bourdieu, Pierre 229
Brauchitsch, General Walther von 49, 262
Brod, Max 247
Buber, Martin 244
Butler, Judith 222

Cham 157, 160, 162, 169, 171, 203, 247, 254–5, 256, 266
Christmas 9, 92, 96–7, 111

class, social 24, 26, 53, 58–60, 61, 89, 91, 92–9, 181, 205, 213, 220, 223, 229–30
  "connections" (znajomości) 46, 58, 219
concentration and extermination camps 123, 144, 204, 224
  Bełżec 264
  Bergen-Belsen, death of Grażyna's father in 202, 205, 211, 272
  death marches 273
  Gross-Rosen 207, 219–20, **308**, **309**
  humor in 117
  Majdanek 266
  soap myth 119, 210, 269
  Treblinka 266
Constantinople 274
co-witnessing 244
currency exchange 182, 186–7, 274
Czechoslovakia 145, 147, 270

Daddy's War 235
Danube (river) 138, 146
deictics 242
diction in *On the Run* 240–1
displaced persons 142, 265, *see also* refugees
Dnieper (river) 123, 146, 268
Dniester (river) 146
dogs, Grażyna's love of 53, 89, 150, 167, 169, 215–16
Domažlice 143, 223
DP, *see* displaced persons

Dresden 57, 133, 269–70
drone (*truteń*) 39, 44, 212, 219
ethnic diversity, *see* multiethnicity
Evhen, *see* Malaniuk
experiencing self, *see* first-person narrative
Eye of the Prophet 35, 43, 261

fairytales 1, 224
  Cinderella 36, 38, 180, 246
  Little Red Riding Hood 2, 179
first-person narratives 223, 239–40, 240–1, 242
  as autofiction 223
fortunetelling 8, 37, 65–8, 128, 129, 131, 224–5
Frank, Anne 237–8
Frank, Hans 222, 263
Furth 135–6, 137, 149, 167–71, 176, 209, 270–1

Ganghofersiedlung 144–9, 230, 271
Gangsterland, *see* Kraków
gender 2–6, 214, 229–30
General Government 222, 261, 263, 265, 274
German
  aircraft 49, 50, 51, 262
  language 128, 149, 160, 167–8, 197, 247
Gestapo 52, 82, 84, 266
Die Glut 234
Goering, Hermann 271
Goethe, Johann Wolfgang von 151, 161, 164, 169, 273, 274
  "Der Erlkönig" 151
  Die Leiden des jungen Werther 273
Grandes Études de Paganini 127, 269
Gross-Rosen, *see* concentration camps
Grottger, Artur 226, 227
Gypsies, *see* Roma

Heine, Heinrich 151, 272
Helcel House for the Poor 60, 264

historical present 243n12, 245–6
Hitler Jugend (Hitler Youth) 48, 51, 82–3, 104, 262
Holodomor 263

Istanbul 274
Italo-Ethiopian War 259

Jews 2–3, 82, 146, 227
  apartments being taken over 41
  blood libel 2, 259
  expropriation 55, 93–4
  family doctor 30–1
  ghettoization and deportation 52, 55, 56, 222
  Grażyna's relationship to 204
  Holocaust victims and survivors 138, 220, 227
  travel with false identity papers 266
Johnson, Barbara 242–3, 244

Kafka, Franz, *see* Brod, Max
Kaunas 47, 62
Keller, Gottfried 266
Kielce 267
Kochanowski, Jan 267
Kraków 222, 261
  Błonia Park 266
  bugler in tower of St. Mary's Basilica 43, 262
  family arrival in 38
  ghetto 204, 222
  Grażyna's return to 203–4
  Jewish Square 263
  Kazimierz 204, 222, 263
  Market Square 42, **288**
  Montelupich prison 77, 266
  Old Town 46
  Planty Park 42, 219, **287**, **295**
  Podgórze 222, 263
  Starowiślna Street 52, 222, 253, 263, **308**, **309**
  Ukrainian Quarter 263, 267
  Ursuline School for Girls 58, 264, **289**, **290**

Kresy 220–1, 225, 227, 230, 247, 260, 261

La Campanella, see Grandes Études de Paganini
Lake Constance, *see* Bodensee
Latin 157–9, 172–3
Light Cavalry Overture (Leichte Kavallerie) 127, 269
liquidating 25, 182–3
Lviv 204, 226

Malaniuk, Yevhen Fylymonovych (Evhen) 143–55, 234, 271–2, **297**
Marx, Karl 146–7
Messerschmitt, Wilhelm "Willi" 262, 271, *see also* German, aircraft
Meyer, Conrad Friedrich 156, 273
Mickiewicz, Adam 225
"The Mighty River Dnieper Roars" song (Реве́ та сто́гне Дніпр широ́кий) 116, 123, 124, 146, 268
multiethnicity 221, 227, 247
Munich 112–14, 134, 137–8, 140, 141, 150, 166

Nansen passport 38, 261
Napoleon 2, 179, 191–2, 259
narrating self, *see* first-person narratives
Native Americans 205
Nazi Judeocide 234, *see also* Jews
New York City 154

occult 128
Ola Gum 48, 49, 262
Operation Barbarossa 52, 222, 263
Oszmiana 7, 29–31, 259, 260–1
Oszmianka (river) 272

paramemoir xi, 235, 236, 238
paratextual material 236
Pawiak, *see* Warsaw
photographs and albums 57, 77–80, 127, 132, 134, 203, 206
Pilsen 134, 143
Piłsudski, Józef 262

Poe, Edgar Allen 163, 273
poetry 85–6, 151, 158, 225, 272
Poland
  1930s border **xiii**
  division of 221, 260–2, 265
    annexation of Western 265
    deportations to Soviet Union 260
    evacuation to Middle East 271
  flag of Second Republic 260
  postwar repatriation to 144
polonization 221
Potsdam Agreement 270
POW camps 40, 58, 59, 85, 95, 147, 182
Prague 126–31, 133–4, 137, 143, 223, 269
prophesying, *see* fortunetelling

Raczkiewicz, Władysław 264
Raczyński 59
refugees 52, 76, 94, 96–7, 138–42, 156–8, 161–2, 167–8, 182, 223, 230–1, 270
  UNRRA and 271
Regensburg 138–42, 149
religion
  belief/unbelief 50, 78, 93, 100, 107–8, 109, 132, 159, 173–4, 175, 206, 219
  (Roman) Catholic priests 10–11, 13, 162, 172–7
  Protestants 93, 173
reparations 188, 196
RGO (Rada Główna Opiekuńcza) 70–2, 265
Rilke, Rainer Maria 152, 272
Roma 2, 8, 11, 17
Russian Revolution 52, 116, 179, 205, 222, 230, 260
  Bolsheviks 143, 147, 260
  loss of Połtowicz family estate in 212

White Russians   20, 38–9, 243–4, 260
Rydz-Śmigły, Edward   262

Schiller, Friedrich von   151, 158, 273
schooling   24, 46–7, 51, 58–60, 92–9, 117, 132, 144–6, 149–50, 156–60, 169–70
second person pronoun, *see* apostrophe
Sienkiewicz, Henryk   269
smuggling   115, 128, 143, 186, 189
Snyder, Timothy   224
Soviet Union   202, 222, 252, 253, 254, 257, 260, 261, 262, 263, 271
Strauss, Johann   138, 163, 269, 271
Suleiman, Susan Rubin   228
Syniukha (river)   272
Syrokomla, Władysław   272

Treuhänder   57, 227, 263
Trotsky, Leon   147
Turkey   3, 90, 220, 261

Ukrainians   143, 145, 149, 154, 227, 263
  relations Poles and   47, 52, 212, 230, 246

Vilnius, *see* Wilno
Vltava (river)   272
Volksdeutsche   146, 230, 270, 271, 272

Walhalla   139, 271
Warsaw, *see* Warszawa
Warszawa
  family arrival in   34
  Ghetto Uprising   82, 266
  Holy Cross Church   267
  Pawiak prison   207, 226, 306
  Warsaw Uprising   117, 226, 268
White, Hayden   225
Wilno   1, 58, 85–6, 245, 259
  arrival of Soviets in   21–2, 54, 181
  family departure from   29, 31–3, 183
  Grażyna's return to   202–3, 205
Wisła (river)   272
Wołożyn   1, 30, 211, 259
  Blood Creek   2, 225

yarrow (*krwawnik*)   2, 225, 259

Der Zigeunerbaron   127, 269

www.ingramcontent.com/pod-product-compliance
Lightning Source LLC
Chambersburg PA
CBHW051559230426
43668CB00013B/1906